HOW TO GET A JOI

In this Series

GET A JOB IN
AUSTRALIA

A guide to employment opportunities and contacts

Nick Vandome

Second Edition

How To Books

Acknowledgement
Commonwealth data included in this publication is copyright and reproduced by permission. Apart from any use as permitted under the *Copyright Act 1968*, no part may be reproduced by any process without prior written permission from the Australian Government Publishing Service. Requests and inquiries concerning reproduction and rights should be directed to the Manager, Commonwealth Information Services, Australian Government Publishing Service, GPO Box 84, Canberra, ACT 2610.

Note
Readers are advised to seek professional advice before making important personal or financial decisions and this book is not in any way to be considered a substitute for such advice. Readers are reminded that law and regulations are liable to change.

British Library Cataloguing-in-publication data
A catalogue record for this book is available from the British Library.

Cartoons by Mike Flanagan.

Published by How To Books Ltd, Plymbridge House, Estover Road, Plymouth PL6 7PZ, United Kingdom. Tel: Plymouth (01752) 735251/695745 Fax: (01752) 695699. Telex: 45635.

First edition 1992
Second edition (revised) 1995

Typeset by Concept Communications Ltd, Crayford, Kent.
Printed and bound by The Cromwell Press Ltd, Broughton Gifford, Melksham, Wiltshire

Preface

to the Second Edition

Australia has attracted the interest of vast numbers of people worldwide in the last forty years: since the end of World War Two five million migrants have settled there. The British, as much as any other nation, are fascinated with Australia and all things Australian. At the beginning of the 1990s this interest remained undiminished, despite an economic recession in Australia that led to higher unemployment and calls for curbs on migration.

However, 1995 has seen a considerable upturn in the economic fortunes of Australia and with the jobless total at a 3-year low of 9.5% the Government has recently decided to increase the migration quotas — the 1994/95 figure is 16% higher than the previous year. The double good news is that the Australian Government is particularly interested in encouraging skilled workers to come and work in the country.

Despite this upturn in the fortunes of the Australian economy, and the job market, the situation is still a far cry from the halcyon days of the 1960s: prospective migrants and workers should not be lulled into a false sense of optimism. There are jobs available but what is needed is careful thought when looking for a job, and a certain amount of research. This book does not promise to land you a top post with a multi-national company but it will arm you with all the relevant information that you need to tackle the job scene in Australia.

I am indebted to a number of people who helped me in gathering much of the factual information for the second edition of this book. This includes a number of unnamed officials in both Australia and Britain. In particular I would like to than Sian Hoskins, who helped bridge the miles between here and Australia and battled with endless red tape to provide me with invaluable information.

Any errors or omissions in the book are the responsibility of the author but I hope it will be of some use to people heading off to forge a living Down Under.

Nick Vandome

Contents

List of Illustrations

1
Economic Overview

ECONOMIC ROOTS

The first 'employees' of Australia were the 800 convicts who sailed with
the First Fleet which arrived in Australia on 26th January 1788. Although
conditions were harsh the new settlers were determined to forge as
prosperous a life as possible in their new home. Those who were released
from the convict settlements, or who went to Australia as willing settlers,
soon found that it was a land rich in natural resources.

Agriculture was the first boom industry and by 1819 a Scotsman named
Captain John Macarthur had built up a flock of over 6,000 merino sheep.
This proved to be only the beginning for the Australian sheep population
and by 1850 there were over 18 million sheep of various varieties,
providing over half the wool imported by England.

The expansion of the sheep population led to increased demands on
the land, which in turn spawned a contingent of pioneers who traversed
the massive spaces of this vast land. One of the results of their exploits
was the discovery of Australia's enormous mineral wealth. In the 1850s
large gold finds were made in New South Wales and Victoria, which
brought a stampede of prospectors from Europe, America and China.
Inevitably this led to the discovery of other minerals: between 1889 and
1920 more than 170 million ounces of silver were mined at Broken Hill
in New South Wales. This was supplemented by equally impressive
amounts of gold, lead and zinc. The company which first exploited this,
Broken Hill Proprietary Limited (BNP) is now the largest corporation in
Australia.

Based partly on their economic wealth Australians gradually began to
have a growing sense of nationhood. On 1st January 1901 the Commonwealth of Australia came into being.

The Australian economy has changed dramatically over the last fifty
years, as it has reacted to events including World War Two, the post-war
boom, the oil crisis of the 1970s and the world-wide recession of the

11

1980s. The main result of these changes is that the economy has switched from a heavy reliance on primary production to a greater dependence on production in the services (tertiary) sector.

Whatever else World War Two did for Australia it had a profound effect on the economy. Manufacturing developed much faster than it would have under normal circumstances and this, coupled with an expansive immigration program at the end of the war, ensured that the 1950s and 1960s were a boom period in Australia. There was a rapid expansion in secondary industry and large-scale investment in export-orientated mining and energy projects. Australia became regarded as an extremely desirable place to live; a country with a strong economy and a high standard of living. It more than justified its tag of the 'Lucky Country'.

Australia, and the rest of the world, was brought down to earth with a bump in the 1970s due to the OPEC oil crisis. As oil prices soared the years of low inflation and low unemployment were turned on their heads as both figures began to rise alarmingly. This continued for most of the 1970s and in the early 1980s there was an investment boom as companies strove to develop Australia's massive reserves of natural resources. However, the expected 'resources boom' was not fulfilled and in 1982/83 the Australian economy experienced a biting recession. Two years later the collapse in commodity prices harmed the economy still further — the subsequent balance of payments crisis led to stringent policy measures to try and redress the situation. These consisted of carefully developed prices-and-incomes policies and structural reforms.

In 1987 the Australian economy took a further buffeting with the world-wide stock market crash of 'Black October'. Hundreds of companies and financial institutions went to the wall and confidence in the economy was severely dented. At the same time there was a sharp down-turn in the agricultural industry — traditionally one of Australia's strongest areas. Farms incomes fell by up to fifty per cent and the economy has been struggling to overcome these events for the past five years.

GENERAL ECONOMIC CONDITIONS

One of the strongest areas of the Australian economy is its natural resources and extractive industries: mineral products account for more than one third of all exports. Australia is one of the world's largest coal exporters and also a major supplier of iron ore, gold, bauxite and alumina. On a rural front Australia is still the largest producer of wool and also a major supplier of wheat, meat and sugar.

In the last decade Australians have recognised the need to keep a close link between wages and taxation. This was typified in 1983 when the **Prices and Incomes Accord** came into being. This was an agreement between the Federal Government and the powerful Australian Council of Trade Unions which set out to modify wage increases in return for various tax trade-offs which resulted in increases in disposable income. This policy still forms the basis for most wage negotiations.

In 1984 the **Prices Surveillance Authority** was established as part of the prices and incomes policy. It is intended to supplement the Prices and Incomes Accord by encouraging prices restraint in response to wage restraint.

In 1989 the **Industries Commission** was formed to advise the Australian Government on matters of structural change within the economy. The Government's intention was to optimise the use of the country's natural resources and expand its productive potential.

Most exchange controls were abolished in 1983, when the Australian dollar was floated. After a sharp initial fall the $A has remained relatively stable — usually between $A2-2.50 to the pound.

The Federal Budget is presented every August. Federal Government spending accounts for approximately a quarter of Australia's Gross Domestic Product, while state, territorial and local government spending accounts for a further fifth. About three-quarters of total public-sector revenue is raised by the Federal Government and a quarter of expenditure goes on payments to state, territorial and local governments. Individual states and territories are responsible for running services such as education, health, housing and transport but they do receive federal funding for this.

Although in theory individual states and territories can levy their own taxes (except customs and excise duties) they rarely do and for over fifty years the Federal Government has been solely responsible for income taxes on companies and individuals. Revenue comes from payroll taxes, taxes on property, financial transactions, motor-vehicle tax and franchise taxes. Australia has agreements with a number of countries to ensure that they avoid double taxation.

The Australian banking system comprises the central bank (the Reserve Bank of Australia) and 35 banks or banking groups which operate under its supervision. There are also approximately 120 money-market corporations.

THE CURRENT SITUATION

It is impossible to discuss the recent Australian economy without mentioning the R-word — recession ravaged the Australian economy at the

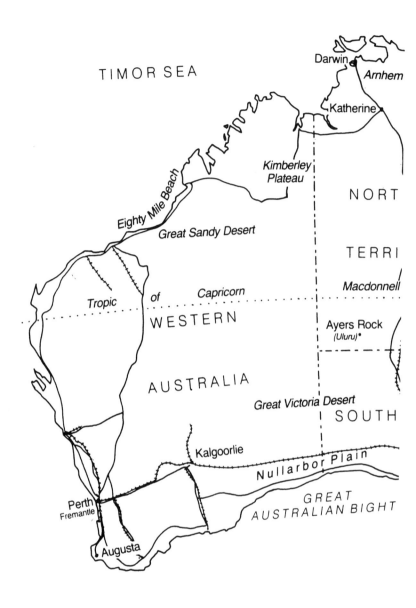

TIMOR SEA

Darwin
Arnhem

Katherine

Kimberley
Plateau

NORT

Eighty Mile Beach

Great Sandy Desert

TERRI

Tropic   of   Capricorn

Macdonnell

WESTERN

Ayers Rock
(Uluru)•

AUSTRALIA

Great Victoria Desert

SOUTH

Kalgoorlie

Nullarbor Plain

Perth
Fremantle

GREAT
AUSTRALIAN BIGHT

Augusta

SOUTHERN OCEAN

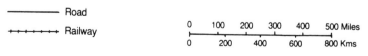

——— Road
+ + + + + + Railway

| 0 | 100 | 200 | 300 | 400 | 500 Miles |
| 0 | 200 | 400 | 600 | 800 Kms |

Fig. 1. Map of Australia.

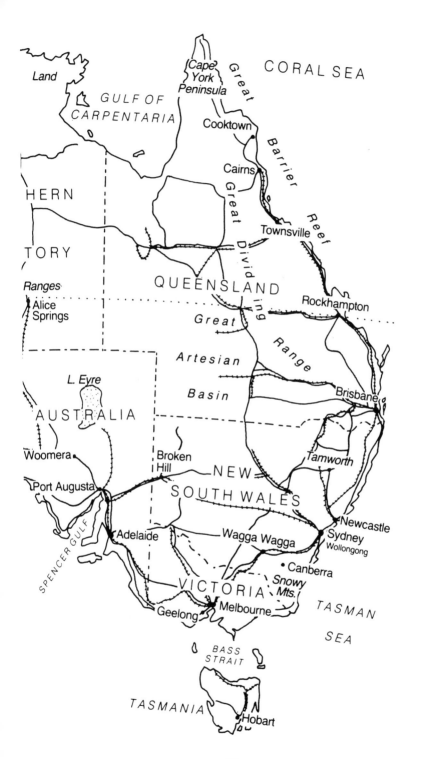

Land

GULF OF
CARPENTARIA

CORAL SEA

Cape
York
Peninsula

Cooktown

Great

HERN

TORY

Cairns

Barrier

Great

Townsville

Reef

Ranges

Alice
Springs

QUEENSLAND

Dividing

Rockhampton

Great

Range

L. Eyre

Artesian

AUSTRALIA

Basin

Brisbane

Woomera

Broken
Hill

NEW

Tamworth

Port Augusta

SOUTH WALES

Newcastle

SPENCER GULF

Adelaide

Wagga Wagga

Sydney
Wollongong

Canberra

VICTORIA

Snowy
Mts.

TASMAN

Geelong

Melbourne

SEA

BASS
STRAIT

TASMANIA

Hobart

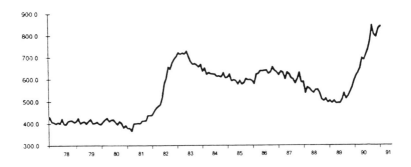

Fig. 2. Australia's unemployment figures.

end of the 1980s and the beginning of the 1990s. One of the main victims of the recession was Bob Hawke who was ousted from power in January 1992 by his former Treasurer, Paul Keating. Australians were becoming increasingly frustrated with high unemployment and high interest rates and it was thought that it was time for a change in an attempt to bring an end to one of the worst recessions in recent years. Mr Hawke was the only Prime Minister in Australian history to have won four consecutive elections and he was the country's second longest serving premier, having held the post for eight years, nine months and eight days.

Paul Keating promised hardline policies to revive the Australian economy and to a certain extent he has delivered a reasonable degree of economic recovery. Both employment and interest rates have come down; at the time of writing the jobless total is at a 3-year low of 9.5% and it is predicted that there will be considerable economic growth over the next decade. This was confirmed in a speech given by the Treasurer, Mr Willis, at the end of 1994: 'The strength of our current economic recovery lies not only in our current economic performance and immediate prospects but also in the fact that this recovery is very soundly based. Unemployment peaked at 11.3% at the end of 1992. It is now down to 9.5%, and with employment expected to rise by 250,000 this financial year, we can certainly look forward to a further reduction in that rate by mid-1995.

'Rather than being a short-term boom and bust recovery it is a durable recovery that gives Australia a real prospect of achieving a strong economic performance for the rest of the century. This is because it is based on the strongest set of economic fundamentals that Australia has experienced for several decades.'

On the immigration front things are also looking up after a few years of hardline policies aimed at curbing immigration levels. As the economic recovery gathers pace it is forecast that immigration levels will rise accordingly. The 1994/95 target for the migration programme (excluding the humanitarian category) was 73,000, an increase of 10,000 on the previous year. A similar increase is predicted for 1995/96 which would take the migrant numbers to 84,000. The Minister for Immigration and Ethnic Affairs, Senator Nick Bolkus, stressed recently the likely trends for the future: 'Increases are likely, keeping them within moderate historical levels but recognising there is an upturn in the economy.'

Overall the outlook for job-hunters from Britain is better than it has been in recent years. The recession seems to have passed, and if people are prepared to put a reasonable amount of work into the job search then there is no reason why they should not be successful. It may not be as easy to get a job in Australia as it was twenty years ago but for the determined job-hunter it can still be the Lucky Country.

2
Entry Requirements

GENERAL

The first thing to consider when looking for a job in Australia is, obviously, getting into the country. For people of working age (men under 65 and women under 60) this can be done through four categories:

1. Independent Migration
2. Concessional Family Migration
3. Business Migration
4. Holiday Working Visa

The first three of these categories operate on a **points system** and applicants will have to achieve a certain score before they are considered. This is to show that they will be able to join the work force quickly and support themselves without government help.

Since the beginning of 1992 the Australian Government has reintroduced the **pool system** for people wishing to migrate to Australia. This applies to all applications lodged after 8th January 1992. The pool system, first introduced in 1989 to give the Government flexible management of their migration policy, gives potential migrants more than one chance to emigrate. Once they achieve the entrance mark to join the pool they are either accepted for emigration because they have enough points to reach the priority pass mark, or if they do not reach this mark, they can remain in the pool and have their points total assessed against any new pass marks which will allow them to emigrate. Commenting on these changes Gerry Hand, the then Minister for Immigration, Local Government and Ethnic Affairs, said, 'The Government's deliberate policy of setting high standard migration selection criteria has had the desired effect of bringing to Australia migrants with record high skill levels over the last three years. This illustrates that the Government will not compromise quality for quantity.'

INDEPENDENT MIGRATION

The current score for independent migrants, at the time of writing, to join the pool system is 95 points. The score for the priority pass mark is 100 points. This is judged under employability skills, age, and language skills.

Skill	*Points*
Trade cert/degree (acceptable), with at least 3 years' sound, continuous relevant experience, on priority list	80
Trade cert/degree (acceptable), with at least 3 years' sound, continuous experience	70
Trade cert/degree (acceptable), with limited experience	60
Diploma (acceptable), with at least 3 years' sound, continuous relevant experience	55
Diploma (acceptable), with limited experience	50
Trade cert/degree/diploma (recognised overseas and requiring only minor upgrading, which must be available in Australia) with at least 3 years' sound, continuous relevant experience	30
Trade cert/degree/diploma (but qualifications held are unacceptable)	25
Other post secondary school qualifications or equivalent experience	25
12 years of primary and secondary education	20
10 years of primary and secondary education	10
Less than 10 years education	0

Graduates who have obtained their qualifications in the five years prior to application will be awarded 40 points for their skills. In addition, they will be required to demonstrate that they have worked continuously for at least six months in the last two years.

Age	*Points*
18 to 29 years	30
30 to 34 years	25
35 to 39 years	15
40 to 44 years	10
45 to 49 years	5
Over 50/under 18	0

Language skills   *Points*

Proficient in English	20
At the above level in 3 of the 4	15
skills of reading, speaking, understanding	
and writing English	
Reasonably proficient in English	10
but minor training required	
Bilingual in 2 languages other than	5
English, or only limited English ability	
Extensive English training required	0
and not bilingual	

CONCESSIONAL FAMILY MIGRATION

The pass mark for this category is 95 points. The pool mark is 90 points. If you are applying in this category you can count the Skill and Age categories above but NOT the Language Skills. In addition, applications are also assessed under:

Relationship factor

If you are:	*Points*
Parent of your sponsor	15
Brother, sister or non-dependent child of your sponsor	10
Nephew or niece of your sponsor	5

Citizenship factor

If your sponsor has been an:	*Points*
Australian citizen for 5 years or more	10
Australian citizen for less than 5 years	5

Settlement factor

If your sponsor (or spouse of your sponsor) has:	*Points*
Been in continuous employment in Australia (including	
self-employment) for the last two years (no unemployment	
or special benefits for more than one month in total)	10

Location factor

If your sponsor has: *Points*
Lived in a state/territory designated area for at least two years   5
State Designated Areas (intended to encourage people, under the Concessional Family category, to settle outside the big cities):

   Queensland (except Brisbane)
   Sunshine Coast and Gold Coast
   Western Australia — south west region, Kalgoorlie and Goldfields
      region, Murchison region, Kimberley and Pilbara region
   South Australia — whole state
   Northern Territory — whole state
   Tasmania — whole state
   Australian Capital Territory — whole state
   Victoria — except Melbourne region

FEES

There are considerable fees involved for people intending to emigrate. Fees for full migration are now £202 and £6 for the initial **Application for Migration** kit. For people living in Australia who want to change their status to permanent resident the fee is now $A370 — $A780 depending on category. Migrants can pay the sum by cheque in sterling — contact your local bank for the current exchange rate.

BUSINESS MIGRATION PROGRAMME (BMP)

In February 1992 the Australian Government introduced new rules and regulations governing business migration. The new category, **Independent— Business Skills** places greater emphasis on the skills of potential business migrants rather than the previous method of judging them solely on how much money they can take with them. They will also have to pass a similar points test to other migrant categories.

Introducing the new scheme, the then Minister for Immigration, Local Government and Ethnic Affairs, commented, 'Applicants under the new category will need to prove that they have attained a certain level of business experience and success, according to specific criteria. They must also pass a points test which will grade them according to the size of turnover of their business, their age, English language ability, and possession of capital available for transfer.

'There will be extra points if their main business background is in a field from which Australia may get particular benefit — the manufacturing sector, trade services or in the development and use of innovative technology.'

In 1995 Business Migration was simplified and expanded to allow a wider range of skilled business people to migrate to Australia.

THE BUSINESS MIGRATION POINTS TEST

Applicants need to obtain at least 105 points from four factors.

Factor one: business attributes

Shareholders/sole proprietors:	*Points*
The principal business had an annual turnover of not less than the amount specified below in not less than two of the four years preceding the application:	
$A5,000,000	60
$A3,000,000	55
$A1,500,000	50
$A750,0000	40
$A500,000	35

Factor two: age (at the time of application)

	Points
Over 30 years but under 45 years	30
Over 45 years but under 50 years	25
Over 25 years but under 30 years	20
Over 50 years but under 55 years	10
Under 25 years or over 55 years	0

Factor three: language

	Points
Better than functional	30
Functional	20
Less than functional but bilingual in two or more other languages	10
Limited	10
None	0

Factor four: capital *Points*

Not less than $A2,500,00	15
Not less than $A1,500,00	10
Not less than $A500,00 but less than $A1,500,00	10
Less than $A500,00	0

Business migrants who pass the points test and are admitted to Australia will have to participate in a comprehensive monitoring system, probably for the first three years of their business operation. According to the current Minister for Immigration and Ethnic Affairs, Nick Bolkus, 'Business people will need to make a three-year financial investment in Australia, which gives them time to consider their longterm business strategy and personal future in Australia.'

The fee for applicants under the Business Skills category is $A1,600.

HOLIDAY WORKING VISAS

These are available to single people, or childless couples, between the ages of 18 and 25. In some exceptional cases people of up to 30 years will be considered.

The main idea behind the Holiday Working Visa is to provide young people with a chance to see Australia and supplement their travels with periods of casual employment. There are nine main conditions which applicants must fulfil:

Conditions

1. The prime purpose of the visit is a temporary stay in Australia and permanent settlement is not intended.

2. Employment is incidental to the holiday and is to be used as a supplement to the money you bring with you.

3. Employment in Australia must not be pre-arranged except on a private basis and on the applicant's own initiative.

4. There must be a reasonable prospect of the applicant obtaining temporary employment to supplement holiday funds.

5. Applicants must show that they have reasonable funds to support themselves for some of their time in Australia, and return airfare. This is approximately £2,000 for one year.

6. Applicants must meet normal character requirements, and health standards where necessary.

7. Full-time employment should not be undertaken for more than three months with one employer.

8. Applicants must leave Australia after their Holiday Working Visa has expired.

9. The maximum length of stay is twelve months.

Applications

Applications can be sent to any Australian Consulate in Britain and with them you will need to include:

- Three recent **passport sized photographs** of yourself, which should be signed on the back.

- **Evidence of funds** for the duration of your stay plus your return airfare. If you do not think you have enough money at the time of application it is a good idea to borrow some money, pay it into a bank or building society account, obtain a statement and then repay the money. However, it is unwise to arrive in Australia without sufficient funds. Immigration officers may not investigate your financial situation when you arrive in the country but if they do they will want to see that you have access to a substantial sum of money.

- A **valid passport**. This should be valid for at least three months *after* your proposed departure date from Australia. If your passport does not comply with this it will be necessary to get a new one.

- A **stamped self-addressed envelope** for the return of your passport.

You should not apply for a Working Holiday Visa more than four weeks before your proposed departure date. Application forms should be filled in carefully as incomplete ones will be returned unprocessed. It is not advisable to telephone to see how your application is progressing. This will only irritate Consulate staff and it will not hasten the arrival of your visa. People holding UK, Greek, Italian, Spanish, Irish, Canadian, Dutch or Japanese passports are all eligible to apply for Holiday Working Visas.

There is a processing fee of £71 for each Holiday Working Visa. This can be paid by cheque to 'Commonwealth of Australia'.

APPLICATION POINTS

All types of visas should be sent to your nearest Australian Consulate or
High Commission:

● Australian High Commission, Australia House, Strand, London
   WC2B 4LA. Tel: 0171 836 7123.

● Australian Consulate, Chatsworth House, Lever Street, Manchester
   M1 2D1. Tel: 0161 228 1344.

3
Employment Law and Conditions

PAY

The main piece of legislation governing wages in Australia is the 1983 Accord, an agreement reached by the Federal Government and the Australian Council of Trade Unions. Its aim is for the unions to cooperate with the Government's employment and anti-inflation policies; in return the Government seeks to help the unions maintain their members' living standards and eventually improve them if possible. It is an agreement that has worked well over the years but it remains to be seen what will become of it now that Bob Hawke has been removed from power.

'Award rates'

Australia is a highly unionised country and because of this most wage rates are set at a minimum level. Federal and state tribunals set rates of pay for various jobs and professions and employers are then obliged to meet these 'award' rates. Seven out of eight Australian workers have their pay agreed by awards, determinations or industrial agreements. However, these figures are only a minimum recommendation and many employers pay well over the award rate.

Awards do not only cover basic rates of pay, they also deal with overtime payments and **penalty rates** — these are higher rates paid for weekend work, shift work or hours which extend past your normal hours of employment.

The award system has a number of advantages for workers. Firstly, they know what they will be paid when they apply for a job and in industries such as the retail trade it ensures that everyone is paid a reasonable wage. Secondly, the payment of penalty rates means that workers can increase their wage simply by working at the weekend, without having to work overtime. Because of this weekend and evening work is eagerly sought by people in trades such as hospitality, whereas in Britain they would be paid at the same rates regardless of the time or the day of the week.

Average wages

According to figures released in 1993 the average nationwide wage for men in full time employment was $A664, including overtime payments, although there can be big differences from state to state. New South Wales and Australian Capital Territory attract the highest wages while the lowest tend to be in Queensland and South Australia.

Women still lag behind men in the wages stakes — on average they earn 84% less than their male counterparts.

HOLIDAYS

The usual holiday entitlement is four to six weeks of paid leave depending on the job and the award to which it relates. But being the fun-loving people that Australians are they do not believe that they should have to scrape by with their basic wage while they are enjoying themselves on their 'hols', so they have introduced a wonderful idea called **leave loading**. This is a an exceptionally agreeable scheme whereby workers are paid an extra 17.5 per cent of their full wage while they are on holiday. All full-time employees are entitled to this bonus which some people would call a luxury but which the workers will tell you is an absolute necessity. Some firms offer a form of sabbatical leave after ten years service with a firm.

There are also national holidays on:

1st January
27th January
Easter Friday
Easter Sunday
Easter Monday
1st May (except Queensland and Northern Territory)
4th May (Northern Territory only)
8th June (except Western Australia)
25th December
26th December (except South Australia)
28th December (South Australia only).

Individual states also have their own bank holidays.

WORKING HOURS

The standard working week is approximately 37 hours but the average hours worked within the workforce vary from 32 hours to 52.5 hours. Hours worked above the standard working week will be paid at overtime rates of either time-and-a-half or double-time, depending on the award for that profession.

Some workers, particularly in the public sector, operate on a **flexi-time** system. This allows them to work a set number of hours in a four week period but within that framework it is largely up to them as to how they make up the hours. There is usually about four hours a day (core time) during which the employee must be at work but other than that they are free to come and go at times which best suit them. Additional days off can also be taken if enough flexi-time has been built up.

TRADE UNIONS

Australia is one of the most highly unionised countries in the world and nearly half of the working population are members of unions. Trade unions have been active in Australia since the middle of the 19th century and they have fought forcefully over the years to improve working conditions and pay. There are some 300 unions in the country, of which 150 are affiliated to the central organisation, the **Australian Council of Trade Unions** (ACTU), which has a total membership of three million members.

The fact that Bob Hawke, who was formerly the president of the ACTU, has taken a backseat in politics may mean that the power of the trade unions will be lessened, but this seems unlikely. Australia has a long history of being strongly supportive of workers' rights.

It was the ACTU which was responsible for forging the 1983 Accord and the national awards on pay and conditions. Every year there is a great show of negotiation between the Government and the ACTU but invariably both parties are relatively pleased with the outcome.

Trade disputes

Industrial disputes are dealt with by state courts and tribunals, as are claims for wages and conditions. If the matters cannot be settled in this way then the matter is taken to the **Conciliation and Arbitration Commission**. This is the highest authority in the industrial set-up and is responsible for settling disputes which cannot be dealt with at a state level. Its most common duty is to arbitrate on wage claims, paying particular attention to the increase in relation to inflation. All the interested parties — employers, unions and the Government — are brought before the Commission and then a judge delivers his verdict. This is the bedrock on which the Accord survives.

Professional workers

Unions still have a great deal of influence — some people would say that they have too much. Workers who do not want to join a union can sign up with a professional association. These are related to professions such as doctors and lawyers and while they are not as powerful as the unions they can have an effective voice.

SICK LEAVE

Australian employees are entitled to one or two weeks' fully paid sick leave a year, depending again on the award in their profession. Most people take full advantage of this allowance and hence the national habit of the 'sickie' — people taking time off even if they are not sick — has developed. This has become such a problem that the Government has recently commissioned a study into the problem. Recent research has shown that 16 per cent of workplaces with five or more employees have between 10 and 25 per cent of their workers away each day. The sickie is less prevalent in industries which have high levels of dismissals and it is most common among public servants.

SUPERANNUATION

This is another scheme which was introduced as a bargaining tool to persuade trade unions to accept moderate wage increases. Under current legislation employers have to contribute at least three per cent of an employee's salary into an **approved superannuation fund**. This is a legal requirement for employers and they are liable to fines if the correct payments are not made.

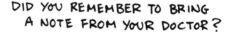

All superannuation schemes are controlled closely and are included in different award arrangements. All employees are entitled to this form of award-based superannuation. These are some of the conditions:

● It must be three per cent of your average monthly wage, paid into a special fund by your employer.

● Failure to pay it by your employer is equivalent to failing to pay the correct wages.

● Award-based superannuation is paid to you from the time you begin work. If your employer is not meeting his/her superannuation obligations you are entitled to a back-payment.

● Superannuation schemes are portable and you do not lose your payments if you change jobs or professions.

● You receive a payout from your superannuation fund when you reach 55 years of age.

● You can choose the type of scheme into which your superannuation is paid.

● If you are self-employed, or you are not part of a recognised superannuation scheme, you can contribute to more than one scheme if you wish.

● In certain cases, tax relief can be claimed against superannuation payments. For specific details contact a tax agent or an accountant.

In the past few years the Australian Government has promoted superannuation because it fears that, due to the aging population, future governments will not be able to afford to pay suitable pensions to retirees. A Government spokesman outlined the importance of superannuation, 'Superannuation is not the exclusive option it used to be. It is taking its place in broad incomes policy.

'It is no longer just a tax-advantaged privilege for a minority. It is part of the social wage, which means it is part of social policy. Workers have paid for their superannuation entitlements by accepting lower wages. Superannuation is deferred income held in trust until it matures.'

FRINGE BENEFITS

The existence of fringe benefits in the Australian economy has declined steeply in recent years, due largely to the introduction of a **Fringe Benefits Tax** (FBT). This is levied on employers at the rate of 47 per cent of the taxable value of fringe benefits offered to employees. These benefits include such things as company cars which are also used for private purposes, expense accounts and private health plans. Because of this high level of taxation the most likely form of 'benefits' that employees can expect are subsidised canteens, living away from home allowances and superannuation deals. Since these are all covered by union awards they are not liable to FBT.

WORKERS' COMPENSATION

Known universally as **compo** this is another prominent feature of the Australian employment landscape. Every accident in the workplace is taken very seriously and workers are invariably paid compensation to cover their medical expenses and their loss of earnings. The system is designed to protect the well-being of employees and because of this the worker is usually deemed to be in the right. He does not necessarily need to prove that his employer was negligent and it does not even matter if he was partly negligent himself.

Each state has its own legislation to cover compensation but they do not vary greatly. If a claim for compensation is rejected then the worker can take his case to a relevant union and the case will be heard before a workers' compensation commission or board.

CONTRACTS OF EMPLOYMENT

Contracts of employment in Australia can be anything from a rough handshake from a fruit farmer, to a lengthy document from a multi-national firm, to a simple public service contract. In some types of work you may not even be offered a formal contract but if you are there are some areas which you should check:

● rate of pay
● hours of employment
● holiday entitlement
● whether you will be working flexi-time or not

Department of Social Security

....

....

Please Quote:
Telephone Ext:

Dear

FORMAL ADVICE TO SHORT TERM EMPLOYEE ON ENGAGEMENT

In accordance with Section 82 AD of the Public Service Act, you have been selected for temporary
employment as

in

A broad description of the tasks on which you will be engaged is set out in the attached.

It is proposed that your employment to perform the attached duties will be for a period of
from   /   /19   to   /   /19   . Before the completion of this period of
engagement, the Secretary (or delegate) of the Department is required to provide to you, either
notice of your termination date, or an indication that the Department will extend your period of
engagement. Your employment will then cease on the date specified in that notice. As a result
of your employment being for a period of less than 12 months, your are not covered by division 8c
of the Public Service Act unless the Department extends your period of engagement and as a result,
your total engagement period exceeds 12 months.

Please sign this notice in the presence of the Regional Manager or the Administrative Officer of the
office, and retain the original.

NB: You may be eligible to join the Public Sector Superannuation Scheme. Please contact your
Personnel Section for further information.

Department to Complete	Employee to Complete
Designation:	Family Name:
Position No:	Given Names:
Hours/Week (If part-time)	Date of Birth
Salary on Commencement	Address
Period of Employment	
Termination Date	

Signature of Employee _____   Date   /   /19

Distribution: White - Employee's Copy; Green - Recruitment's copy; Yellow - Office Copy   E177 (9105)

Fig. 3. Sample Standard Temporary Contract
(courtesy of the Department of Social Security).

- overtime and penalty rates of pay
- meal breaks
- compensation provisions
- provision of uniform/protective clothing
- period of notice required from either party
- rates of severance pay
- superannuation contributions
- specific rules and regulations
- sick leave
- sick pay
- trade union membership
- provision of private medical insurance
- provision of a company car
- pension contributions.

In most jobs, even if part-time (or casual as it is frequently called), you should be offered some sort of contract. If nothing else this will guarantee you some form of payment in the event of employment being terminated abruptly. If you are not offered a written contract then ask for one. It may only be a simple sheet of paper but make sure that you and your employer sign something. Of course there are some areas where you will not be offered a contract. The most obvious is fruit-picking, a job notorious for its lack of control over working conditions. The chances are that you will be at the mercy of your employer but due to the nature of the work and conditions this will probably not be of prime importance.

If you are unhappy with any part of your contract then you should take it to a legal representative or trade union body.

4
Problems in the Workplace

SICKNESS

Australian workers are well provided for in the event of illness and there are two main areas they can guard against financial losses as a result of illness:

1. Medicare

2. Private health plans.

Medicare

Medicare is a form of national health insurance available to every resident of Australia, including temporary residents. You should apply to join Medicare as soon as you arrive in the country. You will need to fill in an application form for a Medicare card and these forms are available at all Medicare offices.

Medicare is partially financed by a tax on all taxable income, which is deducted at source. At present this stands at 1.4 per cent. Once you have joined Medicare it does not mean that you will be entitled to limitless, free medical treatment. It covers basic health needs such as visits to general practitioners, specialists and anaesthetists. However, Medicare only covers 85 per cent of these costs and the remaining 15 per cent usually has to be met by the patient. In most cases the full charge will be levied on the patient and then they will have to claim back the 85 per cent from Medicare.

Medicare also entitles patients to a general ward in a public hospital. However, for operations of a non life-threatening nature, such as hip replacements, there are long waiting-lists and it could be several months until there is a vacancy. Any treatment at a public hospital as a Medicare patient will be free but you will have to show your Medicare card.

Private health insurance

Whether or not to take our private health insurance is very much up to the individual. Medicare is more than adequate for general health needs, but if you think you may need a lot of non-urgent medical attention then private health insurance may be a good idea. But before you commit yourself to the expense of a private plan look around at the various schemes on offer and see which one would suit you the best. Several companies, including **Medibank**, **ANA** and **HBA**, offer a variety of health plans and they should be consulted before any final decision is made. It is worth remembering that any illness has to be weighed against not only the medical costs but also the loss of earning from being off work for perhaps an extended period of time. The average weekly costs, per family, for private health insurance is in the region of $10-20.

Some companies offer their employees membership of a private health plan but this is still very much the exception rather than the rule.

SEXUAL HARASSMENT

Although Australia has gone some way to shed its image of a beer-swilling, macho society, sexual harassment can nevertheless be a problem in the workplace. It is classed as:

● An unwelcome sexual advance or request for sexual favours, or unwelcome conduct of a sexual nature.

It may include some of the following:

● unwelcome comments or questions about a person's sex life;
● suggestive behaviour;
● over-familiarity such as deliberately brushing against someone;
● sexual jokes, offensive telephone calls, photographs, reading matter or objects;
● sexual propositions or continual requests for dates;
● physical contact such as touching, fondling, or unwanted sexual advances.

Although both men and women can be victims of sexual harassment it is usually the latter who are subjected to this type of discrimination. Since the Australian **Sex Discrimination Act 1984** much of this type of behaviour is now illegal and action can be taken against offenders. At its most extreme sexual harassment can take the form of rape or indecent assault.

Since these are criminal offences they should be reported to the police. Sexual harassment in the workplace is unlawful if:

1. You have reasonable grounds for believing that your rejection of it will effect your application for a position, your current job or your future at work.

2. You object to sexual harassment and are then unfairly treated by denial of a job or promotion, sacked, demoted or subjected to further harassment.

Under the Sex Discrimination Act management is obliged to prevent sexual harassment. The employer may be responsible if reasonable steps are not taken to prevent sexual harassment in the workplace.

What can be done?
There are a number of steps that can be followed if you are subjected to sexual harassment at work:

● Make your objections to your supervisor and the person who is harassing you. If this proves to be the same person then take your complaint to a higher authority.

● Check to see if your company and its management has a policy to combat harassment. If not, then lobby to have one created.

● Complain to higher management.

● Seek help from your union.

● Look outside your place of employment for help. Seek a trustworthy counsellor for support and advice about solving the situation.

● Contact the Human Rights and Equal Opportunities Commission or a co-operating agency, where your problem will be dealt with in strictest confidence.

● Keep a record of when and where harassment takes place and do not be dissuaded from tackling the problem.

The Sex Discrimination Commissioner
The **Human Rights and Equal Opportunity Commission** is responsible for administering the Sex Discrimination Act. The Sex Discrimination Commissioner exercises certain statutory powers of inquiry, conciliation

and settlement of sex discrimination complaints on behalf of the Commission. Conciliation is the avenue used in most cases and this is the favoured approach of the Commission.

If you feel you are being sexually harassed you should contact your nearest Commission office or agency and explain the problem to them. They will be able to advise you as to whether you have lawful grounds for making a complaint. You will then be required to submit your complaint in writing before further action can be taken.

Commission Offices

The national office is in Sydney and there are also regional offices in Brisbane, Hobart and Darwin. Complaints under Federal law in New South Wales, Victoria, South Australia and Western Australia are handled on behalf of the commission by the NSW Anti-Discrimination Board and the Equal Opportunity Commissioners in individual states. For the Australian Capital Territory complaints should be made in writing to the Commission's Sydney office:

Commission National Office: Level 24, American Express Building, 388 George Street, Sydney, NSW 2000. Postal address: GPO Box 5218, Sydney, NSW 2000. Tel: (02) 229 7600.

RACIAL DISCRIMINATION

In 1975 the **Racial Discrimination Act** was passed. This prohibits discrimination in employment on the grounds of race, colour, descent or national or ethnic origin.

REDUNDANCY

The thought of redundancy is never a pleasant one but in recent years it has become a more common problem. As firms seek to cut costs they 'rationalise' their operation, which invariably means shedding staff.

The good news is that the Australian Government has laid down guidelines covering payment and conditions covering redundancy. If the worst comes to the worst then people with a period of service with their company will be eligible for severance payments. These rules were set out in 1984 following the Termination Change and Redundancy (TCR) test case and they have recently been confirmed by the Confederation of Australian Industry (CAI). They define redundancy as, 'where an employer has made a definite decision that the employer no longer wishes the job the employee has been doing done by anyone, and this is not due to the ordinary and customary turnover of labour.'

The conditions governing severance pay and periods of notice are both laid down in relation to the length of service by the employee. However, the level of severance pay is not to exceed the amount the employee would have earned if they remained in employment until their normal retirement date.

The TCR ruling also states that after redundancies have been announced employers must allow their employees one day off a week in order to seek alternative employment. Employers must also notify the Commonwealth Employment Service, telling them the number of proposed redundancies, the categories of employees likely to be affected, the period over which the redundancies will occur and also provide employees with a 'statement of employment'.

If an employee receives a superannuation payment when he or she is made redundant then this will be counted against the amount of severance pay; they will receive the full sum *less* the amount received in super-annuation.

The CAI concluded that the TCR test case should be used as a maximum and minimum standard and they stated that it is highly unlikely that any employer would be required to pay more than the levels of severance pay laid down in the test case.

Period of notice

Period of continuous service	*Notice in weeks*
One year or less	one
One year to three years	two
Three years to five years	three
Five years and over	four

Severance pay

Period of continuous service	Severance pay in weeks
One year or less	nil
One year to two years	four
Two years to three years	six
Three years to four years	seven
Four years and over	eight

● Employees over forty-five years of age and with more than two years service are entitled to an extra week's notice or pay in lieu of notice. All severance pay is at ordinary-time rates.

STRIKES AND INDUSTRIAL DISPUTES

If you are involved in an industrial dispute and you are unable to work then you may be eligible to get help from the Department of Social Security. If you are a member of a trade union then you will probably not receive any state benefits — you will have to see your union to see what provisions they make for workers on strike. However, you will receive unemployment benefit if:

● you have been sacked as a result of an industrial dispute which is now over; or
● you have been sacked or stood down in an industrial dispute that your union is not part of.

If your spouse is a member of a union involved in an industrial dispute, you can get paid unemployment benefit for yourself and your dependent children. However, you will not be paid for your spouse.

WORKING ILLEGALLY

There are currently 80,000 illegal immigrants in Australia and it is thought that 60 per cent of them are working illegally. Of this total it is estimated that 8.3 per cent are British. Obviously, people who have migrated to Australia will not make up any of this number but it is thought that people overstaying their holiday working visas account for a large number of the British illegal immigrants. The rest are those who have travelled on tourist visas and decided to stay.

Understandably, the Australian Government is becoming increasingly frustrated by the number of illegal immigrants, and particularly those who are taking jobs away from legitimate workers in times of recession. Gerry Hand, the former Minister for Immigration, Local Government and Ethnic Affairs, confirmed that the Government is cracking down on overstayers. 'Illegal entrants are clearly taking jobs away from Australians and this justifies the tough stance being taken against those who breach Australia's immigration laws. This is a situation which cannot and will not be tolerated.' Although these comments were made in 1992 they are still relevant at the time of writing.

Mr Hand's comments are backed up by the figures: in 1991 4,737 illegal immigrants were caught, up 216 per cent on the figures for 1990. Of these nearly half were deported. Most illegal workers were found to be employed in factories, restaurants and fruit picking areas. The number of Immigration Department field officers has been trebled and methods are being investigated into linking tax file numbers with immigration details.

The message to people who are thinking of overstaying their visas and working illegally in Australia is *don't*. It is increasingly likely that you will be caught, in which case you will probably be unceremoniously deported and not made welcome if you ever try and return.

5
Finance

TAX

Even in the 'Lucky Country' this three letter word is inescapable. The tax year runs from 1st July to 30th June and it pays (sometimes literally) to have a good understanding of the tax system.

For people whose income comes from a salary or a wage tax is levied through a **Pay As You Earn** (PAYE) system which is known as **standard rate taxation**. However the story does not end there because the tax payer has to step daintily through a minefield of Tax File Numbers, Provisional Tax, Tax Forms, Tax Packs, deductions and refunds.

Your Tax File Number (TFN)
The most important thing for migrants to consider is that it is *vital* to obtain a **Tax File Number** as soon as possible upon entering Australia. This is a number which needs to be quoted whenever you apply for a job or fill in the dreaded income tax return. If you do not have one then you will be taxed at the top rate of 47 per cent. You will be able to claim some of this back but you will have to wait until the end of the tax year to do so.

Tax File Numbers can be obtained by filling in an application form available from the Post Office or the local tax office. To do this you will have to have proof of your identity — birth certificate, passport (including residency visa) and driving licence.

Taxation rates
The rates of taxation in Australia at the time of writing are as follows:

Taxable income	Tax
$1-$5,400	Nil
$5,401-$20,700	20 per cent
$20,701-$38,000	34 per cent
$38,001-$59,000	43 per cent
$59,001+	47 per cent

These rates do not include the Medicare levy of 1.4 per cent, and apply to people who have been resident in Australia for the full financial year.

Tax forms and tax pack

All taxpayers in Australia, even if you are a PAYE employee, are required to fill in a tax form at the end of the financial year. In simple terms (nothing about tax forms is ever simple of course) this involves declaring all of your taxable income and also noting any expenses you can claim against your tax. The form for this is something akin to a small encyclopedia — but help is at hand. The Tax Office issues a 96 page booklet entitled *Tax Pack*; this not only includes four copies of tax return forms but also offers invaluable information about filling in your tax form. The scale of the task can be seen from the fact that the front of the Tax Pack declares merrily, 'You may "only" have to answer 15 questions'. In fairness it does take you through the whole operation step by step.

● Tax forms must be completed and returned by **31st October** for the previous tax year. Failure to do so could result in financial penalties.

Provisional tax

Provisional tax is for people who earn more than $999 a year from non-salary or wage income. This includes income from investments, business, primary production and distribution from any source not covered by PAYE.

You will also have to pay provisional tax if you received income from a wage or a salary and:

● the tax payable on your assessment was $3000 or more, and
● the shortfall in tax instalments deducted was $3000 or more.

Provisional tax is calculated when you send in your tax form. Your tax for the year ended is calculated, then, based on that calculation, your tax for the current tax year is assessed. This is the provisional tax. Both amounts of tax are added together and you will receive a bill or a refund as the case may be.

When an **assessment** is made for your next tax return a credit is allowed for any provisional tax you paid the previous year. If you think your rate of provisional tax is higher than the amount of tax you will pay next year you can apply to vary your provisional tax. This is done with a **provisional tax variation form** (PTV) available from any Tax Office.

Fill in (a), (c) and (d) only when Tax Pack asks you to

(a) Are you due a **refund?**

(b) Are you a resident of Australia?

(c) Do you need a Section 169A ruling?

(d) Has a Tax Pack question asked you to fill in this 'Other Attachments' box?

Australian Taxation Office

Income Tax

Return Form

for Individuals

1 July 30 June

Your Tax File Number
This is on the right hand side of your last assessment notice

Your Tax File Number is needed to make sure we correctly identify your tax records

Lodge your return by 31 October

Please print neatly in ink and use BLOCK LETTERS

Your full name   Tick one box   Mr   Mrs   Miss   Ms

Surname or family name

Christian or given names

Your current postal address   If unchanged, print it exactly as on your last notice from the Tax Office

Postcode

Have you changed your postal address from the address you last told us about?   If yes, print the old address exactly as on your last notice from the Tax Office

Postcode

Your home address   If the same as your current postal address, print AS ABOVE. Do not show a Post Office box

Postcode   (f)

Tax Office use only

Full name of your spouse or de facto spouse

Surname or family name

Christian or given names   (f)

Your main occupation

Your date of birth   Day   Month   Year   (f)

Have you changed any part of your name since your last tax return?   If yes, print the full name you used before

Your daytime phone number   (STD   )
Only if convenient. If we need to ask you about your tax return it's quicker by phone

Have you lodged a tax return in Australia before?   If no, print FIRST

If yes, which Tax Office Branch did you send it to?   What year?   19

Do you think this will be your last tax return in Australia?

For example, moving overseas to live   If yes, print FINAL   (f)
and
give details of type, source and expected amount of future income

ETP 5%	B	
ETP1-Code	C	
ETP1-Lit	D	
ETP1-Bal	E	
ETP2-Code	J	
ETP2-Lit	Q	
ETP2-Bal	R	
Average code	H	
INDICS	X	
P/T Indics	Y	
LLP	S	
Eligible income	T	/
Sec. 100(2) Credit	U	
Provisional Tax (Trust)	V	
Checksum (S to V)	W	
OCC Code	Z	
	P	

Read page 6 of Tax Pack, it tells you how to fill in this form

NAT 975   (f)

Fig. 4. Sample Tax Forms.

Income

Show cents　　　　Do not show cents

1 　 USB **A** ✕/☐

2 　 PEN **B** ✕/☐

3 　 SAL **C** ✕
　 SAL **D** ✕
　 SAL **E** ✕
　 SAL **F** ✕

4A 　 LSA **G** ✕
4B 　 LSB **H** ✕

5 　 ETP **I** ✕

6 　 ANN **J** ✕

7 　 ALL **K** ✕

8 *TAX INSTALMENTS DEDUCTED (add 1 to 7 above)* **S** 　 TID

9 　 INT **L** ✕ (f)

10 　 PPD **A** ✕/☐
　 NPPD **B** ✕/☐

　 PPS **C**
　 IMP **D**

11 　 PPS **E** 　 PPN **F** ✕/☐

12 　 PPS **G** 　 NPP **H** ✕/☐

13 　 IEW 　 NET **I** ✕/☐
　 IED 　 WT **J**

14 　 PCL **K** ✕
　 ECG 　 OCL **L** ✕ NCG **M** ✕/☐

15 　 EFS 　 FTC **N** 　 FSI **O** ✕

16 　 IFC **P**
　 NRT **Q** 　 AFI **S** ✕

17 　 GROS 　 DED **T** ✕ REN **U** ✕/☐ (f)

18 　 UNF **A** ✕
　 FRA **B** ✕
　 IMP **C** ✕

19 　 ASS **D** ✕/☐

20 　 ENI 　 OTH **E** ✕/☐

21 *TOTAL INCOME OR LOSS (add the ▼ boxes at 1 to 20 above)* 　 INC **■** ✕/☐

Fig. 4. (continued).

44

Staple the originals of your group certificates (on top) and other attachments here.

Do not send your Tax Pack to the Tax Office.
You can keep it and a copy of your tax return as your personal record.

Use the **checklist** on page 77 of Tax Pack before lodging your tax return.

Page 78 of Tax Pack tells you **where to lodge** your tax return.

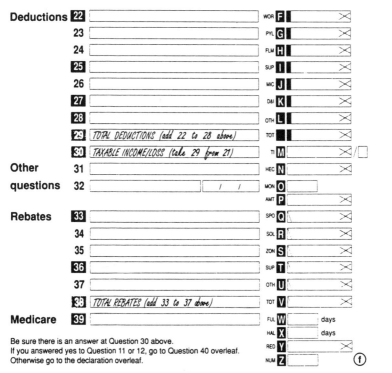

Deductions 22

23

24

25

26

27

28

29 *TOTAL DEDUCTIONS (add 22 to 28 above)*

30 *TAXABLE INCOME/LOSS (take 29 from 21)*

Other 31

questions 32 / /

Rebates 33

34

35

36

37

38 *TOTAL REBATES (add 33 to 37 above)*

Medicare 39

WOR F
PYL G
FLM H
SUP I
MIC J
D&I K
OTH L
TOT
TI M
HEC N
MON O
AMT P
SPO Q
SOL R
ZON S
SUP T
OTH U
TOT V
FUL W — days
HAL X — days
RED Y
NUM Z

Detach here ▼

Be sure there is an answer at Question 30 above.
If you answered yes to Question 11 or 12, go to Question 40 overleaf.
Otherwise go to the declaration overleaf.

Fig. 4. (continued).

45

◄ *Detach here*

Note: This is page 4 of your tax return

Business/professional declaration items (only if you answered yes to Question 11 or 12)

Show investment income and property income only at the Income section on page 2.

You will need to read page 45 of Tax Pack to find out how to answer Questions 50 to 65.

40 Did you cease a business this year?   No ☐   Yes ☐

41 Did you start a business this year?   No ☐   Yes ☐

Office use only **Q**

42 Business name of main business

43 Business address of main business

44 From what profession/source is your *main* business income derived?

45 How much gross income was derived from that main profession/source? $

46 Industry code   Office use only **R**

47 Sub-industry code   Office use only **S**

48 From what profession/source is your *secondary* business income derived?

49 How much gross income was derived from that secondary profession/source? $

Explain:
- what books of account were kept and by whom;
- whether the books were audited and by whom;
- whether the tax return is based on those books or, if not, what basis and information was used.

50 Sales   **A** ⊠

51 Opening stock   **B** ⊠

52 Closing stock   **C** ⊠

53 Cost of sales   **D** ⊠/☐

54 Total business income from primary production   **E** ⊠/☐

55 Total business income from other business   **F** ⊠/☐

56 Salaries and wages paid   **G** ⊠

57 Other labour charges   **H** ⊠

58 Payments to associated persons   **I** ⊠

59 Interest paid   **J** ⊠

60 Repairs   **K** ⊠

61 Motor vehicle expenses   **L** ⊠

62 Depreciation   **M** ⊠

63 Depreciable assets purchased   **N** ⊠

64 Depreciable assets sold   **O** ⊠

65 Gross PPS income   **P** ⊠ ⓕ

Declaration for every taxpayer

I declare that
- all the information I have given is true and correct; and
- I have shown all my income from sources in **and out of** Australia for the year of income; and
- I have the necessary receipts and other records to substantiate any claims made for car and travel expenses incurred in earning income other than as an employee; and
- I have the necessary receipts and other records to substantiate any claims made at Question 22 for car, travel and work expenses (where the total of these expenses is more than $300).

Signature	Date / /

- **Staple** the originals of group certificates and other attachments to page 3 of your tax return.
- Use the **checklist** on page 77 of Tax Pack before lodging your tax return.

Important
The tax law imposes heavy penalties for giving false or misleading information. If the taxpayer is not a resident of Australia the words **'and out of'** may be deleted from the declaration.

About your Tax File Number
The information requested on this form is needed for taxation purposes. The Tax Office is very careful to protect the privacy of personal information. In very limited circumstances, some information may be given to certain government bodies as described in tax law. For more details on Privacy see page 30 of Tax Pack.

- **Do not send** your Tax Pack to the Tax Office.
- Page 78 of Tax Pack tells you **where to send your return.**
- Fill in the questions at the **top of page 1.**

Fig. 4. (continued).

Provisional tax is an area which makes most Australian taxpayers cringe — and with good reason. It is perhaps the greatest factor when it comes to whether you should fill in your own tax form or pass it over to an accountant or tax agent.

Tax agents

When it comes to the time of year for filling in the tax form you can tell who has chosen to fill them in themselves and who has entrusted them to a **tax agent**. The freelancers wander around with worried expressions and furled brows, muttering about petrol allowances and taxable income. Those who have left it in the hands of an agent are usually to be found on the beach or on the golf course, looking forward to a possible refund. The truth of the matter is that you can fill in your own tax form but it is a lot easier, and more often than not a lot more profitable, to let the professionals do it.

Of course, tax agents charge a fee but for the average PAYE taxpayer this will be between $70-$80. Additional fees are charged for additional services but it is worth remembering that fees for tax agents can be claimed as tax deductible.

Apart from saving you lots of grey hairs the main advantage of using a tax agent is that they will be in the best position to try and get you a refund on the tax you have paid, rather than having to pay more. Agents will make sure that you claim for all the deductions to which you are entitled — one of the most common oversights by the individual is not claiming all their deductions. Some of the deductions which can be claimed are:

Deductible expenses
- union dues
- car expenses (but not to or from your place of work)
- travel expenses
- tools and equipment
- uniforms and protective clothing
- home laundry of uniforms
- sickness/accident insurance premiums
- self-education.

Expenses over $300
If your claims for work-related expenses exceed $300 you must keep records to prove your claim. These should include receipts with:

- the date on which the expense was incurred
- the name of the person or business who supplied the goods or service
- the amount of the expense
- details of the goods or services
- the date the document was made out.

For possible auditing purposes these receipts have to be kept for three-and-a-half-years by salary and wage earners and seven years for the self-employed.

Unless you are a financial wizard, or you actually *enjoy* filling in tax forms, it would probably be better to employ the services of a tax agent. They are generally cheaper than accountants, who tend to charge by the hour.

Paying tax

After lodging your tax form you will receive a **Notice of Assessment**. The amount of tax due, if any, will be shown on this assessment, as will the date by which it should be paid. If provisional tax is not included then the due date will be approximately thirty days after you receive the Notice of Assessment. If you have to pay provisional tax and the amount is less than $8,000 then the due date will be no earlier than 31st March. If the amount is over $8,000 then you will be able to make payment in four instalments. These will generally fall on 1st September, 1st December, 1st March and 1st June.

When you come to the dreaded moment of paying your tax you can do so by taking it in by person or by posting it to the tax office which issued your Notice of Assessment. Cheques and postal orders should be made payable to the 'Deputy Commissioner of Taxation' and crossed 'not negotiable'. The bottom section of your assessment should be sent with your payment. If you cannot find it then you should include your name and address and, of course, your Tax File Number.

Late payment of tax
If you feel you are unable to pay your tax by the due date you should write to your tax office immediately, explaining your circumstances. This should include:

- Your name and address.
- Your Tax File Number.
- Your work and telephone number.

- The reasons why you cannot pay your tax.
- How you plan to get the money to pay your tax.
- The amounts you can pay on a regular basis.
- Your first payment.
- The date by which you expect to have paid the full amount.

However, the tax office's charity does not extend to giving you an interest-free period in which to pay your tax: you will be charged an additional tax for late payment. This is 20 per cent per year on the amount unpaid after the due date.

Tax Offices

There are sixteen tax offices throughout Australia where tax returns can be sent if you complete them yourself. Use the one nearest to your area:

GPO Box 9990, Adelaide, South Australia 5001 (also for Northern Territory).
PO Box 9990, Albury, NSW 2640.
GPO Box 9990, Brisbane, Queensland 4001.
GPO Box 9990, Canberra, ACT 2601.
PO Box Chatswood, NSW 2057.
PO Box 9990, Dandenong, Victoria 3175.
GPO Box 9990, Hobart, Tasmania 7001.
GPO Box 9990, Melbourne, Victoria 3001.
PO Box 9990, Moonee Ponds, Victoria 3039 (for Victoria North).
PO Box 9990, Newcastle, NSW 2300.
PO Box 9990, Parramatta, NSW 2123.
PO Box 9990, Penrith, NSW 2740.
GPO Box 9990, Sydney, NSW 2001.
GPO Box 5300, Sydney, NSW 2001 (for Sydney South).
GPO Box 9990, Perth, Western Australia 6001.
PO Box 9990, Townsville, Queensland 4810.

Capital Gains Tax

This is a tax levied on any capital gain realised from the disposal of assets acquired after 19th September 1985. Gains made on the sale of the taxpayer's principal residence are usually exempt from Capital Gains Tax. Other items which are exempt are motor vehicles, superannuation and insurance, personal goods which have a disposable value of $A5,000 or less, and assets acquired before the 20th September 1985.

SOCIAL SECURITY

Australia has one of the best social security systems in the world. The three main types of social security benefits which concern us here are:

● Age pensions
● Job Search Allowance
● Newstart.

The last two are schemes under the **Newstart program** for the unemployed which has replaced the traditional 'dole' unemployment system. (All of the following figures are for up to the end of March 1995.)

Age Pensions

Age pensions are paid to men over 65 and women over 60. Under normal circumstances you must have been a resident of Australia for 10 years. However, special conditions apply and Australia has agreements with a number of countries where residence in one country can count towards residence in Australia. The United Kingdom is covered by this agreement.
Age pensions are assessed according to two criteria:

1.   Income Test
2.   Assets Test.

The Income Test
Under the Income Test a full pension is paid to you if your gross income (not including maintenance) does not exceed $A90.00 a fortnight for a single pensioner and $A156.00 a fortnight (combined) for a pensioner couple. Income above these amounts reduces the pension payable by 50 cents for each dollar.

The Assets Test
Under the Assets Test you will receive a full pension if the current market value of your assessable assets totals less than the following:

Single homeowner	$A115,000
Single non-homeowner	$A197,000
Married homeowner couple	$A163,500
Married non-homeowner couple	$A245,500

Pension Claim

Use this form to claim
- **Age Pension**
- **Disability Support Pension**
- **Wife Pension**
- **Widow B Pension**
- **Sole Parent Pension**
- **Carer Pension**
- **Age Pension (Blind)**
- **Disability Support Pension (Blind)**
- **Widowed Person Allowance**

Put in your claim as soon as you can - because payment cannot be made before you lodge your claim.

Before you can be paid, you must show us
- at least 3 original documents which prove your identity
- details of all your bank, building society and credit union accounts, and any other money you have invested
- your latest rent receipts, rent book or other proof of the amount paid, if you are paying private rent.

Try to bring these things with you when you claim but, if you can't, then lodge your claim and provide them later.

If you are married or living de facto
- you should bring your partner to the office when you claim (if possible)
- your partner will have to fill out a separate form
- we will need to see 3 original documents which prove your partner's identity
- we will also need to see details of all your partner's bank, building society and credit union accounts, and any other money your partner has invested.

If you want an interpreter to help you fill out this form do not answer any questions yet. Bring this form to Social Security as soon as you can.

SA2.9110

Fig. 5. Front of sample Pension Form.

Special Benefit Claim

Put in your claim as soon as you can.

Special Benefit can only be paid from the date Social Security receive your claim.

When you claim, you must show us

- at least 3 original documents which prove your identity
- details of all your bank, building society and credit union accounts, and any other money you have invested
- your latest rent receipts, rent book or other proof of the amount paid, if you are paying private rent.

Try to bring these things with you when you claim but if you can't, then lodge your claim and provide them later.

If you are married or living de facto

- you should bring your partner to the office when you claim (if possible)
- your partner will have to fill out a separate form
- we will need to see 3 original documents which prove your partner's identity
- we will also need to see details of all your partner's bank, building society and credit union accounts, and any other money your partner has invested.

NOTE: If you or your partner is under 21 and you have no dependent children your partner must make their own claim for benefit.

If you want an interpreter to help you fill out this form do not answer any questions yet. Bring this form to Social Security as soon as you can.

SU4.9101

Fig. 6. Front of sample Benefit Claim Form.

If you receive any maintenance then this will affect your pension slightly differently than other income. You will get your full rate of payment if you receive less than $A834.60 per annum maintenance. This is increased by $A278.20 per annum for each child after your first. Maintenance above this allowable amount reduces your payment by 50 cents for each dollar.

Pension rates and payment
As of March 1995 the maximum fortnightly pension for a single person is $A321.60. For a married couple it is $A536.40.

You can claim your pension shortly before you reach retirement age. You can get the relevant forms from any Social Security Regional Office and you will need proof of your identity — passport or driving licence is suitable for this. Your pension will be paid into your bank, building society or credit union account, every second Thursday.

Job Search Allowance

This is one payment made to unemployed people under the Newstart program. To be eligible you must be:

● unemployed and under 18 years of age or
● over 18 and unemployed for less than 12 months
● allowed to live in Australia permanently
● actively searching for work and
● registered with the Commonwealth Employment Service (CES).

The Department of Social Security and CES will apply an **activity test** to make sure that you are actively looking for work, or trying to improve your chances of getting some. These activities will be decided by the CES. In addition you will have to report to the Social Security every fortnight and update them about your job-hunting. Unless you have a good reason for not meeting the activity test your payment will be stopped.

Your payment will be assessed after an Income and an Assets test. The Assets test is the same as the one for age pensions. Under the Incomes test you will be paid the full rate if your gross income does not exceed $A60.00 a fortnight. For each dollar of income between $A60.00 and $A140.00 you will lose 50 cents from your rate. Income over $A140.00 reduces your rate dollar for dollar.

When you apply for Job Search Allowance you will need to take your Tax File Number and your **Employment Separation Certificate**. This comes from your last employer and relates why you left work and how much money you were paid.

You can receive your Job Search Allowance every fortnight by taking a form to the Social Security, detailing your efforts to find work. After this a payment is made into your bank, building society or credit union account. The rates vary according to age, marital status and number of children. The maximum rate for a single person over the age of 21, with no children, is currently $A297.30 a fortnight.

Newstart Allowance
To be eligible for this you must be:

● unemployed
● over 18 years of age
● registered with the CES for twelve months or more
● allowed to live in Australia permanently and
● actively searching for work.

In order to receive your allowance you will have to sign an **action plan** agreement with the CES, which is aimed at improving your job prospects. The Newstart allowance is usually paid from the day after the Job Search allowance stops. The Income and Asset test are the same for both schemes, as are rates of payment.

OTHER FINANCIAL MATTERS

Personal and business finances are one of the biggest worries when planning to work in another country. These worries have been addressed by the Commonwealth Bank of Australia. They not only offer various financial services before you arrive in Australia, such as opening overseas bank accounts and transferring money overseas, but they will also help you get settled when you step off the plane. This includes offering advice on general financial matters as they apply to Australia, such as buying a house, superannuation and investments. The Bank has Migrant Service Centres in each state capital and they also hold Migrant Information Days throughout major cities in Britain. For further information contact:

Financial and Migrant Information Service
3rd Floor, No. 1 Kingsway
London WC2B 6DU
Tel: (0171) 379 0955

They will be able to provide you with an information pack and an invaluable book which covers a wide range of financial matters in Australia.

6
The Official Recruitment Network

COMMONWEALTH EMPLOYMENT SERVICES (CES)

The main cog in the official employment network in Australia is the Commonwealth Employment Services (CES). This is the equivalent of Jobcentres and offers a number of services for the prospective job-seeker. As well as the traditional displays of current vacancies these include:

- Youth Officers
- Career Reference Centres
- Work Information Centres

YOUTH OFFICERS

Youth Officers are located in most CES offices around Australia and they offer advice and information for young people who are entering the job market for the first time. In addition to dispensing advice about current vacancies in various professions and careers around Australia they also give information on cadetships, traineeships and apprenticeships. They not only give you as much information as you will need for your chosen career but they can also put you in touch with prospective employers. It is an excellent service for young people looking for a career in Australia.

CAREER REFERENCE CENTRES (CRC)

Career Reference Centres are situated in various CES offices throughout Australia; they are invaluable specialist reference libraries providing all sorts of information on occupations, study and training. They offer current information about jobs in all Australian states. In addition to experienced staff, job seekers also have audio and video tapes and a comprehensive collection of written material at their disposal. These offer information on employment and vocational training. In addition, there are videos to help people with the whole process of finding a job: writing applications, presentation at interviews and self-assessment.

The CRCs are open from 9-5 and no appointment is necessary, except for large groups. The addresses of the CRCs around Australia are as follows (all telephone numbers are local — prefix with 0106 if telephoning from outside Australia):

New South Wales
1st Floor, 818 George Street, Broadway, Sydney 2007. Tel: 212 2044.
Cnr. King & Darby Street, Newcastle 2300. Tel: 049 254566.
Level 2, Commonwealth Government Centre, Burelli Street, Wollongong 2500. Tel: 042 26 0157.

Victoria
Cnr. Elizabeth and La Trobe Streets, Melbourne 3000. Tel: 03 663 8466.
170 Little Mallop Street, Geelong 3220. Tel: 052 21 3188.

Queensland
280 Adelaide Street, Brisbane 4000. Tel: 07 226 9266.
Home In Centre, 2529 Gold Coast Highway, Mermaid Beach 4218. Tel: 075 52 5400.

South Australia
44 Currie Street, Adelaide 5000. Tel: 08 231 9966.

Western Australia
Ground Floor, 263 Adelaide Terrace, Perth 6000. Tel: 09 425 4670.

Tasmania
85 Macquarie Street, Hobart 7000. Tel: 002 35 7102

Australian Capital Territory
Melbourne Building, Cnr. West Row and London Circuit, Canberra 2600.
Tel: 062 48 7766.

Northern Territory
15 Scaturchio Street, Casuanina, Darwin 5792. Tel: 089 27 1404.

WORK INFORMATION CENTRES (WIC)

Work Information Centres provide a similar service to CRCs but the emphasis is on *local* availability of jobs and careers. WICs are intended to be used by job-seekers as they would a library — ie largely a self-help service. There is both written and audio material, providing in-depth coverage of the local job scene. It is an excellent service for people looking for a job as they are free to go through the literature at their own pace and there is always someone there to help if necessary.

WICs are located in a large number of CES offices throughout Australia:

New South Wales: Metropolitan
44-50 Auburn Road, Auburn 2114. Tel: 646 0111.
15 Green Fields Pde, Bankstown 2200. Tel: 707 4399.
350 Windsor Road, Baulkham Hills 2153. Tel: 639 7266.
113 Main Street, Blacktown 2148. Tel: 622 0800.
38 Green Street, Brookvale 2100. Tel: 938 0100.
195a Burwood Road, Burwood 2134. Tel: 747 2044.
101 Queens Street, Campbelltown 2560. Tel: 046 20 1000.
Lombard House 1st Floor, 70 Archer Street, Chatswood 2067. Tel: 412 6111.
13-15 Wentworth Avenue, Darlinghurst 2010. Tel: 261 5655.
7 William Street, Fairfield 2165. Tel: 278 8111.
11 Albert Street, Hornsby 2077. Tel: 477 1700.
5-7 Railway Pde, Hurtsville 2220. Tel: 580 8366.
24-30 Scott Street, Liverpool 2170. Tel: 602 7222.
244 Pitt Street, Merrylands 2160. Tel: 682 9600.
Cnr. Cleeves Close & North Parade, Mt. Druitt. Tel: 625 1900.
123 Walker Street, North Sydney 2060. Tel: 922 2433.
2-10 Macquarie Street, Parramatta 2150. Tel: 893 4444.
109 Henry Street, Penrith 2750. Tel: 047 32 9800.
432 Parramatta Road, Petersham 2049. Tel: 550 0555.
135 Belmore Road, Randwick 2031. Tel: 398 9888,
35 Devlin Street, Ryde 2112. Tel: 809 7688.
172 Queens Street, St Marys 2760. Tel: 673 1055.
2 Merton Street, Sutherland 2232. Tel: 545 1122.
7 Baker Street, Windsor 2756. Tel: 0452 77 4544.

New South Wales: Country
Wodonga, 520 Swift Street, Albury 2640. Tel: 060 213 400.
1st Floor Cnr. Bearoy and Danger Street, Armidale 2350. Tel: 067 721 300.
154 Russell Street, Bathurst 2795. Tel: 063 31 1588.
Simons Plaza, Auckland Street, Bega 2550. Tel: 0649 218 88.

32 Chlonde Street, Broken Hill 2880. Tel: 080 7155.

154 Canterbury Street, Casino 2470. Tel: 066 621 288.

Cnr. Vernon and Castle Streets, Coffs Harbour 2450. Tel: 066 521 433.

Cnr. Macquarie and Wingewarra Streets, Dubbo 2830. Tel: 068 85 8200.

123 Donnison Street, Gosford 2250. Tel: 043 247 555.

23-25 Motague Street, Goulburn 2580. Tel: 048 212 755.

69 Yambil Street, Griffith 2680. Tel: 069 621 411.

13 Byron Street, Inverell 2360. Tel: 067 223 588.

77 Katoomba Street, Katoomba 2780. Tel: 047 821 011.

40 Wade Avenue, Leeton 2705. Tel: 069 532 899.

66 Woodlark Street, Lismore 2320. Tel: 066 218 7000.

314 High Street, Maitland 2320. Tel: 049 33 6922.

Australia House, Commercial Road, Murwillumbah 2484. Tel: 066 721
    488.

160 Bridge Street, Muswellbrook 2333. Tel: 065 43 3233.

73 Maitland Street, Narrabri 2390. Tel: 067 921 300.

61-63 North Street, Nowra 2540. Tel: 044 216 066.

189 Anson Street, Orange 2800. Tel: 063 61 4144.

206 Clarinda Street, Parkes 2870. Tel: 068 622 055.

143 Horton Street, Port Macquarie 2444. Tel: 065 83 5011.

474 Peel Street, Tamworth 2340. Tel: 067 681 999.

5 Macquarie Street, Taree 2430. Tel: 065 523 366.

25-27 Thompson Street, Wagga Wagga 2650. Tel: 069 21 7766.

Cnr. Alison Road and Margaret Streets, Wyong 2259. Tel: 043 53 1488.

Victoria

48 Bailey Street, Bairnsdale. Tel: 051 52 5155.

16 Victoria Street, Ballarat. Tel: 053 33 2320.

328 Lyttleton Terrace, Bendigo. Tel: 054 43 8566.

252 Dorset Road, Boronia. Tel: 762 93.

1 Bank Street, Box Hill. Tel: 895 0444.

1st Floor, 979 Burke Road, Camberwell. Tel: 813 1366.

1251 Nepean Highway, Cheltenham. Tel: 583 1899.

347 Sydney Road, Coburg. Tel: 383 3011.

61 Gellibrand Street, Colac. Tel: 052 31 4277.

1st Floor, Corio Village, Bacchus Marsh Road, Corio. Tel: 052 75 2901.

288-290 Thomas Street, Dandenong. Tel: 794 8033.

217 Pakenham Street, Echuca. Tel: 054 82 2333.

214 Nicholson Street, Footscray. Tel: 687 7177.

2nd Floor, White Street Mall, Wells Street, Frankston. Tel: 781 3466.

Cnr. Glenroy Road and Blenheim Street, Glenroy. Tel: 300 3911.

190 Gray Street, Hamilton. Tel: 055 72 1644.
89-91 Burgundy Street, Heidelberg. Tel: 50 8888.
90 Firebrace Street, Horesham. Tel: 053 82 0188.
Cnr. Fitzroy and Wellington Streets, Kenang. Tel: 054 52 2066.
Cnr. Carke and Main Streets, Lilydale. Tel: 735 0333.
1st Floor, 177 High Street, Maryborough. Tel: 054 61 2744.
171 High Street, Melton. Tel: 747 8022.
Commonwealth Centre, Ninth Street, Mildura. Tel: 050 22 2922.
31-33 Kirk Street, Moe. Tel: 051 27 4911.
331 Main Street, Mornington. Tel: 059 75 7755.
225-227 Princes Highway, Morewell. Tel: 051 33 9033.
312 Keilor Road, Niddrie. Tel: 379 4119.
2 Mons Parade, Noble Park. Tel: 548 3999.
279 High Street, Northcote. Tel: 489 6222.
358 Whitehorse Road, Nunawading. Tel: 877 7811.
77 Atherton Road, Oakleigh. Tel: 563 2033.
36 Gawler Street, Portland. Tel: 055 23 2044.
251-253 High Street, Preston. Tel: 416 9555.
12-16 Ninth Avenue, Rosebud. Tel: 059 86 4666.
80-82 Ackland Street, St Kilda. Tel: 534 8111.
79 Raymond Street, Sale. Tel: 051 44 6966.
20 Staton Street, Seymour. Tel: 057 92 1744.
Commonwealth Centre, Cnr. Maude and Fraser Streets, Shepparton. Tel: 058 31 1599.
1-7 Elaine Street, St Albans. Tel: 366 4222.
52-55 Main Street, Stawell. Tel: 053 58 2701.
18 Withers Street, Sunshine. Tel: 312 6055.
6-8 McCallum Street, Swan Hill. Tel: 050 32 4571.
Cnr. Hothan and Church Streets, Traralgon. Tel: 051 74 9577.
Cnr. Faithful and Ovens Streets, Wangaratta. Tel: 057 21 5411.
162 Liebig Street, Warrnambool. Tel: 055 62 4266.

Queensland: Metropolitan
Cnr. Ferndale Street and Ipswich Road, Annerley 4103. Tel: 07 892 2255.
Cnr. Russell and Bloomfield Streets, Cleveland 4163. Tel: 07 286 3211.
Cnr. Wickham and Gotham Streets, Fortitude Valley 4006. Tel: 07 852 1251.
2 Smiths Road, Goodna 4300. Tel: 07 818 1099.
Commonwealth Offices, Civic Centre, Kittyhawk Street, Inala 4077. Tel: 07 372 1833.
17 Station Road, Indooroopilly 4068. Tel: 07 878 1999.

Garden Square, Cnr. Kessels Road and Macgregor Street, Upper Mount
    Gravatt 4122. Tel: 07 343 3066.
34 Station Street, Nundah 4012. Tel: 07 266 1277.
99 Sutton Street, Redcliffe 4020. Tel: 07 284 6733.
Station Mall, 21 Station Road, Woodridge 4114. Tel: 07 208 6122.
86 Charlotte Street, Wynnum 4178. Tel: 07 396 7122.

Queensland: Country
282 Ross River Road, Aitkenvale 4814. Tel: 077 79 9744.
29 Mabel Street, Atherton 4883. Tel: 070 91 1277.
100 Macmillan Street, Ayr 4807. Tel: 077 83 1633.
1st Floor Cnr. Quay and Barolin Streets, Bundaberg 4670. Tel: 071 52
    4377.
5 James Street, Caboolture 4510. Tel: 074 95 2555.
Coolangatta Shopping Resort, 2nd Floor Cnr. Griffith and Warner Streets,
    Coolangatta. Tel: 075 36 6400.
Cnr. Archibald Street and Condamine Highway, Dalby 4405. Tel: 074 62
    1122.
100 Goondoon Street, Gladstone 4680. Tel: 079 72 1911.
10-12 Mary Street, Gympie 4570. Tel: 071 82 2322.
High Park Shopping Centre, 72 Herbert Street, Ingham 4850. Tel: 077 76
    2222.
42-44 Ernest Street, Innisfail 4860. Tel: 070 61 1333.
26 East Street, Ipswich 4305. Tel: 07 281 3155.
122 Eagle Street, Longreach 4730. Tel: 074 58 1181.
Commonwealth Centre, Cnr. Victoria and Gregory Streets, Mackay 4740.
    Tel: 079 57 9400.
196-198 Byrne Street, Mareeba 4880. Tel: 070 92 1133.
28 Ocean Street, Maroochydore 4558. Tel: 071 43 3744.
Ace Arcade Bazaar Street, Maryborough 4650. Tel: 071 22 2500.
27-31 Simpson Street, Mount Isa 4825. Tel: 077 43 4511.
44 Lowe Street, Nambour 4560. Tel: 071 41 3177.
225 Musgrave Street, North Rockhampton 4700. Tel: 079 27 9355.
Commonwealth Government Centre, Bell Street Mall, Toowoomba 4350.
    Tel: 076 38 1022.
22 Palmerin Street, Warwick 4370. Tel: 076 61 2211.
304-308 Mulgrave Road, Westcourt 4870. Tel: 070 51 7100.

South Australia
3 Riverview Drive, Berri 5343. Tel: 085 82 3000.
503 Brighton Road, Brighton 5048. Tel: 298 6066.

442 Torrens Road, Kilkenny 5009. Tel: 243 1466.

28 Philip Highway, Elizabeth 5112. Tel: 252 2980.

Cnr. Cowan and Murray Streets, Gawler 5118. Tel: 085 22 1866.

8 Bridge Street, Murray Bridge 5253. Tel: 085 32 4888.

Cnr. Smart and Reservoir Roads, Modbury 5092. Tel: 265 5135.

5-64 Commercial Street West, Mount Gambier 5290. Tel: 087 259 788.

Ramsay Walk, Noarlunga Centre, Noarlunga 5168. Tel: 32 6216.

257 Fullarton Road, Parkside 5063. Tel: 279 2000.

306 Payneham Road, Payneham 5070. Tel: 362 9388.

50 Leadenhall Street, Port Adelaide 5015. Tel: 341 2332.

99 Commercial Road, Port Augusta 5700. Tel: 086 42 6366.

85 Tasman Terrace, Port Lincoln 5606. Tel: 086 82 5677.

60 Florence Street, Port Pirie 5540. Tel: 086 32 5000.

91 John Street, Salibury 5108. Tel: 281 5677.

169 Nicalson Avenue, Whyalla Norrie 5608. Tel: 086 45 7455.

Western Australia: Metropolitan

Stirling Gate Commercial Centre, 257 Balcatta Road, Balcatta 6021. Tel: 09 344 1044.

AMP House Melville City Centre, Davy Street, Booragoon 6154. Tel: 09 364 9777.

32 Burton Street, Cannington 6107. Tel: 09 458 7077.

33 St Quentin Street, Claremont 6010. Tel: 09 383 3033.

Cnr. Lancaster Street and Rockingham Road, Speawood 6163. Tel: 09 335 6444.

Unit 27, Fremantle Malls, William Street, Fremantle 6160. Tel: 09 335 6444.

384 Scarborough Beach Road, Innaloo 6018. Tel: 09 244 1551.

Shop 97 Kwinana Hub Shopping Centre, Gilmore Avenue, Kwinana 6167. Tel: 09 419 1333.

Job Centre, 4 Binley Place, Maddington 6109. Tel: 09 493 2488.

272 Great Eastern Highway, Midland 6056. Tel: 09 274 1344.

Mirrabooka House, 6 Ilkeston Place, Mirrabooka 6061. Tel: 09 344 2722.

Cnr. Walter Road and Russell, Morley 6062. Tel: 09 276 5666.

363 Oxford Street, Mount Hawthorn 6016. Tel: 09 444 5411.

206 Adelaide Terrace, Perth 6000. Tel: 09 325 6755.

23-25 Simpson Avenue, Rockingham 6168. Tel: 09 527 8811.

117-120 Shepparton Road, Victoria Park 6100. Tel: 09 470 4001.

Western Australia: Country

265 York Street, Albany 6330. Tel: 098 41 2577.

Kimberley Regional Centre, Cnr. Frederick and Weld Streets, Broome 6725. Tel: 091 92 1501.

Mutual Acceptance House, Cnr. Stirling and Spencer Streets, Bunbury 6230. Tel: 097 21 4355.

34 Stuart Street, Carnarvon 6701. Tel: 099 41 1107.

51 Prinsep Street, Collie 6225. Tel: 097 34 1255.

Unit 2, Cnr. Hicks and Dempster Streets, Esperance 6450. Tel: 090 71 2422.

73-77 Marine Terrace, Geraldton 6530. Tel: 099 21 1522.

Commonwealth Offices, Cnr. Brookman and Porter Streets, Kalgoorlie 6430. Tel: 090 21 1011.

Realty House, Hedland Place, Karratha 6714. Tel: 091 85 397.

Commonwealth Offices, Konkerberry Drive, Kununurra Drive, Kununurra 6743. Tel: 091 68 1211.

39 Pinjarra Road, Mandurah 6210. Tel: 09 535 4611.

Unit 6, 30 Rose Street, Manjimup 6258. Tel: 097 71 1088.

50A Barrack Street, Merredin 6415. Tel: 090 41 1763.

89 Fitzgerald Street, Northam 6401. Tel: 096 22 1511.

Commonwealth Government Centre, Brand Street, South Hedland 6722. Tel: 091 72 2266.

CES Agent Offices

H and R Block, 17B Albert Street, Busselton 6280. Tel: 097 52 3511.

Kable Agencies, 46 Clarendon Street, Derby 6728. Tel: 091 91 1322.

Richardson Building, 102 Clive Street, Katanning 6317. Tel: 098 21 1944.

Kendle and Co., Estate Agents, 49 Federal Street, Narrogin 6312. Tel: 098 81 2190.

Tasmania

1 Bligh Street, Rosny Park, Bellerive. Tel: 44 6444.

49 Cattley Street, Burnie. Tel: 31 6077.

35 Oldaker Street, Devonport. Tel: 24 6244.

3 Cooper Street, Glenorchy. Tel: 72 8477.

174 Collins Street, Hobart. Tel: 20 5011.

16-18 Main Road, Houville. Tel: 64 1744.

124 Hobart Road, Kings Meadows. Tel: 44 8644.

Shop 1, 32-34 Channel Highway, Kingston. Tel: 29 4455.

93 Cameron Street, Launceston. Tel: 31 5122.

403 Invermay Road, Mowbray. Tel: 26 3611.

345 Elizabeth Street, North Hobart. Tel: 34 8000.

Northern Territory
Ground Floor, FAI Building, Cnr. Gregory Terrace and Bath Street, Alice Springs. Tel: 52 7122.
Ground Floor, Randazzo Building, Katherine Terrace, Katherine. Tel: 72 1655.
Commonwealth Centre, Paterson Street, Tennant Creek. Tel: 62 2499.

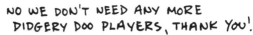

VOCATIONAL SERVICES BRANCHES

These are centres throughout New South Wales which offer vocational guidance including career counselling and the appraisal of abilities, interests and personal characteristics. They are designed to offer a flexible approach for individual job-seekers. These services are provided free of charge and one of the best features of these offices is a 500-page booklet entitled *Background to Careers* which covers more than 350 careers.

Vocational Service Branches can be located at the following addresses throughout New South Wales:

Sydney: City
3rd Floor, 1 Oxford Street, Darlinghurst 2010. Tel: 02 266 8111.
2nd Floor, The Capital Centre, 41 Rickard Road, Bankstown 2200. Tel: 02 707 2500.
Ground Floor, 22 Main Street, Blacktown 2148. Tel: 02 617 8606.
4th Floor, Hurtsville House, 34 McMahon Street, Hurtsville 2220. Tel: 02 570 1963.
3rd Floor, 131 George Street, Liverpool. Tel: 02 602 2777.

3rd Floor, 20-22 Wentworth Street, Parramatta 2150. Tel: 02 689 8617.
1st Floor, Memory Park Arcade, 438 High Street, Penrith 2750. Tel: 047 21 0273.
1st Floor, 39 Chandos Street, St Leonards 2065. Tel: 02 437 5455.

Sydney: Country
1st Floor, State Bank Building, 531 Dean Street, Albury 2640. Tel: 060 21 2999.
1st Floor, NSW Government Offices, Cnr. Faulkner and Dumaresqe Streets, Armidale 2350. Tel: 067 73 7233.
1st Floor, NSW Government Offices, 140 William Street, Bathurst 2795. Tel: 063 33 4376.
130 Brisbane Street, Dubbo 2830. Tel: 068 81 1376.
2nd Floor, GIO Building, 40 Mann Street, Gosford 2250. Tel: 043 24 3688.
NSW Government Offices, 213-215 Auburn Street, Goulburn 2580. Tel: 048 22 1282.
1st Floor, 50 Victoria Street, Grafton 2460. Tel: 066 42 5922.
4th Floor, 29 Molesworth Street, Lismore 2480. Tel: 066 21 7621.
326 High Street, Maitland 2320. Tel: 049 33 6425.
3rd Floor, Harbour Park Centre, 251 Wharf Road, Newcastle 2300. Tel: 049 25 8777.
NSW Government Office Building, Anson Street, Orange 2800. Tel: 063 63 8221.
Suite 2, 146 Gordon Street, Port Macquarie 2444. Tel: 065 84 9100.
2nd Floor, 203 Marius Street, Tamworth 2340. Tel: 067 66 4368.
1st Floor, Housing Commission Building, 72-78 Morgan Street, Wagga Wagga 2650. Tel: 069 21 0607.
State Government Offices, 84 Crown Street, Wollongong 2500. Tel: 042 26 8350.

7
The General Recruitment Network

EMPLOYMENT AGENCIES

Employment agencies proliferate in Australia, particularly for occupations such as secretarial and management. The following list includes a short selection of agencies in various states. For a more extensive list consult the *Yellow Pages* for the relevant state. This can either be done once you get to Australia or check in the nearest large city library in your area to see if they have any copies.

Australian Capital Territory/Canberra

Drake Personnel Ltd, 10 Moore Street, Canberra City. Tel: 062 249 6511. Permanent, temporary and contract staff covering secretarial, accounting, administration, sales, technical, executive and professional.

The Journalists Agency, Canberra New Business Centre, Canberra. Tel: 062 242 1950. All journalistic disciplines.

Keydata Temps, 10 Cohen Street, Belconnen. Tel: 062 251 5133. Specialists in temporary staff covering keyboard operators, word processing operators, secretarial, clerical, receptionists and personal assistants.

Professional Careers Australia, Canberra House, 40 Marcus Clarke Street, Canberra City. Tel: 062 257 1010. Permanent staff covering professional accounting staff, legal, executive, computing, sales and marketing, technical and secretarial. Temporary staff covering professional, technical, secretarial and clerical.

Templine, 33 Ainslie Avenue, Canberra City. Tel: 062 274 4000. Specialists in temporary staff covering word processing operators, secretarial, reception and clerical.

Tourism and Hospitality Service, 39 Jardine Street, Kingston. Tel: 062 295 3633. Permanent and temporary positions for all areas of the hospitality industry.

University of Canberra Student Employment Office, University of Canberra, Kirinari Street, Bruce, Canberra City. Casual and part-time opportunities for a wide range of workers.

New South Wales

Most employment agencies in Sydney have more than one office in the city. The addresses given here are for the most central offices to the city centre. For branch offices, look in the *Yellow Pages* for Sydney.

Accountancy Placements, 443 Kent Street, Sydney. Tel: 02 283 2733. Permanent and temporary accounting positions.

Austwal, Suite 902, 4 Bridge Street, Sydney. Tel: 02 252 4077. Temporary division executive and management recruitment.

Banking Placements, 25 Bligh Street, Sydney. Tel: 02 231 2433. Quality banking and finance personnel.

Brook Street, 4 Martin Place, Sydney. Tel: 02 233 1000. Permanent and temporary staff covering executive secretaries, personal assistants, word processing operators, data entry operators, receptionists, hospitality support staff, clerical staff, accounting, computer, sales and marketing, insurance, legal and medical.

Centacom, 72 Pitt Street, Sydney. Tel: 02 231 5555. Secretaries, receptionists, word processor operators, clerical office, sales and accountancy support.

Computer staff, 72 Pitt Street, Sydney. Tel: 233 6577. Permanent and temporary staff covering data entry, word processing, computer operators, PC support, systems engineers and programmers and software sales and support.

Drake Personnel, 255 George Street, Sydney. Tel: 02 231 6644. Typists, secretaries, word processor operators, data entry operators, clerks, book-keepers, receptionists, telephonists, accounting machine operators and computer operators.

The Journalists Agency, Suite 7, 590 Parramatta Road, Petersham. Tel: 02 550 9749. Writers, sub-editors, photographers and graphic artists.

Library Locums, 74 Redfern Street, Redfern. Tel: 02 699 1855. Permanent and temporary staff covering technicians, librarians and consultants.

Alfred Marks, 167 Kent Street, Sydney. Tel: 02 251 2688. Permanent and temporary staff covering secretarial, clerical, administrative, word processing, executive and industrial.

Professional Catering Staff, 2 Grosvenor Street, Bondi Junction, Sydney. Tel: 02 389 0155. All areas of the catering industry.

Travel Staff, 64 Castlereach, Sydney. Tel: 02 233 1466. Permanent and temporary staff covering travel executives, consultants, reservations, secretarial and support staff.

University of Sydney Graduate Employment Service, Arundel Street, Forest Lodge, Sydney. Tel: 02 692 3481. Casual and temporary employment for students and graduates.

Queensland

Brook Street, 145 Eagle Street, Brisbane. Tel: 07 832 3844. Permanent and temporary staff covering executive secretaries, personal assistants, word processing operators, data entry operators, receptionists, hospitality support staff, clerical staff, accounting, computing, sales and marketing, insurance, legal and medical.

Capablestaff, 5th Floor, Eagle House, 82 Eagle Street, Brisbane. GPO Box 2174 Brisbane. Tel: 07 221 9661. Permanent and temporary staff covering executives, secretarial, engineering, marketing, scientific, accounting, computing, trades, sales and training.

Food and Beverage Staff Placement, Timothy's Catering Service, 919 Sandgate Road, Clayfield, Brisbane. Tel: 07 862 2051. Managers, chefs, bar staff, waiters, cooks and bookkeepers.

Kelly Hospitality Recruitment, Level 5, 135 Wickham Terrace, Spring Hill. Tel: 07 832 2244. Executives, chefs, management, front office, housekeeping, financial, administrative, bar staff, floor staff and cleaning staff.

Law Staff, Level 19, T & G Building, 141 Queen Street, Brisbane. Tel: 07 221 1229. Solicitors, articled clerks, locums, legal secretaries, conveyancing clerks, legal temps, conference stenographers.

Lorraine Martin Personnel, 138 Albert Street, Brisbane. Tel: 07 229 8600. Permanent and temporary staff covering secretaries, receptionists, bookkeeping, word processing, data entry, management, marketing. Also in-house training and resumé preparation.

Manpower, 307 Queen Street, Brisbane. Tel: 07 221 0766. Permanent and temporary staff covering office work and sales, warehouse staff, forklift drivers, labourers, truck drivers and offsiders, process workers and tradesmen.

Alfred Marks, 1st Floor, Newspaper House, 289 Queen Street, Brisbane. Tel: 07 221 1855. Permanent and temporary covering secretarial, clerical, administrative, word processing, executive and industrial.

Masterstaff, Level 21, 10 Eagle Street, Brisbane 4000. Tel: 07 232 0474. Office, industrial, professional, executive and support staff selection.

Mitchell Consultants, 101 Wickham Terrace, Spring Hill. Tel: 07 832 4700. Permanent, temporary and contract staff for office, professional, sales, engineering, trades and computing.

South Australia

Hospitality staffing, 2nd Floor, Wyatt House, 115 Grenfell Street, Adelaide. Tel: 08 224 6161. Specialist recruitment for hotels, motels, restaurants, clubs and functions.

Jon and Associates, 91 William Street, Adelaide. Tel: 08 233 5839. Permanent and contract placements for all disciplines of architecture, engineering and drafting.

Kelly, 157 Grenfell Street, Adelaide. Tel: 08 232 0011. Permanent and temporary staff for secretarial, word processing, bookkeeping, data entry, clerical, receptionists and telemarketing.

Labstaff, 1st Floor, 139 St. Vincent Street, Port Adelaide. Permanent and temporary staff for covering scientific and medical occupations; research, quality control, analytical, production, management, medical, pharmaceutical, food, geochemical and industrial.

Medical Staff Placements, 17 Leigh Street, Adelaide. Tel: 08 212 2142. Permanent and casual medical staff covering state registered nurses, enrolled nurses, occupational therapists, health nurses, receptionists and secretaries.

Metier, 45 King Street, Adelaide. Tel: 08 231 4777. Permanent and temporary staff covering secretarial, word processing and office positions.

Oak Industrial, Suite 4, 155 Fullarton Road, Rose Park, South Australia 5067. Permanent, temporary and contract staff covering manufacturing, engineering, maintenance drafting and technical.

Quality Staff, 29 Marryatt Street, Port Adelaide. Tel: 08 341 2345. Permanent and temporary staff covering executive, sales, secretarial and clerical.

Skilled Engineering, 17 River Street, Hindmarsh. Tel: 08 340 1288. Specialist workers for electrical trades, metal trades, building trades, warehouse and factory staff, supervisors, drafters, engineers, planners, project groups and project management.

Victoria

A La Carte Staff Agency, 343 Little Collins Street, Melbourne. Tel: 03 670 7844. Permanent, temporary and emergency covering management, front office, executive chefs and cooks, waiting staff, bar staff, kitchen hands, canteen assistants and house maids.

Australia Wide Personnel, 79 Mahoneys Road, Forest Hill. Tel: 03 877 2322. Permanent, temporary and contract staff covering engineering, production, technical, sales, marketing, office support, word processing, accounting, administration and management.

Balance Accounting Staff, 51 Queen Street, Melbourne. Tel: 03 629 6611. Permanent and temporary staff covering taxation, audit, financial and management.

Bayside Personnel, 7 Bowen Crs, Melbourne. Tel: 03 867 6066. Permanent, temporary and contract staff covering architectural, engineering, drafting and secretarial.

Cartell Personnel, Suite 314, 3rd Floor 343 Lit Collins, Melbourne. Tel: 03 670 5661. Permanent and temporary staff for all areas of office work.

Carver and Associates, 2nd Floor 37 Queen Street, Melbourne. Tel: 03 614 7211. Permanent, temporary and support staff covering word processing, secretarial, data entry and accounts clerks.

Centacom Staff, 51 Elizabeth Street, Melbourne. Tel: 03 629 6291. Permanent and temporary staff covering secretaries, receptionists, word processor operators, clerical, office, sales and accountancy support.

Drake Personnel, 35 Collins Street, Melbourne. Tel: 03 654 4855 (Main office). Permanent and temporary office staff covering typists, secretaries, word processing operators, data entry operators, clerks, bookkeepers, receptionists, telephonists, accounting machine operators and computer operators.

Kelly Services, 2nd Floor 454 Collins Street, Melbourne. Tel: 03 670 9966. Permanent and temporary staff covering secretarial, office support, clerical, accountants, bookkeepers, insurance staff, finance staff, PC operators, receptionists, sales and marketing.

Masterstaff, 1st Floor, 66 Albert Road, South Melbourne. Tel: 03 690 3455. Permanent, temporary and contract staff for executive and support sectors.

TCS Computerstaff, 1st Floor, 402 Albert Street, East Melbourne. Tel: 03 662 2744. Salaried, temporary and contract staff covering programmers, analysts, computer operators, data entry operators, word processing operators, PC support, sales and engineers.

TriStar Computer Services, 608 St. Kilda Road, Melbourne. Tel: 03 529 8444. Permanent and contract staff covering programmers, analysts, project leaders and DP management.

Western Australia

Bayside Personnel, 7 Havelock Street, West Perth. Tel: 09 321 9983. Contract, permanent and temporary covering architectural, engineering and drafting.

Drake, 108 George's Terrace, Perth. Tel: 09 321 9911. Permanent or temporary staff covering secretaries, word processing, taxation, auditing, management and bookkeeping.

Health Profession Personnel,12 Hardy Street, South Perth. Tel: 09 474
   2343. Permanent and temporary staff covering dental, medical,
   nursing, child care, pharmaceutical.
Hospitality Personnel, Suite 17, The Russell Centre, 159 Adelaide
   Terrace, Perth. Tel: 09 221 2468. Permanent and temporary staff for
   hospitality staff in hotels, pubs, clubs and restaurants.
Insurance, Legal, Mining, Sales and Marketing, Suite 7, 1200 Hay Street,
   West Perth. Tel: 09 481 4262. Permanent and temporary staff covering
   secretarial, clerical, word processing, accounts, executive, administra-
   tion and management.
Pollitt's Employment Agency, 251 Adelaide Terrace, Perth. Tel: 09 325
   2544. Permanent and temporary staff for all areas of the hospitality
   business.
Success Personnel, 26 St. George's Terrace, Perth. Tel: 09 221 1522.
   Permanent and temporary staff for all categories.
Superior Personnel, Suite 6, 678 Beaufort Street, Mount Lawley, WA.
   Tel: 09 370 3121. Permanent and temporary staff for office work and
   word processing.
Technician Personnel Consultants, 5/266 Hay Street, Subiaco, Perth. Tel:
   09 382 4288. Permanent and temporary placements for all types of
   professional staff.
Tomorrow's Staff (incorporating Catertemp), 7th Floor, City Arcade
   Tower, 207 Murray Street, Perth 6000. Tel: 09 321 6391. Twenty-four
   hour relief service for all hospitality and catering staff.
Western Personnel Services, 109 St. George's Terrace, Perth. Tel: 09 321
   4104. Permanent and temporary staff for office, management, technical and industrial, sales, marketing and promotions, nursing and santa.

NEWSPAPERS

With at least two daily newspapers in most major Australian cities and up
to six in Sydney there is no shortage of newsprint to peruse in the Jobs
Vacant Sections. Most of the major newspapers carry extensive employment sections, covering all sectors of the employment market, from
business executives to deck-hands on prawn trawlers.
   The main big city newspapers are:

The Sydney Morning Herald, 235 Jones Street, Broadway, Sydney 2007.
   Tel: 02 282 2822.
The Melbourne Age, 250 Spencer Street, Melbourne. Tel: 03 601 2676.

The Adelaide Advertiser, 121 King William Street, Adelaide. Tel: 08 218
  9760.
The Brisbane Courier-Mail, Campbell Street, Bowen Hills, Brisbane. Tel:
  07 252 6011.
The West Australian, 219 St. George's Terrace, Perth. Tel: 09 482 3111.

Abbreviations in job advertisements

The following is a list of the abbreviations, and their meanings, which
appear most frequently in newspaper job advertisements in Australia.

acc.	according to	cas.	casual
dir	director	gen.	general
adm.	administrative	co.	company
dept	department	hrs.	hours
an. lve.	annual leave	coll.	college
D/L	Driving Licence	immed.	immediate
app.	applicant	comm.	commensurate with
D. O. B.	Date of Birth		interview
appshp	apprenticeship	int.	interview
DP	data processing	conds.	conditions
AP	accounts payable	K (or M)	thousand
A/R	accounts received	CV	Curriculum Vitae
EDP	electronic data processing	knwl	knowledge
apt.	appointment	deg.	degree
em.	employer/ment	maj.	major
asst.	assistant	max.	maximum
ess.	essential	ref/s	reference/s
av.	average	metro.	metropolitan
exc.	excluding	remun.	remuneration
avail.	available	M/F	male/female
exec.	executive	rep.	representative
Awd	Award	mfr.	manufacturer
exp.	experience	reqd	required
bgnr.	beginner	mgmt	management
F/C	full charge	S. A. E.	Stamped Addressed
bfts.	benefits		Envelope
fnl.	financial	min.	minimum
bus.	business	mktg	marketing
F/Pd	fee paid	sal.	salary
F/T	full-time	mth.	month
P/T	part-time	sec.	secretary

sten.	stenography	urg.	urgent
norm.	normal	ph.	phone
svc.	service	vac/y	vacant/vacancy
occ.	occupation	P.O.B.	post office box
tech.	technical	wk.	week/work
opp.	opportunity	pref.	preferred
temp.	temporary	wkly.	weekly
O/T	overtime	prev.	previous
trng.	training	w.p.m.	words per minute
p. a.	per annum	quals.	qualifications
trvl.	travel	recept.	receptionist
pd.	paid	R & D	research and
typg	typing		development
perm.	permanent	yrs	years

Is this you?

Accountant

Actuary

Advertising agent

Farm worker

Radio/TV announcer

Ambulance officer

Architect

Designer

Artist

Fashion illustrator

Air traffic controller

Photographer

Airline steward/ess

Beauty therapist

Bank officer

Builder

Cabinet-maker

Bricklayer

Carpenter

Painter/decorator

Plumber

Nursery nurse

Chiropractor

Childminder

Computer programmer

Data processor

Systems analyst

Community worker

Chef

Conservationist

Performing artist

Dentist

Defence worker

Economist

Film technician

Engineer

Television researcher

Forestry worker

Food technologist

Geologist

Graphic designer

Glazier

Hairdresser

Health worker

Health officer

Horticulturalist

Caterer

Hotelier

Insurance officer

Journalist

Jeweller

Lawyer

Locksmith

Librarian

Doctor

Metalworker

Nurse

Miner

Editor

Musician

Technical writer

Oil driller

Therapist

Optician

Photographer

Pharmacist

Physiotherapist

Printer

Police officer

Prison officer

Public service officer

Psychologist

Surveyor

Leisure manager

Ranger

Researcher

Teacher

Retailer

Australia offers a huge variety of employment opportunities.

8
Careers and Professions

There are a wide variety of careers available in Australia. These can either be entered by people who have gained relevant qualifications or experience in Britain, or training can be undertaken in Australia. In some cases, skills and qualifications will need to be assessed before you can take up an equivalent post in Australia. This will be dealt with in the following chapter. Addresses for the universities and further education establishments mentioned here are given in the chapter on Training.

The wages mentioned here should be used as a guide only, as more and more wage settlements are now being decided by performance.

ACCOUNTING

This covers a wide range of disciplines including accounting staff, accountant assistant, cost accountant, senior accounting executive, chief accountant, financial executive, research, Organisation and Methods, internal auditor, evaluator of projects and programs, and security analyst.

Qualification required: Degree
Where to study: Most major universities and Technical and Further Education (TAFE) colleges in all states.
Current workforce: 65,000+
Future prospects: Very good.
Starting wage: Various depending on the type of accounting.
Further information: The National Institute of Accountants, GPO Box 1128J, Melbourne, Victoria 3001.

ACTUARY

An expert in the theory and practice of statistics. They are called upon to deal with a wide range of statistical problems arising in insurance, superannuation funds, health insurance and a variety of other areas of finance. Most actuaries are employed by insurance companies or in private consultancies.

Qualification required: Degree.

Where to study: Australian University, Bond University, Queensland University of Technology, Macquarie University, University of Melbourne.

Current workforce: 2,000+

Future prospects: Good.

Starting wage: $575+.

Wage after three years: $725.

Further information: The Institute of Actuaries of Australia, Suite 1, 8th Floor, 49 Market Street, Sydney. Tel: 02 264 2411.

ADVERTISING

Account Manager

This is an advertising agency's representative to the client. He or she will be responsible for the overall advertising and marketing campaign of a specific product or image.

Qualification required: Degree

Where to study: Bond University, Charles Sturt University, Deakin University, Edith Cowan University, Queensland University of Technology, Victoria University of Technology — RMIT, University College of Central Queensland, University of New England, University of Western Sydney, Macleay College, Sydney. Also TAFE colleges in all states.

Current workforce: 5,000+.

Future prospects: Good.

Starting wage: $540.

Wage after three years: $700.

Further information: The Advertising Federation of Australia Ltd, 140 Arthur Street, North Sydney, NSW 2060.

Copywriter
The person who writes the scripts for radio, television and printed advertisements.

Qualification required: Degree.
Where to study: As above.
Current workforce: 200+.
Future prospects: Good.
Starting wage: $520.
Wage after three years: $690+.
Further information: As above.

AGRICULTURE AND FARM MANAGEMENT

Farming in Australia has become a tough occupation in recent years and today's farmers need to be managers, book-keepers, mechanics, veterinarians, agronomists and accountants.

Farm management is not just the process of running a farm, but organising land, labour and capital. However, unless you come from a farming family you will have to start near the bottom of the rung if you want to break into farming. The most common way to do this is as a farm hand or a dairy farm worker. This involves long hours and hard work but it can lead to a career in farm management:

Current workforce: 250,000+.
Future prospects: Numbers are likely to decline due to the recession in the farming industry.
Starting wage: $300+.
Wage after three years: $345+.
Further information: Victorian Farmers Federation, 240 Collins Street, Melbourne 3000. Tel: 03 650 9261. NSW Rural Training Committee, GPO Box 1068, Sydney 2001. United Farmers and Stockowners Association, 126 South Terrace, Adelaide 5000.

AMBULANCE SERVICE

Ambulance officer
Undertake similar work to ambulance officers in Britain; attending home,

work and car accidents. They are also likely to be called to incidents such as accidents in bush country or cliff rescues.

Paramedic

Paramedics attend life-threatening emergencies and have to have at least three years' experience as an ambulance officer and have passed all in-service training courses.

Rescue Squad Officers

These officers are involved in getting people trapped in accidents to hospital. Three years' experience as an ambulance officer is required and comprehensive training is given.

Co-ordinators

Co-ordinators work in the centre where the emergency calls are received. They must have three years' experience as ambulance officer and attend an eight week in-service training course.

Qualifications: In-service training and part-time TAFE courses.
Current workforce: 5,500+.
Future prospects: Growth expected.
Starting wage: $375+.
Wage after three years: $520+.
Further information: Career Reference Centres, Careers Advisers, Health
    Commission, in the relevant state.

ANNOUNCER

Can be news readers, disc jockeys or commentators for television or radio. A clear voice and a calm temperament are vital qualities and most announcers begin their careers on country radio stations.

Where to study: The Australian Film, Television and Radio School, PO
    Box 126, North Ryde, NSW.
Current workforce: 2,000+.
Future prospects: Hard to break in to but industry growth is expected.
Starting wage: $500+.
Wage after three years: $600+.
Further information: The Australian Broadcasting Corporation, GPO
    Box 9994, Sydney 2001.

ARCHITECT

Openings for qualified architects but also numerous opportunities for training in Australia.

Qualification: Degree.
Where to study: Universities of Adelaide, Canberra, Melbourne, New South Wales, Newcastle, Queensland, South Australia, Tasmania and Curtain and Deakin Universities.
Current workforce: 10,000.
Future prospects: Reasonable growth but has been hit by the recession.
Starting wage: $415+.
Wage after three years: $520+.
Further information: Royal Institute of Architects, NSW Chapter, 3 Manning Street, Potts Point, NSW.

ART AND DESIGN

Covering commercial artists, community artworkers, community arts officers, graphic designers, textile and fashion designers, industrial designers, illustrators, advertising layout artists, photographers, window dressers and sculptors.

Where to train: As above, plus Ballarat University College, Charles Sturt University, Riverina, Griffith University, La Trobe University College of Northern Victoria, Monash University, Swinburne Institute of Technology, School of Visual Art, East Sydney, The KVB College of Visual Communication and Billy Blue School of Art.
Current workforce: 50,000.
Future prospects: Very good — self-employment is a serious option for many people in art and design.
Starting wage: $450.
Wage after three years: $550.
Further information: School of Art and Design, East Sydney Technical College, Forbes Street, Darlinghurst, NSW. The Crafts Council of Australia, 35 George Street, The Rocks, Sydney. The National Association for the Visual Arts, 1/245 Chalmers Street, Redfern.

AIR TRAFFIC SERVICES

Air Traffic Controllers
Responsible for all aircraft movements inside and outside controlled airspace.

Qualifications: Specialist training courses.

Where to study: University of Tasmania, Civil Aviation Authority — twelve month on-the-job training for former pilots and defence air traffic controllers.

Current workforce: 3,900.

Future prospects: Good.

Starting wage: $575.

Wage after three years: $690.

Further information: Civil Aviation Authority, GPO Box 367, Canberra 2601.

Defence Force Recruiting Centre, 323 Castlereagh Street, Sydney 2000.

Flight attendants

Generally they must be between 1.6m and 1.83m in height, in good health and preferably have previous experience of the catering industry and knowledge of a foreign language.

Qualifications: Special airline training courses.

Where to study: Individual airlines provide their own training.

Current workforce: 8,700.

Future prospects: Good.

Starting wage: $460.

Wage after three years: $525.

Further information: Qantas Airways Limited, Jamison Street, Sydney 2000.

Australian Airlines, Hunter and Philip Streets, Sydney 2000.

East-West Airlines, Level 3, 431 Glebe Point Road, Glebe 2037.

Ansett Airlines and Air NSW, Oxford Square, Oxford and Riley Streets, Sydney 2000.

BANK OFFICER

The way in for most people to the banking trade. This can lead to several areas of banking including administration, secretarial, accountancy, auditing, international banking and portfolio management.

Qualifications: A minimum of four years' secondary schooling. Some banks also operate entrance examinations. In-house training is given for successful applicants. Graduates are greatly in demand by banks and they are usually thought of as head office and senior management material.

Where to study: Australian Catholic University (Mackillop Campus, North Sydney) offers a degree course in Banking and Finance.

Current workforce: Teller: 48,000+. Bank branch managers: 14,000+. Bank accountants: 75,000+.

Future prospects: Very good.

Starting wage: $250+ (Tellers).

Wage after three years: $370+ (Tellers).

Further information: All bank branch managers. Also the Australian Bank Employees Union, PO Box 435, Milsons Point 2061.

BEAUTY THERAPY

People over the age of 21 years old are preferred for most beauty salons. Experience in cosmetic sales or hairdressing are desirable as a basic grounding in the beauty business. Training in beauty therapy is regulated by the **Advanced Association of Beauty Therapists** (AABTh).

Training: Mostly done in salons or in specialised schools.

Where to study: Technical and Further Education (TAFE) colleges throughout Australia.

Current workforce: 7,500+.

Future prospects: Good.

Starting wage: $290+.

Wage after three years: $370+.

Further information: Advanced Association of Beauty Therapists, PO Box 2885, GPO Sydney 2001.

BUILDING TRADES

The building trade in general has been hit badly by the recession in Australia but there are still possibilities for casual employment or a career in building.

Bricklayer

Training: Apprenticeship.

Where to study: TAFE and on-the-job training.

Current workforce: 35,000+.

Future prospects: Little growth expected.

Starting wage: $440+.

Wage after three years: $470+.

Cabinet-maker

Training: Apprenticeship.

Where to study: TAFE and on-the-job training.

Current workforce: 28,000.
Future prospects: Some small growth expected.
Starting wage: $385.
Wage after three years: $440+.

Carpenter/Joiner

Training: Apprenticeship.
Where to study: TAFE and on-the-job training.
Current workforce: 110,000+.
Future prospects: Little growth expected.
Starting wage: $440+.
Wage after three years: $470.

Plumber

Training: Apprenticeship.
Where to study: TAFE and on-the-job training.
Current workforce: 50,000+.
Future prospects: Little growth expected.
Starting wage: $440.
Wage after three years: $470.

Plasterer

Training: Apprenticeship.
Where to study: TAFE and on-the-job training.
Current workforce: 20,000+.
Future prospects: Little growth expected.
Starting wage: $440+.
Wage after three years: $470+.

Painter and decorator

Training: Apprenticeship.
Where to study: TAFE and on-the-job training.
Current workforce: 49,000+.
Future prospects: Little growth expected.
Starting wage: $385+.
Wage after three years: $440+.

Building technician

This is a combination of a tradesperson and the duties of a professional builder.

Training: Apprenticeship and Associate Diploma Courses.
Where to study: TAFE and on-the-job training.
Current workforce: 27,000+.
Future prospects: Little growth expected.
Starting wage: $440+.
Wage after three years: $550+.

Professional builder

These are people, generally with a building related degree, who work on large building projects. They are involved in technological, managerial and economic decisions.

Training: Apprenticeship and Associate Diploma, or Degree, or Graduate
   Diploma.
Where to study: TAFE, on-the-job training and at universities throughout
   Australia.
Current workforce: 35,000+.
Future prospects: Good.
Starting wage: $460+.
Wage after three years: $520+.

Further information for all aspects of the building trade:

● Building Careers Information Centre, 6-12 Atchison Street, St Leonard NSW 2065. Postal address: Box 508, St Leonard.

● The Building Workers Industrial Union, 490 Kent Street, Sydney, NSW 2000.

● The Master Builders Association, 52 Parrish Road, Forest Lodge, NSW 2037.

● TAFE Information Centre, Railway Square, Broadway, NSW 2007.

CHILD CARE

Most child care workers work in child care centres and kindergartens, many of them run by organisations including the Kindergarten Union of NSW, Sydney Day Nursery and the Nursery Schools Association.

Qualifications: Degree, diploma or certificate courses.
Where to study: Universities of Melbourne, South Australia, Western

Australia and Western Sydney, Queensland University of Technology, Northern Territory University, Charles Sturt University, Edith Cowan University, Hedland College, Macquarie University and TAFE colleges.

Current workforce: 50,000.

Future prospects: Good.

Starting wage: Child care worker: $230+. Child care co-ordinator: $460.

Wage after three years: Child care worker: $300. Child care co-ordinator: $550.

CHIROPRACTOR

There are several openings for chiropractors to set up their own practices in Australia. There are also opportunities in clinics, teaching and research.

Qualifications: Degree.

Where to study: Macquarie University, Philip Institute of Technology.

Current workforce: 1400+.

Future prospects: Average.

Starting wage: $550+.

Wage after three years: $715+.

Further information: Philip Institute of Technology, Plenty Road, Bundoora, Victoria 3083.

The Australian Chiropractics Association in individual states.

COMPUTING

This is an area in which jobs and wages depend greatly on experience and qualifications. The wages quoted here are less than experienced staff can expect.

Systems Analysts/Programmers

Qualifications: An accountancy qualification or tertiary training in commerce, economics, computer science, science or engineering is recommended.

Where to study: Most Australian universities and TAFE colleges offer relevant courses.

Current workforce: 57,000+.

Future prospects: Very good.

Starting wage: $575+.

Wage after three years: $725+.
Further information: The Australian Computer Society, 66 King Street, Sydney, NSW 2000.

Computer operators/Word processing operators/Data preparation operators

Training: TAFE and private college courses.
Where to study: As above.
Current workforce: 110,000+.
Future prospects: Very good.
Starting wage: $275+.
Wage after three years: $425+.
Further information: As above and Metropolitan Business College, 74 Wentworth Avenue, Sydney, NSW 2010.

COMMUNITY ARTS

A relatively new career in which artists are employed to design and paint murals, plan and build playgrounds, develop community festivals, write and perform music for community groups and research and write local histories. The people who organise these activities are Community Arts Officers. Most of these posts are at least partly subsidised by the Australia Council.

Qualifications: Degree, diploma or associate diploma.
Where to study: Arts, humanities or social science qualifications at universities around Australia.
Current workforce: 250+.
Future prospects: Good.
Starting wage: $575.
Wage after three years: $690.
Further information: Special Project Officer (Community Arts Officers), Community Development Unit, Australia Council, Lawson Street, Redfern, NSW 2060. NSW Community Arts Association, Box 44, Trades Hall, Goulburn Street, Sydney, NSW 2000.

CONSERVATOR/ART RESTORER

Qualifications: Degree.
Where to study: University of Canberra.
Current workforce: 300+.

Future prospects: Good.
Further information: University of Canberra, PO Box 1, Belconnen, ACT 2616.

COOK/CHEF

This is another area which could be particularly fruitful for migrants — European chefs and cooks are highly thought of and there are openings within all areas of the catering industry for qualified personnel. Training can also be undertaken on arrival in the country.

Training: Apprenticeship (usually four years) and on-the-job training.
Where to study: TAFE colleges in all states.
Current workforce: 55,000.
Future prospects: Good.
Starting wage: $250+.
Wage after three years: $400+.
Further information: Federated Liquor and Allied Industries Union, 19 Argyle Street, Parramatta, NSW 2150. The Catering Institute of Australia, GPO Box 157, Sydney, NSW 2001. The Australian Hotels Association, 60 Clarence Street, Sydney NSW 2000. Restaurant and Catering Trades Association of NSW, 32 Buckingham Street, Surry Hills, NSW 2010.

DANCE

Australia is becoming increasingly appreciative of the performing arts and dance is one area where talented people should be able to find work.

Training: Various, including degree, diploma and courses at private schools.
Where to study: Australian College of Physical Education, Victorian College of the Arts, The Australian Ballet School.
Current workforce: 700+.
Future prospects: Average — outstanding talent is the only way to ensure employment.
Starting wage: $400+.
Wage after three years: $500+.
Further information: The Australian Ballet School, 2 Kavanagh Street, South Melbourne, Victoria. Tel: 03 649 8600. Australian Association for Dance Education, PO Box 287, Jamison, ACT 2614.

DEFENCE FORCES

There are currently 70,000 people in the Australian Defence Forces. To be eligible to join you must be an Australian citizen, or be eligible to become one, pass a medical, pass an aptitude test, have the required education qualifications, be within prescribed age limits and be prepared to serve anywhere. Almost every civilian post has a parallel in the Navy, Army and Airforce and every year the services need to enlist 6,000 new recruits. Training is offered in a wide range of skills.

The most common form of entry into the Defence Forces is through the **Defence Forces Academy** (applicants must usually be between 17 and 20 years of age), apprenticeships, or direct entrants from civilian careers.

Further information: Defence Forces Recruiting Centre, Central Square, 323 Castlereagh Street, NSW 2000, or enquiries can be sent to Director of Recruiting, Box XYZ in any state capital city.

DENTISTRY

Similar to the dentistry business in Britain — dentists or prospective dentists are always in demand.

Qualification: Degree — a five year course within Australia.
Where to study: Universities of Melbourne, Queensland, Sydney, Adelaide and Western Australia.
Current workforce: 6,200+.
Future prospects: Good.
Starting wage: $800.
Wage after three years: $920+.
Further information (including dental assistants): Dean of the faculty of dentistry at the above universities. NSW Dental Assistants Association, Mail Box 47, Trades Hall, Goulburn Street, Sydney 2000.

DRAFTING

Covers a variety of careers including architectural drafter, survey drafter and cartographic drafter.

Qualifications: Associate Diploma of Advanced Certificate courses.

Where to study: TAFE colleges in all states.
Current workforce: 27,000 covering all three categories.
Future prospects: Good.
Starting wage: $450+.
Wage after three years: $575.
Further information: TAFE information centres.

DRAMA

As in other parts of the world there are more people who want to be actors/actresses than there are openings in the profession. This inevitably leads to a large number of people in the drama profession being 'between jobs'.

Training: Degree, Diploma or Associate Diploma.
Where to study: The premier choice is the **National Institute of Dramatic Art** (NIDA). They offer three full-time diploma courses in Acting, Technical Production and Design and two full-time diploma courses in Theatre Crafts and a one year full-time diploma course in Directing. Applicants are accepted from all over the country and they also run courses covering other aspects of drama. Auditions for the Acting and Directing courses are held between November and December in all state capital cities. Various other courses are held at most Australian universities.
Current workforce: 2,200.
Future prospects: Average.
Starting wage: $400+.
Wage after three years: $475.
Further information: National Institute of Dramatic Art, PO Box 1, Kensington, NSW 2033.

ECONOMIST

One profession which is slightly frowned upon by the public as a result of the current recession. Nevertheless their future looks bright.

Qualifications: Degree.
Where to study: Most Australian universities.
Current workforce: 2,500.
Future prospects: Very good.

Starting wage: $600.
Wage after three years: $800+.
Further information: Economics faculty at any university.

ELECTRONIC ENGINEERING

A growing industry with opportunities in areas such as private industry and the consultancy, in hospitals, in radio and television and government departments.

Qualification: Degree.
Where to study: Most Australian universities.
Current workforce: 30,000+.
Future prospects: Good.
Starting wage: $540+.
Wage after three years: $710+.

Electronic Engineering Technician

Qualifications: Associate Diploma or Advanced Certificate (usually two years). Also civilian traineeships with the Department of Commerce.
Where to study: TAFE colleges in all states.
Current workforce: 36,000+.
Future prospects: Good.
Starting wage: $480+.
Wage after three years: $575+.
Further information: Institution of Radio and Electronics Engineers, Australia Commercial Unit 3, 2 New McLean Street, Edgecliff, NSW.

ENGINEERING

This covers several professions: professional engineering; civil engineering; electrical engineering; mechanical engineering; chemical engineering; maritime engineering; mining engineering; metallurgical engineering; agricultural engineering; aeronautical engineering; production engineering and industrial engineering.

Professional engineers are paid according to a nationally agreed pay award and they should hold a qualification which satisfies The Institute of Engineers.

Qualification: Degree.

Where to study: Most Australian universities.
Current workforce: 85,000.
Future prospects: Good.
Starting wage: $520+.
Wage after three years: $720+.
Further information: The Institute of Engineers, 118 Alfred Street, Milsons Point, NSW 2061.
The Association of Consulting Engineers Australia, 75 Miller Street, North Sydney, NSW 2060.

FASHION DESIGNER

Qualifications: Degree, Diploma, Associate Diploma and Certificate courses.
Where to study: TAFE colleges, Victorian College of Technology, University of Tasmania, University of Technology, Sydney.
Current workforce: 3,000+.
Future prospects: Good.
Starting wage: $460.
Wage after three years: $575+.
Further information: TAFE colleges in all states.

FILM AND TELEVISION

An industry which employs people with a variety of skills: scriptwriter; producer; art director; production designer; director; sound recordist; director of photography; and editor.

The best way to break into the film and television industry is to apply to the **Australian Film and Television School** which is the national film, television and radio authority. The aim of the school is to maintain a continuing supply of skilled professionals for these industries. It does not give basic training for people with no experience. A three-year full-time degree course is offered as well as shorter courses, varying from three months to two years. Applicants are aged between 18 to 35 years and need to show a commitment to working in film and television.

Further information: The Australian Film and Television School, PO Box 126 North Ryde, NSW 2113. Tel: 02 805 6446. For an authoritative and readable careers guide see *How to Get Into Films & TV* by Robert Angell, a BAFTA Council Member (How To Books, Plymouth).

FISHING

The creation of a 200-mile Australian fishing zone has led to greater possibilities for the use of fishing resources in the country. The onset of more deep sea fishing means that there is a greater use of modern technology in all sectors of the fishing industry. This now means that there are other careers available than those of fisherman/woman or skipper. These include fishing gear technologist, seafood marketing manager, fisheries biologist and fisheries inspector.

Further information: Australian Maritime College, PO Box 986, Launceston, Tasmania 7250. Tel: 003 26 6493.

FOOD TECHNOLOGY

The hi-tech side of the food industry, this covers all aspects of preserving and processing of all foodstuffs.

Qualifications: Degree, Associate Diploma or Advanced Certificate.
Where to study: Universities of New South Wales, Newcastle, Queensland, Tasmania, Western Australia, and Australian Maritime College, and Ballarat University College.
Current workforce: 10,000+.
Future prospects: Good.
Starting wage: $470+.
Wage after three years: $610+.

FORESTRY

The main areas covered are protection, management, silviculture (growing and tending of trees), wood technology and utilisation, and engineering.

Qualifications: Degree.
Where to study: Specific forestry courses at Australian National University, and universities of Melbourne and Queensland. Also agricultural courses at universities and colleges throughout the country.
Current workforce: 1,000.
Future prospects: Good.
Starting wage: $460.
Wage after three years: $575.

Further information: Institute of Foresters of Australia, PO Box Q213, Queen Victoria Building, Sydney, NSW 2000.

GARDENER/GREENKEEPER

Training: TAFE Certificate Courses, Apprenticeships and on-the-job training.
Where to study: TAFE colleges in all states.
Current workforce: 48,000.
Future prospects: On the decline.
Starting wage: $220.
Wage after three years: $320.
Further information: TAFE Information Centres.

GEOLOGY

The demand for geologists varies according to the demands of the occasionally volatile mining industry. If you are in the right place at the right time there should be plenty of opportunities in the fields of petroleum exploration, mining and mineral extraction, underground water resources and engineering projects.

Qualifications: Degree or Diploma.
Where to study: Courses at universities in all states.
Current workforce: 5,500.
Future prospects: Good.
Starting wage: $560.
Wage after three years: $690.
Further information: Australian Institute of Geoscientists, Suite 10001, Challis House, 10 Martin Place, Sydney, NSW 2000. Tel: 02 231 4695.

GLAZIERS/FLAT GLASS WORKERS

Most glaziers in Australia work for glass merchants. With some experience and capital it is possible to set up your own business after a few years.

Training: Apprenticeship.
Where to study: TAFE colleges in all states.
Current workforce: 6,600.
Future prospects: Good.

Starting wage: $240.
Wage after three years: $425.
Further information: NSW Glass Merchants Association, Private Bag 938, North Sydney 2060.

GRAPHIC DESIGNER/COMMERCIAL ARTISTS

Work in the creation of advertisements for newspapers and magazines, promotional stationery, visual aids, book covers, television graphics, posters, pamphlets and postage stamps. They are usually hired by firms and organisations.

Qualifications: Degree, Diploma or Associate Diploma.
Where to study: Most main universities and the School of Visual Art, The KVB College of Visual Communication, Billy Blue School of Art, Australian College of Photography, Art and Communication.
Current workforce: 20,000.
Future prospects: Very good.
Starting wage: $480.
Wage after three years: $600.
Further information: The Design Institute of Australia in all states.

HAIRDRESSING

There are opportunities for the trainee and also experienced hairdressers — particularly in the large cities. Australians in general take a great deal of interest in their appearance.

Training: Apprenticeship — a four year apprenticeship with a licensed hairdresser.
Where to study: TAFE colleges in all states. There are one year pre-employment courses which are followed by an apprenticeship of two and a half years with a licensed hairdresser.
Current workforce: 42,000.
Future prospects: Very good.
Starting wage: $240.
Wage after three years: $360.
Further information: Australian Workers Union, 245 Chalmers Street, Redfern, NSW 2016.
Hairdressers Association, Suite 904, 9th Level, Aetna Life Tower, Hyde Park Square, Sydney, NSW 2000.

HEALTH SURVEYOR/ENVIRONMENTAL HEALTH OFFICER

They ensure community services maintain good health standards. They are usually employed by municipal councils and government health departments.

Qualifications: Degree or Associate Diploma.
Where to study: Universities of Adelaide, Canberra, New England, Wollongong, Western Sydney and Curtain University of Technology, Edith Cowan University, Griffith University and Queensland University of Technology. Also TAFE colleges in all states.
Current workforce: 5,000.
Future prospects: Good.
Starting wage: $450.
Wage after three years: $575.
Further information: The Australian Institute of Environmental Health, 22 Jarrett Street, Leichhardt, NSW.

HOSPITAL AND HEALTH ADMINISTRATORS

Deal with the provision, management and evaluation of the health service. Most jobs are in hospital administration, Commonwealth, state and regional health services authorities, and private sector organisations.

Qualifications: Degree or Associate Diploma.
Where to study: Curtain University of Technology, La Trobe University, and universities of New England, New South Wales and South Australia.
Current workforce: 3,800.
Future prospects: Good.
Starting wage: $575.
Wage after three years: $745.
Further information: The Education Officer, Australian College of Health Service Administration, c/o Hornsby Hospital, Palmerston Road, Hornsby, NSW 2077.

HOME ECONOMICS

A variety of possibilities involving testing recipes, preparing new products, advising on diet and testing for quality control. Opportunities exist with county councils, equipment and food manufacturers, government authorities, food producers and various food literature publishers.

Qualifications: Degree or Associate Diploma.
Where to study: Hawthorn Institute of Education, Queensland University
of Technology, Victoria College of Technology and universities of
Sydney, Tasmania and Western Australia.
Future prospects: Good.
Further information: Home Economics Association of NSW, GPO Box
2230, Sydney, NSW 2001.

HORTICULTURE

Several careers are available in horticulture: professional horticulturist;
nurseryman; landscape designer; and gardener.

Qualifications: Degree or Associate Diploma, TAFE Certificate Courses,
Apprenticeships and on-the-job training.
Where to study: All major universities and Victorian College of Agricul-
ture and Horticulture.
Current workforce: 48,000.
Future prospects: Poor.
Starting wage: $490.
Wage after three years: $660.
Further information: NSW Association of Nurserymen Ltd, PO Box 13,
Rouse Hill, NSW 2153.
Australian Institute of Horticulture, 257 Pacific Highway, Lindfield,
NSW 2070.

HOTELS AND CATERING

One of the major industries in Australia, particularly in tourist areas.
Opportunities exist for bartenders, chambermaids/chambermen, kitchen
hands and waiters and waitresses on both a casual and permanent basis.
However, experience is often preferred, especially in these times of
recession where employers are looking for stability rather than people
who are going to be moving on after a few weeks.

On a vocational level there are openings for managers, personnel
managers, front office managers, executive chefs, executive housekeepers
and chief engineers. These careers can all be trained for in Australia.

Qualifications: Degree or Associate Diploma.

Where to study: Most major universities plus private colleges including Macleay College (which offers a highly regarded Hospitality Management course), Blue Mountains International Hotel MGNT School, Kenvale College, Australian College of Travel and Hospitality, Bill Healy Travel School, Macquarie Commercial College, Australian Business Academy, Cairns Business College, Gold Coast College of Business, Australian International College of Commerce.

Current workforce (hotel management): 25,600.

Future prospects: Good, particularly for well-trained and qualified professionals at all levels.

Starting wage: From $350.

Wage after three years: From $400.

Further information: Catering Institute of Australia, GPO Box 157, Sydney, NSW 2001.

National Tourism Industry Training Committee, 3rd Floor, 541 George Street, Sydney, NSW 2000.

INDUSTRIAL DESIGN

Concerned with the design of products for manufacturing industry. Designers work for the manufactures or private consultancies.

Qualifications: Degree.

Where to study: Universities of Canberra, New South Wales, Newcastle, South Australia and Western Australia and Curtain University of Technology, La Trobe University of Northern Victoria, and Queensland University of Technology.

Current workforce: Approximately only 180.

Future prospects: Good.

Starting wage: $450.

Wage after three years: $560.

Further information: Australian Design Council, 2-6 Cavill Avenue, Ashfield, 2137.

Design Institute of Australia, 220 Pacific Highway, Crows Nest.

INSURANCE

A variety of occupations exist in the areas of life insurance, fire, marine and accident insurance, and health insurance. The latter has undergone tremendous expansion over the last few years and it is still a major growth industry.

Qualifications: Degree, Certificate and/or on-the-job training.

Where to study: Most major universities, TAFE colleges and the Australian Traineeship Scheme.

Current workforce (including brokers, agents, officers and clerks): 44,000.

Future prospects: Good.

Starting wage: $480.

Wage after three years: $610.

Further information: Insurance Institute of NSW, Level 1, 20 Bridge Street, Sydney, NSW 2000.

INTERIOR DESIGN

These designers work with manufacturers, suppliers and contractors.

Qualifications: Degree or Diploma.

Where to study: Curtain University, Griffith University, Queensland College of Art, Queensland University of Technology, University of South Australia, University of Technology Sydney, Victoria University of Technology.

Current workforce: 500.

Future prospects: Good.

Starting wage: $450.

Wage after three years: $550.

Further information: Design of Australia, GPO Box 9883, Sydney, NSW 2000.

JEWELLERY AND GEMMOLOGY

More openings exist than in many countries since Australia is one of the biggest producers of gems in the world. A gemmologist studies stones to find out what type they are, whether they have been treated in any way, and to identify how best they can be cut. Specialised training is vital.

Qualifications/training: Degree, Diploma, Associate Diploma and apprenticeship certificate courses.

Where to study: Griffith University, Queensland College of Art, University of Tasmania, Victoria College of Technology, and TAFE colleges in all states.

Current workforce: 4,500.

Future prospects: Fair.

Starting wage: $380.

Wage after three years: $440.

Further information: Jewellers Association of Australia Ltd, Federal Secretariat, PO Box E 446 Queen Victoria Terrace, Canberra, ACT 2600.

JOURNALISM

British journalists looking to find work in Australia would be well advised to get hold of a number of Australian publications first. The style of journalism is slightly different from the British variety; it tends to be more direct and colloquial.

Minimum rates of pay are fixed by an industrial award and journalists are promoted from a D grade up to the top level of A grade.

Qualifications/training: University degree or cadetship. There are two types of cadetship — people without a degree will need to undertake three or four years training while for a degree-holder this will probably be cut to one year.

Where to study: Unlike Britain there are a wide range of journalism courses throughout Australia. They are run by most major universities and also the privately run Macleay College.

Current workforce: 14,000.

Future prospects: Good.

Starting wage: $460+.

Wage after three years: $690+.

Further information: The Australian Journalists' Association, 403 Elizabeth Street, Sydney, NSW 2000.

LAW

This is one profession which may require conversions for British qualifications. There are numerous places to do this but an initial approach to The Law Society of NSW, 170 Philip Street, Sydney, NSW 2000 would be a good idea. There are currently 27,000 people working in various aspects of the Australian legal profession and prospects look good.

LIBRARIAN

Qualifications: Degree and Graduate Diploma, Associate Diploma.

Where to study: Ballarat University College, Charles Sturt University,

Curtain University, Edith Cowan University, Monash University College, Northern Territory University, universities of Canberra, Melbourne and South Australia and TAFE colleges in all states.

Current workforce: 11,400+.

Future prospects: Good.

Starting wage: $495.

Wage after three years: $600.

Further information: The Australian Library and Information Association, PO Box E441, Queen Victoria Terrace, ACT 2601.

LOCKSMITH

Training: Apprenticeship.

Where to study: TAFE colleges in all states.

Current workforce: Small.

Future prospects: Good.

Starting wage: $450.

Wage after three years: $520.

Further information: Master Locksmith's Association in individual states.

MEDICINE

With 23-30 areas of specialisation there are numerous avenues for medical staff. However, there is currently an over-supply of doctors although the prospects for the future appear to be encouraging.

Qualifications: Degree.

Where to study: Universities of Adelaide, Melbourne, New South Wales, Newcastle, Queensland, Sydney, Tasmania and Western Australia.

Current workforce: 47,000.

Future prospects: Good.

Starting wage: $720.

Wage after three years: $940.

Further information: The Australian Medical Association, AMA House, 33 Atchison Street, St Leonards, NSW.

METAL TRADES

These cover boilermakers, fitters, machinists, welders, toolmakers and sheet metal workers.

Training: All metal trades are entered by three to four year apprenticeships. These consist of practical training and part-time technical courses.
Where to study: TAFE colleges in all states.
Future prospects: Good for toolmakers, metal fitters and machinists but bleaker for other professions.

MINING

Coal mining in Australia has been badly hit by the world recession and the fall in demand for coal. Competition for jobs is now fierce.

Training: On-the-job training.
Current workforce: 15,000.
Future prospects: Moderate.
Starting wage: $410.
Wage after three years: $560.
Further information: Miners' Federation, 377 Sussex Street, Sydney, NSW 2000.
  Joint Coal Board, 1 Chifley Square, Sydney, NSW 2000.

MOTHERCRAFT NURSING

This involves the care of babies and pre-school children, liaising with parents and families. Two courses of training can be undertaken for mothercraft nursing, a short one of six months and a longer one of twelve months.

Training: Private college courses.
Where to study: The Karitane Mothercraft Society, Tresillian Training Homes.
Current workforce: 48,000.
Future prospects: Very good.
Starting wage: $300.
Wage after three years: $380.
Further information: The Karitane Mothercraft Society, Karitane Training Centre, PO Box 67, Randwick, 2031.
  Tresillian Training Homes, 2 Shaw Street, Petersham 2049.

MOTOR TRADE

Australians are heavily into motor vehicles and this has spawned a motor industry with an assortment of careers including: mechanics, panel beaters, vehicle painters, trimmers, brake mechanics and salesmen.

However, although there are over 7000 outlets for new cars the employment situation is somewhat static presently, due mainly to a drop in the sales of new cars.

Training: Most jobs in the motor industry are entered through
    apprenticeships and on-the-job training.
Where to study: TAFE colleges in all states.
Current workforce: 147,000.
Future prospects: Average.
Starting wage: $210.
Wage after three years: $380.
Further information: Vehicle Builders Employees' Federation of Australia,
    Suite 1, 8th Floor, Labor Council Building, 377-383 Sussex Street,
    Sydney, NSW 2000.
    Motor Traders' Association of NSW, 43 Brisbane Street, Sydney,
    NSW 2000. Motor Vehicle Repair Industry Council, 239 Great North
    Road, Five Dock, NSW.

MUSIC

Similar to drama in that there are a reasonable number of musicians in Australia. Talent will always rise to the top. There are a number of categories to be considered: composers, performers, musicologists and music administrators. Most of these require some form of tertiary education.

Qualifications: Degree or Associate Diploma.
Where to study: Most universities in Australia have music courses.
Current workforce: 5,900.
Future prospects: Average.
Starting wage: $500.
Wage after three years: $520.
Further information: The Musicians' Union of Australia, 5th Floor, Labor
    Council Building, 377-383 Sussex Street, Sydney, NSW.

NATURAL THERAPY

A form of medicine, based on the theory that prevention is better than cure. It is not a recognised health profession and individual professional associations set standards for membership.

Training: A full-time, four year course at private colleges.

Where to study: Consult the Australian Natural Therapists Association and the Australian Traditional Medicine Society for relevant courses.
Current workforce: Under 500.
Future prospects: Good.
Starting wage: $520.
Wage after three years: $620.
Further information: Australian Natural Therapists Association (ANTA), PO Box 522, Sutherland NSW 2232.
The Australian Traditional Medicine Society Limited, PO Box 442, Ryde, NSW 2112.

NURSE (REGISTERED)

Undertake similar work to the nursing profession in Britain.

Qualifications: Diploma or Degree.
Where to study: Most universities in Australia.
Current workforce: 150,000.
Future prospects: Very good.
Starting wage: $440.
Wage after three years: $540.
Further information: Nursing Careers Adviser, NSW Health Department, 73 Miller Street, North Sydney, NSW 2060.

NURSE (ENROLLED)

They work directly under registered nurses. They also work in the community, carrying out various duties in the homes of patients.

Training: On-the-job training and TAFE courses.
Where to study: TAFE colleges in all states.
Current workforce: 47,000.
Future prospects: Very good.
Starting wage: $320.
Wage after three years: $420.
Further information: Nursing Careers Adviser, NSW Health Department, 73 Miller Street, North Sydney, NSW 2060.

OCCUPATIONAL THERAPY

This type of therapist works in hospitals, rehabilitation centres, special schools for children, psychiatric facilities, community health centres, nursing homes and private practices. New areas are currently being developed for occupational therapists; reform and penal institutions, preventative and rehabilitative work in industry, education in the best use of leisure time, education for creative retirement, and programmes for the unemployed.

Qualifications: Degree.
Where to study: Curtain University, La Trobe University and the universities of Newcastle, Queensland, South Australia and Sydney.
Current workforce: 4,000.
Future prospects: Very good.
Starting wage: $560.
Wage after three years: $670.
Further information: NSW Association of Occupational Therapists, PO Box 142, Ryde, NSW 2112.

OIL DRILLER

The oil industry is in a similar volatile state as the mining business and it is hard to predict what will happen in the future. Most oil companies do take on unskilled platform workers and the best way to get these jobs is to be in the right area when they are recruiting.

Training: On-the-job and courses run by the Australian Drilling Industry Training Committee.
Where to study: On-the-job.
Current workforce: 15,000.
Future prospects: Average.
Starting wage: $560.
Wage after three years: $650.
Further information: Australian Drilling Industry Training Committee, Box 1545, Macquarie Centre, NSW 2113.

OPTOMETRIST

Qualifications: Degree.
Where to study: Universities of Melbourne, New South Wales, Sydney and La Trobe.
Current workforce: 1,500.
Future prospects: Good.

Starting wage: $680.
Wage after three years: $800.
Further information: Australian Optometrical Association, Level 8, 26 Ridge Street, North Sydney, NSW 2060.

ORTHOPTIST

This is a health profession which deals with visual and ocular motor anomalies. These include squints, cross-eyes and diseases of the eyes such as defective binocular vision (use of two eyes as a pair).

Qualifications: Degree.
Where to study: La Trobe University, University of Sydney — Cumberland College of Health Sciences.
Current workforce: 1,500.
Future prospects: Good.
Starting wage: $680.
Wage after three years: $800.
Further information: As above and The Orthoptic Clinic, Sydney Eye Hospital, Sir John Young Crescent, Woolloomooloo, NSW.

OPTICAL DISPENSER

Deals with fitting spectacles from an optometrist's prescription.

Qualifications: TAFE Advanced Certificate or Guild of Dispensing Opticians diploma.
Where to study: TAFE colleges in all states.
Current workforce: 1,500+.
Future prospects: Good.
Further information: Guild of Dispensing Opticians, 12 Thomas Street, Chatswood, NSW 2067.

OPTICAL MECHANIC

The person responsible for grinding lenses and assembling spectacles.

Training: Apprenticeship.
Where to study: TAFE colleges in all states.
Current workforce: 1000+.
Future prospects: Average.

Starting wage: $240.
Wage after three years: $440.
Further information: Optical Prescriptions Spectacle Makers Pty Ltd, 66 Reservoir Street, Surry Hills, NSW 2010.

ORGANISATION AND METHODS ANALYST

These analysts carry out studies intended to improve efficiency in businesses and government departments.

Training: Usually on-the-job. Most O and M analysts come from other disciplines such as personnel or accounts. A degree or associate diploma in business management, business administration, personnel or economics.
Where to study: Specific courses are available at Bond University, Deakin University, Griffith University, Queensland University of Technology, University of New South Wales, Victorian University of Technology — RMIT. Other courses in administration and business studies are available from most other Australian universities.
Current workforce: 3000.
Future prospects: Good.
Starting wage: $550.
Wage after three years: $710.
Further information: Any Careers Reference Centre or CES Work Information Centre.

PATTERNMAKING

A patternmaker produces the pattern from which engineers create such products as cylinder blocks, baths, sinks and ships' propellors. Much of the art of the patternmaker has been taken over by computers.

Training: Apprenticeship.
Where to study: TAFE colleges in all states.
Current workforce: 2000.
Future prospects: Poor.
Starting wage: $240.
Wage after three years: $425.
Further information: Master Patternmaking Section, Metal Trades Industry Association of Australia, NSW Branch, 51 Walker Street, North Sydney, NSW 2060.

PERSONNEL OFFICER

Deals with all aspects of employing people: manpower planning, recruiting and selecting, wage and salary administration, training and development, pensions, welfare activities, pensions, medical checks and health and safety regulations. They also deal with problems that occur with employees at work. There are various categories within the range of personnel; managers, specialists, and clerks.

Qualifications/training: Degree, TAFE Certificate and on-the-job training.
Where to study: Most major universities in Australia and TAFE colleges in all states.
Current workforce: Managers: 5000. Specialists: 16,000. Clerks: 15,000.
Future prospects: Very good.
Starting wage (Clerks): $350.
Wage after three years: $500.
Further information: Institute of Personnel Management, 4 Waters Road, Neutral Bay, NSW 1089.

PHARMACIST

Similar to the work of pharmacists in Britain, employed in community practice, hospitals or the pharmaceutical industry.

Qualifications: Degree.
Where to study: Curtain University of Technology, Victorian College of Pharmacy, and universities of Queensland, South Australia, Sydney and Tasmania.
Current workforce: 14,700.
Future prospects: Very good.
Starting wage: $600.
Wage after three years: $750.
Further information: Pharmaceutical Society of Australia, 82 Christie Street, St. Leonards, NSW.

PHOTOGRAPHER

There is a wide range of photographic possibilities including commercial, advertising, fashion, portraiture, newspaper, industrial, and scientific.

Qualifications/training: Degree, Diploma, Associate Diploma, TAFE Certificates and private college courses.

Where to study: Charles Sturt University, Griffith University, James Cook University of North Queensland, Northern Territory University, Queensland College of Art, University of New South Wales, College of Fine Arts, University of South Australia, University of Western Australia, Victoria College, Australian Centre of Photography, Photography Studies College (Melbourne), Australian College of Photography, Arts and Communications and TAFE colleges in all states.

Current workforce: 6,700.

Future prospects: Very good.

Starting wage: $460.

Wage after three years: $550.

Further information: Australian Institute of Professional Photographers, 49 Samuel Street, Ryde, NSW.

PHYSICAL FITNESS INSTRUCTORS

Since Australia is such a health conscious nation there are a wide range of health clubs and centres in all states.

Qualifications: Degree, Associate Diploma or TAFE Certificate.

Where to study: Australian College of Physical Education, and most major universities.

Current workforce: 4000+.

Future prospects: Good.

Starting wage: $240.

Wage after three years: $420.

Further information: Australian Council for Health, Physical Education and Recreation, PO Box 84, Croydon, NSW 2132.

PHYSIOTHERAPIST

Australia has some of the best physiotherapy training in the world.

Qualifications: Degree.

Where to study: Curtain University, La Trobe University, universities of Melbourne, Newcastle, Queensland, South Australia and Sydney (Cumberland College of Health Sciences).

Current workforce: 6500.

Future prospects: Very good.

Starting wage: $580.

Wage after three years: $690.
Further information: Australian Physiotherapy Association, 112 Majors
Bay Road, Concord, NSW.

PODIATRIST

Formerly called chiropodists, podiatrists deal with ailments and diseases
of the feet. Many set up their own practices but to do this they must first
register with the state.

Qualifications: Degree or Diploma.
Where to study: Curtain University, La Trobe University, Queensland
University of Technology and University of South Australia.
Current workforce: 1000.
Future prospects: Good.
Starting wage: $560.
Wage after three years: $670.
Further information: Australian Podiatry Association, 446 Elizabeth
Street, Sydney, NSW 2000.

POLICE FORCE

Australian Federal Police Force (AFP)
In addition to domestic duties the Australian Federal Police Force provides men for the UN Peace Keeping Force in Cyprus. Applicants must
be between the ages of 18 and 35 and be in good physical health. They
should also be Australian citizens.

Qualifications/training: Graduates with degrees in economics, accountancy, computing, law and science are in great demand. The minimum
requirement is completion of Year 12 at school. Training is undertaken at the Police Headquarters in Canberra. This consists of a
sixteen week orientation, theory and practical course and then officers
are posted to either Sydney, Melbourne or Canberra for further
on-the-job training.
Current workforce: 200 new recruits are taken every year.
Future prospects: Good.
Starting wage: $350.
Wage after three years: $500.
Further information: Australian Federal Police Recruitment Consultant,
GPO Box 2845, Canberra City, ACT 2601.

New South Wales Police

State police forces have similar requirements to the Federal ones. In NSW training consists of an eighteen month Police Recruitment Education Programme, involving study and on-the-job training. This is undertaken at the NSW Police Academy at Goulburn.

Current workforce: 40,000.
Future prospects: Good.
Starting wage: $350.
Wage after three years: $500.
Further information: Recruiting Officer, Police Headquarters, 14-24 College Street, Sydney, NSW 2000.

PRINTING

There are five main areas to consider: graphic reproduction operator, printing machinist, book binding, screen printing and table hand. The industry is still relatively labour intensive but in the next few years this could change due to advanced technology.

Training: Apprenticeship.
Where to study: TAFE colleges in all states.
Current workforce (total): 45,000.
Future prospects: Poor.
Starting wage: $240.
Wage after three years: $420.
Further information: Printing and Allied Trades Employers' Federation of Australia, 77 Lithgow Street, St Leonards, NSW.

PRISON OFFICER

A minimum age of 20 years is required and all training is done within the service.

Training: Twelve week full-time course.
Where to study: Prison Service.
Current workforce: 8,000.
Future prospects: Good.
Starting wage: $515.
Wage after three years: $585.
Further information: Probation and Parole Service, Department of

Corrective Services, Roden Cutler House, 24 Campbell Street, Sydney, NSW 2000.
Recruitment Division, NSW Public Service, Goodsell Building, 8-12 Chifley Square, Sydney NSW, 2000.

PSYCHOLOGIST

A wide range of openings exist for trained psychologists: clinical, counselling, vocational, community, organisational, educational, research and applied sports. Due to cutbacks in some social welfare expenditure competition for jobs is getting fiercer, although extensive growth is expected in this field.

Qualifications: Degree — a four years honours degree is needed for admission to the Australian Psychological Society.
Where to study: Most major universities in Australia.
Current workforce: 4,500.
Future prospects: Very good.
Starting wage: $580.
Wage after three years: $700.
Further information: Australian Psychological Society, 30 Atchison Street, St Leonards, NSW.

PUBLIC RELATIONS

PR work is available across the whole spectrum of government and private companies. There are a number of degree and certificate courses on offer, but not all are recognised by the **Public Relations Institute of Australia** (PRIA) which represents about 25 per cent of practitioners. Before you start a course it is wise to check with your state office of PRIA. Graduates are preferred for employment in consultancies.

Qualifications: Degree or TAFE Certificate for sub-professional entry.
Where to study: Bond University, Charles Sturt University, Deakin University, Edith Cowan University, Queensland University of Technology, Victoria University of Technology, University College of Central Queensland, University of Canberra, University of New England, University of Western Australia, TAFE colleges in all states and the private Macleay College.
Current workforce: 16,500.
Future prospects: Very good.

Starting wage: $530.
Wage after three years: $650.
Further information: Public Relations Institute of Australia, PO Box 1728, North Sydney, NSW 2025.

PUBLIC SERVICE

As with the British Civil Service the Australian Public Service (APS) cover a wide range of occupations and professions. Most of them are office based. Some of the areas covered are economic management, foreign affairs, trade, productivity and industry, community services, social security, health, education, territorial administration, transport, employment and industrial relations, environmental concerns, Aboriginal affairs, arts, heritage, and agricultural and fisheries policies.

There are over 175,000 public servants and they fill all kinds of jobs: administrative service officers, computer systems officers, office machine operators (typists, stenographers and wordprocessor operators), data processing operators and technical officers. There are openings for graduates and non-graduates alike. Selection is based on academic qualifications, a selection test and an interview. There are also a number of openings for handicapped applicants.

A number of universities offer degree courses in public administration: Charles Sturt University, Curtain University, Griffith University, Murdoch University, Northern Territory University, Philip Institute of Technology, Queensland University of Technology, University College of Central Queensland and universities of Canberra, New England and Queensland.

Further information: Public Sector Recruitment Office, 17th Floor, Two Hall House, 456 Kent Street, Sydney, NSW 2000.

QUANTITY SURVEYOR

These professionals can either work for themselves as consultants, or for building contractors, developers or government departments or agencies. Qualifications gained in Australia are recognised worldwide.

Qualifications: Degree.
Where to study: Most major universities.
Current workforce: 1600.
Future prospects: Good.

Starting wage: $460.
Wage after three years: $690.
Further information: Australian Institute of Quantity Surveyors, National
   Surveyors House, 27-29 Napier Close, Deakin, ACT 2600.

RADIOGRAPHERS

This job falls into two main categories, diagnostic and therapeutic.
Employment is mainly in hospitals and private practices, and also public
health services and industry for diagnostic radiographers. There are a number of courses available and these are governed by the Royal Australian
College of Radiologists and the Australian Institute of Radiography.

Qualifications: Degree, Diploma.
Where to study: Charles Sturt University, Curtain University, Queensland
   University of Technology, and universities of Newcastle, South
   Sydney, Sydney (Cumberland College of Health Sciences) and Tasmania.
Current workforce: 4,000.
Future prospects: Very good.
Starting wage: $560.
Wage after three years: $730.
Further information: Australian Institute of Radiography, PO Box 2426,
   North Paramatta, NSW 2151.

RADIO/TV REPAIRER

With advanced technology this also covers the repair of hi-fis, business
machines, word processors and videos.

Training: Apprenticeship.
Where to study: TAFE colleges in all states.
Current workforce: 6,000.
Future prospects: Average.
Starting wage: $250.
Wage after three years: $460.
Further information: Electrical Contractors' Association, 51 William
   Street, Sydney, NSW 2000; 155 Wellington Parade South, Jolimont
   3002, Victoria; 213 Greenhill Road, Eastwood 5063, South Australia;
   51 Berwick Street, Fortitude Valley 4006, Queensland; PO Box 364,
   Canberra 2601, ACT; GPO Box 1544R, West Perth 6005, Western
   Australia.

RANGER

Work in all areas of conservation and management in National Parks and the Wildlife Service.

Qualifications: Degree or Associate Diploma.
Where to study: Most major universities.
Current workforce: 1,000.
Future prospects: Average.
Further information: National Parks and Wildlife Service, 43 Bridge Street, Hurtsville, NSW.
Ministry for Conservation, 240 Victoria Parade, East Melbourne, Victoria.

RECEPTIONIST

Good employment prospects in all major cities for receptionists with good training and experience.

Qualifications: Certificate and private college courses.
Where to study: Metropolitan Business College and TAFE colleges in all states.
Current workforce: 145,000.
Future prospects: Good.
Starting wage: $250.
Wage after three years: $380.
Further information: TAFE Information Centres in all states.

RECREATION OFFICERS

As increasing emphasis is being put on the use of leisure time this is one area which could show significant growth in the future. Recreation officers are employed by the Department of Sport and Recreation in various states, by city councils, organisations such as the YMCA and YWCA and psychiatric hospitals.

Qualifications: Degree or Diploma.
Where to study: Universities of Canberra, New South Wales, Newcastle, Queensland, South Australia and Wollongong, Charles Sturt University, Edith Cowan University, Griffith University, James Cook University of North Queensland, La Trobe University and the Australian College of Physical Education.

Current workforce: 1500.
Future prospects: Good.
Starting wage: $490.
Wage after three years: $600.
Further information: NSW Department of Sport, Recreation and Racing, Head Office, 105 Miller Street, North Sydney, NSW 2060.

REAL ESTATE

This includes property managers and real estate salespersons.

Qualifications: Certificate of Registration, Advanced Certificate and Degree courses.
Where to study: Real Estate Institutes in all states, TAFE colleges in all states and Bond University, Curtain University, Queensland University of Technology, and University of Queensland, University of South Australia, University of Technology, Sydney, Victorian University of Technology — RMIT.
Current workforce: 40,000.
Future prospects: Good.
Starting wage: $320.
Wage after three years: $480.
Further information: Real Estate Institute of NSW, 30-32 Wentworth Avenue, Sydney, NSW 2000.

REFRIGERATION/AIR CONDITIONING MECHANICS

Australians like everything to be cool, whether it is their beer or their homes. This means that there is always plenty of work for this group of mechanics.

Training: Apprenticeship and TAFE courses.
Where to study: On-the-job training and TAFE colleges in all states.
Current workforce: 10,500.
Future prospects: Good.
Starting wage after training: $450+.
Further information: The Metal Industry Association of Australia, 51 Walker Street, North Sydney, NSW.
The Australian Institute of Refrigeration, Air-conditioning and Heating, 104 Paramatta Road, Homebush, NSW.
The Refrigeration and Air-conditioning Contractors Association, Box 118, Post Office, Flemington Markets, NSW 2129.

RETAILING

Retail Buyer
Responsible for buying goods from wholesalers and then passing them on for sale to the public.

Training: On-the-job in the form of a trainee managership.
Current workforce: 16,500.
Future prospects: Good.
Starting wage: $335.
Wage after three years: $470.
Further information: Retail Traders Association of NSW, 20 York Street, Sydney, NSW 2000. Also personnel departments of large retailers.

Sales assistants
Training: On-the-job.
Current workforce: 463,000.
Future prospects: Good.
Starting wage: $250.
Wage after three years: $360.
Further information: As above.

SECRETARIAL

The secretarial world has developed to a point where it embraces stenographers, word processor operators and data preparation operators. Top secretaries can progress to become private secretaries or executive assistants.

Secretaries/Stenographers
Qualifications: Degree, Associate Diploma, TAFE Certificate and TAFE courses.
Where to study: TAFE courses in all states, Curtain University, University of New England, University of South Australia and the National Business College — NBC offers a 42 week Diploma course in Secretarial Studies.
Current workforce: 230,000.
Future prospects: Good.
Starting wage: $290.
Wage after three years: $495.
Further information: TAFE colleges in all states.

Word Processor Operators/Data Preparation Operators
Training: TAFE and private college courses.
Where to study: As above.
Current workforce: 110,000+.
Future prospects: Very good.
Starting wage: $280+.
Wage after three years: $420+.
Further information: As above.

SOCIAL WORKER

Most Australian social workers are employed by the government, hospitals and private agencies such as the Royal Blind Society.

Qualifications: Degree — a four year course is offered in all states.
Where to study: Australian Catholic University, Avondale College, Bachelor College, Charles Sturt University, Curtain University, Flinders University of South Australia, James Cook University, Phillip Institute of Technology, Monash University, Queensland University of Technology, La Trobe, and universities of Sydney, New South Wales, Queensland, South Australia, Melbourne and Western Australia.
Current workforce: 9,000.
Future prospects: Very good.
Starting wage: $540.
Wage after three years: $640.
Further information: Association of Social Workers, 66 Albion Street, Surry Hills, NSW 2010.

SPEECH PATHOLOGIST

Deals with all areas of speech disorders.

Qualifications: Degree.
Where to study: Curtain University, University of Sydney — Cumberland College of Health Sciences.
Current workforce: 1,300.
Future prospects: Very good.
Starting wage: $600.
Wage after three years: $700.
Further information: The Australian Association of Speech and Hearing, 112 Majors Bay Road, Concord, NSW.

STOCK AND STATION AGENT

This is a job which involves sales of goods connected with farming: livestock, machinery and fertiliser. The industry is dominated by a few large companies and most employees come from the country areas and have farming experience.

Training: TAFE courses and on-the-job training.
Where to study: TAFE courses in all states and rural studies courses at Charles Sturt University, La Trobe University, University of New England — Orange Agricultural College, University of New South Wales, University of Queensland — Gatton College and Victorian College of Agriculture and Horticulture.
Starting wage: $320.
Wage after three years: $480.
Further information: The Stock and Station Agents Association of NSW, Homebush Saleyards, Homebush, NSW.

STOCK EXCHANGE

The careers encompassed by the Australian Stock Exchange include: juniors (reception and typing), intermediate (departmental secretaries), secretarial and stenographers, clerical, script clerks, accounts staff and research staff. There are also stock exchange operators, who usually work for stock brokers and represent their firms on the floor of the Stock Exchange. This involves using the **Stock Exchange Automated Trading System** (SEATS).

Qualifications: Degree, graduate Diploma, Certificate, and on-the-job training.
Where to study: Securities Institute of Australia.
Current workforce: 22,000.
Future prospects: Very good.
Starting wage: $360.
Wage after three years: $600.
Further information: Securities Institute of Australia, Exchange Centre, 20 Bond Street, Sydney, NSW 2000.

TEACHER

There are a wide range of possibilities for teachers, covering the usual areas of pre-primary teaching, primary teaching, secondary teaching, further education teaching and the teaching of exceptional children, including physically and mentally handicapped. Demand for teachers varies from state to state and good qualifications and/or experience are required.

Qualifications: Degree and a Teaching Diploma.
Where to study: Most universities in Australia.
Current workforce: Pre-primary 10,000. Primary 98,000. Secondary 110,000. Special education 5,500.
Future prospects: Good.
Starting wage: $470.
Wage after three years: $620.
Further information: Teachers Federation branches in individual states.

TEXTILE DESIGNER

Qualifications: Degree, Associate Diploma.
Where to study: Charles Sturt University, University of New South Wales, University of Newcastle, TAFE colleges in NSW, VIC and ACT.
Current workforce: Very small.
Future prospects: Good.
Starting wage: $440.
Wage after three years: $550.

TOWN PLANNER

They are employed by all levels of government.

Qualifications: Degree.
Where to study: Curtain University, Queensland University of Technology, Victoria University of Technology and universities of Melbourne, New England, New South Wales, Queensland, South Australia and Tasmania.
Current workforce: 4,000.
Future prospects: Good.
Starting wage: $490.
Wage after three years: $640.
Further information: The Australian Planning Institute, Darlinghurst Public School Annexe, Cnr. Barcom Avenue and Liverpool Street, Darlinghurst, NSW 2011.

TRAIN DRIVER

The number of new recruits and trainees being taken on by rail authorities throughout Australia is falling because of the recession and the changing levels of manning on trains.

Training: Traineeship.
Where to study: On-the-job training.
Current workforce: 1,300.
Future prospects: Poor.
Starting wage: $370.
Wage after three years: $460.
Further information: State Railway Authorities in all states.

TRAVEL CONSULTANT

Another expanding profession thanks to the expansion of the leisure business.

Qualifications: Degree, Associate Diploma, Certificate and private college courses.
Where to study: Ballarat University College, Bond University, Charles Sturt University, Edith Cowan University, Griffith University, James Cook University of Northern Queensland, Monash University, Footscray Institute of Technology and universities of Canberra, New England, Queensland and Sydney. Also private courses at Metropolitan Business College.
Current workforce: 15,000.
Future prospects: Good.
Starting wage: $250.
Wage after three years: $380.
Further information: National Tourism Industry Training Committee, 3rd Floor, 541 George Street, Sydney, NSW 2000.

VALUER

Deals with assessing the value of land and buildings, based on the current economic climate.

Qualifications: Valuers Certificate of Registration, Associate Diploma and Degree courses in Land Economy.

Where to study: Real Estate Institutes, TAFE colleges in all states, Bond University, Curtain University, and universities of Queensland, South Australia and Sydney.
Current workforce: 2,000.
Future prospects: Good.
Starting wage: $300.
Wage after three years: $510.
Further information: Australian Institute of Valuers and Land Economists, 300 George Street, Sydney, NSW 2000.

VISUAL MERCHANDISING

Including both visual merchandisers and ticket writers this profession is concerned with presenting goods in an attractive fashion to the buying public. This covers window dressing and posters for point of sale advertising.

Qualifications: Certificate courses and on-the-job training.
Where to train: TAFE colleges in all states.
Current workforce: Small.
Future prospects: Good.
Starting wage: $315.
Wage after three years: $450.
Further information: Retail Training Council, PO Box C154, Clarence Street, Sydney, NSW 2000.

WINE MAKER

Australia produces some of the best wines in the world and the wineries of Victoria, New South Wales, South Australia and Western Australia are good starting points for prospective or qualified wine makers.

Qualifications: Degree or Associate Diploma.
Where to study: Charles Sturt University, University of Adelaide — Roseworthy Campus.
Current workforce: Small.
Future prospects: Good.
Further information: The above universities.

WOOL CLASSER

This involves all aspects of wool preparation and classification in the shearing shed. All states have wool classing courses run by TAFE and also some Agricultural Pastoral Colleges. They vary in length from six months full-time to two years part-time.

Qualifications: Certificate and Associate Diploma courses.
Where to study: University of New England — Orange Agricultural College, University of New South Wales, Victorian College of Agriculture and Horticulture and TAFE colleges in all states.
Current workforce: 1,200.
Future prospects: Poor.
Further information: Australian Wool Corporation, 55 Clarence Street, Sydney, NSW 2000.

ZOOLOGY — ANIMAL CARER

Qualifications: Certificate courses.
Where to study: TAFE colleges in all states.
Current workforce: 2,600.
Future: Average.
Starting wage: $220.
Wage after three years: $300.
Further information: TAFE Information Centres.

9
Recognition of Overseas Skills and Qualifications

NATIONAL COUNCIL OF OVERSEAS SKILLS RECOGNITION (NCOSR)

In many professions there are no restrictions for foreign workers entering the Australian workplace. However, certain professions require their workers to be registered and possess the necessary qualifications. For people trained in Australia this is no problem but for workers trained in Britain this could pose difficulties. In order to address this question the Australian Government established the **National Council of Overseas Skills Recognition** (NCOSR) in 1989, in order to make it easier for overseas-qualified people to ease themselves into the Australian workplace.

The belief on which NCOSR was formed is to promote recognition of skills on the basis of demonstrated competence. The long term goal is to replace reliance solely on paper qualifications by assessment processes for skills and work experience. The recognition of these skills is done by:

- Simplifying administrative processes and improving flexibility between occupations in professional, para-professional, technical and trades areas.

- Giving a reasonable chance to all skilled workers by encouraging the development of consistent national skills standards which do not discriminate between skills gained in Australia or overseas.

- Improving the information, counselling and referral services necessary to give migrants and prospective migrants the support they deserve in order to make a choice of career.

- Developing fair, open and easily understandable skills assessment procedures.

- Providing improved support services, such as better access to education and training for bridging and refresher purposes, where these will assist migrants obtain recognition of their skills.

- Promoting occupational deregulation wherever possible.

NCOSR's Client Service

NCOSR offers comparative and competency assessment services to professionally and technically qualified prospective migrants and to overseas-trained people already resident in Australia, in the following areas: architecture, computing, general academic qualifications, nursing, radiography, social welfare, technical occupations, dentistry, dietetics, occupational therapy, pharmacy, physiotherapy, podiatry, veterinary science and occupational English.

The service consists of giving clients advice, counselling, comparative assessment and referral services, all geared towards overcoming skill recognition difficulties in all professional, para-professional and technical occupations. They will also direct clients who need further qualifications to obtain full recognition skills.

NCOSR deals with 15,000 cases each year, the majority of them migrants who want to gain the relevant qualifications or have their current qualifications assessed. If migrants want to have their qualifications assessed they should write directly to NCOSR, asking for an application form. This should be completed and returned. The assessment can take anything from a few days to several months, depending on the types of qualification being dealt with. Approximately 73 per cent of all assessments are successful and a charge of no less than $A100 is levied for each assessment. The individual charges may change without notice.

Contact address
National Council of Overseas Skills Recognition
First Floor, Derwent House, University Avenue, Canberra City, ACT.
Postal Address: GPO Box 1407, Canberra City, ACT, 2601.
Tel: 06 276 8111. Fax: 06 276 7636.

ASSESSMENT OF INDIVIDUAL PROFESSIONS AND CONVERSION OF QUALIFICATIONS

Accountancy

Accountants working in Australia need to be members of either the **Australian Society of Certified Practising Accountants** (ASCPA) or the **Institute of Chartered Accountants in Australia** (ICAA). If you are an accountant wanting to migrate to Australia you must meet the ASCPA or the ICAA membership requirements in order to get the highest possible points score for skills on your points test. In order to do this you must hold an academic qualification comparable to an Australian Bachelor degree. Your degree must also meet the specific requirements of these two organisations.

However, it is virtually impossible for overseas-trained accountants to meet these membership needs immediately because both the ASCPA and the ICAA require a prospective member to be trained in Australian company law and Australian taxation law. Because of these requirements the Department of Immigration, Local Government and Ethnic Affairs will accept overseas-trained accountants for migration on the basis of their skills if their qualifications need only minor upgrading — three or fewer subjects to be studied at tertiary level to meet ASCPA or ICAA requirements.

You can have your current situation assessed by either organisation by writing to:

● Educational Assessment Officer, The Australian Society of CPAs, 170 Queen Street, Melbourne, Victoria 3000.

● National Education Co-ordinator, The Institute of Chartered Accountants in Australia, GPO Box 3921, Sydney, NSW 2001.

A fee of $A100 will be charged and you will need to provide: family name, full address, date and country of birth, name and address of present employer, brief employment history, the institution where you studied, course name and the award your received, duration of course, name of any professional accountancy organisations of which you are a member, certified copies of your original degree or certificate, a list of all subjects studied and grades awarded.

After the assessment the ASCPA or the ICAA will write to you and tell you whether your qualifications have been recognised and what upgrading you will require.

Architecture
If you have overseas architectural qualifications these are assessed in Australia by the **Architects Accreditation Council of Australia** (AACA) in co-operation with NCOSR. General qualifications are evaluated under one of the following categories:

- Overseas qualifications considered equivalent to an approved architectural qualification in Australia, which are listed on the AACA Approved Overseas Architectural Qualifications List.

- Overseas qualifications not on the AACA Approved List but which have been accepted in individual cases in the past and are listed on the AACA Individually Approved Qualifications List.

These lists are held at AACA, who can be contacted by writing to:

- The Registrar, Architects Accreditation Council of Australia, PO Box 373, Manuka, ACT 2603.

If you apply from overseas your application should be sent to NCOSR, along with a $A100 fee. If you do not have your qualifications assessed as part of your migration then you should contact the Registrar of AACA when you arrive in Australia. If your qualifications are on the Approved List then you will be asked to contact a state or territory Registration Board to enquire about the requirements for registration. You will need to gain practical experience in Australia and also pass the AACA Architectural Practice Examination before you can register.

Computing
Although there are no registration requirements for computer professionals in Australia and no formal minimum requirements it is a good idea to have qualifications which meet the minimum membership of the **Australian Computing Society** (ACS). This is currently an Associate Diploma, or alternatively you could sit the Society's Examination in Computing.

If you have trained as a computer professional overseas you will be assessed by NCOSR or according to NCOSR guidelines. If you apply before you enter Australia, as is recommended, you should send the following documentation: final certificate for academic awards, course transcript showing subjects studied and examination results, official employer references, dates of employment, details of major projects undertaken, the technology you have been using, your personal role in projects and software and computer equipment utilised.

You should include a fee of $A100 with you application and if you receive a favourable assessment from NCOSR then they will inform the Australian diplomatic mission where you have applied that you have met the minimum requirements to practise as a computer professional in Australia.

For further information contact NCOSR or the ACS at: PO Box 319, Darlinghurst, NSW 2010.

Dentistry

The national professional body for dentists in Australia is the **Australian Dental Association** (ADA). Any registered dentist is eligible for membership.

If you have trained as a dentist overseas your qualifications may meet Australian requirements — qualifications from some British universities are immediately acceptable while others are not. If you are not eligible to be registered immediately then you can either take an Australian dental degree or sit written and clinical examinations conducted by the Australian Dental Examining Council (ADEC). You can take these examinations if you have completed four years' full-time academic training and you are in the process of migrating.

The ADEC examination consists of an English test, a preliminary examination and a clinical examination. The fee at the time of writing is $A2000 for all parts of the examination. If you pass you will then be eligible to apply for registration with any of the eight Australian dental boards.

Due to the cost involved in the ADEC examination it is a good idea to contact NCOSR first to see if it is necessary to sit it or not.

Dietetics

Dietitians are only required to be registered to practise in Victoria and the Northern Territory; in the rest of Australia there are no legal limits on the practice of the profession. However, if you want to work in government-controlled hospitals you will be expected to have qualifications acceptable to the **Dietitians Association of Australia** (DAA), or the dietitians' boards of Victoria or Northern Territory. If you hold overseas qualifications then you will have to pass a NCOSR examination before being eligible for membership of the DAA or registration with the boards. You can only take this examination if you are a permanent resident of Australia, or if you are going through the migration procedures, or if you have been given permission to engage in employment in Australia.

In order to sit the Examination you should write to the Registrar of Dietetic Qualifications at NCOSR and include: a certified copy of your degree, diploma or professional qualification, details of the course content, official evidence of any internships, official evidence of any registration/licensure, official evidence of extra qualifications and official evidence of any change of name. At the time of writing the fee for the Dietetics Examination is $A200.

Nursing

The main national professional nursing body in Australia is the **Australian Nursing Federation** (ANF). To work as a nurse in Australia you must be registered with the nurse-registering authority in the state or territory where you intend to practise. If you have qualified as a nurse in a country with a health care delivery system similar to Australia's in culture, technology, licensing and language then you could be considered for immediate registration in Australia. The countries which meet these requirements are Canada, Ireland, New Zealand, South Africa, United Kingdom and the USA.

If you have been trained in the United Kingdom you can be registered after your arrival in Australia, in some cases, after only an interview with the registering authority. Registration fees range between $A25-40. You will need certified copies of all original nursing documents when you register.

For further information contact: Australian Nursing Federation, 373-375 St George's Road, North Fitzroy, Victoria 3068. Tel: 03 482 2722.

Pharmacy

The **Australian Pharmacy Examining Council**, which is associated with NCOSR, was established to help pharmacists educated overseas to become registered in Australia so that they could practise their profession. The Council has established an examination for overseas-trained pharmacists to demonstrate that they have the knowledge to practise in Australia.

The Council examination is open to any pharmacist who has completed a pharmacy course which included at least three years' full-time academic study and is eligible for registration as a pharmacist in the country in which that qualification was obtained. You must also be eligible to migrate to Australia.

The council's examination procedure is as follows:

- Stage 1 examination — a written multiple-choice question examination covering basic pharmaceutical sciences. There are two papers, each taking two hours and consisting of 100 questions.

- Interview and counselling.

- Twelve months' supervised practice in an Australian pharmacy.

- Stage 2 examination — a practical and oral examination covering the practice of pharmacy.

The fee for the Stage 1 examination is $A250 and for the Stage 2 examination $A500. The average success rate is 60 per cent.

For further information contact NCOSR or: Executive Director, **Pharmaceutical Society of Australia**, 44 Thesiger Court, Deakin, ACT 2605.

Physiotherapy

All practising physiotherapists in Australia must be registered with the relevant state or territory body. If not they cannot practise or use the title physiotherapist. Each state and territory has different registration laws and registration in one state does not automatically allow you to practise in another. To do this separate registration is required. The professional body is the **Australian Physiotherapy Association** (APA).

The Australian Examining Council for Overseas Physiotherapists Incorporated (AECOP) has a procedure whereby physiotherapists who qualified overseas may prove their competence to practise in Australia.

If you are an overseas-educated physiotherapist you can apply to register in Australia if you obtain the AECOP Final Certificate.

To have your overseas qualifications assessed, you must complete an Application for Assessment form; these are available from Australian diplomatic posts, or AECOP and APA offices in Australia. You must apply as part of an application to migrate and once this application is accepted you can approach NCOSR with your application for assessment. You must also provide supporting documentation consisting of: your final diploma or degree, a transcript of your course, showing subjects and hours, examination results detailing practical, theoretical and clinical education, documented evidence of any internships, references or evidence of employment since your graduation, evidence of any registration/licensure, documented evidence of any change of name.

To be eligible to take the AECOP examination procedure you must satisfy them that:

● The physiotherapy course you took was similar in theory and practice to the physiotherapy curricula in Australia.

● The physiotherapy course included an appropriate electrotherapy component.

● Your course would qualify you to practise as a physiotherapist in the country where the course was taken.

● You completed at least two years' full-time postgraduate clinical practice or the equivalent part-time, within three years of the date of application. (If you qualified less than two years before your application then this does not apply.)

All eligible overseas physiotherapists applying for registration in Australia have to follow at least one of the following procedures:

1. Take the AECOP screening examination — two papers, each with approximately 150 multiple-choice questions. You can sit the examination at an overseas Australian Government office. The fee at the time of writing is $A200.

2. Supervised Clinical Practice.

3. The AECOP Clinical Examination. This is only available in Australia and it is recommended that supervised clinical practice is undertaken before this examination is sat. The fee at the time of writing is $A450.

For further information contact: The Executive Officer, Australian Examining Council for Overseas Physiotherapists, GPO Box 1407, Canberra City, ACT 2601.

Podiatry

Each Australian state has separate legislation covering the recognition of podiatry qualifications. Registration in one state does not automatically make you eligible for registration in another. Each state has a registration board and NCOSR helps these boards to assess overseas-qualified podiatrists through an examination procedure. If you are an overseas-trained podiatrist you must take this examination. It consists of an English test, if needed, a Stage 1 examination — written, and a Stage 2 examination — clinical and oral.

There are three levels of eligibility for this NCOSR examination for podiatrists:

1. If you have finished a three-year, full-time tertiary course from an institution in the United Kingdom, *and* you have current registration or you are eligible for registration in the country where you qualified, then you will only have to sit the Stage 2 examination.

2. If you have completed at least a three-year, full-time tertiary course at an institution outside the United Kingdom *and* have current registration, then you will have to sit the Stage 1 and Stage 2 examinations.

3.   If you have had different but comparable podiatry training, this will
     be considered separately.

If you wish to take the podiatry examination you should apply for a
form from NCOSR or your nearest Australian embassy or consulate. You
must send certified copies of the following documents with your application: final diploma or degree obtained on completion of podiatry course,
transcript of the course showing subjects and hours and detailing practical
and theoretical examination results, evidence of further education and
training, post graduate qualifications, evidence of registration/licensure,
evidence of current registration, evidence of employment experience after
graduation, two recent employment references, documented evidence of
change of name where applicable.

The fee for the Stage 1 examination is $A200 while the fee for Stage
2 is $A450.

For further information write to NCOSR or contact: Executive
Director, Australian Podiatry Council, Suite 11, 96 Camberwell Road,
Hawthorn, Victoria 3122.

Radiography

The organisation which represents the professional and ethical practice of
radiography is **The Australian Institute of Radiography** (AIR), 212
Clarendon Street, East Melbourne, Victoria 3002.

To become a registered radiographer in Australia, you first have to
meet the minimum entry requirements of all appropriate Australian
tertiary institutions. Since 1986 this is a diploma-level course with at least
three years' full-time study.

If you have an overseas qualification your application will be assessed
through NCOSR and you will be advised in one of the following ways:

● You could be advised that your qualifications, training and
   experience in radiography make you eligible for membership of the
   AIR.

● You could be told that you have the qualifications and training which,
   prima facie, meet the requirements for eligibility for AIR membership. However, you may need twelve months' clinical supervision
   when you arrive in Australia.

● You may be told that you do not reach the required standard but that
   you could possibly reach it by completing successfully an accredited

bridging course conducted by a recognised college in Australia.

● You could be advised that you are well below the standard and you would need to complete successfully a retraining program in Australia before you would be considered for institute membership.

The minimum academic standard is used as a basis for assessment but other factors, such as the type of your course, will also be considered. Your recent experience must be broadly based and include basic experience in one or more forms of digital imaging.

● If you graduated since 1986, you must have had at least two years' full-time practical experience within five years of the consideration of your application.

● If you graduated between 1976 and 1985, you must have had three years' full-time experience in the five years before consideration of your application.

● If you graduated in 1975 or earlier and you have had many years of virtually uninterrupted radiographic experience including the five years before consideration of your application, then your case will be considered on its merits.

For further information contact NCOSR or AIR.

Social Welfare

Australian social work courses require at least four years of education at tertiary institutions which award a Bachelor degree as the basic social work qualification. The **Australian Association of Social Workers** (AASW) requires at least four years of degree-level, full-time study or its part-time equivalent for association membership. This study must lead to a distinct qualification in social work.

The assessment of an overseas qualification is based on how it compares with an Australian social work program. If your qualification is assessed at a three-year degree level of Australian study you can take a one-year course at an Australian university to bridge the gap. There is a shorter supplementary course if your needs are in field work only. These programs are arranged through the AASW.

For further information about how your social work qualifications will be assessed contact NCOSR or: The Australian Association of Social

Workers, PO Box 84, Hawker, ACT 2614. Qualified welfare workers should contact: The Australian Institute of Welfare and Community Workers, GPO Box 2557, Canberra, ACT 2601.

Teaching

Teachers who have been trained overseas and want to work in Australia must have tertiary teaching qualifications comparable to those offered by Australian universities. Not only this, but you will also have to adapt to different teaching traditions, a different educational structure and a different organisational system.

Many overseas teaching qualifications are generally acceptable in Australia but the authorities do not automatically recognise particular qualifications. All qualifications are assessed on how they compare with Australian teacher education standards.

If your qualifications are accepted by a registration board or employing authority this does not guarantee that you will find a teaching post. This will depend on a number of other factors including job availability and your own suitability for a particular post. If you are accepted in one state or territory this does not mean that you will be automatically accepted in another as each has its own requirements.

Registration or employing authorities usually require teachers from abroad to have completed a course of teacher education equivalent to an Australian course.

If you wish to migrate to Australia as a teacher your qualifications must meet the criteria of the government school system in at least one state or territory. If you want an assessment of your qualifications for migration purposes then you should read the *Procedures Advice Manual* published by the Department of Immigration, Local Government and Ethnic Affairs, available at all of the offices of that Department in Australia or overseas. It gives valuable information on the overseas teaching qualifications which can be assessed by migration officers. Other qualifications are assessed by NCOSR.

If you are applying for assessment to NCOSR then you will need to supply the following documents: Form 44 — the Application for Assessment of Professional, Para-professional or Technical Skills and Qualifications, available from all migration offices; certified copies of — original award certificates for all qualifications, original transcripts of mark sheets listing all subjects studied and grades awarded and any details of supervised teaching practice, the letter from the Australian migration authorities requesting that you have your application assessed; and the fee advised by the migration officer.

Once you arrive in Australia you can apply for registration and/or employment with the following authorities:

New South Wales
Department of School Education, PO Box 6000, Parramatta, NSW 2124.

Victoria
Government schools: Teachers' Registration Board, 49-51 Spring Street, Melbourne, Victoria 3000. Non-government schools: Registered Schools Board, Rialto Tower, 525 Collins Street, Melbourne, Victoria 3001.

Queensland
Board of Teacher Registration. PO Box 389, Toowong, Queensland 4066.

South Australia
Teachers' Registration Board, 1st Floor, 45 Wakefield Street, Adelaide, South Australia.

Western Australia
Human Resources Services Branch, Ministry of Education, 151 Royal Street, East Perth, Western Australia 6000.

Tasmania
Government schools: Department of Education, GPO Box 169B, Hobart, Tasmania 7001. Non-government schools: Teachers and Schools Registration Board, GPO Box 169B, Hobart, Tasmania 7001.

Australian Capital Territory
Teaching Service Section, Ministry for Health, Education and the Arts, PO Box 20, Civic Square, ACT 2608.

Northern Territory
Personnel Branch, NT Department of Education, PO Box 4821, Darwin, Northern Territory 0801.

Technicians
The profession of technician in Australia covers medical technical officers and technicians, science technical officers and technicians, electrical and electronic engineering associates and technicians, mechanical engineering associates and technicians, building, architectural and surveying associates and technicians.

Overseas qualifications for technicians are assessed against the requirements for obtaining an appropriate award from one of the Australian TAFE colleges. NCOSR assessments are available to the following categories:

- Prospective migrants who have been advised by an Australian diplomatic mission to seek assessment of their qualifications.

- Overseas-trained people who are already living in Australia and want their qualifications assessed for employment.

When you apply for migration you will be told which documents are required for assessment of your qualifications and skills. The fee for assessment by NCOSR in this field is $A100.

Veterinary Science

All veterinarians in Australia must be registered with a veterinary surgeon's board before they can practise. Bachelor degrees from United Kingdom universities are acceptable but if you gained your degree from the University of Dublin or the University of Ireland then you should contact the registrar of the veterinary surgeon's board in the state or territory where you wish to practise. If you graduated from any other university then you will be required to sit the National Veterinary Examination.

For further information contact: The Executive Officer, Panel in Veterinary Science, NCOSR, PO Box 1407, Canberra, ACT 2601.

Veterinarians with qualifications from United Kingdom universities who are eligible for immediate registration in Australia should contact the Registrars in the relevant states and territories:

New South Wales
Board of Veterinary Surgeons of New South Wales, PO Box K220, Haymarket, NSW 2000.

Queensland
Veterinary Surgeons' Board of Queensland, c/o Department of Primary Industries, GPO Box 46, Brisbane, Queensland 4001.

South Australia
Veterinary Surgeons' Board of South Australia, GPO Box 1671, Adelaide, South Australia 5001.

Western Australia
Veterinary Surgeons' Board of Western Australia, 28 Charles Street, South Perth, Western Australia 6151.

Tasmania
Veterinary Board of Tasmania, GPO Box 192B, Hobart, Tasmania 7001.

Australian Capital Territory
Veterinary Surgeon's Board of the Australian Capital Territory, GPO Box 825, Canberra, ACT 2601.

Northern Territory
Veterinary Surgeon's Board of the Northern Territory, PO Box 4160, Darwin, Northern Territory 5794.

Victoria
Veterinary Board of Victoria, 272 Brunswick Road, Brunswick, Victoria 3056.

RECOGNITION OF TRADE SKILLS

The metal and electrical trades have a system by which overseas-trained tradespeople can have their qualifications recognised in Australia. This is done by obtaining an **Australian Recognised Tradesman's Certificate**. This can only be issued if you permanently reside in Australia, but eligibility for recognition can be assessed prior to migration. The certificates are issued under the Tradesmen's Rights Regulation Act 1946, and the term tradesman applies to both male and female workers.

The trades covered by the act covers five groups: engineering, boilermaking, sheetmetal, blacksmithing and electrical. The overall policy for determining the conditions under which a person is assessed is laid down by Central Trades Committees for each of these five groups. Local Trades Committees determine individual applications and issue Australian Recognised Tradesman's Certificates to persons who meet the requirements.

You may be eligible for an Australian Recognised Tradesman's Certificate if you have completed trade training outside Australia and/or have worked as a tradesperson overseas for specified periods in a recognised trade, and:

● your training and employment is assessed as equivalent to that of an Australian apprenticeship, or

● you have gained an acceptable standard and range of skills with, subsequently, six years employment on work ordinarily performed by a tradesperson in any one of the listed metal trades, or seven years employment on work ordinarily performed by a tradesperson in any one of the listed electrical trades. You must also be capable of doing the work of the relevant trade in Australia.

Definition of 'tradesman'

The Central Trades Committee defines a tradesman as a broadly trained and/or experienced tradesperson who has gained, as a minimum, sufficient knowledge and skills to:

● read working instructions and technical drawings common to his or her trade;

● plan independently the method and order of progressing a job;

● take measurements and readings using measuring instruments of appropriate accuracy;

● mark out, lay out and set up trade work;

● select appropriate materials, tools, machines and/or equipment;

● make appropriate settings on tools, machines and/or equipment;

● carry out trade work independently; and

● check and/or test trade work in relation to the standards applying to his or her trade.

When you apply to have your trade qualifications assessed you should initially contact your nearest Australian High Commission, Consulate or Embassy. You may need to have them assessed before being permitted to migrate but even if this is not the case it is a good idea to get an assessment so that you can estimate your chances of recognition when you arrive in Australia.

How to get a Trade Test

Once you are in Australia you will need to satisfy a Local Trades Committee that you meet the requirements to be issued with an Australian

Recognised Tradesman's Certificate. In order to do this you can undertake a **Trade Test** when you get to Australia. For this you will need the following documents:

- evidence of your identity and age;

- evidence of completion of your technical and vocational education, including final certificates or diplomas, and the details of the duration of the course and subjects passed;

- evidence of completion of any trade or trade-related courses, including final certificates or diplomas;

- evidence of completion of your apprenticeship or traineeship, including contracts of apprenticeship or traineeship and final certificates or diplomas, and details of the main parts of the training program and their duration;

- evidence of your trade or trade-related employment, from all your previous employers. (This should be a statement of service on the official letterhead paper of your employers, without any alterations or erasures, and signed by an identifiable senior member of the firm's management. The statement must show trade classification or classifications in which you were employed, period of employment, including exact dates in each classification, and a detailed description of your training. It is not necessary to obtain a statement of service from your present employer, if this would cause problems in your present job.)

- evidence of trade or trade-related self-employment, such as: a personal statement on a properly signed statutory declaration providing details of the exact commencement and completion dates of business, classification in which you were self-employed, number of staff employed and their classifications, and a full description of work, tools and equipment used; Certificate of Business Registration covering each year of self-employment; statement on letterhead paper from your accountant or legal representative certifying the name and nature of your business, the exact dates and period of self-employment and the capacity in which you were self-employed, statements from suppliers confirming the nature of your business and dates of trading period; and statements from clients, on letterhead paper, confirming full details of the work you performed for them and dates and periods worked;

● evidence of trade training and/or employment in the Defence Forces, including discharge certificate if applicable;

● evidence of licensing or registration.

If you cannot obtain some of the required documents, your application may still be considered if you submit a statutory declaration giving the reasons why evidence is unobtainable.

Trades
The following are the trades covered by the Tradesmen's Rights Regulation Act, and which require an Australian Recognised Tradesman's Certificate.

Engineering
Adjuster
Coppersmith
Electroplater, first class
First class machinist (Boring)
First class machinist (Drilling)
First class machinist (Grinding)
First class machinist (Milling)
First class welder (Engineering)
Fitter (Diesel)
Fitter and first class machinist
Fitter
Fitter (Instruments)
Fitter and turner
Ground engineer (Airframe)
Ground engineer (Engines)
Ground engineer (Airframes and Engines)
Ground engineer (Instruments)
Locksmith
Machine setter
Mechanic (Marine and other Engines), excluding persons engaged solely on maintaining motors of less than 200cc capacity
Motor cycle mechanic
Pattern maker
Refrigeration mechanic or serviceman

Repairer (Security work)
Scalemaker
Scalemaker and adjuster
Scientific instrument maker
Turner

Boilermaking
Angle-ironsmith
Boilermaker
Boilermaker and structural steel tradesman
Marker-off (a tradesman, the greater part of whose time is occupied in
    marking-off or template making, or both)
Structural steel tradesman
Welder, first class

Blacksmithing
Angle-ironsmith
Annealer
Annealer and case hardener
Blacksmith
Case hardener
First class welder (Smithing)
Forger
Smith, other
Toolsmith
Tradesman heat treater

Sheetmetal
Body maker, first class
First class welder
Panel beater
Sheetmetal worker, first class

Electrical trades
Armature winder
Armature winder (Automotive)
Electrical fitter
Electrical fitter (Automotive)
Electrical fitter and armature winder
Electrical fitter and armature winder (Automotive)
Electrical fitter (Instruments)

Electrical mechanic
Ground engineer (Electrical)
Ground engineer (Instruments)
Ground engineer (Radio)
Refrigeration mechanic or serviceman
Telegraph mechanic
Tradesman (Radio)
Tradesman (Television)
Tradesman (Radio and Television)

OFFICES OF LOCAL TRADES COMMITTEES

New South Wales (including ACT)
10th Floor, 255 Pitt Street, Sydney, NSW 2000. Postal address GPO Box 9879, Sydney, NSW 2001.

Victoria
13th Floor Rialto Building North Tower, 525 Collins Street, Melbourne, VIC 3000. Postal address GPO Box 9879, Melbourne, VIC 3001.

Queensland
11th Floor, 127 Creek Street, Brisbane, QLD 4000. Postal address GPO Box 9879, Brisbane, QLD 4001.

Western Australia
8th Floor, 190 St. Georges Terrace, Perth, WA 6000. Postal address GPO Box 9879, Perth, WA 6001.

South Australia
Mezzanine Floor, Hooker House, 33 King William Street, Adelaide, SA 5000. Postal address GPO Box 9879, Adelaide, SA 5001.

Tasmania
Level 6, Stock Exchange Building, 83-85 Macquarie Street, Hobart, TAS 7000. Postal address GPO Box 9879, Hobart, TAS 7001.

Northern Territory
Kriewaldt Chambers, 6 Searcy Street, Darwin, NT 0800. Postal address GPO Box 9879, Darwin, NT 0801.

10
Vocational Training

TECHNICAL AND FURTHER EDUCATION (TAFE)

The network of Technical and Further Education (TAFE) colleges throughout Australia are the main means for vocational training in the country. They provide an enormous variety of courses which are aimed at providing training for a specific job or vocational area. There are over 1200 different courses which can be taken at over 1000 colleges and associated centres in Australia.

TAFE colleges offer three main qualifications:

1. **Diploma Courses.** These usually consist of three years of full-time study or five years of part-time study.

2. **Associate Diploma Courses.** These usually consist of two years of full-time study or four years of part-time study.

3. **Advanced Certificate Courses.** These are courses which lead to state registered awards — endorsements, statements of attainment and college statements. Endorsements are granted for courses which follow on from another specified TAFE course.

On completion of one TAFE course you can then progress to a higher-level course within the TAFE system.

Special entry requirements
Although TAFE courses are generally geared towards school-leavers and students they are available to anyone. Special admission can be granted to people over 20 years old who do not have the necessary entry requirements for a specific course but who can show evidence of a suitable educational background and/or abilities gained in occupational or life experience.

The TAFE year

The period of study at TAFE colleges is divided into four terms, roughly equivalent to those in the public school system. Some courses follow a semester pattern; two semesters per year, each of 18 weeks, with a break of one or two weeks in the middle. Most courses begin in February but some start in July.

Due to the fact that many people who attend TAFE colleges are already employed it is possible to take a number of part-time courses at night. Fees for Diploma and Associate Diploma courses are approximately $A30 per year. You may also have to pay for books, tools and any other equipment which you will need.

For anyone who is thinking of undertaking vocational training in an attempt to improve their job prospects in Australia then TAFE is an invaluable service.

For more information about TAFE in each state or territory contact:

Australian Capital Territory
ACT Institute of TAFE, PO Box 826, Canberra City, ACT 2601.

New South Wales
TAFE Information Centre, 849 George Street, Railway Square, Broadway, NSW 2007.

Northern Territory
TAFE Division, Northern Territory Division Department of Education, 69 Smith Street, Darwin, NT 0800.

Queensland
TAFE Information Centre, PO Box 33, North Quay, QLD 4002.

South Australia
TAFE Information Centre, Education Centre, 31 Flinders Street, Adelaide, SA 5000.

Tasmania
Hobart Technical College, 75 Campbell Street, Hobart, TAS 7000.

Victoria
Vocational Orientation Centre, 328 Queen Street, Melbourne, VIC 3000.

Western Australia
TAFE Information Centre, WA Department of Education, Cable House, Victoria Avenue, Perth, WA 6000.

UNIVERSITIES

Most Australian universities and colleges offer a range of vocational courses. The range of qualifications offered in most cases are degrees, diplomas, associate diplomas, transfer courses, postgraduate courses and conversion courses. The following is a selection of universities who place particular emphasis on vocational subjects.

New South Wales and ACT

Australian National University, Canberra Institute of Arts, GPO Box 4, Canberra, ACT. Tel: 06 249 5111.

Charles Sturt University, Private Mailbag 7, Bathurst 2795. Tel: 063 31 1022.

Macquarie University, Balaclava Road, North Ryde 2113. Tel: 02 805 7111.

University of New England, Armidale 2351. Tel: 067 73 333.

University of New South Wales, Anzac Parade, Kensington 2033. PO Box 1. Tel: 02 697 2222.

University of Newcastle, McMullan Building, Rankin Drive, Shortland 2308. Tel: 049 68 0401.

University of Sydney, Science Road, University of Sydney 2006. Tel: 02 692 2222.

University of Technology, Sydney, Broadway Campus, 15-73 Broadway 2007. PO Box 123. Tel: 02 20 930.

University of Wollongong, Northfields Avenue, North Wollongong 2500. PO Box 1144. Tel: 042 27 0555.

Victoria

Ballarat University College, PO Box 663, Ballarat 3350. Tel: 053 33 9000.

Deakin University, Pigdons Road, Geelong 3217. Tel 052 47 1111.

La Trobe University, Bubdoora 3083. Tel: 03 479 1111.

Monash University, Wellington Road, Clayton 3168. Tel: 03 565 4000.

Philip Institute of Technology, PO Box 179, Coburg 3058. Tel: 03 353 9222.

Swinburne Institute of Technology, Box 218, Hawthorn 3122. Tel: 03 819 8911.

University of Melbourne, Parkville 3052. Tel: 03 344 4000.

Victoria College, 221 Burwood Highway, Burwood 3125. Tel: 03 285 3333.

Victoria University of Technology, GPO Box 2476V, Melbourne 3001. Tel: 03 662 0611.

Queensland

Griffith University, (including Gold Coast University College), Kessels Road, Nathan 4111. Tel: 07 875 7111.

James Cook University of North Queensland, Townsville 4811. Tel: 077 81 4111.

Queensland University of Technology, GPO Box 2434, Brisbane 4001. Tel: 07 223 2111.

University of Queensland, Queensland Agricultural College, St. Lucia 4067. Tel: 07 377 1111.

Bond University, Private Bag 10, Gold Cost Mail Centre 4217.

South Australia

Flinders University of South Australia, Sturt Campus, Sturt Road, Bedford Park 5042. Tel: 08 275 3911.

University of Adelaide, GPO Box 498, Adelaide 5001. Tel: 08 228 5333.

University of South Australia, North Terrace, Adelaide 5000. Tel: 08 236 2211.

Western Australia

Curtain University of Technology, Kent Street, Bentley 6012. Tel: 09 351 1466.

Murdoch University, South Street, Murdoch 6150. Tel: 09 332 2421.

University of Western Australia, Nedlands 6009. Tel: 09 380 3050.

Edith Cowan University, Person Street, Churchlands 6018. Tel: 09 383 8333.

Tasmania

University of Tasmania, GPO Box 252C, Hobart 7001. Tel: 002 20 2101.

Northern Territory

Northern Territory University, PO Box 40146. Casuarina 0811. Tel: 089 46 6666.

Adult entry

Most of the above universities operate special adult entry admission schemes whereby people over a certain age are admitted on the basis of work experience and qualifications other than purely academic ones. The universities which are most likely to offer this type of entry are: University of Technology Sydney, University of Sydney, University of New South Wales, Curtain University of Technology, University of New England, Queensland University, Edith Cowan University, Macquarie University and University of South Australia.

Part-time

The following are the biggest providers of part-time education: University of Technology Sydney, University of Sydney, University of New South Wales, Curtain University of Technology, University of New England, Queensland University, Victoria University of Technology, Melbourne University, Queensland University of Technology, Edith Cowan University, Macquarie University, La Trobe University and University of South Australia.

GOVERNMENT VOCATIONAL SCHEMES

Through the Department of Employment, Education and Training, the Federal Government is very aware of the need to give unemployed people a chance to get back into the workforce. There are a number of schemes intended to do this.

Jobstart

This is a scheme which offers employers subsidies to employ long-term unemployed of all ages. To qualify you have to have been unemployed for six months in the last nine months. If the CES thinks that you are particularly disadvantaged then this may be waived. Wage subsidies range from $50 to $320 depending on the award rate for the job and the age of the applicant. The employer has to pay the current award rate of pay so they cannot cut corners as far as the employee is concerned.

JobTraining

This provides vocational training for people of all ages through established and specially created courses. The same eligibility conditions as for JobStart apply.

Innovate training: Projects-National skills

These are projects designed to target skill shortages in specific area that are having an adverse effect on the economy. Once this has been done short-term training is given in these areas. In recent years this has included the following programs:

- National Skills Shortages.
- Labour Adjustment Programs.
- Heavy Engineering Adjustment and Development Programs.
- Textile, Clothing and Footwear Labour Adjustment programs.

These not only provide updated training for people who have been working in these industries but, perhaps more importantly for migrants from Britain, they act as bridging courses for qualified workers from overseas seeking to make their qualifications acceptable to the Australian employment market. There are also programs to upgrade the skills of existing workers.

Job Search Training Program

This program is designed to give unemployed people all the assistance they need for finding work and to equip them with the necessary job-finding skills. These are two main schemes within the program:

1. Job Search Training Courses
These are courses given by local community and educational groups that run for a total of twenty-two hours. Applicants must be:

- registered unemployed
- have an idea of what they want to do
- possess the necessary skills, qualifications and experience for the job they are seeking
- be prepared to take an active part in the training program
- able to speak, read and write English.

The course covers various aspects of job-hunting including: filling in application forms, writing letters of application and CVs, telephoning employers and interview technique.

2. Job Clubs

This is a longer program — three weeks — which is intended to give the long-term unemployed and special groups such as single parents and the disabled the necessary job-seeking skills. The course consists of a combination of theory and practice and those on it have access to everything they need for applying for jobs: postage, stationery, telephones, photocopiers, and typewriters.

The Australian Traineeship System

This is a new form of vocational training for young people aged between sixteen and nineteen. It is designed to help young people find vocational employment and also bring benefits to industry by providing them with well trained staff. The system has been designed through consultation between employers, trade unions, the education sector, trainers and young people themselves.

Trainees of the scheme receive twelve months of quality training in non-trade occupations. This is made up of on-the-job training and also practical study at TAFE colleges or approved training centres. The training includes:

- job specific training in a range of occupational skills
- training in general skills such as numeracy
- the development of personal work effectiveness skills.

Trainees who complete the course satisfactorily receive a certificate from the State/Territory Training Authority, which is recognised nationally.

Some of the traineeships currently on offer are: Australian Public Service, automotive, banking, business equipment maintenance, clerk — legal office, computer programming, electrical goods manufacturing, financial services, food service assistant, furniture removals, insurance, local government, office skills, plastics, retails sales assistant, rural, small offset printing, software support, textiles and clothing, timber merchandising and travel industry.

APPRENTICESHIPS

Apprenticeships are widespread in Australian trades and there are two main types:

1. **Indentured** — where an agreement is signed by the apprentice and the employer.

2. **Trainee** — no agreement is signed and there is no guarantee of continued employment.

Apprentices have to be at least 15 years old and they can complete an apprenticeship technical training course by:

● day release
● block study
● external study.

Most apprenticeships last four years but some can be shorter.

11
Applying for Work

Although the basics of applying for a job in Australia are essentially the same as in the UK the main point to remember is that the Australian character is slightly different to its British counterpart. The lack of class barriers means that Australians are more interested in whether you are able to do the job, than in what school or university you went to. Also, pretension and affectation will be given short shrift — down-to-earth honesty and straightforwardness are the orders of the day.

HOW TO APPLY

When making written applications for a job, whether it is on a speculative basis or on an official application form, it pays to be:

- precise
- positive
- honest.

Australians are not great ones for waffle and padding. They are more interested in one short sentence coming straight to the point rather than two paragraphs skirting around the issue. They also like to see an upbeat, positive attitude. Don't say things like, 'I was not very good as a manager in Britain but I hope to get better.' Instead say, 'In the present economic climate I feel I have a variety of skills to offer, which will greatly benefit your business.' Then go on to list those skills, but again, briefly.

Some people think that it is permissible to be economical with the truth on job application forms. This may be true in that some things will never be checked. However, if it is something that is important for the job then sooner or later you will be found out. If it is not important then it is not worth lying about in the first place. Australians set great store by honesty and a solid, reliable worker is often preferred to a well-qualified but shady one.

HANDLING YOUR INTERVIEW

The rules for applications apply just the same for interviews, as do the
normal things you would do for an interview in Britain:

- Be well dressed.
- Have clean and tidy hair.
- Be punctual.
- Find out the name of your interviewer if possible and use it.
- Find out as much as possible about the company to which you are
  applying.
- Do not fidget or move around unnecessarily during the interview.
- Have proof of your qualifications.
- Be prepared to ask questions.
- Do not tell other interviewees what questions you were asked.

Dress

The main differences will come from the novelty of a different environment and culture. The first difference will be in your attire for the
interview. At home you would probably wear something respectable and
non-descript — the safe option. But you should dress appropriately for
your environment. If you are in Sydney or Melbourne in the middle of
winter then this may be similar to Britain and so the safe option would be
in order. However, if you were in Brisbane at the height of summer or
further north in the sub-tropical belt of Australia then a grey suit may look
slightly incongruous. This is not to suggest that you should turn up in a
beach shirt and thongs (flip-flops) but a certain relaxation of the normal
interview wear could be allowed. To get an idea of what would be
acceptable take a look around and see what people in the profession you
are applying to are wearing. Follow suit, literally.

Attitudes

The second difference in the interview may be the attitude of your
interviewer. He or she will want to find out what kind of a person you are,
not the cut of your school tie. Questions may be direct and to the point
and answers should be in a similar vein, but try not to be too blunt.

One important consideration for interviews is to avoid being too
critical. This applies particularly to the country you have come from; you
will not ingratiate yourself to your interviewer by declaring, 'Britain is
such a dump, I'm glad I got away.' Contrary to popular belief Australians
do not dislike Poms as they would like to pretend, but they are opposed

to 'whinging' of any kind. They will not be inclined to employ people who come across as negative.

THE AUSTRALIAN WAY OF WORK

Three of the most commonly used colloquialisms in the Australian workplace are, 'sickie', 'bludger' and 'dobber'.

● The **sickie** is a piece of wonderful Australian logic which reasons that since there is an allowance for you to take a certain numbers of days off a year through sickness that you should take them whether you are actually ill or not. Perhaps they are just putting into words what goes unsaid in other countries but the sickie is as much a part of the Australian workplace as income tax or overtime payments. Whether you conform to the sickie philosophy or not is a personal choice, but when in Rome. . .

● A **bludger** is someone who is lazy and does not do their job properly. It is often used as a playful term of abuse and should not be taken too seriously. However, if your employer begins to think of you as a bludger then this could have an adverse effect on your prospects. It is better to get known for doing 'hard yakka' rather than for being a bludger. Hard yakka is a term for hard work or hard graft.

● A **dobber** is a much more serious offender in the workplace. In effect it is a grass who goes to the boss to tell tales on his fellow workmates. Australian workers have very strong bonds of solidarity and if anyone breaks the unspoken code that all workers stick together come what may they will be treated at best with silence and at worst with violence.

Means to an end

In many ways Australians have a good attitude to their jobs in the overall scheme of things: it is a task to be taken seriously but it should not be allowed to take over your life. However, the attitudes vary in different professions. In 1991 the Australian Bureau of Statistics published a survey which showed that 1.3 million Australians worked more than 49 hours a week. Most of these were managers and administrators. Professionals averaged 37 hours a week while labourers and those in related work clocked in at an average of 31 hours a week. If you are prepared to accept an honest wage for an honest week's work then, as they say, 'She'll be right, mate!'

Australians like to socialise after a hard day at the office/factory/-kitchen/vineyard and they invariably do this with their workmates. This is not just a case of a few tinnies of Fosters after work; they will invite you to barbecues at their home or to a day at the beach at the weekend. This type of invitation should be treated exactly as it is intended — an open gesture of friendship. Australians are not hung up on workplace hierarchy and once it is time to go home then everyone is very much an equal.

Mateship

Depending on your point of view, the concept of Australian mateship is either an example of an unique form of male bonding, or an outdated example of extreme macho chauvinism. It is prevalent in all aspects of Australian society and the workplace is no exception. Thankfully though mateship seems to be on the decline as Australian men begin to realise that friendship does not have revolve exclusively around swill tubes of Fosters and sticking up for your mate no matter what he has done.

You may be confronted by mateship on two levels: aimed against migrants and women. As a migrant you will be accepted happily enough into the workplace but there may be some elements who are not prepared to trust you fully until you have proved your true worth in the mateship stakes (what this involves is a mystery to those not initiated into the inner circle but is has been rumoured that this involves surviving forty days and forty nights in the outback or drinking a tanker of Castlemaine XXXX in one go.)

The overcoming of mateship from a female perspective is slightly harder. First you will have to prove that you are as good as the mateship fraternity, then prove you are better, and then be prepared to let them take the limelight. Whatever you do make sure that you are not intimidated by mateship — the mateship brigade admires spirit and boldness as much as anything else.

The concept of mateship may seem somewhat archaic in the 1990s and its impact is definitely lessening in the workplace. However, it must be remembered that this is a society that until the 1950s banned women from drinking in the majority of its pubs. The baser side of mateship may be dying, but it is not dead.

CHECKLIST FOR THE AUSTRALIAN WORKPLACE

1.   Although working in Australia can be similar to Britain in many ways there are subtle differences in style, approach and attitudes.

2. Be positive and upbeat but not showy or pushy.

3. Concentrate on your future rather than dwell on your past achievements, or otherwise.

4. Be prepared to listen and learn — do not say things like, 'Back home we used to do it this way. . .'

5. You will be rewarded for reliable, hard work so try and capitalise on this.

6. Do not criticise people for taking sickies — it is as much a part of Australian life as Fosters and Paul Hogan.

7. You may get away with being a bludger but definitely not a dobber.

8. Enjoy your job but make sure you take advantage of your life outside the workplace.

9. Accept the fact that mateship exists in the workplace but try not to get involved.

10. Hope Australia wins as many major sporting events as possible — when Alan Bond won the America's Cup Bob Hawke announced a public holiday the following day.

How to Pass That Interview

Judith Johnstone Grad IPM

Everyone knows how to shine at interview — or do they? When every candidate becomes the perfect clone of the one before, you have to have that extra 'something' to raise your chances above the rest. Using a systematic and practical approach, this How To book takes you step-by-step through the essential pre-interview groundwork, the interview encounter itself, and what you can learn from the experience afterwards. The book contains sample pre- and post-interview correspondence, and is complete with a guide to further reading, glossary of terms, and index. Judith Johnstone has written extensively on employment-related subjects; she has been an instructor in Business Studies and adult literacy tutor, and has long experience of helping people at work.
£6.99, 128pp illus. 1 85703 110 8. 2nd edition

How To Books Ltd, Plymbridge House, Estover Road, Plymouth PL6 7PZ, United Kingdom. Tel: (01752) 735251/695745. Fax: (01752) 695699. Telex: 45635.

12
Casual Work Opportunities

Not all people who are looking for work in Australia are intending to migrate there and find permanent jobs. Young people arriving Down Under with holiday working visas are more interested in short-term casual employment, to supplement their travels.

As with migrant employment the casual job market has been hit by the recession and there is no longer any guarantee that you will be able to get a job within five minutes of walking off the plane. Although some industries, such as catering, have been particularly hard hit the casual job-seeker can, with a certain amount of dedication and hard work, spend a profitable year working around Australia.

THE JOB SEARCH

Commonwealth Employment Service

As with permanent employees, people with holiday working visas can take advantage of the CES offices around the country and the services they have to offer. For jobs in catering, fruit-picking and labouring the CES will either be able to offer you specific jobs or, failing that, direct you to the areas where workers are most needed. Although casual employees can use any CES, there are some that cater specifically for their needs:

* CES Templine, 9th Floor, Santos House, 215 Adelaide Street, Brisbane, Queensland 4002. Tel: 07 229 5188.
* CES, 128 Bourke Street, Melbourne, Victoria 3000. Tel: 03 666 1222.
* CES Templine, 2nd Floor, 45 Grenfell Street, Adelaide, South Australia 5000. Tel: 08 231 9070.
* CES, 818-820 George Street, Railway Square, Sydney, NSW 2000. Tel: 02 281 6088.

- CES, 1st Floor, 186 St. George's Terrace, Perth, Western Australia 6000. Tel: 09 325 6155.
- CES Templine, 1st Floor, 40 Cavenagh Street, Darwin, Northern Territory 0801. Tel: 089 46 4866.
- CES, 175 Collins Street, Hobart, Tasmania 7000. Tel: 002 20 4068.

Private agencies

The private employment agencies are worth considering for people looking for temporary employment, particularly in secretarial and clerical work. There are also agencies which specialise in placing casual workers for jobs such as cleaning and gardening. If you are going to be stationed in one place for a reasonable period of time then you will have a better chance to get established with an agency and provide yourself with a steady stream of temporary work.

All major agencies advertise in the local *Yellow Pages* and a selection of them are listed elsewhere in this book.

Opportunism

Sometimes the best way to find casual employment is to keep your eyes open, your ears close to the ground and all other parts of your body in a state of readiness. Look for private advertisements in shop windows or youth hostels noticeboards, or ask fellow travellers for tips about the job market in areas they have visited.

Being the straightforward people that Australians are, sometimes the best way to find job leads is to go into the nearest pub, sit yourself down with a drink and see what happens. This may sound like advice from a brewery PR man but it could be a good investment to buy a few drinks and get chatting with the locals. You may not be offered a job there and then but you may well gain some local knowledge that will point you in the right direction.

It can also pay to promote your own talents. Put notices in local shops offering to cut lawns, paint walls or dig ditches. Alternatively go door-to-door offering your services for any odd-jobs that might need to be done. Even if you do not get snowed under with work you will undoubtedly have some interesting experiences doing this. Another method would be to put an advertisement in a local newspaper. Perhaps something along the lines of: 'Willing worker seeking serious employment in the odd-job business. Nothing is too big, too small or too ludicrous. Years of experience in several continents. Competitive rates that will not break the mortgage.' If this does not work in one area then try it somewhere else where people are more understanding.

FRUIT PICKING

This is traditionally a boom area for casual employment. Not only that, but it is a good way for the overseas worker to see a side of Australian life which they would not see in a big city. The work is hard and dirty and the financial rewards vary from the mediocre to the excellent. To find fruit picking work you should go to the CES office nearest to the area in which you want to work. They will advise you on job availability. Due to problems in other sectors of the economy more and more people are now turning to fruit-picking for a living. This means there are less places for casual workers from abroad. This at least is the official line you will hear from the CES. Unofficially, the nature of fruit-picking and the poor conditions under which the workers live means that pickers are frequently walking off the job. The best way to land a picking job is to go to a fruit growing area and start knocking on a few farm doors. People have even been approached on the street in fruit picking towns and offered jobs. The best time is towards the end of the season when the growers are getting desperate to get their crops in and the pickers are getting fed up with their task.

Fruit picking as a means of employment during a year in Australia is not only a good idea from the financial point-of-view, it also has the big advantage of being the type of work that you would not come across at home. Making use of a holiday working visa is not so much about how much you earn but rather what you do. Fruit picking will be an experience you will never forget, no matter how hard you try.

Harvest times and areas

New South Wales

Harvest period	Crop	Area	Nearest CES or Agency
Jan	Apricot, prunes and peaches	Griffith	Griffith
Feb-Mar	Prunes	Young	Young
	Grapes	Griffith	Griffith
		Leeton	Leeton
	Cherries	Forbes	Parkes
	Peaches	Forbes	Parkes
Feb-Apr	Apples	Oranges	Oranges
	Pears	Forbes	Parkes
Feb-May	Apples	Forbes	Parkes

Harvest period	Crop	Area	Nearest CES or Agency
Mar-Apr	Apples	Batlow	Tumut
	Beans	Forbes	Parkes
	Zucchinis	Forbes	Parkes
	Peas	Forbes	Parkes
Mar-June	Cotton	Wee Waa	Narrabri
Sep-Apr	Oranges	Griffith	Griffith
Sep-Dec	Asparagus	Dubbo	Dubbo
Oct-Dec	Asparagus	CowraCowra	
		Forbes	Parkes
Nov-Dec	Cherries	Young	Young
Nov-Jan	Cotton chipping	Wee Waa	Narrabri
	Cherries	Oranges	Oranges
Nov-Feb	Cotton chipping	Moree	Moree
Nov-Mar	Onions	Griffith	Griffith
Nov-Apr	Tomatoes	Forbes	Parkes
Dec-Mar	Oranges	Leeton	Leeton

Victoria

Harvest period	Crop	Area	Nearest CES or Agency
Jan-Mar	Pears, peaches	Shepparton	Shepparton
		Ardmona	Shepparton
		Tatura	Shepparton
		Kyabram	Kyabram
		Invergordon	Kyabram
		Cobram	Cobram
Jan-Apr	Table grapes	Sunraysia	Mildura
		Robinvale	Mildura
Feb-Apr	Tomatoes	Shepparton	Shepparton
		Ardmona	Shepparton
		Tatura	Shepparton
		Kyabram	Kyabram
		Echuca and	
		Tongala	Echuca
		Rochester	Rochester

Harvest period	Crop	Area	Nearest CES or Agency
Feb-Mar	Grapes	Nyah District	
		Swan Hill	Swan Hill
		Lake Boga	Swan Hill
		Robinvale	Robinvale
		Sunraysia	Mildura
Jan-Apr	Tobacco	Ovens, King Wangaratta and Kiewa Valleys	
Mar-Apr	Apples	Red Hill	Rosebud
		Main Bridge	Rosebud
Sep-Nov	Asparagus	Dalmore	Dandenong
Oct-Dec	Strawberries	Echuca	Echuca
		Kyabram	Kyabram
		Silvan	Lilydale
Nov-Feb	Cherries and berries	Wandin	Lilydale
		Silvan	Lilydale
		Healesville	Lilydale
Nov-Dec	Tomato weeding	Echuca	Echuca
		Rochester	Echuca
		Tongala	Echuca
Queensland			
Jan-Feb	Grapes	Stanthorpe	Warwick
Feb-Mar	Pears	Stanthorpe	Warwick
Feb-Mar	Apples	Stanthorpe	Warwick
Mar-Apr	Ginger	Nambour	Nambour
Apr-Nov	Beans	Mary Valley	Gympie
May-Dec	Sugar cane	Ingham	Ingham
		Innisfail	Innisfail
May-Dec	Small crops	Ayr	Ayr
Jul-Sep	Ginger	Nambour	Nambour
Jul-Oct	Strawberries	Nambour	Nambour

Harvest period	Crop	Area	Nearest CES or Agency
Aug-Dec	Asparagus	Warwick	Warwick
Aug-Nov	Small crops	Ayr	Ayr
Sep-Nov	Potatoes/onions	Lockyer Valley	Toowoomba Gatton
Sep-Nov	Tobacco	Mareeba	Mareeba
Oct-Dec	Tomatoes	Bundaberg	Bundaberg
Dec	Stone fruits	Stanthorpe	Warwick
Dec-Feb	Mangoes	Ayr	Ayr
South Australia			
Feb-Mar	Wine grapes	Southern Vales	Noarlunga
Feb-Mar	Dried fruits	Riverland	Berri
Feb-Mar	Apples,pears	Adelaide Hills	Payneham
Feb-Apr	Wine grapes	Riverland	Berri
Feb-Apr	Peaches	Riverland	Berri
Feb-Apr	Wine grapes	Barossa Valley	Gawler
Jun-Aug	Navel oranges	Riverland	Berri
Jun-Sep	Pruning	Riverland	Berri
Sep-Jan	Oranges (Juicing and packing)	Riverland	Berri
Oct-Feb	Strawberries	Adelaide Hills	Payneham
Dec-Feb	Apricots	Riverland	Berri
Tasmania			
Feb-May	Potatoes	Scottsdale	Mowbray
Jan-Mar	Strawberries	Ringarooma	Mowbray
Mar-Apr	Hops	Scottsdale Derwent Valley Devonport	Mowbray Glenorchy Devonport

Harvest period	Crop	Area	Nearest CES or Agency
Mar-Apr	Grapes	Pipers River	Mowbray
		Tamar Valley	Mowbray
Feb-Apr	Grapes	Berridale	Glenorchy
Mar-Apr	Pears, apples	Huon Valley	Huonville
Feb-May	Apples	Eastern Shore	Eastern
		Bicheno	Eastern
		Tasman Peninsula	
Dec-Jan	Raspberries	Elizabeth Town	Launceston
		Derwent Valley	Glenorchy
		Devonport	Devonport
Jun-Aug	Brassica	Devonport	Devonport

Western Australia

Harvest period	Crop	Area	Nearest CES or Agency
Feb-Mar	Wildflowers	Coorow	Geraldton
Feb-Apr	Grapes	Albany	Albany
		Mt Barker	Albany
		Swan Valley	Midland
Feb-May	Apples	Manjimup	Manjimup
		Pemberton	
		Bridgetown	
		Donnybrooke	Bunbury
Mar-Jun	Rock lobster	Geraldton	Geraldton
Mar-Jun	Oats, wheat barley	Merredin	Merredin
		Northam	Northam
Mar-Oct	Prawning, scalloping	Carnarvon	Carnarvon
Apr-Jun	Oasts, wheat barley	Wagin	Collie
		Gnowangerup	Gnowangerup
		Katanning	Katanning
		Williams	Collie
		Narrogin	Collie
		West Arthur	Collie
		Geraldton	Geraldton

Harvest period	Crop	Area	Nearest CES or Agency
Apr-Jun	Oats, wheat	Bindoon Lower Chittering	Midland
Apr-Jun	Oats, wheat	Moora	Midland
Apr-Nov	Watermelons	Coorow	Geraldton
May-Jun	Oats, wheat	Salmon Gums	Esperance
May-Sep	Zucchini, squash watermelons rockmelon	Kununurra	Kununurra
Jul-Dec	Wildflowers	Coorow	Geraldton
Sep-Nov	Mangoes	Kununurra	Kununurra
Oct-Dec	Oats, wheat, barley	Merredin	Merredin
Jun-Dec	Tomatoes	Carnavon	Carnavon
Aug-Nov	Wildflowers	Machea	Midland
Oct-Jan	Oats, wheat, barley	Geraldton	Geraldton
Nov-Dec	Oats, wheat, barley	Albany	Albany
15th Nov- 30th Jun	Rock lobster	Fremantle Dongara Kalbarri Mandurah Jurien Bay Geraldton	Fremantle Fremantle Fremantle Mandurah Geraldton Geraldton
Nov-Dec	Wheat, barley	Moora Northam Esperance	Midland Northam Esperance
All year bananas		Kununurra	Kununurra

Pay and conditions for fruit pickers

The amount you earn from fruit picking will vary depending on your speed and the crop you are picking. In the majority of cases you will be paid according to your output. Some crops are more profitable than others — grapes are considered to be one of the most profitable crops because they are relatively easy to get to and pick. Even a novice grape-picker could expect to earn at least $A350 a week. At the other end of the scale are the likes of apples and oranges. These are notoriously unprofitable for the beginner because you have to keep going up and down a ladder to get the fruit. Placing the ladder is considered to be an art in itself.

Conditions can vary as much as pay but do not expect any five-star treatment, as one grape-picker in Mildura explained, 'When I reached the farm I was confronted by a corrugated-iron shed which I thought was the tractor shed. In fact, it turned out to be the staff accommodation. For the first few days I had to sleep on the concrete floor, but then I was afforded the ''luxury'' of having a rusty bedstead on which to lay my sleeping bag. To be honest I was lucky to have any type of free accommodation because most unexperienced pickers have to provide their own tent.

'We usually ate together in a fly-infested kitchen and after the first week we gave up cooking altogether and lived off hamburgers and, of course, grapes. Most of the growers in the area were tough men who always tried to get away with whatever they could. In the end three of us got fed up with our boss's behaviour and walked out. We ended up sitting on the pavement on the main street and after five minutes we had another offer of employment. Fruit picking tends to take you into cowboy country but it is well worth the experience.'

As well as taking your own accommodation it is also helpful, if not essential at times, to have your own transport too. Check with the CES first to find out the local conditions.

HOSPITALITY WORK

This is one area in which people on holiday working visas have traditionally found a variety of casual work. Whether it is as a potwasher (dishwasher) in a five-star hotel or a barman at the tourist resort at Ayers Rock, catering staff are in demand in all areas of the Australian hospitality industry.

Although experience is not always necessary for this type of work it does pay to look clean, tidy and respectable when applying for jobs. If you do have experience as a barperson, a chef or a waiter/waitress then take references with you to convince employers of your suitability. Lots of other people will be looking for the same types of jobs as yourself, so you will need a certain amount of luck and, at times, determination to land a job in hospitality. Check local newspapers and the CES; if there are no suitable vacancies then put on your glad rags and your best smile and go knocking on some doors. It is conceivable that you could spend several days without success but do not become down-hearted. Keep trying and do not be afraid to go to the same place two, three or four times — workers are frequently leaving or being fired from bars and restaurants and if you arrive at one of these moments then you could be in luck.

One of the things that is beginning to count against holiday working visa holders is that some of their predecessors have only spent a week, or even a couple of days, in a particular job before moving on. Although there is no reason why they should not do this it does not endear casual workers to a lot of employers. This is most apparent in tourist areas such as the Queensland island resorts and Cairns. As one nightclub manager explained, 'About two years ago most of my staff were travellers on holiday working visas and it can get extremely tiring if they work for a fortnight and then leave. There is never a problem in replacing them but the paperwork involved in putting on new staff can be considerable. My advice to people who know they will only be in an area for a short period of time is to avoid employment — you will only ruin it for people who come after you.' How you convince employers that you will turn up for work for a longer period of time is up to individuals but it is best not to lie.

Another factor counting against casual workers is the current recession and a downturn in the Australian tourist industry. This has led to more native Australians chasing fewer openings and there have been some cases of travellers being unable to find this type of casual work in certain areas.

In order to try and maximise your chances of employment in the hospitality industry you should:

● Look at it as a serious option, not a continuous party for which you expect to be paid.

● Be well prepared — if you have had relevant experience then take documents to show this. If you have no experience try and get some before you go.

● Be prepared to do any job, even if it is cleaning fish-heads or peeling mountains of potatoes.

● Make sure you are neat and tidy.

● If possible, take black trousers, black shoes and a white shirt/blouse with you.

● Be determined in your job-hunting — there are hospitality jobs to be had, they are just a bit harder to track down at present.

● Be prepared to convince employers that you will be around for more than a couple of days.

OTHER JOB POSSIBILITIES

Factory work

If you have a high boredom threshold then you could consider working in a factory packing anything from pineapples to soap. A good source of information about job availability is fellow travellers who have 'been there and done it', as they say. It is also worth following the fruit picking cycle — a lot of this produce will be packed for consumption in other parts of the country or overseas. The pay tends to be good for this type of work but you may be driven crazy if you do it for too long.

Fishing

There are some jobs to be had on prawn fishing vessels out of Broome, Darwin, Cairns and Townsville. The main jobs for men are net-mending and prawn-sorting, while women are usually taken on board as cooks. A set of good sea-legs and willingness to work hard are the best qualifications for this type of work but it is worth remembering that you may be at sea for several weeks at one time. Payment is in the form of a fixed wage or a share of the catch. Since the number of prawns being caught is smaller than it used to be a more stable option is to take the former. If you are a female member of crew you should make it perfectly clear what your role on board is going to include — and, more importantly, what it will *not* include. You can look for this type of work through the CES, or approach privately-owned boats or large companies, although these will probably tell you that you have to be a member of a seamans unions.

Jackaroo/Jillaroo

For people with farm experience of some description it may be possible to get a job as a jackaroo or a jillaroo (a sheep station assistant). Although it sounds romantic the chances are that you will not be riding across the outback on your trusty steed. In reality there can be a lot of sitting around on a sheep station — if not you will be doing all the jobs that no-one else can be bothered with. Ask someone who has done it before you commit yourself.

Labouring

This area of employment is being hit harder than most as a result of the recession. As the building trade contracts so the need for labourers dwindles. You could try visiting building sites to see if there is any work going but the best bet is to go to a relevant CES *early* in the morning. If there is any need for labourers they will be picked from the pool of men who gather at or before 6am. This is done on a day to day basis but it could lead to some useful contacts.

Mining

The more robust and adventurous could try and find work in the mining areas of north Western Australia or the Northern Territory. Due to recent contraction in the industry there are few jobs advertised in the local newspapers or CES so it is a case of going to the mines themselves. Since they can be hundreds of miles from any major city this is quite a risk if you do not find a job. On the other hand you will have a memorable experience getting there and back. Another possibility is the gold mining town of Kalgoorlie in Western Australia or Charters Towers in Queensland. If you are feeling particularly dedicated you could go looking for gold yourself, as one traveller, Andy Schmitke, did in the hills near Townsville in northern Queensland: 'I bought a second-hand gold dredger (approximately $A800) and four of us headed for the hills in best goldrush tradition. The work consisted of finding a suitable looking stream and then using the dredger to sift through the mud. We did it for eight weeks and although we did not make a fortune we did earn a few hundred dollars, and got a real buzz from the pioneering feeling.'

Miscellaneous opportunities

Travellers in Australia have been known to get jobs drinking beer in commercials or singing cockney songs in an 'English' pub. Keep an open mind about job opportunities and not just in terms of the type of job you would do at home. It may even be worthwhile brushing up on a few choruses of 'Knees up, Mother Brown'!

   Although casual employment is an important part of a working holiday in Australia it should be looked upon as a benefit rather than a necessity. Make sure you take enough money to support you for a reasonable length of time during your visit. If you arrive with only a few dollars in your pocket, hoping to find work immediately, then you may quickly find yourself in a miserable situation if you cannot find a job. There is still plenty of work available for holiday working visa holders but it should be approached in the same way as looking for a permanent job somewhere.

CHECKLIST

1. Be aware of the current economic situation in Australia.

2. Be prepared to work at getting work — do not consider it as your right.

3. Use the CES to find out about the availability of jobs in various areas.

4. Be willing to promote yourself and use your initiative.

5. Take with you any documents which could help your job-hunting.

6. Ask your fellow travellers about their experiences of working and looking for work in Australia.

7. Do not be easily put off if you initially find it difficult to find a job.

8. Make sure you have finances to support you during your first few months in Australia.

9. Be prepared to accept Australian work ethics.

10. Make the most of your time working — if you are not enjoying it then move on.

13
Relocation

Relocation for any job is a difficult business even if it is in your own country. However, if your relocation is international then the problems tend to multiply. Due to the complex nature of moving yourself, your family and all your possessions to Australia there are a number of companies who specialise in all aspects of removal and also personal travel.

REMOVAL

Unless you want to ship a Chieftain tank you can transport virtually anything to Australia. This includes:

- cars
- motorbikes
- animals
- boats
- complete household goods
- excess baggage
- miscellaneous items.

There are a number of firms who specialise in shipping goods to Australia and it is worth using their experience. A few points should be considered when choosing a company and organising your removal:

1. Shipping costs are usually calculated on volume and so you will have to give your removal firm precise details of the items you need moved, or the sizes of trunks, cartons and tea-chests which you plan to use.

2. If you are planning on a substantial shipment it is advisable to get estimates from various companies before you commit yourself.

3.   You must tell the removal company your final destination in Australia because this could effect the overall cost. For instance, if you plan on settling in a port city such as Perth or Sydney then the cost of moving the goods from the port to your home will be small. On the other hand, if you are going to be living in Alice Springs then the extra transport cost will be considerable: charges are based on mileage from the port of entry.

4.   Check varying prices and conditions of service from at least four different companies.

5.   It is worth making initial enquiries over the phone but make sure you have precise information about what you want.

6.   Do not ask for a quote too far ahead of your time of departure (over six months) because prices will invariably have increased by then.

7.   Alternatively do not leave things too late — remember, it will take your goods up to three months to arrive in Australia.

8.   As well as the charge by the removal firm there may be additional costs in the form of storage, quarantine (for any animals shipped), demurrage and Customs duty.

Removal companies

General

Abels International, 4a North Orbital, Napsbury Lane, St. Albans, Herts AL1 1XB. Tel: 01727 837417.

All Route Shipping (NI) Ltd, 14-16 West Bank Road, Belfast Harbour Estate, Belfast BT3 9JL. Tel: 01232 370223.

Anglo Pacific International Plc, Unit 1 Bush Industrial Estate, Standard Road, North Acton, London NW10 6DF. Tel: 0181 965 1234.

Avalon. Tel: London 0181 451 6336; Manchester 0161 945 9685; Scotland 01324 634170.

Bishop Blatchpack, Kestrel Way, Sowton Industrial Estate, Exeter, Devon EX2 7PA. Tel: 01392 420404.

Copsey & Company Ltd, Danes Road, Romford, Essex, London RM7 0HL. Tel: 0800 289 658.

Crown Worldwide Movers/Scotpac International Movers, Gartsherrie Road, Coatbridge, Glasgow. Tel: 0141 776 7191.

Davies Turner, Worldwide Movers, Overseas House, Stewarts Road, London SW8 4UG. Tel: 0171 622 4393.

Doree-Bonner, 0800 289541 (Enquiries and quotations).

Double E Overseas Removals Ltd, Movements House, Ajax Works, Hertford Road, Barking, Essex IG11 8BW. Tel: 0181 591 6929.

Econopak Removals Limited, Unit K, Abbey Wharf Industrial Estate, Kingsbridge Road, Barking, Essex IG11 0BT. Tel: 0181 591 3434.

Harrison, Lennon and Hoy, Rochester Way, Dartford, Kent DA1 3QY. Tel: 0181 460 8535.

Hoults Removals. Tel: Central London 0171 607 7321; North London 0181 367 7600; Northwest London 0181 965 4523; Birmingham 0121 359 7541; Manchester 0161 865 0071; Edinburgh 0131 225 6764; Glasgow 0141 336 3335.

Interpak, 3 Standard Road, London NW10 6EX. Tel: 0181 965 5550.

John Mason International Ltd, 2 Mill Lane Industrial Estate, Mill Lane, Croydon, Surrey CR0 4AA. Tel: 0181 667 1133.

McConnell Removals Limited, Unit 11 Mullusk Park, Newtownabbey, Northern Ireland. Tel: 01232 843631.

Personal Shipping Services, 8 Redcross Way, London Bridge, London SE1 9HR. Tel: 0171 407 6606.

Pickfords, 492 Great Cambridge Road, Enfield, Middlesex EN1 3SA. Tel: 0181 367 0045 (Head Office)/ 0800 28 92 29 (Enquiries).

Animal freight specialists

Golden Arrow Shippers, Lydbury North, Shropshire SY7 8AY. Tel: 015888 240 and 606.

Ladyhaye Livestock Shipping, Hare Lane, Blindley Heath, Lingfield, Surrey RH7 6JB. Tel: 01342 832161.

Par Air Livestock Shipping Services, Stanway, Colchester, Essex. Tel: 01206 330332.

Pinehawk Livestock Shippers, Church Road, Carlton, Newmarket, Suffolk CB8 9LA. Tel: 01223 290249.

Skymaster Air Cargo Ltd, Room 15, Building 305, Cargo Centre, Manchester Airport, Altrincham, Cheshire WA15 8UX. Tel: 0161 436 2190.

Transpet, 160 Chingford Mount Road, London E4 9BS. Tel: 0181 529 0979/0112.

Whitelea Skydogs, Cross Green, Matlock, Derbys DE4 2JT. Tel: 01629 734000.

Since overseas removal companies can go bust just as easily as anyone else it is advisable to choose a company which is a member of **The Association of International Removers** (AIR). This not only means that the company has been carefully vetted and specialises in international removal but also that it is covered by the AIR Customer Payment Guarantee. This protects your full payment and in the event of a company ceasing trading AIR will take over responsibility for management of your removal.

TRAVEL ARRANGEMENTS

Once you have arranged for your goods and possessions to be transported to Australia it is time to think about getting yourself the 10,000 miles to the other side of the world. The main considerations when doing this are:

- cost
- comfort
- speed

Cost will probably be the most important factor for most people but until you have spent forty hours and numerous transit stops in getting to Australia you do not know the real meaning of jet-lag. When booking a flight of this nature it pays to deal with travel agents who specialise in long haul travel. Not only will they be able to offer you the best deal (hopefully), they will also be able to give you some hints and tips from their own experiences. Some of the companies who have a good reputation for helping people get to Australia as quickly, cheaply and as comfortably as possible are:

- Anglo Pacific, 23 Earls Court Road, London W8 6ED. Tel: 0171 937 9893.

- Australian Air Fare Centre, 102 New Street, Birmingham B2 4HQ. Tel: 0121 633 3232. Special services for migrant travellers, including 40kg baggage allowance and 50 per cent child discount.

- Austravel, 50 Conduit Street, London W1. Tel: 0171 734 7755.

- Bridge The World Travel Centre, 1-3 Ferdinand Street, Camden Town, London NW1. Tel: 0171 911 0900.

- STA Travel, 86 Old Brompton Road, London SW7; 117 Euston Road, London NW1; 75 Deansgate, Manchester; 25 Queens Road, Bristol; 88 Vicar Lane, Leeds; 19 High Street, Oxford; 38 Sidney Street, Cambridge. For information about flights to Australia — Tel: 0171 937 9962.

- Taprobane Travel, 4 Kingly Street, London W1R 5LF. Tel: 0171 437 6272/3.

- Trailfinders, 42-50 Earls Court Road, London W8 6EJ. Tel: 0171 938 3366. 194 Kensington High Street, London W8 7RG. Tel: 0171 938 3939.

ACCOMMODATION

Short-term accommodation can be one of the biggest worries for people arriving in Australia, particularly if they are migrating and they have not arranged to buy property yet, or do not have family with whom to stay.

As a sample these are some of the rates you can expect to pay for various types of accommodation in different Australian cities. These rates are generally for people looking for accommodation from one to four weeks.

Sydney

Studio From $A275 per week (two people).
One bedroom, self-contained units From $A350 per week (two people).
Two to three bedroom, self-contained units From $A475 per week (two people).
Hotel/motel units From $A400 per week (double).
Note Rates are more expensive for accommodation which is near to the city centre or beach holiday areas.

Brisbane

One bedroom apartments From $A260 per week.
Two to three bedroom apartments From $A330 per week (two persons).
Four bedroom apartments (Limited supply) From $A500 per week.
Note Since Brisbane is Australia's holiday state a large part of the year is classified as peak — the more notice you give the better chance you have of being offered a lower rate.

Perth
One bedroom apartment From $A230 per week.
Two to three bedroom apartments From $A290 per week.
Hotel/motel units From $A300 per week (double).

Melbourne
One bedroom apartment From $A200 per week.
Two to three bedroom apartments From $A300 per week.
Hotel/motel units $A320 per week.

Adelaide
One bedroom apartments From $A220 per week.
Two to three bedroom apartments From $A260 per week.
Hotel/motel units From $A375 per week.

Other contacts for accommodation
The magazine *Australian Outlook* offers an accommodation service for most areas of Australia, for which they charge a £15 fee. For further information contact: Consyl Publishing, 3 Buckhurst Road, Bexhill-on-Sea, East Sussex TN40 1QF. Tel: 01424 223111.

SETTLING IN

Although it will not be as obvious as in some other countries, you will experience culture-shock when you first arrive in Australia: the climate, the politics, the way people talk, general attitudes, the media, the food, the culture and a hundred and one other areas that may seem similar to those at home but which have numerous subtle differences. For instance, Australians speak English but they also have one of the most colourful and expressive colloquial vocabularies in the world.

The best way to come to terms with your new environment is to become absorbed in it slowly rather than to try and change into a 'true-blue' Aussie overnight. Take time to look around you to see how people act and what type of behaviour is acceptable and unacceptable. Watch a variety of television programmes and read newspapers to find out what is going on in the country and what makes it tick. But most of all, talk to people. This is the best way to learn things and it will pay to be an interested observer initially. Avoid being opinionated or over-bearing — you are the new kid on the block and you should try and make a good impression. If you do, it will stand you in good stead for the future.

It may take several months, or even a few years, before you feel properly settled in your new surroundings but it is something that should be done gradually and persevered with.

14
The Future

No workforce can afford to stagnate and thoughts of the future should always be in everyone's mind. This has recently been addressed by the Australian Department of Employment, Education and Training which has produced a booklet entitled *Australia's Workforce in the Year 2001*. Despite the recent recession this extensive survey predicts that employment growth in the next ten years will match that of the last ten. However, the mix of employment seems set to change, with greater growth occurring in skilled trades and professions.

It seems that Bob Hawke's intention in the 1980s to turn Australia into 'the clever country' is going to become true by the turn of the century. Jobs and careers requiring degrees and diplomas look set to show greater growth than less skilled employment. However, due to increased levels of training there will be greater competition for the available places.

The largest areas of expansion will occur in construction, wholesale, community services and recreation and personal services.

THE TOP GROWTH JOBS

The following list is from *Australia's Workforce in the Year 2001*. The top group 90-100 is expected to have just over 19 per cent of all jobs in the next decade. The 80-90 group is expected to have a growth of 14.7 per cent, while the figure for the 70-80 group will be 12.3. Occupations with the best prospects are professionals, sales workers and tradespersons. The worst prospects occur for machine operators and labourers — although construction labourers will benefit from the expansion in the construction industry as a whole.

Rated 90-100
University teachers, psychologists, economists, doctors and specialists,

dental practitioners, geologists and geophysicists, veterinarians, physiotherapists, lawyers, speech pathologists, pharmacists, other natural scientists, chemical engineers, optometrists, school teachers, social workers, mathematicians, statisticians and actuaries, occupational therapists, mining engineers, architects and landscape architects, librarians, civil engineers, TAFE teachers, metallurgists and materials scientists, chiropractors and osteopaths, legislation and government officials, electrical and electronic engineers, other social professionals, mechanical engineers, other engineers, other health practitioners, quantity surveyors, radiographers, podiatrists, accountants, cartographers and surveyors.

Rated 80-90
Computing professionals, aircraft pilots, aircraft maintenance engineers, electrical mechanics, child care co-ordinators, electrical fitters, specialist managers, medical technicians, toolmakers, plumbers, automotive electricians, refrigeration mechanics, general managers, metal fitters, welfare para-professionals, other business professionals, vehicle mechanics.

Rated 70-80
Extra systemic teachers, carpenters and joiners, hairdressers, panel beaters, registered nurses, engineering technicians, bricklayers, other transport technicians, vehicle body builders, securities and finance dealers, precision metal trades, metal coasting trades, boilermakers, cabinetmakers, meat trades, journalists, vehicle painters, other metal trades, painters and decorators.

Rated 60-70
Printing trades, vehicle trimmers, enrolled nurses, sheetmetal trades, other artists, glass trades, floor and wall tilers, wood machinists, plasterers, other electrical trades, bakers and pastrycooks, upholsterers, other wood trades, other para-professionals, other insurance salespersons, other tradespersons, dental nurses, managing supervisors.

Rated 50-60
Roof slaters and tilers, sales representatives, cooks, police, child care, refuge and related workers, horticulturists, metal finishing trades, stenographers and typists.

Rated 40-50
Other personal service workers, stationary plant operators, numerical clerks, other clerks, filing clerks, other food trades.

Rated 30-40

Receptionists, construction and mining labourers, farmers and farm managers, despatch clerks, mobile plant operators.

Rated 20-30

Other salespersons, road and rail drivers, data processing clerks, agricultural labourers.

Rated 10-20

Other labourers, sales assistants.

Rated 0-10

Machine operators, trades assistants, cleaners, tellers.

JOB GROWTH BY 2001

(From *Australia's Workforces in the Year 2001*).

			Employment	
Occupation	Growth 1991-2001	1986	2001	

Managers				
1. Legislators	29.0%	1,895	4,175	
2. General managers	19.0%	34,428	61,772	
3. Specialist managers	16.9%	187,679	214,042	
4. Farmers and managers	-10.9%	261,268	218,886	
5. Managing supervisors	28.2%	297,428	485,894	
Total	12.1%	782,697	974,769	
Professionals				
6. Geologists/geophysicists	12.8%	3,477	4,041	
7. Other natural scientists	30.2%	27,199	44,236	
8. Architects	31.0%	9,590	13,800	
9. Quantity surveyors	31.0%	9,590	13,800	
10. Cartographers/surveyors	16.1%	7,301	10,430	
11. Chemical engineers	28.4%	1,949	2,859	
12. Civil engineers	28.9%	18,933	33,829	
13. Electrical/electronic engineers	30.0%	19,894	41,427	
14. Mechanical engineers	25.9%	11,991	24,542	
15. Mining engineers	38.6%	1,900	6,922	

16.	Metallurgists	29.6%	2,498	6,640
17.	Other engineers	27.9%	12,476	26,791
18.	Doctors and specialists	19.8%	32,942	42,312
19.	Dental practitioners	19.6%	6,384	9,628
20.	Pharmacists	52.2%	10,754	13,165
21.	Occupational therapists	51.6%	2,771	7,270
22.	Optometrists	46.9%	1,475	4,224
23.	Physiotherapists	47.3%	5,908	13,751
24.	Speech pathologists	58.6%	1,335	3,582
25.	Chiropractors and osteopaths	19.9%	1,392	1,938
26.	Podiatrists	12.5%	1,008	1,388
27.	Radiographers	12.4%	4,321	7,035
28.	Veterinarians	59.4%	3,022	6,226
29.	Other health practitioners	46.7%	3,934	9,600
30.	School teachers	25.6%	219,579	311,058
31.	University teachers	29.8%	22,746	38,414
32.	TAFE teachers	20.6%	20,576	39,951
33.	Extra systemic teachers	20.6%	29,476	52,026
34.	Social workers	83.1%	6,499	23,623
35.	Lawyers	32.5%	23,493	39,883
36.	Other social professionals	-18.7%	17,141	17,081
37.	Accountants	52.6%	65,992	167,871
38.	Computing professionals	59.4%	40,712	134,945
39.	Other business professionals	39.7%	42,059	76,705
40.	Journalists	25.8%	10,087	20,174
41.	Other artists	28.6%	39,019	67,587
42.	Economists	78.6%	2,412	4,391
43.	Psychologists	93.0%	3,891	8,461
44.	Mathematicians, statisticians and actuaries	66.3%	2,040	4,244
45.	Librarians	74.3%	9,324	17,194
46.	Other professionals	44.3%	30,040	41,782
Total		33.0%	780,174	1,382,454

Para-professionals

47.	Medical technicians	11.1%	18,349	36,783
48.	Engineering technicians	8.7%	92,587	94,153
49.	Aircraft pilots	7.4%	5,085	5,786
50.	Other transport technicians	-4.5%	11,532	9,910

51.	Registered nurses	20.5%	139,923	192,808
52.	Police	14.2%	34,811	52,821
53.	Welfare para-professionals	53.8%	17,025	34,726
54.	Child care co-ordinators	44.5%	2,012	4,018
55.	Other para-professionals	14.5%	110,486	118,576
Total		16.1%	431,709	549,582

Tradespeople

56.	Toolmakers	18.3%	10,069	13,700
57.	Metal fitters	16.6%	102,510	125,712
58.	Sheetmetal trades	20.2%	16,966	24,533
59.	Boilermakers etc	15.4%	57,686	78,015
60.	Metal-casting trades	8.3%	2,141	1,781
61.	Metal-finishing trades	12.0%	2,973	2,999
62.	Aircraft maintenance			
	engineers	14.0%	8,339	10,235
63.	Precision metal trades	22.8%	9,151	11,438
64.	Other metal trades	15.7%	2,320	1,946
65.	Electrical fitters	10.0%	19,848	15,278
66.	Automotive electricians	25.3%	5,112	10,772
67.	Refrigeration mechanics	30.7%	8,364	18,754
68.	Electrical mechanics	25.6%	54,221	97,701
69.	Other electrical trades	5.2%	66,978	77,486
70.	Carpenters and joiners	27.9%	82,272	131,087
71.	Bricklayers	40.2%	23,500	43,759
72.	Painters and decorators	26.2%	38,230	64,762
73.	Plasterers	36.6%	14,274	48,564
74.	Plumbers	32.1%	43,891	69,158
75.	Roof slaters and tilers	36.9%	4,561	6,608
76.	Floor and wall tilers	41.2%	5,711	15,224
77.	Printing trades	15.0%	36,694	54,781
78.	Vehicle mechanics	24.4%	85,133	132,367
79.	Panel beaters	26.7%	17,653	29,448
80.	Vehicle painters	19.2%	8,585	12,375
81.	Vehicle body builders	20.3%	4,308	6,246
82.	Vehicle trimmers	18.1%	2,088	3,454
83.	Meat trades	12.3%	27,873	35,841
84.	Bakers/pastrycooks	5.3%	13,874	24,819
85.	Cooks	28.1%	54,448	72,358
86.	Other food trades	-0.1%	1,626	2,064
87.	Horticulturists	11.1%	42,330	49,827

88.	Wood machinists	28.5%	5,571	9,906
89.	Cabinet makers	27.5%	16,981	23,001
90.	Other wood trades	21.2%	3,900	7,007
91.	Upholsterers	20.5%	5,070	8,155
92.	Glass trades	24.9%	5,108	11,420
93.	Hairdressers	47.9%	38,018	65,204
94.	Other trades	9.5%	72,800	88,821
Total		21.2%	1,020,757	1,482,795

Clerks

95.	Stenographers/typists	17.8%	258,853	334,476
96.	Data-processing clerks	15.4%	74,873	112,346
97.	Numerical clerks	16.4%	272,757	518,682
98.	Filing clerks	14.6%	46,472	69,736
99.	Dispatch clerks	11.8%	83,724	83,164
100.	Receptionists	8.0%	142,001	186,434
101.	Other clerks	16.4%	265,655	221,177
Total		15.2%	1,144,335	1,526,015

Sales workers

102.	Securities and finance dealers	18.4%	10,814	34,350
103.	Other insurance sales people	10.3%	47,802	69,328
104.	Sales representatives	19.5%	79,155	144,819
105.	Sales assistants	28.0%	339,896	640,673
106.	Tellers	18.9%	114,086	155,150
107.	Other salespersons	28.7%	135,997	210,993
108.	Child care and related workers	24.6%	28,855	80,199
109.	Enrolled nurses	21.0%	35,763	57,591
110.	Dental nurses	16.1%	8,961	15,723
111.	Other personal service workers	18.4%	26,731	42,988
Total		24.0%	828,061	1,451,816

Machine operators

112.	Road and rail drivers	11.5%	208,762	284,164
113.	Mobile plant operators	15.7%	95,526	115,392
114.	Stationary plant operators	-2.9%	57,527	58,741

115. Machine operators	2.1%	190,722	161,990
Total	7.5%	552,537	620,287

Labourers

116. Trades assistants	1.7%	236,263	285,125
117. Agricultural labourers	-16.8%	79,332	104,561
118. Cleaners	6.7%	164,236	217,001
119. Construction/mining labourers	21.6%	97,464	170,635
120. Other labourers	15.2%	385,726	488,159
Total	8.4%	963,020	1,265,482
Grand total	15.9%	6,503,290	9,253,200

Glossary of Employment Terms

Accord This is the agreement reached between the Federal Government and the Australian Council of Trade Unions in 1983. Its main aim is to offer tax trade-offs in return for moderate wage increases. It was instigated by Bob Hawke and its future is now uncertain.

ACTU Australian Council of Trade Unions. The equivalent of the British TUC.

A/H After hours. Used by many tradespeople who can be contacted for jobs after normal working hours.

Annual leave This is generally a minimum of four weeks paid leave a year. See also **Leave loading**.

Assets test A means test on pensioners which can reduce their pensions in line with their assets.

Award rate This is the minimum rate of pay which can be offered to employees. Each profession has a different award rate which also deals with conditions of employment as well as pay.

Bludger Someone who avoids work at every opportunity.

Commonwealth Employment Service (CES) This is the major feature in the public sector recruitment network. It has offices throughout the country and offers advice as well as advertising the current job vacancies.

Compo Workers compensation. A popular concept among Australian workers; even the smallest injury will be put under the compo spotlight.

Dobber Anyone who tells tales on their fellow workmates. In a society which prides itself on workers' solidarity dobbing is looked upon as a cardinal sin and anyone who is accused of this is likely to be sent to Coventry, or perhaps Sydney.

Dragging the chain Someone who does not do their fair share of the work — something that may be done by a **bludger**.

Equal Employment Opportunity (EEO) A Commonwealth Government policy to discourage discrimination in employment. Employers following this policy consider job applicants on their ability and regardless of sex, race, marital status and other such factors.

Flat-out-like-a-lizard-drinking Someone working their socks off.

Flexitime An arrangement where workers can start and leave work at earlier or later times to normal. Debits or credits of working hours can be built up within specified limits enabling a 'flex day' to be taken off on occasions. Flexitime conditions vary from company to company and depend on the relevant award for that industry. Flexitime is most common in the public service.

Full-time employment Any job where you work more than 30 hours a week.

Group certificate A yearly statement of earnings issued by the employer and used by the employee to prepare the dreaded tax return.

Gun The best, and fastest, worker. Frequently applied in industries such as fruit-picking or anything where you have to produce a certain amount a day.

Hard yakka Hard work — definitely not done by a **bludger**.

Job sharing As employment rises, more and more people are embracing the concept of job sharing, whereby two or more people share the duties and responsibilities of one job. The hours and conditions are arranged to suit the employees.

Leave loading This is a particularly Australian concept which allows for an extra 17.5 per cent to be added to workers' annual holiday pay. An extremely civilised arrangement.

Long service leave Three months paid leave usually granted after either 10 or 15 years of continuous employment with one firm.

Medicare The system of national health care. Provides for free hospital treatment and 85 per cent of general practitioners' fees. A tax of 1.4 per cent is levied on all wage earners in order to finance Medicare.

O A suffix used with a variety of occupations, such as journo, milko, garbo (garbage collector), muso, and so on.

Offsider An assistant.

Overtime Any hours worked in excess of regular full-time hours. Overtime rates are usually at time-and-a-half or double-time.

Part-time work (also called **casual employment**) Any job where you work less than 30 hours a week. You do not always have the same rights as full-time workers but awards for part-time work usually contain sufficient provisions to protect workers.

Penalty rates Due to the **accord** and **award** agreements, workers are paid at higher rates if they work at weekends, at night or on shift work. Workers are often happy to work at unsociable hours because of penalty rates.

Piece work Work where you are paid on how much you produce.

Severance pay Compensation paid by a firm to an employee whose services are no longer required because of technological changes or other factors.

Shift work Most shift work is divided into three sections — day, afternoon, and night shift. All shifts are usually eligible for **penalty rates** but night shift attracts the highest rate.

Sickie An unscheduled day off when you do not feel like going to work because of a hangover, the sun is shining or you just do not feel like working. An increasing problem in the Australian workforce, since some workers believe that it is their right to take a certain number of sickies a year.

Sick leave Paid leave when you are suffering from the sickie malaise. It also applies when you are genuinely sick although there is a limit to how many sick days you can have a year.

Smoko A tea break — some industries would be brought to a halt if its workers were not allowed their smoko. Smoking is not obligatory.

Special leave This is extra leave which is granted in exceptional circumstances, such as the death of a close relative, attendance at jury service, or private study.

Superannuation A scheme financed by either employers, or employers and employees, which assures the employee an income after retirement.

TAFE: Technical and Further Education colleges. This is the main vocational education body in Australia. It covers a wide range of professions and has a large number of colleges in all states.

Tax agent Someone to fill in your tax form. Although they charge a fee it is usually well worth it, not only for the time they can save you but also because of the refund which they may be able to calculate.

TFN: Tax File Number A number which you must have if you intend to work in Australia. It can be obtained by filling in a form from any tax office in Australia.

Useful Addresses

Australian Bureau of Statistics, PO Box 10, Belconnen, ACT 2616. Tel: 06 252 6112.

Australian High Commission, Australia House, Strand, London WC2B 4LA. Tel: 0171 379 4334.

Australian Consulate, Chatsworth House, Lever Street, Manchester M1 2DL. Tel: 0161 228 1344.

Australian Department of Employment, Education and Training, PO Box 9880, Canberra, ACT 2601. Tel: 062 837008.

Department of Industrial Relations, GPO Box 9879, Canberra, ACT 2601. Tel: 06 243 7333.

Department of Immigration, Local Government and Ethnic Affairs, Central Office, Benjamin Offices, Chan Street, Belconnen, ACT 2617. Tel: 062 574111.

Department of Social Security, Australia House, Strand, London WC2B 4LA.

Department of Social Security, Juliana House, Bowes Street, Philip, ACT 2606. Tel: 062 891444.

Department of Trade, Edmund Barton Building, Kings Avenue, Barton, ACT 2600. Tel: 062 723911.

Financial and Migrant Information Service, Commonwealth Bank of Australia, 1 Kingsway, London WC2. Tel: 0171 379 0955.

National Council of Overseas Skills Recognition (NCOSR), GPO Box 1407, Canberra City, ACT. Tel: 06 276 7636.

Trade

Agent-General for New South Wales, New South Wales House, 66 Strand, London WC2N 5LZ. Tel: 0171 839 6651.

Agent-General for Victoria, Victoria House, Melbourne Place, Strand, London WC2B 4LG. Tel: 0171 836 2656.

Agent-General for Queensland, Queensland House, 392-393 Strand, London WC2R 0LZ. Tel: 0171 836 1333.

Agent-General for Western Australia, Western Australia House, 115-116 Strand, London WC2R 0AJ. Tel: 0171 240 2881.

Australian Trade Commission (AUSTRADE), Australia House, Strand, London WC2B 4LA. Tel: 0171 887 5326.

Further Reading

MAGAZINES AND NEWSPAPERS

Australian News, Outbound Newspapers Limited, 1 Commercial Road, Eastbourne, East Sussex BN21 3XQ. Tel: 01323 412001.

Australian Outlook, 1 Buckhurst Road, Town Hall Square, Bexhill-on-Sea, East Sussex TN40 1QF. Tel: 01424 223111.

Brisbane Courier-Mail, Campbell Street, Bowen Hills, Brisbane.

The Adelaide Advertiser, 121 King William Street, Adelaide.

The Melbourne Age, 250 Spencer Street, Melbourne.

The Sydney Morning Herald, 235 Jones Street, Broadway, NSW 2007.

The West Australian, 219 St. George's Terrace, Perth 6000.

BOOKS

Australian Careers Guide, David Royce Publishing, 44 Regent Street, Redfern, NSW.

How to Live and Work in Australia by Laura Veltman, How To Books, Estover Road, Plymouth PL6 7PZ. 4th edition 1994.

How to Get a Job Abroad by Roger Jones, How To Books (as above).

How to Spend a Year Abroad by Nick Vandome, How To Books (as above).

How to Study Abroad, Teresa Tinsley, How To Books (as above).

How to Teach Abroad, Roger Jones, How To Books (as above).

Cost of Living and Housing Survey, Commonwealth Bank of Australia.

Telecom National Business Directory, Telecom Australia (available from most large libraries).

Jobsons Year Book of Public Companies, Dun and Bradstreet (Publications), 24 Albert Street, South Melbourne, Victoria 3205.

Smart Start, Hobsons Press (Australia), 270 Pitt Street, Sydney, NSW 2000.

What Job Suits You?, Hobsons Press (Australia), 270 Pitt Street, Sydney, NSW 2000.

Job Prospects — Australia, Hobsons Press (Australia), 270 Pitt Street, Sydney, NSW 2000.

What Jobs Pay, Hobsons Press (Australia), 270 Pitt Street, Sydney, NSW 2000.

The Job Book — Life After School, Hobsons Press (Australia), 270 Pitt Street, Sydney, NSW 2000.

Business Destination Australia/New Zealand, Business Migration Program, Australian Consulates, Embassies and Commissions.

Index

Holiday Working Visa, 18, 23-25
Holidays, 27
Hospital administrator, 94
Home economics, 94-95
Horticulture, 95
Hotel and catering, 95-96, 162-164

Income tax, 41-49
Independent Migration, 18, 19-20
Industrial design, 96
Industrial relations, 39
Industries Commission, 15
Insurance, 96-97
Interior design, 97

Jewellery, 97
Job Search, 146-147
Job Search Allowance, 53-54
Job Start, 145
Journalism, 98

Keating, Paul, 16, 17

Law, 98
Leave Loading, 27
Librarian, 98-99
Locksmith, 99
'Lucky Country', 12 16, 17

Mechanics, 89-90, 114
Medicare, 34
Medicine, 99
Metal trades, 99-100
Migration, 18-25
Mining, 100, 165
Mothercraft, 100
Motor trade, 100-101
Music, 101

National Office of Overseas Skills
    Recognition (NOOSR), 122-135
New South Wales, 67-68, 143, 156-157
Newspapers, 71-72
Newstart, 54
Natural therapy, 101
Northern Territory, 144
Nursing, 102, 127

Occupational therapy, 102-103

Oil driller, 103
Optometrist, 103-104
Orthopist, 104
Optical, 104-105
Organisation and Methods, 105

Painter, 82
Patternmaking, 105
Pay, 26
Penalty rates, 26
Pensions, 50-53
Personnel, 106
Pharmacist, 106, 127-128
Photographer, 106-107
Physical fitness, 107
Physiotherapist, 107-108, 128-129
Plasterer, 82
Plumber, 82
Podiatrist, 108, 129-130
Police, 108-109
Pool system, 18
Prices Surveillance Authority, 15
Printing, 109
Prison officer, 109-110
Psychologist, 110
Public relations, 110-111
Public Services, 111

Quantity surveyor, 111-112
Queensland, 68, 143-144, 158-159

Radiographer, 112, 130-131
Radio/TV repair, 112
Ranger, 113
Receptionist, 113
Recreation officers, 113-114
Recruitment, 63-74, 154-155
Recruitment agencies, 66-71
Real estate, 114
Redundancy, 38-39
Relocation, 167-173
Removal, 168-170
Retailing, 115

Secretarial, 115-116
Sickies, 151
Social security, 50-54
Social Welfare, 131-132
Social work, 116

How to Get a Job in America
Roger Jones

Updated and revised, this book helps you to turn your dream into reality by explaining the work possibilities open to non-US citizens. Drawing on the experiences of individuals, companies and recruitment agencies Roger Jones reveals the range of jobs available, the locations, pay and conditions, and how to get hired. The book includes the latest on immigration procedures. 'Essential for anyone who is thinking of working in the US.' *Going USA.* 'Outlines with some thoroughness the procedures a future immigrant or temporary resident would have to undertake. . . For young people considering a US exchange or summer employment the section on vacation jobs is particularly worthwhile.' *Newscheck/Careers Service Bulletin.* 'Very good value for money.' *School Librarian journal.*

224pp illus. 1 85703 1687. 3rd edition

How to Get a Job in Europe
Mark Hempshell

Packed throughout with key contacts, sample documents and much hard-to-find information, this book will be an absolutely essential starting point for everyone job-hunting in Europe, whether as a school or college leaver, graduate trainee, technician or professional — and indeed anyone wanting to live and work as a European whether for just a summer vacation or on a more permanent basis. 'A very useful book . . . a valuable addition to any careers library — well written, clear and interesting.' *Phoenix/Association of Graduate Careers Advisory Services.* 'I learned a lot from the book and was impressed at the amount of information that it contained.' *Newscheck/Careers Service Bulletin.* Mark Hempshell is a freelance writer who specialises in writing on overseas employment.

208pp illus. 1 85703 128 8. 2nd edition.

How to Retire Abroad
Roger Jones

Increasing numbers of people are looking for opportunities to base their retirement overseas — away from many of the hassles of life in the UK. This book meets the need for a really comprehensive and practical guide to retiring abroad — from the initial planning stages, to choosing the right location and property, and adapting to a completely new environment. Such a big change in lifestyle can involve many pitfalls. Written by a specialist in expatriate matters, this handbook will guide you successfully step-by-step through the whole process of finding a new home, coping with key matters such as tax, foreign investment, property, health care, and even working overseas. The book is complete with a country-by-country guide. Roger Jones is a freelance author specialising in expatriate information.

176pp. 1 85703 051 6.

ArtScroll Mesorah Series®

Expositions on Jewish liturgy and thought

Rabbi Nosson Scherman/Rabbi Meir Zlotowitz
General Editors

PURIM

PURIM — ITS OBSERVANCE AND SIGNIFICANCE / A PRE-SENTATION BASED ON TALMUDIC AND TRADITIONAL SOURCES.

Published by

Mesorah Publications, ltd

A PROJECT OF THE

Mesorah
Heritage
Foundation

Compiled by
Rabbi Avie Gold

Overview by
Rabbi Nosson Scherman

FIRST EDITION
First Impression . . . January 1991
Second Impression . . . January 1993
Third Impression . . . January 1997

Published and Distributed by
MESORAH PUBLICATIONS, Ltd.
4401 Second Avenue
Brooklyn, New York 11232

Distributed in Europe by
J. LEHMANN HEBREW BOOKSELLERS
20 Cambridge Terrace
Gateshead, Tyne and Wear
England NE8 1RP

Distributed in Israel by
SIFRIATI / A. GITLER — BOOKS
10 Hashomer Street
Bnei Brak 51361

Distributed in Australia & New Zealand by
GOLDS BOOK & GIFT CO.
36 William Street
Balaclava 3183, Vic., Australia

Distributed in South Africa by
KOLLEL BOOKSHOP
22 Muller Street
Yeoville 2198, Johannesburg, South Africa

ARTSCROLL MESORAH SERIES ®
"PURIM" / Its Observance and Significance

© Copyright 1991, by MESORAH PUBLICATIONS, Ltd.
4401 Second Avenue / Brooklyn, N.Y. 11232 / (718) 921-9000

ISBN
0-89906-607-0 (hard cover)
0-89906-608-9 (paperback)

Typography by Compuscribe at ArtScroll Studios, Ltd.
4401 Second Avenue / Brooklyn, N.Y. 11232 / (718) 921-9000

Printed in the United States of America by Moriah Offset
Bound by Sefercraft, Quality Bookbinders, Ltd. Brooklyn, N.Y.

„לַיְּהוּדִים הָיְתָה אוֹרָה וְשִׂמְחָה וְשָׂשׂוֹן וִיקָר"
The Jewish people had light, joy,
happiness and honor (Esther 8:16).

אמר רב יהודה: אורה זו תורה, שמחה זה יום טוב, ששון זו
מילה, ויקר אלו תפלין.
Rabbi Yehudah said: light is Torah; joy — this is the
festival; happiness — this is milah; honor — this is
tefillin (Megillah 16b).

Dedicated in honor of the
bar mitzvah of our בכור

Ephraim Yechiel נ"י

Just as Purim remains the beacon of hope
that penetrates all dark times with the light of Torah,
so may Ephraim Yechiel's simcha
be the beginning of a long and healthy life
of greatness in Torah and Yiras Shamayim.

We express our gratitude to
Hashem Yisborach for His infinite blessings
and to our parents
Anna and Joseph Glatt שיחיו
and
Ethel and Marshall Korn שיחיו
whose guidance, devotion, and kindness
have made this day possible.

Margie and Aaron Glatt

Table of Contents

✌ Preface

Adar is the national month of rejoicing. In the words of the Talmud (*Taanis* 29a): מִשֶּׁנִּכְנָס אֲדָר מַרְבִּין בְּשִׂמְחָה, *When Adar begins, we increase in joyousness*. Although this joy is in no small measure due to our salvation from the wicked schemes of, as well as the downfall of, our eternal foe Amalek, as personified by the arch-villain Haman, there's another reason for celebration. The Talmud (*Shabbos* 88a) states that Purim marks the reaffirmation of Israel's acceptance of the Torah, on an even loftier level than when it was accepted at Mount Sinai. For at that time, God overturned the mountain and suspended it above their heads like a barrel. He then said, 'If you accept the Torah, all will be well. But if not, there shall be your grave.' In other words, the Torah was accepted under duress, which could have given later generations an excuse for not adhering to its mandates. Nevertheless, the Talmud continues, in the days of Ahasuerus they reaccepted the Torah out of great love for God. Thus, the joy of Adar in general and Purim in particular is the joy of *Kabbalas HaTorah*, receiving the Torah.

It is our fervent wish that this volume will enhance the celebration of Purim both through a deeper appreciation of the mitzvah obligations of the day and as a vehicle for Torah study. Thus we are proud to add this volume to the others in this series: *Rosh Hashanah; Yom Kippur; Succos;* and *Chanukah.*

❦ ❦ ❦

The author was assisted by all the members of the Mesorah Publications staff, each in his or her own field of expertise. Nevertheless, special thanks are due two people: REB ELI KROEN who extended himself beyond the call of duty to assure an aesthetically pleasing book; and NICHIE FENDRICH who did a yeoman job typing both the original manuscript and the subsequent revisions. To the two of them we offer our sincere appreciation.

No words can adequately acknowledge my wife's contribution. While I was taken up with research, writing and revisions, she had to assume many of the roles that usually fall on the man of the house. That

in addition to her regular household functions, chessed projects and, as
Morah Nechie, responsibility for the building block aleph-beis education of a classful of budding *talmidei chachamim*.

יְשַׁלֵם ה׳ פְּעֳלָה וּתְהִי מַשְׂכָּרְתָּה שְׁלֵמָה מֵעִם ה׳ אֱלֹקֵי יִשְׂרָאֵל

Avie Gold   אברהם יצחק גאלד
8 Shevat 5751   ח׳ שבט ה׳תנש״א
Brooklyn   ברוקלין

An Overview/
Purim — The Essence of Reality

I. Diaspora Festivals

Special
Meanings

The author of *Chiddushei HaRim* once said that the 'Diaspora festivals,' Purim and Chanukah, have a special for meaning for Jews who still await the coming of *Mashiach*. Because they were instituted by the Sages to commemorate miracles and bring to mind aspects of spiritual potential that came to the fore in times of danger to our national existence, they have a particular relevance

When we have the festivals without the Temple, we lack the full extent of their spiritual gifts.

to us in times of dispersion and dependence on the nations of the world. True, the Torah's festivals have greater holiness, but when we have the festivals without the Temple, we lack the full extent of their spiritual gifts. The full degree of their holiness includes the Temple service and, in the case of the three pilgrimage festivals of Pesach, Shavuos, and Succos, the obligation to visit Jerusalem and the Temple, to bring personal offerings and experience the surge of sanctity that engulfed the Jew who ascended the Temple Mount and entered its precincts.

This condition is reminiscent of *Ramban's* teaching that only in *Eretz Yisrael* can one achieve the primary significance and effect of the performance of the Torah's commandments, because the Land is suffused with holiness. Compared to that, the performance of the commandments outside of the Land, though equally obligated by the Torah, is so inferior that it is as if they are being performed only so that they will not be strange to us when we return to our Land.

Thus, *Ramban* explains that the Patriarchs, who performed all the commandments even before the Torah was given, could make exceptions *outside* of *Eretz Yisrael*, if a particular act was necessary for their task of laying the foundation of the Chosen People. This is why when he was the 'guest' of Laban in Aram, Jacob could be married to two sisters, an act that the Torah would later forbid. In *Eretz Yisrael* he would not have done so, even before the giving of the Torah. Indeed, Rachel died just as the family entered the Land, so that in the Holy Land Jacob, was married only to Leah.

Perceptiveness

Rabbi Elchanan Wasserman explained how the Patriarchs could have kept the commandments — even Rabbinic ones — before they were given; how did they know what the Torah would mandate and what it would forbid? The answer lies in the superior nature of the Land and their perception of that holiness. So refined and attuned to God's will were their instincts that they could sense, as it were, what deeds would siphon holiness into themselves and their surroundings. In the Land, this atmosphere was so palpable to those who were attuned to it, that they knew what was beneficial and what was harmful. In other countries, the holiness is far weaker, so the sensitivity to it was not as keen.

How did the Patriarchs know what the Torah would mandate and what it would forbid?

This may be likened to dear friends who understand one another instinctively, with little or no conversation, whereas casual acquaintances may communicate endlessly, and still lack clarity. The Talmudic scholar looks at a passage and sees its nuances immediately; the uninitiated person, no matter how brilliant he is or how accomplished he is in other fields, looks at the same passage and sees a puzzle. A great musical conductor can hear one false note smothered in a hundred-piece orchestra; someone else may barely appreciate perfection. Great men have said that they were able to comprehend their Torah studies more deeply and quickly in *Eretz Yisrael* than they had been able to outside the Land; the holiness of the Land was having its effect on people with the proper spiritual antennae.

As people whose souls dominated their bodies and

who existed only to serve God, the Patriarchs and Matriarchs sensed the holiness that is everywhere in *Eretz Yisrael*, and they knew without being instructed what deeds would accentuate it and what deeds would interfere with it.

Preparation for Exile

The condition of Exile deadens our spiritual perceptions; that is the nature of being deprived of the Temple, of prophecy, of closeness to God. To survive as a Jew in exile requires a discipline and a quest that would not be needed in Messianic times. *R' Yaakov Kamenetzky* זצ"ל used to find this illustrated by the fourteen years that Jacob spent in intense Torah study in the academy of Shem and Eber. Why was this necessary? Was Eber a greater sage than Isaac? Did the sixty-seven year old Jacob — who had devoted himself since childhood to Torah study — need Eber to teach him?

Rav Kamenetzky explained that Jacob was entering a new era of his life. He was on the way into exile, leaving Isaac, Rebecca, and *Eretz Yisrael* for the home of his duplicitous uncle Laban in the idolatrous land of Aram. To survive in such new surroundings, he would need a new sort of preparation; he would need a 'Torah of exile.' To achieve a fuller appreciation of this seemingly esoteric idea, one need only look to the history of recent times. Amid the population displacements of our century, some people who made their mark in the Orthodox societies of Eastern Europe were able to adapt well to their new homes in Israel, America, and elsewhere, becoming leaders and shaping people here as they had done there. Others, however, fell by the wayside. They could be productive and successful in spiritually compatible surroundings, but could not cope with the antagonistic values of the West. Some of them remained whole on the personal level, although they were unable to make an impact on Western society; others succumbed to a greater or lesser degree. Jacob knew that he was embarked on a mission of nation-building in a hostile environment, one that was unimaginably different from the home of Isaac and Rebecca. To prepare himself, he went to a new academy — the academy of exile.

Purim and Chanukah are the holidays of a people

To survive in such new surroundings, Jacob would need a new sort of preparation; he would need a 'Torah of exile.'

that graduated with honors from the academy of exile. Purim demonstrates Israel's recognition that the hand of God guides events everywhere, though unobtrusively. Chanukah shows that there can be an exile of the spirit even in the Holy Land, and that Jews can overcome it by fiercely and unequivocally declaring their allegiance to the Torah, no matter what the obstacles. These are the concepts that have sustained us through the over nineteen centuries without a Temple, scattered throughout the globe.

Let us seek the lesson of Purim, therefore, one of the 'Galus festivals' that is closer to our needs and that is indispensable if we are to chart our way to the Messianic promises of holiness and homeland.

II. Who Is in Control?*

It is among the ways of repentance that at a time when distress comes, and they cry out and sound the shofar because of it, people should know that God afflicted them because of their evil deeds, as it is written, 'Your iniquities influenced these [travails] ...' (Jeremiah 5:25). It is this that will cause the distress to be removed from them.

But if they do not cry out and do not sound the shofar, but say, 'This happened to us because of normal causes, and this distress occurred coincidentally', this is the way of cruelty and causes them to adhere to their evil deeds, and this distress will cause the accumulation of further distresses. Thus it is written in the Torah [after a long list of the terrible consequences of national sinfulness], 'Yet you [still] behave casually with Me! Then I will behave toward you with a fury of casualness' (Leviticus 26:23-24). This means, 'When I bring upon you distress in order to induce you to repent, if you say that it is

---

* The remainder of the Overview is based on the thoughts of Rabbi Gedaliah Schor in *Ohr Gedalyahu.*

*casual [i.e., that the disaster was nothing
more than coincidental], I will multiply upon
you a fury because of that casualness of
yours' (Rambam, Hil. Taaniyos 1:2-3).*

Cruelty and Coincidence

Through lifetimes of experience, observation, and reading, we have developed ways of understanding happenings. The great majority of us have no doubt that the primary determinant of events is cause-and-effect: a tire blew out and a car crashed; a cigarette was not extinguished and a house burned down; a man smoked heavily and he suffered premature illness and death. Since every event seems to be the result of a prior cause, we have become confident that if we can regulate causes, we can control events. This arrogance has become reinforced with the triumphs of science and technology. So it is that supercomputers probe the economy, their programmers and researchers convinced that ways can be found to interpret data well enough to predict and control the vagaries of the business cycle. Social scientists analyze human behavior, certain that if they can amass and organize enough statistics, they can know what makes people behave as they do and develop ways to influence them otherwise. The world is sure that it can control almost anything, if it knows enough and develops the ways to act on its knowledge.

*Since every event
seems to be the
result of a prior
cause, we have
become confident
that if we can
regulate causes, we
can control events.*

The truth, however, is otherwise. As *Rambam* states in the passage cited above, there are two ways to view calamity. One may say that it happened 'because of normal causes, and this distress occurred coincidentally.' This is hardly a stupid way of understanding events; it is the method of academics and officials, of pundits and strategists, of genuinely brilliant and level-headed people. It is the way of all but a select, wiser few, because we *do* see the world through the lenses of cause-and-effect; that is the way of the material world.

*We do see the
world through the
lenses of cause-
and-effect; that is
the way of the
material world.
But it is not the
way of the Torah
and its world view.*

But it is not the way of the Torah and its world view.

Let us note carefully how *Rambam* describes that approach. He does not call it wrongheaded or foolish. He says, 'this is the way of **cruelty** and causes them to adhere to their evil deeds.' What is cruel about it?

Let us imagine someone suffering from the symptoms of advanced heart disease. The cure might involve diet, a sharp change of harmful habits, perhaps expensive and dangerous surgery. Unpleasant and difficult. Then along comes a savior. He provides medications to relieve the pain and servants to carry the work load. How kind? No, how cruel! Because by masking the symptoms he guarantees that the condition will worsen and end in pain and death. So, too, in dealing with danger and calamity, one who provides soothing nostrums and facile analyses is not foolish, but cruel.

When misfortune comes upon the nation, we are to see it as emanating from God. There must be a reason.

As *Rambam* shows from the Torah, God tells us that man *can* introduce a pattern of coincidence into the universe: *Yet you [still] behave casually with Me. Then I will behave toward you with a fury of casualness.* That passage comes from the Admonition that warns Israel of the most dire punishments if the nation should stray from God's path. Sprinkled through the long and frightening litany is the refrain that God's wrath is not to be treated as if it were a 'normal, casual' occurrence. When misfortune comes upon the nation, we are to see it as emanating from God. There must be a reason. The suffering is a message that we are to search our attitudes and behavior to find the reason for God's wrath. As the Talmud puts it, 'It is not the wild ass that kills, but the sin that kills' (*Berachos* 33a).

Nature

Can a logical person see the hand of God and deny its existence? Certainly. God wears a glove called nature. The Divine Name אֱלֹהִים, which signifies God's mastery over the universe, has the numerical value of 86, the same as that of הַטֶּבַע, *the laws of nature.* Nature truly exists; it is God's way of exercising His control over creation. Can one find natural causes for events? Yes; almost always there are good causes for every effect. When God dispatches angels to do his bidding, they take the form of fires, winning lottery tickets, business upturns, winds that push balls over goal posts, aggressors — the entire panoply of causes and effects that make headlines and history books. So we are always challenged to see the Hand inside the glove.

God wears a glove called nature.

We are always challenged to see the Hand inside the glove.

If we recognize God's control of events and let that awareness bring us closer to His will, then God acts accordingly. He treats us with Divine Providence and looks after us. This does not necessarily mean that everything will happen as we would wish it to. Not every investment will be profitable and not every personal relationship will be satisfying. But we will have faith that they are all directed by a Higher Intelligence and that everything happens for a purpose that is ultimately good, because God wills it so.

Mirror Image

God's behavior toward people mirrors their own actions.

The man or woman of genuine faith, the human being who elevates himself above the mirage of cause-and-effect, merits a Divine response. For God's behavior toward people mirrors their own actions. In the famous homiletical interpretation of the *Baal Shem Tov*, the Psalmist's declaration that צִלְּךָ 'ה, *HASHEM is your shade* (Psalms 121:5), can be rendered as *HASHEM is your shadow*. Just as a shadow mimics a person, so God's conduct toward someone varies according to the person himself. If he is kind to others, God will be generous with him; if he is tightfisted to others, God will not be gracious with him. If he believes that God is everywhere and in control of everything — as the Sages say, "Every blade of grass has an angel that commands it, 'Grow' " — then God will shower His personal attention upon him.

And, conversely, if someone is convinced that every occurrence has a natural reason that is its *only* true cause, then he is the person that God speaks of in that chilling refrain in the Admonition: our casualness toward God's message to us, a message that is delivered by motley agents, will beget a wrath of casualness on His part.

We refused to see Him when He paraded in front of us, seeking our attention! Instead we saw presidents and prejudice, madmen and missiles, and we engaged in the eternally comforting search afor scapegoats.

This means that if we find the reason for everything in natural causes, then God, our 'Shadow,' will treat us in kind. He will abandon us to chance, remove His Providence from us, and leave us to the mercies of our enemies and the vagaries of uncontrolled nature. Tragedy after tragedy will occur, and we will demand, 'Where was God?' But we refused to see Him when He paraded in front of us, seeking our attention! Instead we saw presidents and prejudice, madmen and missiles, and we engaged in the eternally comforting search for scapegoats. We treated His sovereignty as if it were not

Only if we acknowledge God in every happening does Divine Providence manifest itself in everything, and guide the most righteous people step by step. real, as if it were the abstract stuff of editorial judgments and doctoral theses, so He left us to our own devices and the mercies of our enemies. Only if we acknowledge God in every happening does Divine Providence manifest itself in everything, and guide the most righteous people step by step (see *Ramban* and *Rabbeinu Bachya* to *Genesis* 18:19).

The Sages teach that one who denies the possibility of תְּחִיַּת הַמֵּתִים, *the Resuscitation of the Dead*, will not live when God brings the dead back to life (*Sanhedrin* 90b). On the surface this would seem to be a case of a measure-for-measure punishment: one who denies God's ability to give life will be denied life. R' Tzaddok HaKohen understands it differently. Through his prior sins, this offender had previously forfeited his privilege of coming to life again at the End of Days. It is not surprising, therefore, that he refuses to believe in the possibility of it happening. Those who lack faith in God cannot see Him controlling events. Those whose spirit has died cannot believe in the potential of life after the physical part of their existence — the only part they acknowledge — is no longer alive. It is normal for people to deny what they cannot perceive. God need not punish them; they have punished themselves.

Narrow Line

This basic principle of Judaism should not be misunderstood, however. While it would seem to postulate that one should live by faith alone and not see to his livelihood or health, such a course is erroneous. The Talmud teaches that R' Shimon bar Yochai was angry with those who tended to their fields and livelihoods. 'What will become of Torah study?' he demanded angrily. But a Heavenly voice charged that such an attitude would result in a withering of the world. R' Yishmael counseled differently. People must live as human beings, working their fields and tending their affairs in a natural manner and, despite this, they must still make God and Torah the central factors in their lives. The Talmud concludes the discussion saying, 'Many followed R' Yishmael and succeeded; many followed R' Shimon and did not succeed' (*Berachos* 35b).

People must live as human beings, working their fields and tending their affairs in a natural manner and, despite this, they must still make God and Torah the central factors in their lives.

Even though a man's years and days are decided beforehand by God, one should be engaged in obtaining food, clothing, and shelter according to his needs. He should not leave it to God, saying, 'If God wishes me to live, He will sustain me without food, so I will not trouble myself to find food.' Similarly, one should not put himself in danger and rely on his trust in God [to insure that he will be unhurt] . . . Thus [when God sent the prophet Samuel to anoint David as king, an act that could be construed as a rebellion against King Saul and punishable by the death penalty], Samuel protested, *'How can I go? Saul will hear and will kill me!'* (*I Samuel* 16:2). This was not a failure of trust on [Samuel's] part. To the contrary, God's reply [that Samuel take a calf with him and say that he had gone to bring it as an offering to God] showed that Samuel's concern was justified and proper (*Chovas HaLevavos, Shaar HaBitachon* 4).

Chovas HaLevavos explains at length the narrow line between trust and foolhardiness. Man is required to work and strive for his livelihood and to take measures to preserve his health and seek medical assistance if it is in danger. But he must also recognize that after all his exertions, it is God Who decides who will live and who will die, who will succeed and who will fail, who will be wealthy and who will be poor. We must do our part because that, too, is part of the natural law that God's wisdom imposed on His Creation. But just as nature should not blind us to the presence and power of God Who created nature, so our exertions to help ourselves should not make us forget that God is in the wings, and only He determines whether or not our efforts will succeed. To do otherwise is to imitate the wisdom of the man who discovered that it is the spoon, not the sugar that sweetens the tea, because the tea did not become sweet until after someone stirred it.

Our exertions to help ourselves should not make us forget that God is in the wings, and only He determines whether or not our efforts will succeed.

III. Creation of Falsehood

וַיִּקְרְאוּ שְׁמוֹ עֵשָׂו, הָא שָׁוְא שֶׁבָּרָאתִי בְּעוֹלָמִי.

They called his name Esau (Genesis 25:25).
[God said]this represents the emptiness [שָׁוְא]
that I have created in My world (Bereishis
Rabbah 63:12).

אֵת כָּל אֲשֶׁר קָרָהוּ בֶּן בְּנוֹ שֶׁל אֲשֶׁר קָרְךָ

[In relating how Haman reported to his wife
and friends the events of the day, the Book of
Esther states that he told them] everything
that had happened [קָרָהוּ] to him (Esther
6:13). Haman was the grandson of [Amalek,
of whom the Torah says,] אֲשֶׁר קָרְךָ, who
happened against you (Midrash).

Happen-
stance

E sau is a creation of falsehood, for God willed that
there be in the world an aspect of Creation that is
without true content, that masquerades as powerful and
laden with meaning, but that is a mirage, without inner
truth. Esau represents the false, empty idea that
everything is the product of coincidence, that there is no
hand of God. And if there is no Divine intervention in
human affairs, then man is free to do as he pleases.
Amalek, Esau's offspring and standard bearer, carried on
this mission throughout history, for Amalek's enmity to
Israel is a battle against what Israel represents in Creation.
Israel proclaims the Oneness of God; Amalek proclaims
that God is nowhere in nature.

*Amalek's enmity to
Israel is a battle
against what Israel
represents in
Creation. Israel
proclaims the
Oneness of God;
Amalek proclaims
that God is nowhere
in nature.*

In describing Amalek's sneak attack on Israel after the
Exodus, the Torah says, אֲשֶׁר קָרְךָ בַּדֶּרֶךְ, who happened
against you on the way (Deuteronomy 25:18). The word
קָרְךָ is from the same root as מִקְרֶה, happenstance, or
coincidence, for that is what Amalek signified: the
concept that nothing is ordained by God, that everything
is left to nature and chance. Haman the Amalekite
continued this family tradition. He lived by the law of
chance, the proposition that the external appearance is all
there is; there is no content beyond what the eye can see
and instruments can measure.

*Haman the
Amalekite continued
this family tradition.*

Therefore the Torah says of Amalek:

רֵאשִׁית גּוֹיִם עֲמָלֵק וְאַחֲרִיתוֹ עֲדֵי אֹבֵד

Amalek is the first among nations, but its fate is to be destroyed (Numbers 24:20).

Because people are easily deceived by the illusion of content and the promise that man controls his own destiny, Amalek is first and foremost among nations, but Amalek is doomed to ultimate destruction, because no matter how long it may bloom, falsehood cannot prevail forever. Amalek will crumble and be erased from human memory, because it is *the emptiness that [God] created in [His] world.* The time will come when Amalek's alluring exterior will be stripped away, and without his exterior, nothing is left.

The time will come when Amalek's alluring exterior will be stripped away, and without his exterior, nothing is left.

As *Maharal* expressed it, God promises that He will erase Amalek *from* **beneath** *the heaven (Exodus 17:14);* the nation of falsehood never had an existence *above* the heavens — the place of truth. It existed only in places that did not perceive truth, and it is only from there — beneath the heaven — that it need be exterminated.

Power of Error

Nevertheless, Amalek has great power during the centuries when he holds sway. He can create the illusion that his gospel of happenstance has validity, for God decreed that people have the possibility of error just as they have the potential for truth. Man's mission on earth is to differentiate, to choose what is right and discard what is false. By definition, freedom of choice implies freedom to err, and that is possible only if falsehood can be tempting. That is Amalek's assignment.

The Midrash comments that there is none but God even 'in the vacuum of the world' (*Devarim Rabbah* 2:19). What is this vacuum of which the Midrash speaks? R' Gershon Henoch of Radzin explained that there is an area where it seems as if God is not involved, where man can do as he pleases. This is the sphere of Amalek and his followers, where the omnipotence of God is hidden, so that man can delude himself that he has free sway without fear of God. No, the Midrash declares, even Amalek's sphere of influence is not truly his. Behind the illusion there is only God.

Even Amalek's sphere of influence is not truly his. Behind the illusion there is only God.

IV. Where Is He?

... הֲיֵשׁ ה' בְּקִרְבֵּנוּ אִם אָיִן? וַיָּבֹא עֲמָלֵק וַיִּלָּחֶם עִם
יִשְׂרָאֵל בִּרְפִידִם

... is HASHEM in our midst or not? Then
Amalek came and waged war against Israel
in Rephidim (Exodus 17:7-8).

The chapter [of Amalek's attack] is juxta-
posed to a question [in which Israel wondered whether God was truly present among
them. This juxtaposition is meant] to teach
[that God said:] "I am always among you,
prepared for all your needs — yet you say, 'Is
HASHEM in our midst or not?!' By your lives,
the dog will come and bite you and you will
cry out to Me. Then you will know where I
am!"

What is this like? A man lifted his child
onto his shoulders and set out on the road.
The child saw an object and said, 'Father, get
it for me,' and his father gave it to him. This
happened a second time and a third time.
They met a man and the child said to him,
'Have you seen my father?' The father said,
'Don't you know where I am?' He cast him
down, and a dog came and bit him (Rashi
from Mechilta).

Amalek's attack followed a series of Israel's
grievances against God that seem to have become
progressively more serious. Yet they are apparently
incomprehensible. There was a year in Egypt during
which Moses brought plague after plague upon the
Egyptians. God protected the Jews from the stones and
arrows of the pursuing Egyptians. He split the sea for
the Jews and gave them the wealth of Egypt. He gave
them manna and made bitter water drinkable. And
after all that, they had the temerity to demand, 'Is
HASHEM in our midst or not?' Incredible, isn't it? Very
apt is the parable cited by Rashi, of a father who is
outraged by his child's lack of awareness of who has
been protecting him and giving him gift after gift.

*... And after all
that, they had the
temerity to
demand, 'Is
HASHEM in our
midst or not?'
Incredible, isn't it?*

In the light of the above, however, it is quite understandable. Of course the Jews knew that God was Master of the heavens and that it was He Who tore up the law of nature when they needed miracles. The plagues and the Splitting of the Sea were miracles of an unprecedented magnitude that, in aggregate, have not been duplicated ever since. That God had wrought them was never in doubt. But they asked whether He is *in their midst*, as well — in everyday life, in the ordinary things that seem to be so natural that we take them for granted. Only God could split the sea, but was it also God who gave water from wells, made the sun come up every morning, and gave strength to a farmer's arms?

They asked whether He is in their midst, as well — in everyday life, in the ordinary things that seem to be so natural that we take them for granted.

In other words, after 210 years in Egypt, they had fallen into the trap of Amalek's empty idea that there is a vacuum in the world, a vacuum uninhabited by God. The result was that they were attacked by Amalek.

That may well have been a forerunner of the Jewish condition throughout the millennia: We find comfortable beliefs or friendly nations and put our faith in them. Time goes by and we learn to our chagrin and pain that the True Inhabitant of the vacuum will not permit us to escape our destiny. The beliefs turn out to be charades and the friends turn out to be enemies. How many times have Jews found spurious salvations, only to be disabused, often drowned in seas of blood?

How many times have Jews found spurious salvations, only to be disabused, often drowned in seas of blood?

Moses' Hands

Our true hope is to find our heavenly roots. In that first war against Amalek in the Wilderness, Moses appointed Joshua to lead the battle, while he, Moses, held the staff of God and, together with Aaron and Hur, climbed up a hill, where he prayed for God's help. The Torah relates that when Moses raised his arms, Israel was victorious, and whenever he lowered his arms, Amalek was victorious (see *Exodus* 17:8-13).

The Mishnah (*Rosh Hashanah* 29b) states, 'Did the hands of Moses make war or lose the war? Rather the verse tells you that as long as Israel looked upward and dedicated their hearts to their Father in heaven, they were strong, and if not, they would fall.

As long as Israel looked upward and dedicated their hearts to their Father in heaven, they were strong, and if not, they would fall.

At first glance the Mishnah's question seems a bit strange. Moses had been God's emissary to perform a multitude of miracles in Egypt and afterwards; is it truly so surprising that his intervention could have turned the tide of war?

The point, however, was not to defeat Amalek through miracles; God could have done that very easily, just as he obliterated the Egyptians. But Amalek did not arise as a military threat. Amalek came because Israel doubted that God was with them in every activity; the dog came because the child wondered where his father was. The only way Israel could survive and eliminate the danger of Amalek — a military danger that existed only because of the spiritual failure of the Jews — was to eliminate the spiritual failure that had enabled Amalek to strike.

Amalek did not arise as a military threat. Amalek came because Israel doubted that God was with them in every activity.

Moses raised his hands not as a tactic in war but as a signpost of the spirit. His upraised arms were a signal. When the people heeded their unspoken message and lifted their spirits heavenward, they overcame Amalek — not merely the bearer of physical swords and arrows, but the enemy who insisted that everything was happenstance.

V. The Weapon of Fasting

The Source

On the verse saying that Moses, Aaron, and Hur were on the hilltop (*Exodus* 17:10), *Rashi* cites the *Mechilta* that we derive from this incident that three people must lead the congregation in the special prayers of a fast day [that had been enacted to beg for Divine mercy in a time of attack or calamity] — and it is certain that the Jews fasted that day, as Jews always do in time of mortal danger.

This is the first time in the Torah where we find an allusion to a fast. *R' Tzadddok HaKohen* frequently cites the principle that the first time something is mentioned in the Torah must be regarded as its source, and that this placement sheds light on the purpose and application of the particular law or fact. That the Torah alludes to a fast in connection with the war against Amalek indicates that fasting is especially relevant to Amalek and the struggle against it. Moreover, it implies

That the Torah alludes to a fast in connection with the war against Amalek indicates that fasting is especially relevant to Amalek and the struggle against it.

that fasting is a major weapon against Amalek.

The story of Purim is closely related to that first battle against Amalek. Haman was an Amalekite and, as the Sages teach, he was carrying out the legacy of his forebears in his plot to wipe out the Jewish people. Haman, a descendant of the Amalekite king Agag, was born only because King Saul, in a much earlier battle against Amalek, was overcome by mistaken pity and could not bring himself to kill Agag. [See Overview to ArtScroll *Megillas Esther*.] In line with R' Tzaddok's principles, the tactics employed by Moses and Joshua should guide us in the eternal battle against Amalek.

In the struggle of Mordechai and Esther against Haman, too, a fast played an important role. In the struggle of Mordechai and Esther against Haman, too, a fast played an important role. Esther consented to risk an uninvited visit to King Ahasuerus only if Mordechai would gather all the Jews of Shushan for a three-day fast; and thereafter the miracle happened in quick succession.

As we see from the *Rambam* cited above, the purpose of a fast is to counteract the false notion — the *cruel* one as *Rambam* characterizes it — that calamity has natural causes, that there is no point in praying or fasting because God has no hand in the affairs of the 'real' world. In the jargon of today, one might say that *Rambam* refers to the claim that religion has the competence to decide the kosher status of pots and cutlery, but should not meddle in affairs of state. It is clear from *Rambam* that the fast has the function of withdrawing man from dependence and reliance on his body and turning his attention and devotion to God. That is why the source of fasting is found in a war against Amalek, and the centrality of fasting is stressed again in the book that gave us the first of our 'Galus festivals.'

Our primary weapon against Amalek and its ideology is recognition of God's omniscience. Our primary weapon against Amalek and its ideology is recognition of God's omniscience. Onc we recognize that He is everywhere and that His power and presence fill every vacuum, we have defeated our inner Amalek, the source of the outer Amalek's strength. Having done that, the battle is more than half won; Amalek is potent only as long as the success of its deception enables it to lead. When its ideas are exposed as fraudulent, it is on the way to its final downfall and disappearance. Let Jews realize that *they*, not Amalek, are the cause of Jewish woe, and salvation is on the way. To accomplish this, the Jews fasted in Moses' day, in Esther's day, and in every period of our history. When enough of us learn this lesson and observe it with complete sincerity, Amalek will begin to disappear.

Let Jews realize that they, not Amalek, are the cause of Jewish woe, and salvation is on the way.

An Integral Part

This concept has a halachic application, as well. *Ran* quotes *Raavad* who wonders how the Sages instituted the Fast of Esther on the day before Purim when there is a general rule that it is forbidden to fast either the day before or the day after a halachically recognized day of joy, such as Purim? *Raavad* responds that this fast is unique for two reasons: The fast is a commemoration of the miracle that took place on it; and, secondly, just as the Jews accepted upon themselves the holiday of Purim, so too they accepted upon themselves the fast and prayer, as reported in the Book of Esther.

According to the above, *Raavad's* reasoning is illuminated. The fast is an integral part of the miracle, because the weapon against Haman's machinations was the realization engendered by the fast: that God is present in all circumstances. [See the Overview to *The Megillah* for a lengthy discussion of this concept.] The fast could not be removed from Purim, because without the fast and the faith it represented there would have been no Purim.

The fast could not be removed from Purim, because without the fast and the faith it represented there would have been no Purim.

The lesson of Amalek is still current. We still seek definition of our destiny in the wisdom of professors and pundits. We still look for allies in chanceries and legislatures. This tendency is the true *Galus* mentality. Let us combat it with the lesson of the first *Galus* festival. Amalek is a danger because it convinces us of its message, a message that is nothing more than air filling an impressive balloon. Moses showed the way, and Mordechai and Esther followed it. Let us do the same, and in that merit let us pray that a *Galus* festival will lead us out of *Galus* forever, with the coming of *Mashiach*, speedily, in our time.

Rabbi Nosson Scherman

Shevat, 5751 / February 1991

❧ Background and Insights

The Four Torah Portions
Taanis Esther
The Seven Mitzvos of Purim
Hallel — Omitted on Purim
Thoughts on the Megillah
Until He No Longer Knows
Family and Local Purims
Masquerading
Purim in Gematria

✧ Background and Insights

אַרְבַּע פָּרְשִׁיוֹת / The Four Torah Portions

✧ Four Sabbaths just prior to and during the month of Adar (the Second Adar in a leap year) have been assigned special Torah portions to be read as *maftir*, with related passages from the Prophets to replace the regular *haftarah*. The portions are: *Shekalim, Zachor, Parah* and *HaChodesh*.

Shekalim

✧ פָּרָשַׁת שְׁקָלִים, *Parashas Shekalim (Exodus* 30:11-16), deals with the half-shekel per capita tax that paid for the purchase of communal offerings. Since the annual collection of this tax commenced on the first of Adar, this reading on the Sabbath preceding Rosh Chodesh Adar (or Rosh Chodesh itself, when it falls on the Sabbath) served during the Temple era as an announcement of that collection and as a reminder to pay the tax. Nowadays, the reading serves as a remembrance of the tax. Additionally, when the *Beis HaMikdash* will be rebuilt in Messianic times, the half-shekel will once again serve its original purpose. Thus, the reading of *Parashas Shekalim* each year protects us against ignorance of the obligation at that time.

Another reason for this reading is based on a Talmudic teaching: God knew that Haman would offer *shekalim* for the right to destroy Israel. Therefore, He anticipated his *shekalim* with those of Israel [i.e., He ordained that the Jews should give *shekalim* for a holy purpose before Haman gave *shekalim* for a profane purpose], as the Mishnah (3:9) says, 'On the first of Adar the announcement is made that the *shekalim* must be given' [God thus negated Haman's plan.] (*Megillah* 13b). And thus, *Parashas Shekalim* is read on the Sabbath before Rosh Chodesh Adar (or Rosh Chodesh itself, when it falls on the Sabbath).

☐ The *haftarah* reading for *Parashas Shekalim* is from *II Kings* 12:1-17. That chapter discusses the *shekalim* collected by Jehoyada the *Kohen Gadol* during the reign of Jehoash, king of Judah.

☐ When Rosh Chodesh Adar coincides with the Sabbath, three Torah Scrolls are taken out: one for the regular weekly reading; a second for the Rosh Chodesh portion (*Numbers* 28:9-15); and a third for *Parashas Shekalim.* In this case, the passage of Rosh Chodesh is read before *Parashas Shekalim,* because of the rule תָּדִיר וְשֶׁאֵינוֹ תָּדִיר תָּדִיר קוֹדֶם, *the more frequent mitzvah takes precedence over the less frequent.* But since only one *haftarah* can be read and the *haftarah* must always be related to the last Torah passage read, the frequency rule is waived and the *haftarah* of *Parashas Shekalim* is read.

The same rule applies when *Parashas HaChodesh* is read on Rosh Chodesh Nissan (see below).

Zachor

◄§ פָּרָשַׁת זָכוֹר, *Parashas Zachor* (*Deuteronomy* 25:17-19), sets forth the commandment to exterminate Amalek. Since Haman was descended from Amalek, reading this portion on the Sabbath immediately preceding Purim juxtaposes the commandment to eradicate Amalek with its fulfillment, namely, the wiping out of Haman. The name זָכוֹר, literally, *Remember,* is taken from the first word of the portion.

☐ The *haftarah* reading for *Parashas Zachor* is from *I Samuel* 15:2-34. That chapter describes King Saul's battle against Amalek and his misjudgment in allowing Agag, king of Amalek, to remain alive for one night. During that night Agag cohabited, and the child resulting from that union became the forebear of Haman.

☐ Most authorities reckon the *Parashas Zachor* reading as much more than a mere reminder. The Torah states זָכוֹר, *remember,* and follows it with אַל תִּשְׁכַּח, *do not forget* (v. 19), a seeming redundancy. The Talmud explains that 'forgetting' is a function of the heart, while 'remembering' implies an oral pronouncement. Thus, the reading of *Parashas Zachor* is a Scriptural commandment. Therefore, residents of a village who do not have a local *minyan* must come to a large town for this Sabbath, in order to hear the reading (*Shulchan Aruch, Orach Chaim* 685:7).

Parah

◄§ פָּרָשַׁת פָּרָה, *Parashas Parah* (*Numbers* 19:1-22), contains the laws of the פָּרָה אֲדֻמָּה, *Red Cow,* whose ashes were used in the purification rites of those who became טָמֵא, *contaminated,* by contact with a corpse. The reading of this portion served to remind anyone who had contracted such *tumah*-contamination to undergo the seven-day purification process before the approaching Pesach.

☐ The *haftarah* reading for *Parashas Parah* is from *Ezekiel* 36:16-35. That passage includes that verse: *I shall sprinkle pure water upon you, that you be cleansed: from all your contamination and from all your filth I will cleanse you* (v. 25).

☐ According to some authorities, this reading, like *Parashas Zachor*, is a Torah obligation. Therefore, villagers should go to the city to hear the reading.

HaChodesh

⋖§ פָּרָשַׁת הַחֹדֶשׁ, *Parashas HaChodesh* (*Exodus* 12:1-20), begins with the *mitzvah* of counting the months of the year from Nissan — הַחֹדֶשׁ הַזֶּה, *This month shall be unto you the head of the months . . .* (v. 2) — hence the name *Parashas HaChodesh*. Thus the appropriate time for this reading is the Sabbath before Rosh Chodesh Nissan (or Rosh Chodesh itself when it coincides with the Sabbath). The remainder of the passage enumerates the laws and particulars of the *pesach* offering.

☐ The *haftarah* reading for *Parashas HaChodesh* is from *Ezekiel* 45:16-46:18. That passage discusses the *pesach* offering and Pesach festival of the future.

☐ The sequence of the Four Portions presents a historical problem: Since *Parashas HaChodesh* speaks of the first day of Nissan while the first Red Cow was burnt on the second of Nissan, shouldn't *Parashas HaChodesh* precede *Parashas Parah*? The Talmud Yerushalmi explains that the reading of *Parah* was advanced to underscore the paramount importance of purity. Thus, people who hear the reading will be reminded to cleanse themselves before Pesach.

Taanis Esther

> *Then Esther spoke to reply to Mordechai, 'Go, assemble all the Jews who may be found in Shushan and fast for me; do not eat and do not drink for a three-day period, night and day. I and my maids will also fast thus . . .'* (*Esther* 4:15-16).

⋖§ Why were the Jews of that era deserving of extermination? Because they derived pleasure from Ahasuerus' feast (*Megillah* 12a). The Talmud does not say that they were guilty of eating or drinking, but 'because נֶהֱנוּ, they *derived pleasure*.' Eating and drinking could possibly have been justified with the claim that they were subject to royal intimidation and therefore were afraid to abstain. Their unjustifiable sin was that they *enjoyed* themselves when they took part in the festivities (*Pirchei Levanon*).

☐ Usually the most important aspects of a fast day are the repentance, prayer and charity that accompany the fast. For, in the words of the Rosh Hashanah-Yom Kippur prayer *Unesaneh Tokef*, 'וּתְשׁוּבָה וּתְפִלָּה וּצְדָקָה מַעֲבִירִין אֶת רֹעַ הַגְּזֵרָה', *Repentance, prayer and charity, remove the evil of the decree!'* Yet here the verse stresses the fast!? Since their abstinence at this time would serve as atonement for indulging themselves and enjoying Ahasuerus' banquet, the fast was the essence of their repentance (*Me'am Lo'ez*).

☐ Ahasuerus held his banquet during the third year of his reign (see *Esther* 1:3) and Haman promulgated the decree to annihilate the Jews in Ahasuerus' twelfth year (ibid. 3:7). Nevertheless, Esther — as well as the Talmudic Sages who interpreted her actions — realized the connection between these two events. Esther understood this cause and effect relationship because she was a prophetess (see *Megillah* 14a). But what insight led the Sages to draw this same conclusion? Perhaps the answer lies in the different phraseology used to describe the Jews of Shushan. In chapter nine (vs. 13, 15, 18) the verse calls them, הַיְּהוּדִים אֲשֶׁר בְּשׁוּשָׁן *the Jews that are in Shushan*, while in reference to both the feast and the fast (1:5 and 4:16) the verse states, הַנִּמְצָאִים בְּשׁוּשָׁן, *who may be found in Shushan*. The similarity of expression in these seemingly disparate events may have inspired the Sages to assign one as the cause of the other (*Matzreif Dahava*).

☐ Esther's three-day fast was unprecedented and unequalled in its duration and intensity. Moreover, under ordinary circumstances this fast would be contrary to *halachah,* in more than one way:
   (a) A series of fast days [decreed because of a national emergency] should not be decreed for consecutive days, because a majority of the people cannot endure such a thing. Rather [the fasts should be decreed] for Monday, the following Thursday and the following Monday, and so on in this manner, Monday, Thursday, Monday until they are pitied (*Maimonides, Hilchos Taaniyos* 1:5). Yet Esther called for a three-day fast, night and day.
   (b) We do not promulgate public fasts on Sabbaths or Festivals (ibid. 1:6). Yet Esther's three-day fast included the first two days of

Pesach. [This is evident from the date of Haman's evil decree, the thirteenth of Nissan (*Esther* 3:12). On that day Mordechai donned sackcloth and asked Esther to intercede with the king. Thus, the three-day fast took place on the fourteenth of Nissan (*erev* Pesach), the fifteenth (first day Pesach) and the sixteenth (second day Pesach — see *Rashi* to *Megillah* 15a).] The Midrash relates that Mordechai protested to Esther regarding fasting on Pesach, but she replied, if there are no Jews, why should there be a Pesach?

(c) Fasting on the first night of Pesach transgresses two positive mitzvos — one ordained by the Torah, the second by the Rabbis; as Maimonides states: There is a Scripturally ordained positive *mitzvah* to eat *matzah* on the fifteenth night of Nissan . . . [This applies] everywhere in every era. This eating is not contingent upon the *pesach* offering, but is an independent *mitzvah* . . . (*Rambam, Hil. Chametz Umatzah* 6:1). The eating of *marror* is not an independent Scripturally ordained *mitzvah*, but is dependent upon the eating of the *pesach* offering, i.e., there is a positive *mitzvah* to eat the meat of the *pesach* with *matzah* and *marror*. But the Rabbis ordained the eating of *marror* by itself on this night, even when there is no *pesach* offering (ibid. 7:12). Ester's decree to fast on *seder* night prevented the observance of these two *mitzvos*, as well as the four cups of wine and the *afikoman*.

Since Esther's fast involved so many transgressions and abandonments of *mitzvos*, by what right did she request it and Mordechai promulgate it? Perhaps the answer lies in Rava's interpretation of the verse, עֵת לַעֲשׂוֹת לַה' הֵפֵרוּ תּוֹרָתֶךָ, *It is a time to act for* HASHEM, *they have voided Your Torah* (Psalms 119:126). Rava said that this verse is to be expounded from beginning to end [i.e., the first clause is a consequence of the second] and from end to beginning [i.e., the second clause is a consequence of the first]. From beginning to end it is expounded: *It is time for* HASHEM *to act* [and exact vengeance from the wicked, because] *they have voided Your Torah*. From end to beginning it is expounded: *They* [the righteous] *have voided Your Torah*, [because] *it is a time* [for them] *to act for* HASHEM'S [sake] (*Berachos* 63a, *Rashi*).

Thus, God fulfilled the first interpretation of this verse; since they voided His Torah be participating in Ahasuerus' feast, it was time for Him to act in strict judgment by allowing Haman to order their extermination. Esther, in turn, fulfilled the latter interpretation; she voided parts of the Torah, because in that way she would save God's people from destruction (*Matzreif Dahava*).

Whence The Taanis Esther Of Today?

◦§ On the thirteenth of Adar, the very day Haman sought to annihilate every Jew — man, woman and child — events were turned about, and the Jews gained the upper hand over their enemies (*Esther* 9:1). But victory was not given them on the proverbial silver platter. They had to organize and defend themselves; to destroy, slay and exterminate every armed force of every people and province that threatened them (ibid. 8:11). In short, they had to wage war.

But in times of war the Jewish nation was wont to fast, to pray, to evoke the Divine compassion and mercy that would enable them to defeat their foe. Thus, the Sages teach that when the Jews battled against Amalek (*Exodus* 17:8-16), Moses declared a fast day. Similarly, in the time of Mordechai and Esther, the people certainly fasted when they went into battle. And in memory of that fast Israel customarily fasts on this day.

Although all of Israel participated in the fast, it has been named in honor of Esther as a reminder that God sees and hears each individual in his straits, if he fasts and repents wholeheartedly, as they did in those days (based on *Mishnah Berurah* 686:2).

An Alternative Interpretation

◦§ Fast days may be classified in two groupings, based upon both the original reasons for their respective enactment and their present-day purpose and intent.

One type of fast commemorates a national tragedy brought about by public waywardness. Examples of such fasts are the four that recall the Destruction of the *Beis HaMikdash* (both First and Second) — the Seventeenth of Tammuz, the Ninth of Av, the Third of Tishrei (*Tzom Gedaliah*) and the Tenth of Teves. The national purpose of these fasts today is rectification of, and atonement for, the sins that brought about the Destruction. Each individual should fast with the intention that the fast will humble his corporeality — allowing for the enhancement of his holy image. Since the *Beis HaMikdash* has not been restored, we may assume that the sins that brought about its Destruction have not been fully expiated.

Other fasts were established to heighten man's spirituality by purifying his corporeality and affording it some measure of spirituality. This is the purpose of refraining from eating matzah on the day before Pesach: that the matzah eaten at the Seder in fulfillment of the mitzvah should be eaten with an appetite that adds spirituality to the bodily function of eating. Similarly, the Midrash (*Pirkei DeRabbi Eliezer*) teaches that the nation fasted three days in preparation for the Giving of the Torah at Mount Sinai. That fast was not to atone for any particular sin or class of sins. Rather, it was to purify and sanctify their material bodies, to elevate them to a more rarefied plane where they would become receptacles for the Torah's holiness.

The Fast of Esther precedes Purim, about which the Megillah (9:27) states: קִיְּמוּ וְקִבְּלוּ הַיְּהוּדִים עֲלֵיהֶם. *The Jews confirmed and accepted upon themselves*. The Talmud explains that they confirmed at that time what they had already undertaken long since, namely, their acceptance of the Torah. At Sinai, God had overturned the mountain, suspended it above them like a barrel and said, "If you accept the Torah, it is well; but if not, there shall be your grave." But this provided them with an excuse for non-observance: namely, since the Torah was imposed by threat of death, its acceptance was not binding. Nevertheless, this excuse was negated when, at Purim time, the Jews confirmed and accepted the Torah upon themselves anew, this time of their own free will (*Shabbos* 88a). This being the case, the day of Purim — just like the day of Shavuos when the Torah was given at Sinai — became an auspicious day throughout the generations for each Jew to reaffirm his acceptance of the Torah. As such, Purim is preceded by a fast day, when the material body is elevated to a sublime plane and readied to receive the Torah (based on *Tur Barekes* 686:1).

The Seven Mitzvos of Purim

⥄ The festival of Purim is one of the seven mitzvos מִדִּבְרֵי סוֹפְרִים, *ordained by the Rabbis*. Although the reading of *Megillas Esther* is the first obligation that comes to mind when Purim is mentioned, and both *Rambam* (Maimonides) and the *Shulchan Aruch* classify all the laws and customs of Purim under the heading *Hilchos Megillah*, closer examination will reveal that the laws of Purim comprise seven distinct mitzvos. Six of these are positive mitzvos; one is a negative requirement.

In order of their appearance during Purim, the six positive mitzvos are: (1) עַל הַנִּסִּים, adding the paragraph beginning *Al HaNissim* to the day's *Shemoneh Esrei* prayers and to *Bircas HaMazon* (Grace after Meals); (2) קְרִיאַת הַמְּגִלָּה, *reading the Megillah*, the Scroll of Esther, at night and again in the morning; (3) קְרִיאַת הַתּוֹרָה, *reading the Torah* passage regarding Amalek's attack on Israel soon after the nation was redeemed from Egypt (*Exodus* 17:8-16); (4) מִשְׁלוֹחַ מָנוֹת אִישׁ לְרֵעֵהוּ, *sending food portions to friends*; (5) מַתָּנוֹת לָאֶבְיוֹנִים, *giving gifts to the poor;* and (6) סְעוּדָה, *a festive meal.*

The negative *mitzvah* is the prohibition against delivering eulogies and fasting.

Al HaNissim

◆§ On those special days that include a *mussaf*-offering (e.g., the three Pilgrimage Festivals), the prayers added to the *Shemoneh Esrei* מֵעֵין הַמְאוֹרָע, *to reflect the event of the day,* are recited either during the central blessing dedicated to the holiness of the day (on *Yom Tov*) or during the blessing רְצֵה, *Be Favorable*, dedicated to the Temple service (on *Chol HaMoed*). However, when a *mussaf*-offering is not brought (e.g., Chanukah and Purim), the events of the day are mentioned during *Modim*, the thanksgiving blessing (*Tosefta Berachos* 3:14).

☐ (וְ)עַל הַנִּסִּים, (*And*) *for the Miracles,* is a declaration of thankfulness for the miracles, both obvious and hidden, by which God saved the Jews from physical annihilation on Purim and spiritual destruction on Chanukah. Therefore, it is inserted into מוֹדִים, *Modim*, the blessing of *Shemoneh Esrei* devoted to expressions of gratitude and into נוֹדֶה, *Nodeh*, the blessing of *Bircas HaMazon* that is dedicated to giving thanks for the Land of Israel, the Exodus, the covenant of circumcision, the Torah, life, grace, kindness and food.

The first paragraph of *Al HaNissim* is a roster of the types of favor God showered upon the nation: miracles, redemption, mighty deeds, salvation, wonders, consolations and victories in battle. Thus it is recited on both Chanukah and Purim.

The second paragraph, however, specifies the particular events of each festival, and so appears in two versions: one beginning בִּימֵי מָרְדְּכַי וְאֶסְתֵּר, *In the days of Mordechai and Esther,* to be recited on Purim; the other, בִּימֵי מַתִּתְיָהוּ, *In the days of Mattisyahu,* for Chanukah.

Hallel — Omitted on Purim

◆§ The prophets ordained that the six psalms of *Hallel* [113-118] be recited on each Festival, and to commemorate times of national deliverance from peril. Moreover, before David redacted and incorporated these psalms into the Book of Psalms, *Hallel* was already known to the nation: Moses and Israel had recited it after being saved from the Egyptians at the sea; Joshua after defeating the Kings of Canaan; and Deborah and Barak after defeating Sisera. Later, Hezekiah recited it after defeating Sennacherib; Chananiah, Mishael and Azariah, after being saved from the wicked Nebuchadnezzar; and Mordechai and Esther, after the defeat of the wicked Haman (*Pesachim* 117a).

These psalms were singled out as the unit of praise because they contain five fundamental themes of Jewish faith: the Exodus, the Splitting of the Sea, the Giving of the Torah at Sinai, the future Resuscitation of the Dead, and the coming of the Messiah (ibid. 118a).

Hallel is omitted on Rosh Hashanah and Yom Kippur because they are days of judgment and it is inappropriate to sing joyful praises on days when our very survival is being weighed on the scales of judgment.

The Talmud gives three reasons for the omission of *Hallel* on Purim.

(a) It is omitted because, despite the miracle of the day, the Jewish people remained in exile as servants of Ahasuerus, and thus the deliverance was only partial. In the words of the Talmud: Regarding the Exodus from Egypt the verse reads, הַלְלוּ עַבְדֵי ה׳, *Give praise, you servants of HASHEM* [i.e., for the fact that we have become servants of HASHEM] (*Psalms* 113:2) and not servants of Pharaoh. But concerning the Purim miracle, אֲכַתֵּי עַבְדֵי דַאֲחַשְׁוֵרוֹשׁ אֲנַן, *As yet we are servants of Ahasuerus* [*Rashi:* We were saved only from death — but not from servitude].

(b) The reading of the *Megillah* of Purim takes the place of *Hallel*.

(c) *Hallel* is not recited over a miracle that occured outside the Land of Israel.

If so, why is *Hallel* recited over the miracle of the Exodus from Egypt? — Until Israel entered the Land, all lands were appropriate for the recital of *Hallel*. However, once the nation entered the Land, only it is deemed suitable for saying *Hallel* (*Megillah* 14a).

On Chanukah, however, the military victory was more complete; there is no *Megillah* reading; and the miracle took place in the Land of Israel. Therefore *Hallel* is recited. Additionally, the *Hallel* recited on Chanukah commemorates the miracle of the lights, which marked the renewal of the Temple.

The Megillah

מֵהֹדוּ וְעַד כּוּשׁ — *From Hodu to Cush* (1:1).

Although this phrase is usually rendered, 'from India to Ethiopia,' the Talmud records a dispute regarding their actual locations. One view separates them, placing each בְּסוֹף הָעוֹלָם, *at the end of the world,* i.e., a whole world apart. The other says that they were adjacent to each other. According to this second opinion the verse should be understood: Just as Ahasuerus readily controlled two neighboring provinces, so did he exercise complete control over all hundred and twenty-seven provinces (*Megillah* 11a).

Rama justifies each view in light of the other. The actual distance between Hodu and Cush may be a stone's throw. But, since the world is a globe, in the opposite direction, they are separated by the entire world (*Mechir Yayin*).

☐ **שֶׁבַע וְעֶשְׂרִים וּמֵאָה מְדִינָה** — *One hundred and twenty-seven provinces* (1:1).

Rabbi Akiva was once delivering a lecture when he noticed his students drowsing. In order to rouse them, he asked, 'Why was it seen fit that Esther should rule over one hundred and twenty-seven provinces? Because thus said God: Let the daughter of Sarah who lived one hundred and twenty-seven years come and reign over one hundred and twenty-seven provinces' (*Midrash*).

Why would these words alert the drowsing students more than the topic of the day? — Rabbi Akiva wanted to impress upon his students the importance of time and the duty to use every second to best advantage. It was because Sarah's one hundred and twenty-seven years were perfect and completely sin-free that her grand-daughter could hold sway over one hundred and twenty-seven provinces. Each second meant a family; each minute, a farm; each day, a village. Had Sarah idled away her time, Esther's kingdom would have been diminished. Time is too precious to waste. Sarah's well-spent time was rewarded during Esther's reign. Each of us, too, is presented with the fleeting gift of time — and the mission of utilizing it fully and well. Who can say what the rewards will be for each minute well-spent; or the penalty for each minute wasted?

This admonition brought Rabbi Akiva's students to attention (*Chiddushei HaRim*).

☐ **בִּשְׁנַת שָׁלוֹשׁ** — *In the third year* (1:3).

It was the third anniversary of his ascension to the throne. He celebrated this anniversary with an annual feast, but in this third year, he had multiple cause for celebration:

According to his (erroneous) calculation, the seventieth year of the Jews' exile had passed, thus belying the prophets who had foretold the exile's end after seventy years (see *Megillah* 11a) and Ahasuerus rejoiced in this frustration of Jewish hope; he had completed the building of his magnificent throne; he was finally secure in his reign; he took Vashti as his queen. Thus the causes for such a lavish feast (*Midrash; Ibn Ezra*).

☐ שְׁמוֹנִים וּמְאַת יוֹם — *A hundred and eighty days* (1:4).

The Sages teach that Nebuchadnezzar buried one thousand and eighty different treasures in the bed of the river Euphrates. God revealed this hiding place to Cyrus, predecessor of Ahasuerus, as a reward for having given orders to rebuild the Temple. Ahasuerus inherited this fortune from him and displayed it to the guests at this party. The Midrash tells us that he showed them six treasures a day. This is derived from the six superlatives mentioned in the previous verse: עֹשֶׁר, *riches*; כָּבוֹד, *glory*; מַלְכוּתוֹ, *kingdom*; יְקָר, *splendor*; תִּפְאֶרֶת, *excellence*; גְּדוּלָתוֹ, *majesty*. At this pace, it took him exactly one hundred and eighty days to go through all his wealth, for 180 x 6 equals 1,080 (*Vilna Gaon*).

☐ Another explanation of the feast's length is based upon the well-known Talmudic dispute between Rabbi Eliezer and Rabbi Yehoshua:

R' Eliezer says: In Tishrei the world was created; in Tishrei the Patriarchs [Abraham and Jacob] were born; in Tishrei the Patriarchs died; on Pesach Isaac was born; on Rosh Hashanah [before the Exodus] the slavery of our ancestors in Egypt was ended; in Nissan they were redeemed and in Tishrei they are destined to be redeemed.

R' Yehoshua says: In Nissan the world was created; in Nissan the Patriarchs were born; in Nissan the Patriarchs died; on Pesach Isaac was born; on Rosh Hashanah Sarah, Rachel and Hannah were remembered; on Rosh Hashanah [before the Exodus] the bondage of out ancestors in Egypt was ended; in Nissan they were redeemed and in Nissan they are destined to be redeemed (*Rosh Hashanah* 10b-11a).

Ahasuerus at first thought that the seventy-year period of exile foretold by the prophets would end in Nissan, for in that month the Jews were destined to be redeemed. So he began his feast at the beginning of Nissan (*Menos HaLevi*). Nevertheless, his joy was incomplete because of his apprehension that the count might have begun with Tishrei. If so, the seventy years were incomplete. Thus, he extended the feast for one hundred and eighty days, or six months and three days (for a month of the lunar calendar is 29 1/2 days). These ended on the third day of Tishrei. To these Ahasuerus added another seven-day feast for the residents of Shushan. The seventh of these days then was not only the Sabbath (see 1:10 below), but was also the Tenth of Tishrei, or Yom Kippur. Thus when Ahasuerus saw the Jews of Shushan eating, drinking and making merry on Yom Kippur, he was sure that his kingdom was safely in his hands for now the Jews would never be redeemed (*Yeshuah Gedolah*).

☐ מִשְׁתֶּה . . . חוּר כַּרְפַּס וּתְכֵלֶת . . . מִטּוֹת זָהָב — *A drinkfest . . . white linen, fine cotton, blue wool . . . couches of gold and silver, on floors of green and white marble, studded with precious gems* (1:5-6).

Such are the machinations of the *Yetzer Hara* (Evil Inclination) in its quest to trap man into lust for material possessions. He begins to tempt man with fine food and drink. Then he causes him to desire fancy clothing. This leads to an appetite for gold and silver, and for fancy furniture. But the *Yetzer Hara* does not stop even when he has succeeded in causing man to desire precious stones, for even when one's vaults are full, one still wants to be able to pave his floors with gems (*Vilna Gaon*).

☐ בַּיּוֹם הַשְּׁבִיעִי — *On the seventh day* (1:10).

It was the Sabbath. God always metes out punishment מִדָּה כְּנֶגֶד מִדָּה, *measure for measure*. The wicked Vashti used to take the daughters of Israel, strip them of their clothing and make them work on the Sabbath. It was on the Sabbath, therefore, that her punishment overtook her, and, for the same reason, it was put into the King's heart to have her appear in public, stripped of all clothing (*Megillah* 12b).

Just as Esther's accession to royalty was related to the number of provinces in Ahasuerus' kingdom (see 1:1 above), so was Vashti's downfall. For two full years and one hundred eighty-seven days of the third year, Vashti perpetrated her disgusting treatment of the daughters of Israel. Since the lunar year contains 354 days, the total number of days she ruled as queen was 895. Thus, she had worked her wickedness for one hundred twenty-seven weeks and six days [895 ÷ 7 = 127 r6]. For each week she would be deprived potentially of one province, but in actuality she was not to be dethroned until her measure of evil was filled. And so, on the 128th Sabbath of her reign, she lost her kingdom and her head (*Likutei Anshei Shem*, cited in *Yaynah shel Torah*).

☐ וַתְּמָאֵן הַמַּלְכָּה וַשְׁתִּי — *But Queen Vashti refused* (1:12).

When Ahasuerus sent for her, he called her וַשְׁתִּי הַמַּלְכָּה, *Vashti the Queen* (v.11), implying that her title was of secondary importance. He was suggesting that she was simply 'Vashti', a commoner, who had been elevated to the throne because it pleased him to do so.

She, on the other hand, referred to herself as הַמַּלְכָּה וַשְׁתִּי, *the Queen Vashti,* to make it plain that she was of royal blood even before her marriage, and that her dignity was not to be trifled with.

Further on, when he wished to spare her, Ahasuerus referred to her as Queen Vashti (v.15), reminding his advisors that she was a queen — the daughter of a great ruler, a royal personage in her own right (*Vilna Gaon*).

According to the Talmud (*Megillah* 12b), Vashti's refusal was not based on modesty, but on physical blemishes which miraculously appeared on her body. One view is that she contracted leperous rashes all over her body; the other opinion states that the angel Gabriel came to her and caused her to grow a tail.

R' Pinchas Menachem of Piltz (cited in *Yaynah shel Torah*) explains that just as Esther merited to rule because she was descended from the Matriarch Sarah, so did Vashti receive a tail because she was the granddaughter of Nebuchadnezzar. The *Book of Daniel* (ch. 4) describes how Nebuchadnezzar metamorphosed into a beast of the wilderness. In like fashion his descendant Vashti also became beast-like by growing a tail.

☐ וַיֹּאמֶר מְמוּכָן — *Memuchan declared* (1:16).

A Tanna taught: 'Memuchan is Haman. Why was he called Memuchan? — Because he was destined [מוכָן] for destruction. Rav Kahana said: 'From here we see that an ignoramus always thrusts himself to the forefront.' [Memuchan is mentioned last in verse 14, yet he speaks first here] (*Megillah* 12b; *Midrash*).

Everywhere else his name is spelled מְמוּכָן, but here מוּמְכָן. This strange arrangement of the letters forms the two words מוּם כֵּן, *a blemish is here.* The blemish is his discourtesy in speaking out of turn, for the Torah is not tolerant of boorishness (*Masoras HaBris*).

☐ לִהְיוֹת כָּל אִישׁ שֹׂרֵר בְּבֵיתוֹ — *That every man should rule in his own home* (1:22)

The relevance of this part of the decree is difficult to understand. Rabbah said that had it not been for this decree, even a shred would not have remained of the Jews. People said: 'What does he mean by sending us word that every man should rule in his own home? Of course he should! Even a weaver in his own home must be boss!' (*Megillah* 12b).

The commentaries explain that upon reading this first decree, everyone saw how foolish the king was. Later, therefore, when they read his second decree about exterminating the Jews on the thirteenth of Adar, they were afraid that the king had issued this decree while intoxicated and that he would change his mind and reverse the order the next morning. Were it not for this mockery, they would have responded immediately to the second decree by 'jumping the gun,' and would not have waited for the appointed date to exterminate the Jews (*Me'am Loez*).

☐ וּשְׁמוֹ מָרְדֳּכַי — *Whose name was Mordechai* (2:5).
In Scripture, the names of the wicked are given before the word שֵׁם, *name*; as it says: נָבָל שְׁמוֹ, *Nabal was his name;* גָּלְיָת שְׁמוֹ, *Goliath was his name;* שֶׁבַע בֶּן בִּכְרִי שְׁמוֹ, *Sheva son of Bichri was his name.* But the names of the righteous are preceded by the word שֵׁם, as it says: וּשְׁמוֹ מָנוֹחַ, *and his name was Manoach;* וּשְׁמוֹ קִישׁ, *and his name was Kish;* וּשְׁמוֹ אֶלְקָנָה, *and his name was Elkanah;* וּשְׁמוֹ שָׁאוּל, *and his name was Saul;* וּשְׁמוֹ בֹּעַז, *and his name was Boaz;* וּשְׁמוֹ יִשַׁי, *and his name was Jesse;* וּשְׁמוֹ מָרְדֳּכַי, *and his name was Mordechai.* They thus resemble their Creator of whom it is written וּשְׁמִי ה', *My Name* HASHEM . . . (*Midrash Rabbah; Midrash Abba Gorion*).

☐ מָרְדֳּכַי — *Mordechai* (2:5).
Where is Mordechai alluded to in the Torah? — In the verse מָר דְּרוֹר, *flowing myrrh* (*Exodus* 30:22), which the *Targum* renders as מֵירָא דַכְיָא, *Mira Dachia* [which both in spelling and sound resembles מָרְדֳּכַי, *Mordechai* (*Chullin* 139b).
Just as myrrh is the foremost of spices, so Mordechai was the foremost of the righteous of his generation (*Midrash*).

☐ בֶּן יָאִיר בֶּן שִׁמְעִי בֶּן קִישׁ — *Son of Yair, son of Shim'i, son of Kish* (2:5).
The verse skips over generations here. The word בֶּן therefore means 'son' in the sense of 'descendant' rather than the literal meaning. The Midrash interprets homiletically: בֶּן יָאִיר, *the son who illuminated* (from אור, *to light*) *the eyes of Israel;* בֶּן שִׁמְעִי, *the son whose prayers were heard* (from שמע *to hear*); בֶּן קִישׁ, *the son who banged*

(from נקש, *to knock*) on the gates of heaven and was answered.

A casual glance indicates that the order of events has been reversed by the Midrash. First Mordechai stormed the gates of heaven; then his prayers were accepted; finally, the Jews' eyes lit up with relief. Why then does the Midrash invert the order?

The Midrash follows the arrangement of names as they appear in the *Megillah* which traces Mordechai's ancestry working backwards from Mordechai himself. But when the names are placed in chronological order of when they lived, the events they symbolize also fall into their proper places (*Sefas Emes*).

☐ הֲדַסָּה — *Hadassah* (2:7).

There is a difference of opinion among the Sages (*Megillah* 13a) whether Hadassah was her proper name and Esther was added later, or vice-versa. Both names are descriptive of her virtues. Hadassah is derived from the Hebrew word הָדָס, *myrtle*; Esther from אִסְתַּהַר, *Istahar* [as beautiful as the moon (*Rashi*)].

Just as the myrtle [הָדָס] has a sweet smell but a bitter taste, so Esther was sweet to Mordechai but bitter to Haman (*Midrash*).

Where is Esther alluded to in the Torah? — In the verse וְאָנֹכִי הַסְתֵּר אַסְתִּיר פָּנַי בַּיּוֹם הַהוּא, *And I will surely hide* (אַסְתִּיר) *My face on that day* [*Deuteronomy* 31:18] (*Chullin* 139b).

In Esther's lifetime God seemingly diverted (הִסְתִּיר) His attention from Israel because of their evil ways. But, through the efforts of Mordechai (see above) and Esther, His presence was revealed when he saved Israel from Haman's evil plot. Thus the Scriptural book that relates the Purim story is called מְגִלַּת אֶסְתֵּר, which may be translated 'the revelation (from גלה, *to uncover*) of that which was concealed' (*Yismach Yisrael*).

☐ שֶׁבַע הַנְּעָרוֹת — *The seven maids* (2:9).

The Talmud explains that there were seven so that she could count the days of the week through rotating their schedule, for the same one always served her on a given day. The commentators wonder why Esther — a prophetess — would need such a system to keep track of the Sabbath. Esther was keeping her identity as a Jewess hidden. Forever mindful that *laziness leads to indolence,* she kept herself busy throughout the week. Afraid that her maids would notice that on the Sabbath she performed no work and they would guess she was Jewish, she appointed a different maid for each day of the week. Those who ministered to her during the week did not see her rest on the Sabbath; the Sabbath maid, meanwhile, assumed that just as she did no work on the Sabbath, she did no work on *any* days of the week (*Yaaros Devash*).

☐ ... לֹא הִגִּידָה אֶסְתֵּר — *Esther had not told of her family or her nation* (2:10).

Many reason are given for keeping Esther's Jewishness secret: Mordechai must have realized that if Esther was chosen to be queen it could only be that she was to be instrumental in saving Israel from some impending calamity. He reasoned that if her origins as a Jew were known, Ahasuerus would never choose her and she would lose her opportunity (*Rokeach*).

— Mordechai had Esther keep her relationship to him a secret so others would not be secretive in his presence (*Yosef Lekach*).

— Her secrecy enabled her to observe her religion in secret. Had she declared her faith, she would have been forced to transgress (*Ibn Ezra*).

— She did not declare her *royal* lineage (as a descendant of the family of King Saul) so that the king might think that she was of humble origin and send her away (*Rashi*).

— Moreover, having seen Ahasuerus' contempt for royalty — he killed Vashti who traced her ancestry to Nebuchadnezzar — Esther would probably feel safer if she was thought of as a commoner. Should any misunderstanding arise between her and the king, he might excuse her as being unaware of royal protocol. But Vashti, who was groomed to the throne from birth, could not be forgiven the slightest lapse (*Matzreif Dahava*).

☐ וּבְהַגִּיעַ תֹּר אֶסְתֵּר בַּת אֲבִיחַיִל — *Now when the turn came for Esther, daughter of Avichail* (2:15).

Why is her family background and her father's name given for the first time only here? — One also wonders why the fact that Mordechai adopted Esther is repeated at this point.

The reason is to let us know that precisely *because* she was acutely aware of her background, she asked for nothing. She kept in mind that her father was Avichail, and that her relative and savior and adoptive father was Mordechai. With these images before her, she did not request any artificial beauty aids, in the hope of lessening her chances of finding favor in the eyes of Ahasuerus so that she would be rejected and possibly even be sent home to her family (*Menos HaLevi*).

☐ וַיִּוָּדַע הַדָּבָר לְמָרְדְּכָי — *The plot became known to Mordechai* (2:22). Being a member of the Sanhedrin, Mordechai knew seventy languages. Bigsan and Teresh spoke in their native Tarsian tongue in Mordechai's presence, not expecting him to understand them (*Megillah* 13b).

On one of his visits to Warsaw, Sir Moses Montefiore asked the Gerrer Rebbe, known as the *Chiddushei HaRim*, why the Polish chassidim do not teach their children the national language of their country. 'Don't we find that in order to serve on the Sanhedrin, one had to understand seventy languages? And didn't the miracle of Purim occur through Mordechai's knowledge of Tarsian?'

The *Chiddushei HaRim* replied, 'It is the very incident that you just mentioned from which we learn not to teach foreign languages to our children. For had that been the Jewish way, Bigsan and Teresh would certainly not have spoken openly in Mordechai's presence!'

☐ וּמָרְדֳּכַי לֹא יִכְרַע — *But Mordechai would not bow down* (3:2).

Why is this verse written in future, יִכְרַע, lit., *will bow*, rather than past tense, כָּרַע, *bowed*? — The future tense signifies a decision not to bow under any circumstances, rather than a decision taken for a particular occasion (*Shaar Bas Rabbim*).

At the request of Esther, Ahasuerus himself freed Mordechai from the obligation of prostrating himself before Haman (*Midrash Chazis*).

This explanation may be inferred from the verse itself. The words כִּי כֵן צִוָּה לוֹ הַמֶּלֶךְ, *for this is what the King had commanded concerning him*, apply to the end of the verse rather than the beginning. Thus: *This is what the King had commanded concerning him:* וּמָרְדֳּכַי לֹא יִכְרַע, *That Mordechai should not bow*. This also explains the use of the future tense יִכְרַע (*Yeshuah Gedolah*).

☐ בַּחֹדֶשׁ הָרִאשׁוֹן הוּא חֹדֶשׁ נִיסָן . . . לְחֹדֶשׁ שְׁנֵים עָשָׂר הוּא חֹדֶשׁ אֲדָר ☐ — *In the first month, that is the month of Nissan . . . to the twelfth month, that is the month of Adar* (3:7).

God made the lots fall on a date eleven and a half months later. This would give the Jews almost a full year in which to repent their ways and return to *Hashem* (*Ibn Ezra*).

☐ יֶשְׁנוֹ עַם אֶחָד — *There is a certain people* (3:8).

There was never a slanderer so skillful as Haman. He said to Ahasuerus, 'Come, let us destroy them.'

I am afraid of their God,' the King answered, 'lest He do to me as He did to my predecessors.'

Haman said: 'יְשֵׁנִים, they are asleep [i.e., they are negligent; a play on the word יֶשְׁנוֹ, *there is*] in regard to observing the precepts.

'There are Rabbis among them [who *do* keep the precepts],'
Ahasuerus replied.

'עַם אֶחָד, *they are one people* [and all hang together],' said Haman
(*Megillah* 13b).

☐ טַבַּעְתּו — *His signet ring* (3:10).

Transference of the King's signet ring was symbolic that Haman
now had full authority to act on the King's behalf (*Rashi*).

Our Rabbis said: Ahasuerus hated the Jews more than the wicked
Haman. Usually the buyer gives a pledge to the seller, but here the
seller gave the pledge (*Midrash*).

When Haman offered a huge sum of money for the privilege of
destroying the Jews throughout the Persian Empire, it was exactly
what Ahasuerus had hoped. Like two men, one of whom had a mound
in his field and the other had a hole in his field . . . Said the owner of
the hole to the owner of the mound, 'Sell me your mound for money.'
Replied the other, 'Take it for nothing and welcome to it' (*Megillah*
14a).

☐ פַּתְשֶׁגֶן . . . גָּלוּי לְכָל הָעַמִּים ☐ — *The copies . . . published to all [the]
peoples* (3:14).

Haman was afraid to openly and publicly decree the annihilation of
the entire Jewish people. In the confidential decree to *the satraps,
governors, and high officials,* (verses 12 and 13), he clearly spelled out
his intent to utterly destroy the Jews on the thirteenth of Adar. On
the copies of the documents, which were publicly displayed in every
town square and were published to all the peoples, however, it was
written only that on the thirteenth of Adar they must all be prepared
for military action whose nature will then be revealed. That is why
the next verse follows with וְהָעִיר שׁוּשָׁן נָבוֹכָה, *but the city of Shushan
was bewildered,* for no one knew who would be involved in this
action (*Vilna Gaon*).

☐ *Mordechai And The Three Schoolboys*

After Haman's letters had been written by his scribes, he and his
cohort rejoiced. They came upon Mordechai who was walking
before them. Mordechai spied three children returning home from
yeshivah, and ran after them. Haman and his henchmen saw
Mordechai running after the children, so they followed behind to
discover what Mordechai would request of them.

When Mordechai reached the children he asked each of them,
'Recite the verse you studied today!'

One responded, *'Do not fear sudden terror, or the holocaust of the wicked when it comes'* (*Proverbs* 3:25).

The second replied, *'Plan a conspiracy and it will be annulled; speak your piece and it shall not stand, for God is with us'* (*Isaiah* 8:10).

The third said, *'Even till seniority, I remain unchanged; and even till your ripe old age, I shall endure; I created you and I shall bear you; I shall endure and rescue* (ibid. 46:4).

Upon hearing these verses, Mordechai laughed and rejoiced with great joy. Said Haman to him, 'What is this joy that you have displayed at the words of these children?'

Mordechai answered, 'I rejoice at the good tidings they have informed me; I need not fear the evil plan that you have plotted against us.'

Immediately the wicked Haman flared angrily and said, 'I shall stretch out my hand against these children first!' (*Esther Rabbah* 7:13).

Why were three verses necessary? Couldn't Mordechai have gotten his positive response from one child?

According to the Vilna Gaon these three verses allude to three different wars against Amalek and his descendants.

Amalek's first attack against Israel came shortly after the Exodus from Egypt. He attacked suddenly — as it is written, *He encountered you unexpectedly on the way* (*Deuteronomy* 25:18). Regarding this the first lad said, *'Do not fear sudden terror.'*

Amalek's second attack against Israel came when the Clouds of Glory that had protected Israel during their forty-year sojourn in the wilderness dispersed upon the death of Aaron. At that time Amalek devised a scheme to nullify the Jew's prayers against them. They disguised themselves as Canaanites, hoping that Israel would pray that God save them from the Canaanite foe. Since the Amalekites are not Canaanites, the supplications would be in vain. This plot backfired when Israel prayed, 'Protect us from this enemy, whomever he may be.' Thus the second child said, *'Plan a conspiracy and it will be annulled.'*

Finally, the third schoolboy told Mordechai, just as God protected Israel in those two wars, so will He protect us against Haman who, in his letter to the peoples stated, 'Their God has aged; He can no longer protect them.' Therefore, the third boy recited the verse, *'Even till seniority, I remain unchanged.'*

□ וּמָרְדֳּכַי יָדַע אֶת כָּל אֲשֶׁר נַעֲשָׂה — *And Mordechai knew all that been done* (4:1).

It was told to him a dream (*Rashi*).

The words כָּל, *all*, implies that Mordechai not only knew what had been done by Haman, but he also knew the entire scenario, from its inception to its conclusion. In other words, he was made aware both of Haman's machinations and of his downfall (*Yalkut*).

If so, why did Mordechai decree fasting, prayers, sackcloth and ashes? — Had the information been revealed to Mordechai through prophecy, he may not have decreed the fasts, etc. However, since it came to him through a dream, he was unsure of the dream's veracity. For the Talmud (*Berachos* 55a) states that no dream is devoid of nonsense. Thus, Mordechai was not certain that the outcome would be as his dream predicted (*R' Chanoch Henoch of Aleksander*).

□ *Biding Time*

Hashem often will allow a long passage of time before punishing a sinful act. Such delay is not due to His inability to act, ח״ו, but to His limitless mercy, for the sinner is thus given ample time to reflect and repent.

Unfortunately, many people do not use this respite wisely, and soon forget what they have perpetrated. Thus, there deeds go unatoned for. Eventually, heaven gives some sign as a reminder of past misdeeds. Often, the common folk will not realize the connection between the original act and the later warning signal. Only a very wise person will make the link. And this is precisely what occurred during the Purim story.

The *Megillah* spans a history of nine years, from the third to the twelfth year of Ahasuerus' reign. A layman could never recognize that the Jews' refusal to obey Mordechai's plea not to attend Ahasuerus' feast would result in a dramatic, but seemingly uncon-nected, series of events over the next nine years.

The common people 'knew' that Haman's decree was caused by Mordechai's obstinate refusal to bow. They held him responsible for the mortal danger to the nation. Mordechai knew better. He knew that the decree was in punishment for the Jews' weakness in enjoying the forbidden feast. He knew that refusal to bow was the first step in a chain of courage and repentance that, alone, could save his people.

When he and Esther wrote the *Megillah*, he began the story with the feast of Ahasuerus because the participation of the Jews living in Shushan was the cause of the evil decree, which was annulled as a result of their sincere repentance — a full nine years later.

The *Megillah* teaches us that our leaders discern much more than we; ultimate salvation lies in submission to their authority (*Der Alte funn Kelm* cited in *Michtav MeEliyahu*, vol. 1, pg. 76).

□ *Esther's Request*

Esther told Mordechai, '*Go, assemble all the Jews to be found in Sushan, and fast for me; do not eat or drink for three days*' (*Esther* 4:16). These three days were the thirteenth, fourteenth and fifteenth of Nissan. [According to *Rashi* (*Megillah* 15a, 16a) the days were the fourteenth, fifteenth and sixteenth.]

Mordechai sent a reply to Esther, 'But one of those days is the first day of Pesach!'

She responded, 'Elder of Israel, why do we need Pesach [if there will be no Jews left to observe it]?'

Mordechai immediately conceded . . . then he prayed, 'Lord of the World, it is revealed and known before the Throne of Your Glory, that my refusal to bow to Haman was not done with a haughty heart or arrogant eye. Rather it was done out of my reverence for You. I did not bow to him in order not to give to a human being the honor reserved for You . . .

'And now, our God, save us from his hand! Let him fall into the pit he has dug, and let him be caught in the trap he has set for Your pious people. Make this agitator aware that You have not forgotten the oath that You have have taken on our behalf: *And even with that, when they will be in the land of their enemies, I will not have despised them nor abhorred them to destroy them, to annul my covenant with them, for I am HASHEM, their God* (*Leviticus* 26:44).'

What did Mordechai do then? He assembled the children, withheld bread and water from them, dressed them in sackcloth and sat them in the dust. They wept and studied Torah.

At that time, Esther was exceedingly apprehensive about the evil that had sprouted against Israel. She removed her royal garments and jewelry, donned sackcloth, let down her hair and filled it with dust and ashes. She fasted and fell in supplication before God.

'*Hashem*, God of Israel! You have ruled from ancient days; You have created the world. Please help Your maidservant who is an orphan — with neither father nor mother. Like a pauper begging from house to house, so do I go from window to window in

Ahasuerus' palace seeking Your mercy. Now, *Hashem*, please grant Your poor maidservant success, and save the sheep of Your flock from these enemies who have stood up against us, for nothing can prevent You from saving the many or the few. May You Who are the Father of orphans stand to the right of this orphan who has placed her trust in Your kindness. Grant me compassion before this man, for I fear him. Humble him before me, for You are the One Who humbles the haughty (*Esther Rabbah* 8:7).'

☐ יָבוֹא הַמֶּלֶךְ וְהָמָן הַיּוֹם — *Let the King and Haman come today* (5:4).

Esther answered the King that, indeed, she had something very important, to ask of him, but that this was not the right time. It would be more opportune if he were to visit her. During a social visit at her banquet he would be more relaxed. Then she would present her request. The King ordered his servants to 'hurry Haman' so the banquet could start early thus allowing Esther to make her request and relieve her of her sadness (*Vilna Gaon*).

☐ *Why Did Esther Invite Haman? — Twelve Reasons*

The Talmud (*Megillah* 15b) questions Esther's motive in inviting Haman to her two banquets. Twelve answers are offered.

(i) R' Eliezer says: She spread a snare for him — as it is said, *May their table become a snare before them* (*Psalms* 69:23).

(ii) R' Yehoshua says: She learned from her father's family — as it is said, *If your enemy is hungry, feed him bread,* [*if he is thirsty, give him water to drink. For thus you pour coals on his head . . .*] (*Proverbs* 25:21-22).

(iii) R' Meir says: That he not be able to take counsel and rebel.

(iv) R' Yehudah says: That her Jewishness not be recognized.

(v) R' Nechemiah says: That Israel not say, 'We have a sister in the king's palace,' and thus stop seeking God's compassion.

(vi) R' Yose says: So that he would be within her reach at all times.

(vii) R' Shimon ben Menasia says: Perhaps the Omnipresent will see [how I am forced to flatter this wicked man (*Rashi*)] and perform a miracle for us.

(v) R' Yehoshuah ben Karchah says: I will show favoritism for him so that both he and I will be killed [i.e., she was willing to be martyred if that were the only way to rid the world of Haman].

(ix) Rabban Gamliel says: She thought,'He is a fickle king.' [If I don't convince him to kill Haman in a fit of anger, Haman will use the delay to appease the king (*Rashi*).]

(x) Rabban Gamliel said further that we are beholden to the

explanation found in a *baraisa* that cites R' Eliezer HaModai: She wished to arouse the king's jealousy and the envy of the nobles.

(xi) Rabbah said: *Pride goes before destruction [and haughtiness before stumbling]* (Proverbs 16:18).

(xii) Abaye and Rava both say: *I shall set their drinkfests in their heat, [and I will make them drunk that they may celebrate — then they shall sleep an eternal sleep, and they shall not awaken]* (Jeremiah 51:39).

Rabbah bar Avuhah met Elijah the Prophet and asked him, 'According to which view did Esther actually act?'

Elijah answered, 'According to all the opinions of all the Sages cited.'

☐ *In The Afternoon —*
On other festivals, the main meal in honor of the day is eaten around noontime following the *Mussaf* prayers. On Purim, however, when the morning and early afternoon is taken up with the other mitzvos of the day — *Megillah, mishloach manos,* and *matanos laevyonim* — the *seudah* is served later in the day. *Minchah* should be recited earlier that usual, followed by the festive *seudah*. The meal should also extend a bit into the night (*Shulchan Aruch* 695:2; *Mishnah Berurah* 8).

The *Vilna Gaon* explains that an allusion to this ruling may be found in *Megillas Esther*. The Purim *seudah* commemorates the feast given by Esther for Ahasuerus and Haman. Her feast took place on the third day of the fast, two hours before nightfall. Although the full fast lasted seventy-two hours, Esther and her maidens ate after only seventy hours because of the feast. She wouldn't dare serve food to the king and refuse to partake of it herself, for then she should be suspected of poisoning the king's food.

Esther's eating two hours before the fast ended is alluded to in her words to Mordechai, '*I, with my maids, will also fast,* בֵּן, *thus*' (*Esther* 4:16). The word בֵּן has a *gematria* (numerical equivalent) of seventy, i.e., I, with my maidens, will fast seventy hours.

☐ אֶל הַמִּשְׁתֶּה אֲשֶׁר עָשִׂיתִי לוֹ . . . אֶל הַמִּשְׁתֶּה אֲשֶׁר אֶעֱשֶׂה לָהֶם — *To the banquet that I have prepared for him . . . to the banquet that I shall prepare for them* (5:4,8).

Esther's invitation to the first banquet was extended to the king and Haman, yet she stated that it was 'prepared for him'. Logically, Ahasuerus would interpret this wording to refer to himself.

Haman was only invited, thought the king, because — as the highest official in the land — it would be his duty to carry out Esther's request. But when Esther issued her second invitation, it was for a banquet she would 'prepare for them'. This time she equated Haman with Ahasuerus. Esther calculated that this would arouse the king's jealousy against Haman, so that he would be willing to kill him.

When Ahasuerus heard Esther say לָהֶם, for them, he became suspicious, as she had hoped. Not only was the king slighted by seeing his advisor treated as his peer, but he began to think about the earlier invitation. Perhaps when she had prepared the banquet לוֹ, for him, she meant Haman. If so, she had placed the king lower than Haman. Thus, Esther's plan worked (based on Menos HaLevi).

□ כְּבוֹד עָשְׁרוֹ וְרֹב בָּנָיו . . . אֲשֶׁר נִשְּׂאוֹ עַל הַשָּׂרִים . . . לֹא הֵבִיאָה אֶסְתֵּר . . . כִּי □ אִם אוֹתִי — The glory of his wealth and his large number of sons . . . that the king had raised him over the officials . . . Esther invited no one . . . but myself (5:11-12).

Haman had not recounted the glories of his wealth, children and power simply to make conversation. Obviously, his wife and friends were well aware of his family and status. Rather, he told them all this just to lead up to the point of how debilitatingly frustrated he was at Mordechai's refusal to acknowledge his superiority (Yosef Lekach).

Another reason for telling them of his glory was to prove that he could easily dispose of his arch-enemy, Mordechai through כְּבוֹד עָשְׁרוֹ, the glory of his wealth, for he had sufficient financial means to bring about Mordechai's downfall; וְרֹב בָּנָיו, his large number of sons, for all were very capable; and אֲשֶׁר נִשְּׂאוֹ עַל הַשָּׂרִים, that the king had raised him over the officials, thus endowing him with the power to kill anyone he wishes. 'Lastly', Haman said, 'even the Queen herself would not save Mordechai. It was I, alone, not Mordechai, whom she invited to the banquet.' Eventually, Haman was proved wrong in all these cases: His wealth was given to Mordechai; his sons were hung; the King who had raised him over the officials humbled him before Mordechai; and Esther exposed him as her enemy, intent on her people's death (Akeidas Yitzchak).

□ A Wicked Wife's Advice

Haman had three hundred sixty-five advisors, one for each day of the year, with whom be would take counsel. But none could advise as well as his wife Zeresh. She said to him, 'If this man about whom you seek advice is of the seed of the Jews, you will not succeed against him unless you go after him with a wise plan. You must do something to him that has never been tried against any of his nation. Should you throw him into a fiery furnace, Chananiah, Mishael and Azariah have already been saved from prison. Should you throw him into the lion's den, Daniel has already ascended from there. Should you imprison him in a dungeon, Joseph has already been delivered from prison. Should you lock him into an iron pot and light a fire under him, Menashe has already emerged from one after praying hard. Should you exile him to the wilderness, his ancestors were fruitful and multiplied there. And they have withstood so many other trials — Moses, the sword of Pharaoh: David, the mighty Goliath; Isaac, the knife at the *Akeidah*. Even if you should blind him, the blinded Samson has already slain thousands of Philistines. Rather, you must hang him from a gallows, for we do not find that any of his people were ever saved from a gallows' (*Esther Rabbah* 9:2)

☐ גָּבֹהַּ חֲמִשִּׁים אַמָּה — *Fifty cubits high* (5:14).

Haman searched for a fifty-cubit beam but could not find one. So his son, Parshandasa, who was the governor of the Mt. Ararat area, supplied him with a beam from the remains of Noah's Ark, which was fifty cubits wide (*Midrash Abba Gorion*).

☐ *Which Tree Is Most Fit?*

But which tree would Haman use for his gallows?

Said the Sages: When Haman decided to prepare a gallows, God summoned all the trees in creation before Him and asked, 'Who volunteers to have this wicked man hang from him?'

The fig tree replied, 'I volunteer, for it is from my fruits that Israel offers the first-fruit *bikkurim*. Moreover the verse compares Israel to me: *As ripe figs at the beginning of their season have I seen your forefathers (Hosea 9:10).'*

The grape vine replied, 'I volunteer, for Israel is compared to me: *The vine You caused to journey forth from Egypt (Psalms 80:9).'*

The pomegranate replied, 'I volunteer, for Israel is compared to me: *Your temples are like a piece of pomegranate (Song of Songs 4:3).'*

The nut tree replied, 'I volunteer, for Israel is compared to me: *I descended into the nut orchard (ibid. 6:11).'*

The esrog tree replied, 'I volunteer, for Israel uses me for a *mitzvah . . .'*

The myrtle replied, 'I volunteer, for Israel is compared to me: *He stood among the myrtles at the water (Zechariah 1:8).'*

The olive tree replied, 'I volunteer, for Israel is compared to me: *A* fresh olive tree with fruit beautiful to look upon does HASHEM call you (Jeremiah 11:16).'

The apple tree replied, 'I volunteer, for Israel is compared to me: Like an apple among the fruitless forest trees, so is My beloved among the children (Song of Songs 2:3).'

The palm tree replied, 'I volunteer, for Israel is compared to me: Such is you stature, likened to a palm tree (ibid. 7:8).'

The shittim and beroshim trees replied, 'We volunteer, for the Tabernacle and Temple were built with us.'

The date-palm and the cedar replied, 'We volunteer, for we are compared to the righteous: A righteous man will flourish like a date-palm, like a cedar in Lebanon he will grow tall (Psalms 92:13).'

The willow replied, 'I volunteer, for Israel is compared to me: Like willows upon streams of water (Isaiah 44:4). Moreover, they take me to fulfill the mitzvah of the Four Species with the lulav.'

Then the thorn appeared before God and said, 'Master of the Universe, although I have nothing on which to base my claim, I volunteer to have this contaminated person hang on me. My name is 'thorn' and he is a painful thorn; it is appropriate that the thorn hang from the thorn.'

Thus, when Haman's henchmen sought wood for a gallows, all they were able to find was a thorn tree.

When the tree was brought before Haman, he set it up at the doorway of his palace. Then he measured himself against it, to show his servants how Mordechai would hang from it. A Divine Voice called out, 'This tree is appropriate for you. It has been prepared for you since the six days of Creation'(Esther Rabbah 9:2).

□ The School Children Pray

After building his gallows, Haman went to seek Mordechai. He found him sitting in the study hall with twenty-two thousand children before him. Haman had them all thrown into iron chains and assigned soldiers to guard them. Then he said, 'Tomorrow I shall slay all of these children first. Then I shall hang Mordechai.'

Their mothers brought food and drink for them and said, 'Our children, eat and drink before you die tomorrow, so that you not die of starvation.'

The children spontaneously placed their hands on their sefarim and swore, 'By the life of our teacher Mordechai, we shall neither eat nor drink. Rather, we will die fasting.'

They all began crying, until their screams ascended to heaven during the night. At that time, God's attribute of mercy reigned as He arose from His Throne of Judgment and sat on His Throne of Mercy, saying, 'What is this sound of kids and lambs that I hear?'

Our teacher Moses stood before God and said, 'Master of the Universe, these are neither kids nor lambs, they are the children of Your people. Today is the third day of their three-day-three-night fast. Tomorrow the enemy wishes to slaughter them like kids and lambs.'

At that time, God took the letters which had been sealed in clay, that contained the decrees, tore them up, and threw Ahasuerus into a state of confusion. So that *on that night sleep eluded the king . . .* (*Esther Rabbah* 9:3).

☐ נָדְדָה שְׁנַת הַמֶּלֶךְ — *Sleep eluded the King* (6:1).

A thought occurred to Ahasuerus: What is the meaning of Esther having invited Haman to the feast? Perhaps they are conspiring to kill me? He thought again: If that is so, don't I have any friend who would tell me? Then he thought again: Perhaps someone has done me a valuable service and gone unrewarded. If I am guilty of such ingratitude, then I may have forfeited the friendship of loyal subjects; they will not inform me of conspiracies against me. He, therefore, *ordered the record book, the annals to be brought* (*Megillah* 15b).

☐ בִּגְתָנָה וָתֶרֶשׁ — *Bigsana and Teresh* (6:2).

Previously [in 2:21] he is referred to as 'Bigsan'; why the addition of an א at the end of his name? — Haman's sons were the scribes who recorded the incident; they wished to make light of Mordechai's involvement so they wrote that Mordechai had denounced בִּגְתָן אוֹ תֶרֶשׁ, *Bigsan or Teresh,* not really knowing which was the guilty party. Thus, they implied an innocent man was executed as a result of Mordechai's vague suspicions — therefore Mordechai was unworthy of any reward. When the incident was read now, the letters of the incriminating word אוֹ, *or,* miraculously separated. The א moved at the end of Bigsan, and the ו to Teresh. Now the chronicle read, בִּגְתָנָא וָתֶרֶשׁ, *Bigsana and Teresh,* i.e., Mordechai saved the king's life by denouncing both equally guilty plotters. He is eminently deserving of reward — which he has never received (*Alshich; Menos HaLevi*).

☐ According to the *Malbim*, the king had forgotten who was responsible for saving his life in the Bigsan-Teresh incident. All he remembered was that Esther had told him and, since Haman was responsible for his choosing a new queen, the king promoted him

and bestowed enormous power upon him. The *Malbim* differen-
tiates between the דִּבְרֵי הַיָּמִים, *Book of Records*, the official
chronicle of the nation's history, which was kept under the
jurisdiction of the prime minister, and the סֵפֶר הַזִּכְרֹנוֹת *the annals*,
[literally, *book of remembrances*] the King's personal diary which
was kept in the monarch's personal possession. Haman had
rewritten *the Book of Records* and inserted his own name to conform
with his self-serving version. Now, however, when the king had his
personal diary read to him, he discovered that Mordechai, not
Haman, was responsible for saving his life. Thus becoming aware of
Haman's fraud in the Bigsan-Teresh affair, Ahasuerus was quite
willing to accept the even more damning accusation that Esther
would make against Haman the next day. This teaches a great lesson
about Divine intervention: precisely at the crucial moment when
Haman built a gallows to hang Mordechai, God reversed the course
of events.

☐ אֲשֶׁר הֵכִין לוֹ — *Which he had prepared for him* (6:4).
     The word לוֹ, *for him*, is seemingly superfluous. According to the
Talmud: A Tanna stated: He had prepared it for himself (*Megillah*
16a).
     The Talmud tells us that Haman, without realizing it, was divinely
influenced to prepare the gallows for ultimate use on himself.
Elsewhere in the Megillah, the Heavenly decree that was originally
against the Jews was reversed and turned against their enemies. The
preparation of the gallows was different. The Talmud tells us that
from the moment of its preparation, its intended victim was Haman
(*Vilna Gaon*).
     — Traditionally, every Mitzvah requires הֲכָנָה — previous prepara-
tion; unlike sins, which are committed spontaneously Therefore, our
Sages (*Megillah* 16a) state that Haman prepared the gallows *for
himself.* If there was הֲכָנָה, *preparation,* it follows that a mitzvah was
being readied. The mitzvah was the destruction of the memory of
Amalek [of whom Haman was a descendant] (*Belzer Rebbe*).
     — According to the *Gerrer Rebbe*, Haman intended to trick
Ahasuerus into ordering him to hang Mordechai. He came to the
king to complain that Mordechai's obstinance in disobeying the royal
edict had so upset Haman, that he was willing to take his own life. In
fact, he had already constructed a gallows for this purpose. Certainly,
thought Haman, the king would never let me carry out my suicide
threat. Instead, he will suggest that I hang Mordechai.

☐ אָבֵל וַחֲפוּי רֹאשׁ — *Mourning and with his head covered* (6:12).

As Haman was leading Mordechai through the streets, his daughter saw them from an overhanging roof. She thought the man on the horse was her father and the man leading him was Mordechai. So she took a chamber pot and emptied it on her father's head. He looked up at her, and when she realized it was her father, she threw herself from the roof to the ground and killed herself (*Megillah* 16a).

☐ עוֹדָם מְדַבְּרִים עִמּוֹ — *While they were still talking with him* (6:14).

While he was considering their advice that he dismantle the gallows. God's plan caused the chamberlains to take him away to the party before he could implement their suggestion. This was because of the divine intention that the gallows was destined for Haman (*Vilna Goan*).

☐ תִּנָּתֶן לִי נַפְשִׁי בִּשְׁאֵלָתִי וְעַמִּי בְּבַקָּשָׁתִי — *Let my life be granted to me as my request and my people's as my petition* (7:3).

The sequence of Esther's request seems to indicate that she placed her personal safety before the nation's! The truth is, however, that she showed great tact in arousing the king by first making a plea for her own life. The word בַּקָּשָׁה, *petition,* is stronger than שְׁאֵלָה, *request.* She requested her own life in terms of a שְׁאֵלָה. When the king immediately responded that he would go to any ends to save her life, she said that her life was secondary to her. She had something far more important to ask, a בַּקָּשָׁה for the salvation of her people. If her people were to be destroyed, then her own life would matter little to her; she would die a slow death from utter despair (*Yosef Lekach*).

☐ כִּי נִמְכַּרְנוּ . . . לְאַבֵּד וְאִלּוּ לַעֲבָדִים . . . הֶחֱרַשְׁתִּי — *For be were sold . . . to be annihilated: had we been sold as slaves. . ., I would have kept quiet* (7:4).

Why did Esther express Haman's genocide in terms of a sale? Wouldn't the phrase כִּי נִגְזַר עָלֵינוּ, *for it has been decreed upon us,* have been more appropriate? — When Haman requested permission from Ahasuerus to exact vengeance from the Jews, he did so orally, saying, 'If it pleases the king, יִכָּתֵב לְאַבְּדָם, *let it be recorded that they be annihilated.'* At the same time he offered the king a huge sum of money, which implied that he wished to buy them as his slaves. Haman's intention was a clear case of doublespeak. For the word לְאַבְּדָם (with an א), *to annihilate them,* is homophonous with לְעַבְּדָם

(with an ע) *to enslave them.* Thus, if the king would have balked at exterminating such a large segment of the population, Haman would excuse himself by saying, 'I said לְעַבְּדָם not לְאַבְּדָם.' But when Haman instructed the scribes he told them to write לְאַבְּדָם with an א. To avoid any ambiguity when the heralds would announce Haman's plan, he had the scribes add the words לְהַשְׁמִיד לַהֲרֹג, *to destroy, to slay,* to the document (*Oheiv Yisrael*).

☐ וְהָמָן נִבְעַת מִלִּפְנֵי הַמֶּלֶךְ וְהַמַּלְכָּה — *Haman trembled in terror before the king and queen* (7:6).

In the presence of both of them, together, he trembled. Had he been confronted by either of them privately, he could have talked his way out of the bind. To the queen he could have innocently pleaded that he did not know the Jews were her people, but had he known he would never have issued the decree. To the king he could have claimed that, although the Jews were Esther's people, they were nevertheless worthy of extinction. But since both the king and queen were there he couldn't defend himself: How could he tell the king, in the queen's presence, that her people were evil? And how could he say to the queen, in the king's presence, that had he known they were her people, he never would have condemned them? Having said they were thoroughly evil it would have been traitorous for him to allow their survival! Therefore, he trembled in terror, for in their joint presence he was unable to defend himself. But as soon as the king stepped out of the room (v. 7), Haman seized the opportunity to beg for his life by telling Esther that he didn't known the Jews were her people. Before he had a chance to get very far, however, the king returned (*Vilna Gaon*).

☐ וַיֹּאמֶר חַרְבוֹנָה . . . גַּם הִנֵּה הָעֵץ . . . גָּבֹהַּ חֲמִשִּׁים אַמָּה — *And Charbonah said . . . 'Furthermore, the fifty-cubit-high gallows'* (7:9).

The Talmud (*Megillah* 16a) states that Charbonah was among the conspirators to hang Mordechai. Now that he saw that the plot had failed and that Haman was in disfavor, he became his enemy and, before Haman could open his mouth and implicate Charbonah, he advised the king to hang Haman (*Yad Hamelech*).

But how do the Sages know that Charbonah was in on the original plot? — The Maggid of Dubno explained with a parable:

A blind man hired a lad to be his guide. One day, the blind man realized that twenty silver coins were missing from his purse. 'Oh! My money, my money!' cried the hapless one. 'It's gone. How will I ever pay my creditors? Some scoundrel has taken advantage of my handicap and stolen my money.' In his despondency, he cried and cried.

The lad, it was he who had stolen the money, heard his master's cries and became apprehensive. 'Perhaps a policeman will hear his wailing and will come to investigate. Then I will be caught as the thief and jailed.' So he said, 'My master, I have good news for you. I have just found the missing twenty silver coins; here they are.'

The blind man responded by giving the lad a telling blow with his walking stick. 'If you aren't the thief, how do you know exactly what coins were missing?'

Similarly, since Charbonah was able to supply the exact dimensions of the gallows, the Sages realized that he was a co-conspirator.

☐ וְאַתֶּם כִּתְבוּ עַל הַיְּהוּדִים כַּטּוֹב בְּעֵינֵיכֶם — *You may write concerning the Jews whatever you desire* (8:8).

The king gave them *carte blanche* permission not to annul, but to override Haman's decree by wording a new decree in any manner they thought effective. This, of course, faced Mordechai and Esther with the dilemma of framing an edict that would not challenge the legal standing of Haman's decree but that would effectively neutralize it.

They were able to solve this problem by a simple punctuation mark. The original decree stated, לְהַשְׁמִיד לַהֲרֹג וּלְאַבֵּד אֶת כָּל הַיְּהוּדִים, *to destroy, to slay, and to annihilate all the Jews,* which implies genocide of the Jewish people. However, when Mordechai and Esther rewrote the decree, they inserted a pause before the word הַיְּהוּדִים, *the Jews.* Thus, the decree read, 'to destroy, to slay and to annihilate all — the Jews.' That is, the Jews should destroy, etc.

And who placed this stratagem into their heads? — The idea came unwittingly from Ahasuerus himself, when he said, 'You may write concerning הַיְּהוּדִים, i.e., the punctuation of the term הַיְּהוּדִים, whatever you desire' (*Alshich*).

☐ Although Ahasuerus gave permission to override Haman's decree in Nissan, Mordechai and Esther waited more than two months, until the twenty-third of Sivan, before writing the all-important edict with out which death still hovered over the head of the Jews. One reason for the delay is that Mordechai was waiting for the return to Shushan of Haman's couriers. He felt that it was essential for his letters to be delivered by the same couriers. That would add legitimacy to the contents of the second letter, despite the fact that it apparently contradicted the intent of Haman's royal decree (*Yosef Lekach*).

☐ לְהַקָּהֵל — *To organize* (8:11).

Only by organizing and unifying themselves in begging for God's assistance could the Jews be victorious despite being seriously outnumbered (*Yosef Lekach*).

☐ הָרָצִים ... יָצְאוּ מְבֹהָלִים וּדְחוּפִים — *The couriers ... went forth bewildered and in haste* (8:14).

When Haman's decree was dispatched (3:15), the word מְבֹהָלִים, *bewildered,* is not used. The couriers were not at all bewildered by a decree calling for the annihilation of Jews, because Jews are frequently massacred. So when Haman issued his decree they dutifully *went forth in haste.* But here, when Mordechai's decree in favor of, and protecting, the Jews was issued — an act without precedent, — *they went forth bewildered and in haste,* for they did not understand the King's intentions (*Menos HaLevi*).

☐ לַיְּהוּדִים הָיְתָה אוֹרָה — *The Jews had light* (8:16).

Rav Yehudah said: אוֹרָה, *light,* refers to Torah; שִׂמְחָה, *gladness,* to holidays; שָׂשׂוֹן, *joy,* to circumcision; and יְקָר, *honor,* to tefillin (phylacteries) [i.e., they were finally able to resume the study of Torah without hindrance; so with the holidays, circumcision and tefillin] (*Megillah* 16b).

Why, then, didn't the *Megillah* specifically mention that the Jews had 'Torah, holidays, circumcision and *tefillin*'? — The essence of the redemption was that the Jews attained a heightened realization of the true nature of light, gladness, joy, and honor. They once thought that the true source of light is the sun; after the miracle, they realized that Torah is the only true light. Even the most brilliant material light is but a faint approximation in allegorical terms of spiritual light. So it was with the other commandments. The Jews felt gladness, joy, and honor only in the performance of mitzvos (*S'fas Emes*).

☐ אִישׁ וְאֵת פַּרְשַׁנְדָּתָא ... עֲשֶׂרֶת בְּנֵי הָמָן — *Men, including Parshandasa ... the ten sons of Haman* (9:6-10).

In hand-written parchment *Megillos,* the names of Haman's ten sons are written in a column, one under the other, in larger than usual letters. And in some congregations the listeners customarily recite this passage aloud, in addition to the four verses (1:5, 8:15-16; 10:3) universally recited by the congregation. Although not all authorities agree that the listeners should recite the ten-sons' passage (see, e.g., *Chayei Adam*), the Gaon of Rogatchov makes a most ingenious observation about this custom and the use of large letters for writing the passage about the ten sons.

First, he explains that the custom of saying this passage aloud is based on the law requiring the [names of the] ten sons of Haman to be recited with one breath (*Megillah* 16b). With respect to this obligation, he explains, the reader cannot serve as a proxy to fulfill the obligation of the listeners, as he does for the rest of the *Megillah*. The mitzvah of reading in itself may be fulfilled by proxy through the principle, שׁוֹמֵעַ כְּעוֹנֶה, *listening is equal to saying*. But the obligation of one breath cannot be fulfilled by proxy, as the author proves, from various sources.

Having thus established why all the listeners say this section of the *Megillah* aloud, the author cites *Tosafos* (*Berachos* 46b) that the word נֶאֱמָן in the blessings over the *Haftarah* is 'written large' because in earlier times the whole congregation used to stand up and say the words נֶאֱמָן אַתָּה aloud. We see, then, that the use of large letters indicates a passage which the congregation says aloud, and since the passage of ten sons must be said aloud, it must be written with large letters (*Tzafnas Paaneach,* cited in *HaMoadim BeHalachah*).

☐ הַקְּרוֹבִים וְהָרְחוֹקִים — *The near ones and the far ones* (9:20).

All Jews are capable of absorbing the sanctity and spiritual aura of the day, whether they are on an elevated plane, near to heaven, or on a lower one, far from where they should be. Each is able 'to observe and fulfill the days of Purim' (*Munkaczer Rav*).

☐ וּמִשְׁלֹחַ מָנוֹת אִישׁ לְרֵעֵהוּ וּמַתָּנוֹת לָאֶבְיוֹנִים — *For sending delicacies to one another, and gifts to the poor* (9:22).

Why such emphasis on sending presents of food and gifts of charity on Purim, more than any other holiday? — The Mishnah (*Avos* 1:2) teaches that the world stands on three things: Torah study; the Temple service; and kind deeds.

Yet, regarding Purim, the Talmud (*Megillah* 3b) states that reading the *Megillas Esther* supersedes both Torah study and the Temple service. If so, the world remains standing on the single pillar of kind deeds. Hence, we must reinforce that pillar with charity and the exchange of food portions (*Rabbi Avraham Mordechai of Ger*).

עַד דְּלֹא יָדַע / Until He No Longer Knows

The Obligation to Drink

◦§ A man is obligated to drink on Purim until he no longer knows [the difference] between אֲרוּר הָמָן, *cursed be Haman,* and בָּרוּךְ מָרְדְּכַי, *blessed be Mordechai (Megillah* 7b). This well-known statement of Rava is examined by the literature of *halachah* from three aspects: (a) its status as law; (b) its source; and (c) its proper interpretation.

Is the law according to Rava, or not? *Rif* and several other *Rishonim* (early authorities) rule according to Rava. And thus is the *halachah* established in *Tur* and *Shulchan Aruch (Orach Chaim* 695). But the decision was not unanimous. *Baal HaMaor, Ran,* and others cite Rabbeinu Ephraim to the effect that the Talmud in fact rejects Rava's statement as *halachah.* Rabbeinu Ephraim's reason for this conclusion is that the *Gemara* there goes on to tell the following story. Rabbah and Rav Zeira held a Purim feast together, and became drunk. Rabbah rose up and slew Rav Zeira. The next day, he prayed over his slain friend and Rav Zeira came back to life. The following year, Rabbah again invited his colleague to join him for the Purim feast. Rav Zeira sent back the answer: 'It is not every day that a miracle happens.' From the time of this occurrence — according to Rabbeinu Ephraim — Rava's law was annulled. *Bach* adds: It is for this reason that the *Gemara* places the story about Rabbah and Rav Zeira immediately after Rava's pronouncement — to make clear that it is not accepted as *halachah.*

☐ Another interpretation of the story:

A logical argument is brought by *Pri Chadash* against Rabbeinu Ephraim and his adherents. On the contrary, this author argues, from this very story one must draw the opposite conclusion, namely, that the law actually is that one is obligated to become very drunk on Purim, and that is the reason why there were misgivings about holding the Purim feast together a second time — for, in his (obligatory) drunkenness, Rabbah was liable to repeat the sort of deed that would require a miracle to correct it. But if it were true, as Rabbeinu Ephraim claims, that from that event onward Rava's law was annulled, why should Rav Zeira have had misgivings? Let him avoid the danger by not drinking.

Parallels with Esther's Banquet

◈§ *Ksav Sofer* attempts to clarify the position of *Rif*. He presents various approaches, most of them homiletical. One of his explanations is the following: Rava is consistent with his own theories; Rabbah with his; and likewise, the *halachah* follows a consistent theory. How so? The *Gemara* gives a long list of explanations of why Esther invited Haman [to the banquet with King Ahasuerus].

Abaye and Rava answered: '[Her reason was the verse:] בְּחֻמָּם אָשִׁית אֶת מִשְׁתֵּיהֶם וְהִשְׁכַּרְתִּים לְמַעַן יַעֲלֹזוּ וְיָשְׁנוּ שְׁנַת עוֹלָם וְלֹא יָקִיצוּ נְאֻם ה', *In their heat I will make their feasts, and I will make them drunken, that they may rejoice, and sleep an eternal sleep, and not awake, says* HASHEM *(Jeremiah 51:39).* Thus according to Rava's theory, the miracle came about through the drinking of wine, and that is why he says, 'A man is obligated to drink . . . ' One who drinks heavily is then protected by the principle, שׁוֹמֵר מִצְוָה לֹא יֵדַע דָּבָר רָע, *One who keeps a mitzvah shall experience no evil (Ecclesiastes 8:5),* which implies that no mishap can occur through the mitzvah of becoming intoxicated at the Purim feast.

But Rabbah gives an entirely different answer to explain why Esther invited Haman to the banquet, namely, to swell Haman's pride, for לִפְנֵי שֶׁבֶר גָּאוֹן וְלִפְנֵי כִשָּׁלוֹן גֹּבַה רוּחַ, *Pride goes before destruction, and haughtiness of spirit before downfall (Proverbs 16:18),* so that according to Rabbah Haman's drinking was not a factor at all, and not relevant to the miracle. Hence, there is no mitzvah to drink on the day that commemorates the miracle, and one who does drink does not come within the principle, *One who keeps a mitzvah shall experience no evil.* Thus, Rabbah by his own theory did not have the protection of a mitzvah and was susceptible to the mishap that occurred through him.

As for the *halachah*, the *Gemara* relates that Rabbah bar Avuha asked Elijah the Prophet which of the many interpretations given did Esther really have in mind. Elijah replied, '[Her reasons were those of] all the *tannaim* and all the *amoraim*' who had given answers. Since this includes Rava's reason, we see that after all there is a mitzvah to drink on Purim, and one need not fear a mishap, for 'One who keeps a mitzvah will experience no evil.'

Limitations on Drinking

◈§ Rav Ephraim Zalman Margolios, in *Yad Ephraim*, writes that the *Gemara* tells the story of Rabbah and Rav Zeira, not to nullify Rava's *halachah* but on the contrary, to reinforce it. Rava's intention, according to this author, was to set a limit to the drinking. The expression '. . . until he no longer knows the difference between cursed be Haman and blessed be Mordechai' means *to* that point — but not including that point. Thus the story of Rabbah and Rav Zeira comes as a warning example of one who went beyond that point, and experienced a downfall.

☐ The majority of the halachic authorities rule according to Rava. But even those who say that his law is rejected by the Gemara agree that there is a general obligation to eat and drink on Purim. For example, *Shibbolei HaLeket* 201, though ruling in agreement with Rabbeinu Ephraim, nevertheless states that a man is obligated to rejoice on Purim and to regale himself with many kinds of food and drink, as it is written: לַעֲשׂוֹת אוֹתָם יְמֵי מִשְׁתֶּה וְשִׂמְחָה — *that they should make them days of feasting and joy* (*Esther* 9:22). People should eat and drink, rejoice and sing at their own tables and in their friends' houses . . .

This refinement of the concept of joy as being for the sake of thankfulness to *Hashem* is expressed even by those who hold, like Rava, the law of עַד דְּלֹא יָדַע, . . . *until he no longer knows. Sheiltos* (*Vayakhel*), for example, cites Rava's opinion as law, and nevertheless writes: 'All the House of Israel are obligated to eat and drink on Purim and to give thanks and praise to Heaven for all the miracles that the Holy One, Blessed is He, has done for them, as it is written . . . *that they should make them days of feasting and joy.*'

The Source of the Obligation to Eat and Drink

◆§ What is the source of the obligation to rejoice on Purim through eating and drinking? We have seen already that in citing this *halachah*, *Sheiltos* and *Shibbolei HaLeket* based themselves on the verse, *they should make them days of feasting and joy* (*Esther* 9:22). However, in the *Gemara* (*Megillah* 5b) we find that from this phrase — *days of feasting and joy* — only a negative obligation is derived: the prohibition against delivering eulogies and against fasting. Furthermore, the positive mitzvah (of rejoicing) is distinct from the negative one (of not fasting or eulogizing), for the positive obligation of rejoicing applies essentially in each type of city — walled or unwalled — only on the specific Purim date reserved for that city; the unwalled cities on the fourteenth, the walled, on the fifteenth. However, the negative obligation against fasting and eulogizing fully and essentially applies in both types of city on both days.

Nevertheless, while the negative mitzvah is indeed derived from the verse through exegetical reasoning, the positive mitzvah is not such a derivation, but is no less than the simple meaning of the verse itself, מִשְׁתֶּה וְשִׂמְחָה, *feasting and joy.*

Purim vs. Other Festivals

◦§ In fact, we find another place where the Talmud itself makes this assumption: that the simple meaning of the phrase יְמֵי מִשְׁתֶּה וְשִׂמְחָה, *days of feasting and joy,* is that feasting and joy are obligatory on Purim. In Tractate *Pesachim* (68b) there is a dispute whether feasting on the festivals in general is optional or mandatory. Rabbi Eliezer holds that *Yom Tov* is given either כֻּלּוֹ לה׳, *entirely for Hashem* (i.e., for Torah study), or כֻּלּוֹ לָכֶם, *entirely for you* (*Rashi*: 'that one should rejoice on the festival through eating and drinking'); while Rabbi Yehoshua maintains that every festival must include both Torah study and feasting. But, the *Gemara* goes on: All agree (that is, even Rabbi Eliezer) that on Purim 'for you' is obligatory. What is the reason? — The verse says: *days of feasting and joy.*

☐ Concerning the joy of *Yom Tov* in general (an obligation learned from the verse וְשָׂמַחְתָּ בְּחַגֶּךָ, *And you shall rejoice on your festival* (*Deuteronomy* 16:14), the *Gemara* (*Pesachim* 109a) says: 'There is no joy without meat and wine'. Likewise, for Purim. In *Rambam's* words: 'How does one fulfill the obligation of the Purim feast? By eating meat, and serving a good meal in accordance with one's means' (*Hil. Megillah* 2:5). Meat is given to the poor, too, for the Purim feast.

☐ The joy of Purim exceeds that of *Yom Tov* by one feature: 'A man is obligated to drink on Purim until . . .' It would appear that the source of our being 'obligated to drink' is the word מִשְׁתֶּה in the verse about Purim. [This word is usually translated 'feasting,' but its root — שתה — is the word for 'drinking.'] The verse about *Yom Tov* mentions joy alone (וְשָׂמַחְתָּ בְּחַגֶּךָ — *And you shall rejoice on you festival . . .*) while the verse about Purim mentions both *feasting* (i.e., drinking) *and joy.*

The Meaning of the Obligation to Drink

◦§ Even if he had not specified the required amount ('until he no longer knows . . .'), the plain meaning of Rava's word for 'drinking' לִבְסוּמֵי, is 'to become intoxicated.' *Aruch*, the medieval dictionary of the

Talmud, defines the term as 'referring to intoxication'; *Rashi* too, in his comment on Rava's dictum, says the word means 'to become intoxicated with wine.' *Rambam* rules accordingly: 'One must drink wine until he becomes drunk . . .'

However, not all the authorities agree. *Kol Bo* writes: The statement, 'A man is obligated to drink on Purim . . .' does not mean to become intoxicated, for drunkenness is completely forbidden; no sin is worse, for it leads to sexual misconduct and spilling of blood and various other transgressions. Rather, [Rava meant that] one should drink a little more than he is accustomed to, so that he will be very joyful. Thus he will also give joy to the poor, comforting them and speaking to their hearts — and this is joy in its full perfection.

Meiri expresses a view similar to that of *Kol Bo*. *Meiri* says: 'In any case, we are not commanded to become drunk and to lower ourselves in our joy; for the joy we were commanded to experience is not that of wildness and nonsense, but that of pleasure through which one arrives at love of God and thankfulness for the miracles that He has done for us.'

Halachic Definitions of 'Not Knowing'

◆§ What is this required amount defined by 'until he no longer knows . . .,' and what is meant by 'knowing' the difference between 'cursed be Haman' and 'blessed be Mordechai'? The interpretations — in the literature of the *halachah*, in the homiletical insights of *derush*, and in the teachings of Chasidism — have multiplied beyond counting. One scholar of an earlier generation (*VaYitzbor Yosef*) used to give a new interpretation of Rava's statement every year. From centuries of commentary, we shall present a few examples.

Rambam understands Rava to mean: until one falls asleep and thus no longer knows the difference between 'cursed' and 'blessed'. This same idea is expressed, in the name of *Maharal*, by *Rama* in *Shulchan Aruch* (695): . . . one falls asleep, and since he is asleep does not know the difference between 'cursed be Haman' and 'blessed be Mordechai.'

A different interpretation points out that the numerical value of the letters of 'cursed be Haman' (אָרוּר הָמָן) is exactly equal to that of 'blessed be Mordechai' (בָּרוּךְ מָרְדְּכַי); each phrase totals 502. One has become sufficiently drunk when he can no longer do the necessary arithmetic to prove this (*Abudraham; Agudah*).

☐ Two other explanations base themselves on the assumption that in Rava's time there was a *piyyut*, liturgical poem, in which alternate verses ended with the words 'cursed be Haman' and 'blessed be Mordechai.' The first of these explanations says that one needed clear-headed sobriety not to make a mistake in the rhymes (*Minhagim*). The second asserts that one must become drunk to the point that he sometimes begins to confuse the refrains, singing 'blessed be Mordechai' in the verses that should end 'cursed be Haman,' and vice versa (*Bach* citing *Tzeidah LaDerech*).

□ *Taz* takes another approach. A person should give praise to *Hashem* for the twofold good that He did for us: the downfall of Haman and the aggrandizement of Mordechai; and one must continue giving praise joyfully, without interruption, until one can no longer distinguish between the two benefits; at that point the mitzvah has certainly been fulfilled. This last approach tells us the proper measure, not of drinking, but of time: one should not cease acknowledging *Hashem's* benefits until he can no longer distinguish between those benefits. A similar definition in terms of time is given by the author of *Sfas Emes*. He says that the obligation to drink applies throughout the entire day, unless one reaches the point of 'he no longer knows . . .' at which time the obligation is fulfilled.

Interpretations in Works of Derush

◆§ So much for halachic works. Interpretations have multiplied also — or even more so — in the homiletical books of *derush*. One such book is *Yaaros Devash*, in which the author approaches Rava's statement in various ways. One of these is as follows. At first sight, it seems that one may raise an objection to the whole idea of 'cursed be Haman' and 'blessed be Mordechai.' The objection is that these two phrases are contradictory and mutually exclusive. If Haman is cursed, then it cannot be that Mordechai is blessed; and likewise, if Mordechai is blessed, it cannot be that Haman is cursed. How so? If Ahasuerus did not himself desire the decree לְהַשְׁמִיד לַהֲרֹג וּלְאַבֵּד — *to destroy, kill, and annihilate* (*Esther* 3:13), but was simply duped by Haman's trickery and lies, then certainly 'cursed be Haman' — but on the other hand there was no need for any extraordinary exertions on the part of Mordechai. For if even the least of the servants had revealed to the king that Haman wished to spill the innocent blood of an entire people, this would have been sufficient to turn all the king's wrath against Haman.

But perhaps, on the contrary, there was evil in the heart of Ahasuerus towards the Jews, and he himself wished to be rid of them, as we find in the Talmud: To what may Ahasuerus and Haman be compared? To the story of two men, one of whom had a mound in the midst of his field, while the other had a ditch in the midst of his. The owner of the ditch thought, 'If only I could purchase that mound' the owner of the mound thought, 'If only I could purchase that ditch.' After a time, the two got together. Said the owner of the ditch to the owner of the mound, 'Sell me your mound.' He answered him, 'Take it for nothing, and good riddance.' If this was the case, that Ahasuerus was only waiting for an opportunity to get rid of the Jews, then certainly 'blessed be Mordechai' for preventing him, but now there is no justification for 'cursed be Haman' for, even without Haman, the king did not lack agents. Thus, the two phrases in Rava's dictum cannot be true at once.

Now the real meaning of the drinking on Purim is to know how to distinguish one kind of drinking from another — by understanding the reason for drinking, to know when to drink and when not to. This is just what the Jews of Mordechai and Esther's time did not do; instead, they sinned by enjoying the feast of that wicked king.

This, then, is the true meaning of the two phrases. 'Cursed be Haman' in that he tempted Israel by means of a feast, hoping that they should sin; and 'blessed be Mordechai' who admonished them not to drink, as the Sages expound: לַעֲשׂוֹת כִּרְצוֹן אִישׁ וְאִישׁ, . . . that they should do according to each man's will (ibid.) — the expression each man means Mordechai (who wished that they should not drink) and Haman (who wished that they should).

Thus, we can arrive at a measure of how much one should drink on Purim. One should drink until one no longer understands the correct explanation of 'cursed be Haman' and 'blessed be Mordechai' — that it refers to the original feast of Ahasuerus, whose 'law' was arranged by Haman — and hence cannot answer the objection posed before, that the two phrases are seemingly contradictory. At this point one certainly need drink no more, for one can thus no longer understand why he drinks.

Family and Personal Purims

~§ Individuals — and certainly whole towns — who had been threatened with disaster but were miraculously delivered may institute a personal 'Purim' for themselves and their offspring on the anniversary of that event. (Note that *Pri Chadash* disputes this ruling.) The annual *seudah* in honor of that miracle has the status of a *seudas mitzvah* ... (as attested to by *Yam shel Shlomo*, Bava Kamma #37; *Chayei Adam* 155:41).

The Danzig Family Purim

~§ Rabbi Avraham Danzig, author of *Chayei Adam*, concludes that volume with the above-quoted paragraph, then relates an incident in his lifetime in which he fulfilled that *halachah*:

And thus, we [i.e., the Danzig family] celebrate the sixteenth day of Kislev in commemoration of the miracle wrought for us on that day in the year 5564 (November 30, 1803). A great fire broke out [in Vilna] in the courtyard where I live when a cask of gunpowder exploded. Many lives were lost and many building were destroyed, including one that I owned. [Rabbi Danzig had always refused to receive a salary for teaching and other rabbinic functions. Although he was a member of Vilna's *beis din*, he supported his family as a successful merchant.] The room in which most members of my family were sitting at the time of the explosion suffered great damage. A ceiling beam and parts of two walls collapsed. My daughter Vitka was trapped beneath the rubble and only a hair's breadth separated her from death. My wife sustained open wounds to her face, her upper lip had multiple lacerations, and all her bottom teeth were broken. I was in another room with my son; the windows and door were smashed and the walls split open. My son's back was gashed in two places by the debris. Not one of us escaped without a loss of blood.

Hashem, in His great mercy and compassion, considered our blood as if it were the blood of an atonement offering. He watched over us and we all remained alive. My monetary losses at that time reached several thousand rubles — *Hashem* had exchanged דָּמִים for דָּמִים [the word דָּמִים means 'money' but is also the plural form of דָּם, *blood*, thus, God exacted money instead of blood]. Although we were saved, due to our copious sinfulness thirty-one people perished in our courtyard ...

The obvious Providence shown the survivors is too great for words; whoever was worthy of being saved was saved, while many outsiders 'happened to be' in the courtyard and were killed. *Hashem's* eyes view the ways of each man individually.

In order to relate the wondrous deeds of *Hashem*, in fulfillment of the verse, *He has made a memorial for His wonder (Psalms 111:4)*, I have undertaken (but without the stringency of an oath) upon myself and my offspring to dedicate at least half of each sixteenth of Kislev to *Hashem* [i.e., to spend at least half the day in prayer and Torah study] and, for those who are able, to fast . . . On the night following, immediately after *Maariv*, all of us are to assemble, light candles as on other festivals [without reciting a blessing, of course], and to chant the entire שִׁיר הַיִּחוּד, *Song of Unity*, and שִׁיר הַכָּבוֹד, *Song of Glory*, and sixteen psalms (111, 116, 117, 23, 34, 66, 100, 103, 121, 130, 134, 138, 139, 143, 148, 150). Then, whoever can afford to is to serve a *seudah* for Torah students, and to give charity in proportion to the assets with which *Hashem* has blessed him. May *Hashem* heal His people's afflictions.

[This day is sometimes called Pulver ('powder') Purim.]

The Tosefos Yom Tov's Purim

◆§ Rabbi Yom Tov Lipmann Heller, best known for his magnum ·opus *Tosefos Yom Tov* on the Mishnah, was a rabbi in Prague. During the Thirty Years' War (1618-1648), heavy taxes were placed upon the Jewish communities of Bohemia to help offset the cost of the war. Collection of the tax was left to the Jewish community leaders and rabbis, among whom the *Tosefos Yom Tov* held a prominent position. A loan with which to pay the tax was obtained and each Jew was assessed and ordered to pay his share.

Many of the poorer members of the community opposed the assessment. They accused Rabbi Yom Tov of favoring the wealthy and tried in vain to have him removed from office. When their efforts failed, some of them resorted to slander. They accused him before Emperor Ferdinand II of showing open contempt for the state and of insulting Christianity.

On the fifth of Tammuz 5389 (June 25, 1629) he was imprisoned and a court of Catholic priests pronounced the death sentence on him and banned all of his books. However, the emperor commuted this sentence and imposed a large fine instead. Rabbi Yom Tov was also prohibited from serving as a rabbi in Prague. Additionally, the ban placed on his books by the tribunal of priests was lifted; but the offensive fragments, upon which his conviction was based, were ordered deleted.

Forty days after being imprisoned, the *Tosefos Yom Tov* was released and returned to Prague. He established the fifth of Tammuz as a fast day for all the members of his family. He also wrote a volume, *Megillas Eivah* ('Scroll of Enmity'), in which he relates the details of his accusation, imprisonment and acquittal.

Other Family Purims

◄§ On the tenth of Adar 5370 (1710) David Brandeis, a shopkeeper in Mlada Boleslav, Bohemia, and his family were saved from death after being accused of killing a gentile by serving him poison plum jam. This day has become known as Povidl ('plum jam') Purim.

☐ On the first of Iyar, the Segal family of Cracow celebrates their rescue from almost drowning while escaping from a pogrom in 5417 (1657).

☐ The Meyuchas family of Jerusalem observes their personal Purim on the sixteenth of Adar in commemoration of the day in 5584 (1724) on which their forebear Raphael Meyuchas escaped from death at the hands of highwaymen.

☐ The oldest family Purim on Record is probably the one celebrated on the first day of Elul, in memory of Shmuel HaNaggid's escape from a conspiracy to kill him in the year 4799 (1039).

Local Purims

◄§ Historians record almost a hundred Special Purims each of which is commemorated by either an entire country or city.

☐ One of the most famous of these is Purim Saragossa (in Northeast Spain). On the seventeenth of Shevat 5180 (1420), an informer accused the Jews of mocking King Alfonso V by carrying empty Torah cases at a reception for the king. When the cases were confiscated and found to contain scrolls, the Jews were saved from certain punishment. A scroll describing the miraculous salvation was written at that time.

☐ The Jews of Algiers celebrate Purim Edom on the fourth of Cheshvan and Purim Tammuz on the eleventh of Tammuz. On those days in 5301 (1541) and 5535 (1775) respectively, the Algerian Jewish community was spared when the Turkish rulers repulsed the Spanish invaders who, had they won the war, would certainly have devastated the Jewish quarter.

☐ Ancona, a seaport in Italy, was struck by an earthquake on the twenty-first of Teves 5440 (December 29, 1690). The Jewish community miraculously escaped destruction, and Purim Ancona is celebrated on that day.

☐ A rioting mob attacked the Jewish community of Avignon, France, on the eighth of Shevat 5517 (1757), but the Jews enjoyed Providential protection and escaped. That day became a holiday in Avignon.

☐ In 5284 (1524), governor Ahmed Pasha of Cairo, Egypt, attempted to extort a large sum of money from the Jewish director of the mint, Abraham Castro. Ahmed threatened to eradicate the Jewish community of Cairo if he did not receive the money by the twenty-eighth of Adar. On that very day, Ahmed was assassinated by his own soldiers who were loyal to the sultan against whom the governor was planning a rebellion. That day is celebrated as Purim Mitzrayim by Egyptian Jews.

☐ Frankfort on the Main, Germany, was the scene of a ruthless attack on the Jewish ghetto in the year 5374 (August 5, 1614). Vincent Fettmilch, an anti-Jewish guild leader, led a mob which forced all Jews to leave the city. The emperor issued an order for Fettmilch's arrest, and on March 16, 1616, the "new Haman" along with six of his henchmen were hanged. The Jews were ceremoniously returned to the city and established the twentieth of Adar as Purim Winz (Vincent), also called Purim Fettmilch.

Masquerading On Purim

◆§ One of the best known and most popular customs of Purim is disguising oneself in gentile garb or otherwise masquerading as someone we are not. Various reasons are given as the basis of this practice.

The Talmud relates Rabbi Shimon bar Yochai's response to his disciples' question: Why were the Jews of that generation sentenced to death?

He replied, 'You tell me!'

They said, 'Because they derived pleasure from the evil one's [i.e., Ahasuerus'] banquet.'

'If so,' he asked, 'only those in Shushan should have been sentenced, not those who lived elsewhere?'

They said, 'Then you tell us!'

He replied, 'Because they bowed to the idol in the days of Nebuchadnezzar (see *Daniel* ch. 3).'

'But does God show favoritism in this matter? [If they bowed, they were truly deserving of death. If so, why were they exonerated?]'

'They only bowed for outward appearance [in fear of the king's wrath]. Similarly, God only threatened them for outward appearance]!' (*Megillah* 12a).

Thus it has become customary to change our outward appearance on Purim (*Bnei Yisaschar* cited in *Taamei HaMinhagim*).

God's Hidden Face

◆§ The Talmud (*Taanis* 9a) states the principle: There is no matter mentioned in the Writings that is not alluded to in the Pentateuch.

Based on this, the Talmud (*Chullin* 139b) asks: 'Where is there an allusion to Esther in the Torah?' And answers, 'The verse states, וְאָנֹכִי הַסְתֵּר אַסְתִּיר פָּנַי, *And I shall surely hide My face!* (*Deuteronomy* 31:18).'

Thus we see that a 'hidden face' is in the spirit of Purim.

Earlier Masquerades

◆§ Haman was not the first Jew-hater in his family. He was a member of the Amalekite nation whose history of hatred began even before the birth of its forebear Amalek. Esau, grandfather of Amalek, harbored deep and malicious hate for his brother Jacob. Esau justified that feeling by pointing to the blessing that Jacob 'stole' from him. At that time Jacob, under instructions from their mother Rebecca, disguised himself as Esau. By masquerading as gentiles on Purim, we acknowledge that Jacob's action was completely righteous, and that the blessings truly belonged to him.

Moreover, it was Esau's practice to mask his true intentions with a slick tongue, as the verse states: כִּי צַיִד בְּפִיו, *for there was entrapment in his mouth* (*Genesis* 25:28).

Amalek's Disguise

◦§ During the fortieth year of the nation's sojourn in the Wilderness, Aaron died. The Clouds of Glory that had protected the people dispersed, for they had been granted in the merit of Aaron.

Amalek, sensing that the Jews were now devoid of Divine protection, decided to attack. However, they feared the Jewish power of prayer, for they had seen how, forty years earlier, Moses' prayers has caused Amalek's downfall (see *Exodus* 17:8-16). To avert another defeat, the Amalekite warriors donned Canaanite clothing. They figured, 'When the Jews see us coming against them, they will pray to be delivered from the Canaanite army — a vain supplication.'

Before they were able to attack however, the Israelite scouts penetrated their lines and overheard them speaking to each other in the Amalekite tongue. When the scouts reported back to the Jewish camp, the nation prayed, 'We don't know whether we are facing Amalek or Canaan. Please, *Hashem*, save us from our foe, whomever they may be.

This is another source of the custom of disguising ourselves on Purim when we 'remember' the mitzvah of eradicating the memory of Amalek.

Other Allusions

◦§ *Matzreif Dahava* relates the custom of masquerading on Purim to the many events in the Purim story involved changes of clothing:
— Vashti refused to appear before the king without any (*Esther* 1:12, see *Rashi*).
— Each maiden brought to Ahasuerus could request any wardrobe she thought might make her attractive to him (2:13).
— Mordechai and the Jews rent their garments and donned sackcloth (4:1-3).
— Esther sent Mordechai a change of clothes, but he refused to accept it (4:4).
— Esther dressed herself in royal gowns before approaching Ahasuerus (5:1).
— Haman was forced to dress Mordechai royally and parade him around town (6:10-11).
— Haman's face was covered with a veil when Ahasuerus turned against him after Esther's accusation (7:8, see *Ibn Ezra*).
— Mordechai left the king's presence clad in royal apparel of blue

and white with a large crown and a robe of fine linen and purple (*Esther* 8:15).

Purim In Gematria

In almost every alphabet, each letter is assigned a particular place in the sequence of letters. Most of today's languages developed from earlier, ancient tongues, and not all bothered to keep the internal structure of their alphabets the same as that of the borrowed-from languages. Moreover, even the arrangements of letters in the earlier alphabets had neither scientific nor logical bases.

The Holy Tongue, however, assigns each letter its position among the others based upon the unique numerical value of that letter. Thus, the א, with a value of one, is first; ב, two, is second; and ג, three, is third. A complete table of these values appears below. This system of numbers is called *gematria*. Thus, the *gematria* of ג is three.

$$\text{א} = 1 \quad \text{ב} = 2 \quad \text{ג} = 3 \quad \text{ד} = 4 \quad \text{ה} = 5 \quad \text{ו} = 6 \quad \text{ז} = 7 \quad \text{ח} = 8$$
$$\text{ט} = 9 \quad \text{י} = 10 \quad \text{כ} = 20 \quad \text{ל} = 30 \quad \text{מ} = 40 \quad \text{נ} = 50 \quad \text{ס} = 60$$
$$\text{ע} = 70 \quad \text{פ} = 80 \quad \text{צ} = 90 \quad \text{ק} = 100 \quad \text{ר} = 200 \quad \text{ש} = 300 \quad \text{ת} = 400$$

☐ A natural consequence of this correlation between letters and numbers is the *gematria* of words. That is, the total of the numerical equivalents of the respective letters of the word. For example, the gematria of אַבָּא, *father* is four (1 + 2 + 1).

☐ *Gematria* often plays a significant role in Torah study on levels of רֶמֶז, *allusion,* דְּרוּשׁ, *exegesis,* and סוֹד, *kabbalistic teachings.* In some rare cases it is used in determining the פְּשַׁט, *simple meaning,* of a verse. And an occasional *halachah*, law, is supported through a *gematria* proof. Some examples of *gematriaos* related to Purim follow below.

127 Provinces

The *Vilna Gaon* cites a Midrash that locates one hundred of Ahasuerus' provinces on continental land masses. The remaining twenty-seven were islands in the sea. He then cites the verse, *King Ahasuerus levied (מַס) a tax on the land (וְאִיֵּי) and the islands of the sea* (*Esther* 10:1) as proof of this statement. The gematria of מַס, *tax*, is 100; and the gematria of וְאִיֵּי, *and the islands*, is 27.

מס = 40 + 60 = 100

ואיי = 6 + 1 + 10 + 10 = 27

This verse may then be interpreted: *King Ahasuerus had* מַס, *100 on the mainland,* וְאִיֵּי, *and 27 in the sea.*

On The Sabbath

◦§ Vashti was killed on the Sabbath, because God always metes out punishment, measure for measure. Every Sabbath day Vashti would strip her Jewish maids of their clothing and force them to work. Therefore, on the Sabbath, God caused the king to demand that she appear in public stripped of her clothing (*Megillah* 12b).

Arameiz Badavar finds in Vashti's name an allusion to her profanation of the Sabbath. The *gematria* of וַשְׁתִּי, 716, is the same as that of שַׁבָּת בָּזָה, *she insulted the Sabbath.*

ושתי = 6 + 300 + 400 + 10 = 716

שבת בזה = 300 + 2 + 400 + 2 + 7 + 5 = 716

Haman — Remembrance Of Amalek

◦§ After the first battle against Amalek, HASHEM *said to Moses, '. . . I shall surely eradicate the remembrance of Amalek . . .'* (*Exodus* 17:14).

Baal HaTurim notes that this verse alludes to Haman, for the words מָחֹה אֶמְחֶה, *I shall surely eradicate,* have the same *gematria* as זֶה הָמָן, *this is Haman,* 107.

מחה אמחה = 40 + 8 + 5 + 1 + 40 + 8 + 5 = 107

זה המן = 7 + 5 + 5 + 40 + 50 = 107

Only The Crown

◦§ When Ahasuerus asked Haman what to do for the man he wished to honor, Haman thought the king was referring to him (*Esther* 6:6). And since the king had already raised Haman above all the other officials in his kingdom (3:1), Haman lacked nothing. In fact, he considered himself on a par with Ahasuerus. [Even his name alluded to royalty: הָמָן, *Haman,* has a *gematria* of 95, the same as הַמֶּלֶךְ, *the king* (Arameiz Badavar).] The one thing Haman did not have was the king's crown. And that he coveted greatly. So Haman replied that the man the king desires to honor should be dressed royally 'with the royal crown on his head' (6:8). However, when he mentioned this part of the reward,

Ahasuerus' face reddened. Haman did not refer to the crown again, nor did he place it on Mordechai's head (see *Rashi* to 6:9).

Arameiz Badavar points out an allusion to Haman's lust for the crown, the only thing separating him from the king:

The first time Haman is mentioned in *Megillas Esther* (3:1), he is called, הָמָן בֶּן הַמְּדָתָא הָאֲגָגִי, *Haman son of Hammedasa the Agagite.* The *gematria* of this phrase is 619, exactly one less than the *gematria* of כֶּתֶר, *crown* — 620.

המן בן המדתא האגגי = 5 + 40 + 50 + 2 + 50 + 5 + 40 + 4 + 400 + 1 + 5 + 1 + 3 + 3 + 10 = 619

כתר = 20 + 400 + 200 = 620

The Test Of Sobriety

⮜ The Talmudic dictum, חַיָּב אָדָם לִבְסוּמֵי בְּפוּרְיָא עַד דְּלֹא יָדַע, בֵּין אָרוּר הָמָן לְבָרוּךְ מָרְדְּכַי, *A man is obligated to become intoxicated on Purim until he does not know the difference between 'cursed be Haman' and 'blessed be Mordechai,'* is the subject of much halachic dispute (see above pages 64-70) regarding the amount one must actually drink to fulfill his obligation.

According to *Abudraham* one is required to drink enough so that the will become too intoxicated to be able to compare two columns of figures to determine whether they are equal. The Talmud expresses this tersely as the difference between אָרוּר הָמָן, *cursed be Haman,* and בָּרוּךְ מָרְדְּכַי, *blessed be Mordechai,* two phrases with the same *gematria,* 502.

ארור המן = 1 + 200 + 6 + 200 + 5 + 40 + 50 = 502.

ברוך מרדכי = 2 + 200 + 6 + 20 + 40 + 200 + 4 + 20 + 10 = 502.

Pesachyah/Mordechai

⮜ A Mishnah states: פְּתַחְיָה, *Pesachyah,* was [the administrator] over the bird offerings [in the Temple]. This Pesachyah is Mordechai [of the Purim story]. Why is he called Pesachyah? Because he was able to open up (פָּתַח) mysteries and investigate them (*Shekalim* 5:1).

Pachad Yitzchak (cited in *Taamei HaMinhagim*) presents a riddle based on this Mishnah:

'Pesachyah is Mordechai' conforms to the verse, *Though your beginning will be small, your end will increase greatly* (*Job* 8:7)!!

The solution to this riddle is that the first three letters of Mor-dechai, מרד, have the respective *gematriaos* 40, 200, 4. These are ex-actly half of the *gamatriaos* of the corresponding letters of Pesachyah, פתח — 80, 400, 8. The last two letters of Mordechai כי, have *gematriaos* exactly double those of the corresponding letters of *Pesachyah* י-ה — 10, 5. Thus, *Though your beginning* מרד *will be very* small (only half of פתח), *your end* כי *will increase greatly* (double as much as י-ה.

✒ Selected Laws and Customs

◄§ Selected Laws And Customs

This digest cannot cover all eventualities and should be regarded merely as a guide to enable the reader to familiarize himself with the complex laws of the mitzvos central to Purim. It should not be taken as a substitute for the source texts, but as a learning and familiarizing tool. For halachic questions, one should consult the *Shulchan Aruch* and its commentaries and/or a halachic authority.

The laws and customs have been culled, in the main, from the most widely accepted authorities: the *Shulchan Aruch Orach Chaim* [here abbreviated O.C.] and *Mishnah Berurah* [M.B.].

When a particular *halachah* is in dispute, we generally follow the ruling of *Mishnah Berurah*. On occasion, however (usually when *Mishnah Berurah* does not give a definitive ruling), we cite other opinions.

◄§ Adar

1. When Adar begins, we increase in joyousness (*Taanis* 29a; M.B. 686:8).

2. If a Jew has a court case pending against a gentile, he should try to have it adjudicated during the month of Adar (*Taanis* 29b; M.B. 686:8).

◄§ Taanis Esther

3. In the days of Mordechai and Esther, the Jews gathered on the thirteenth of Adar to defend themselves and to take vengeance upon their enemies. To accomplish this they had to seek God's compassion and help. Therefore they repented, fasted and prayed for Divine assistance on that day. In remembrance, all Israel has accepted that day as a fast day through the generations.

This fast is called תַּעֲנִית אֶסְתֵּר, *the*

Fast of Esther, as a reminder that *Hashem* sees and hears the plight and prayer of every person in the time of his straits, if he fasts and returns to God wholeheartedly, as our ancestors did in those days (M.B. 686:2).

4. Nevertheless, this fast is less stringent than the four fasts mentioned in the Prophets (10 Teves, 17 Tammuz, 9 Av, 3 Tishrei). Therefore it is proper to be lenient when necessary, as in the case of pregnant women, nursing mothers, a woman within the first thirty days of childbirth, or a person whose eyes ache painfully. Such people should not fast. Nevertheless they should repay the fast by fasting at some later date (O.C. 686:2; M.B. 4). Additionally, a groom during his seven days of *Sheva Berachos* (i.e., the first seven days after marriage) need not fast (*Kitzur Shulchan Aruch* 141:2).

5. Despite the leniencies mentioned above, all other healthy

people should participate in this communal fast. Even travelers who find the fast difficult must nevertheless fast (O.C. 686:2; M.B. 6).

6. When the thirteenth of Adar falls on the Sabbath, the fast is observed on the previous Thursday, the eleventh of Adar (O.C. 686:2).

ﻋ Purim Eve

7. The home should be prepared before Purim as before every Yom Tov: the table should be set for the evening meal; candles should be lit (but no blessing recited); and Sabbath clothing should be worn in honor of the *Megillah* reading (O.C. 695:2).

ﻋ Machatzis HaShekel

8. It is customary for every man to donate מַחֲצִית הַשֶּׁקֶל, a *half-shekel*, before Purim, as a remembrance of the half-shekel head tax of Temple times [for the purchase of communal Temple offerings]. Since the shekel is not used universally as currency, we use a 'half' coin of the established currency in the particular country and time that it is given. [Thus, in the United States today, half dollar coins are used.] Custom calls for each man to donate three half-shekels. The coins are customarily donated before *Minchah* on the day before Purim (O.C. 694:1).

A boy who has not reached his legal majority (i.e., his thirteenth birthday; according to some views, his twentieth birthday) is exempt from *machatzis hashekel*; however, his father may donate for him if he

wishes to, and this is the preferred custom. Moreover, once the father has done so, he *must* continue to donate for his minor son in subsequent years (O.C. 694:1; M.B. 5).

ﻋ Maariv

9. The regular weekday *Maariv* is recited — with עַל הַנִּסִּים inserted into the *Modim*, Thanksgiving, blessing of *Shemoneh Esrei*. If this prayer was omitted, *Shemoneh Esrei* should not be repeated (O.C. 693:2; 682:1). However, if the omission is discovered before the word HASHEM in the concluding formula (בָּרוּךְ אַתָּה ה' הַטּוֹב . . .) has been said, one should return to עַל הַנִּסִּים and proceed from there (O.C. 682:1). [One who has omitted עַל הַנִּסִּים may, if he so desires, recite עַל הַנִּסִּים after the verse יִהְיוּ לְרָצוֹן at the conclusion of *Shemoneh Esrei*. (M.B. 683:4).]

During בִּרְכַּת הַמָּזוֹן, *Grace after Meals*, the עַל הַנִּסִּים prayer is recited during the second blessing, which begins נוֹדֶה לְךָ. If it is forgotten, and the omission is not discovered until after the word HASHEM in the concluding formula, *Bircas HaMazon* should be continued until the end of the paragraph בַּמָּרוֹם. Then the phrase הָרַחֲמָן (הוּא) יַעֲשֶׂה לָנוּ נִסִּים וְנִפְלָאוֹת כְּשֵׁם שֶׁעָשִׂיתָ לַאֲבוֹתֵינוּ בַּיָּמִים הָהֵם בַּזְּמַן הַזֶּה should be recited, followed by בִּימֵי מָרְדְּכַי (O.C. 682:1, however, the version printed in most *siddurim* varies slightly from this wording).

After *Shemoneh Esrei*, the *chazzan* recites the Full *Kaddish*, and the *Megillah* is read (see below). After the *Megillah* reading, וְאַתָּה קָדוֹשׁ is recited [on Saturday night וַיְהִי נֹעַם and וְאַתָּה קָדוֹשׁ followed by וְיִתֶּן לְךָ and הַבְדָּלָה (in those *shuls* that usually recite these during *Maariv*)] and the chazzan repeats *Kaddish*, but this time omitting the verse תִּתְקַבֵּל (*O.C.* 693:1; *M.B.* 1).

◈§ The Megillah Reading

10. Every man and woman is obligated to hear the *Megillah* reading at night and again by day. Therefore, even those single girls who do not usually attend synagogue services should go to the shul on Purim, or have the *Megillah* read for them at home (*O.C.* 687:1; 689:1; *M.B.* 689:1).

11. Parents are obligated to bring even young children to *shul* to train them in the mitzvah of hearing the *Megillah* reading. However, very young children who tend to disrupt the services and disturb the congregants should not be brought to the synagogue (*O.C.* 689:1,6; *M.B.* 17-18).

12. The nighttime *Megillah* reading may not begin before nightfall (צֵאת הַכּוֹכָבִים), even for one who is weak from fasting. Although ideally one should not break the fast until after the *Megillah* reading, one who is in pain may ease his hunger with a cup of coffee or even an egg-sized piece of bread before the reading (*O.C.* 682:4; *M.B.* 14).

13. The preferable place to hear the *Megillah* is in the synagogue, in accordance with the verse,

A multitude of people is the King's glory (*Proverbs* 14:28). If this is not possible, at least a *minyan* of ten adult men should be present (*O.C.* 690:18; *M.B.* 64). If even this is impossible, each individual should read the *Megillah* from a kosher scroll and recite the three blessings (see #15 below) that precede it. But if only one of those present knows how to read it, he should read it and the others should listen to his reading with the intention to fulfill their obligation (*O.C.* 689:5).

The blessing recited after the *Megillah* reading is recited only in the presence of a *minyan* (*O.C.* 692:1).

14. The synagogue reader customarily unrolls his *Megillah* and folds it column over column before reading from it. This is in accordance with the verse that calls the *Megillah* אִגֶּרֶת הַפּוּרִים, *the Purim Letter*. (In ancient time, an אִגֶּרֶת was folded or bound, and a מְגִלָּה was rolled.) Those listening, however, do not have to fold their *Megillos* (*O.C.* 690:17; *M.B.* 55).

15. Before reading the *Megillah*, both at night and by day, the reader recites three blessings: עַל מִקְרָא מְגִלָּה, *regarding the reading of the Megillah*; שֶׁעָשָׂה נִסִּים, *who has wrought miracles*; and שֶׁהֶחֱיָנוּ, *who has kept us alive* [the full text appears on page 97] (*O.C.* 692:1).

After the reading, the *Megillah* is rolled up and the blessing הָרָב אֶת רִיבֵנוּ, *Who takes up our grievance*, is recited [p. 132] (*O.C.* 692:1; 690:17).

16. The reader of the *Megillah* must have in mind that his reading will fulfill the obligation of those who listen to it. Similarly, the listener must intend to fulfill his obligation (*O.C.* 689:2; *M.B.* 4). Moreover, the listener must hear every word, for even a one-word lapse invalidates his fulfillment, and he must hear the *Megillah* reading again from the missed word on (*O.C.* 690:3; *M.B.* 5). Therefore, the reader should be careful not to begin reading after Haman's name until the tumult has stopped completely; otherwise, some congregants may miss a word (*M.B.* 690:60).

17. It is advisable for each congregant to have a kosher *Megillah* scroll before him, so that he may read along in an undertone. In this way he will be certain not to miss a single word. If this is not possible, the listener should follow the reading from a printed *Megillah*, but should not read along. Nevertheless, he may read a word or phrase from the printed *Megillah* if he was unable to hear the reader because of the noise (*M.B.* 690:60).

18. One who is following the reading from an invalid scroll or from a printed volume should not read aloud for two reasons: (a) It is difficult to concentrate on someone else's words while speaking; and (b) another person may mistake this one's voice for the reader and concentrate on listening to it, thus not fulfilling his obligation (*O.C.* 690:4; *M.B.* 13).

19. During the public reading, four verses are recited aloud by the congregation and repeated by the reader. They are: . . . אִישׁ יְהוּדִי (2:5); . . . וּמָרְדְּכַי יָצָא (8:15); הָיְתָה (8:16); and . . . כִּי מָרְדֳּכַי (10:3) but see #21 below (*O.C.* 690:17). Among the reasons for this custom are: (a) פִּירְסוּמֵי נִיסָא, *broadcasting the miracle;* since these verses are all seminal passages in the Purim story, reciting them aloud serves to underscore and announce the miracles that took place (*M.B.* 689:16); (b) just as various customs have arisen at the Pesach Seder to keep the children awake until the end, so too does this public recitation keep the children alert and attentive (ibid.); (c) the verses are read aloud as an additional expression of the joy of the day (*M.B.* 690:58).

20. When the reader reaches the verse, בַּלַּיְלָה הַהוּא (6:1), he should raise his voice, for the main part of the miracle begins there. And when he reaches הָאִגֶּרֶת הַזֹּאת (9:26), he should raise or shake the *Megillah* slightly (*M.B.* 690:52).

21. The reader should recite the passage that names Haman's ten sons, . . . [חֲמֵשׁ מֵאוֹת אִישׁ] וְאֵת וַיְזָתָא עֲשֶׂרֶת (9:6-10) in one breath, to indicate that they were hanged simultaneously. However, if he fails to do so the reading remains valid (*O.C.* 690:15).

In some synagogues this passage is recited aloud by the congregation before the reader reads them. Some authorities endorse this custom; others censure it (see *M.B.* 690:52).

22. If one has fulfilled his obligation and will read the *Megillah* for someone who did not hear the *Megillah* yet, many authorities maintain that the listener should recite the blessings. However, others state that it is customary for the reader to recite the blessings even in this case (*O.C.* 692:3; *M.B.* 11).

23. When the *Megillah* is read for a woman or group of women, with no man fulfilling his obligation through that reading, the blessings are recited by the reader, with the first blessing changed from עַל מִקְרָא מְגִלָּה, *regarding the reading of the Megillah*, to לִשְׁמוֹעַ מְגִלָּה, *to hear the Megillah*, for many authorities maintain that a woman is obligated to hear the reading, but not to read it (*M.B.* 682:11).

◈ Purim On The Sabbath

24. When Purim coincides with the Sabbath (such as Sushan Purim in Jerusalem) a *Megillah* scroll is *muktzeh* and may not be moved. On any other Sabbath a *Megillah* scroll is not *muktzeh* and may be moved. However, when Purim falls on a Saturday night, the *Megillah* may not be brought to the synagogue on the Sabbath, even in a locality where there is a valid *eruv*. Such carrying is classified as מֵכִין מִשַּׁבָּת לְחוֹל, *preparing for a weekday on the Sabbath*, and is forbidden (*Machatzis HaShekel* 682).

◈ Shacharis

25. The weekday *Shacharis* is recited with the addition of

עַל הַנִּסִּים in the *Shemoneh Esrei* [if forgotten, see #9 above] (*O.C.* 693:2). During the *chazzan's* repetition, some congregations recite *Krovetz*.

26. After the *chazzan's* repetition, the *chazzan* recites Half *Kaddish*. תַּחֲנוּן and אֵל אֶרֶךְ אַפַּיִם are omitted. Unlike Chanukah and the Three Pilgrimage Festivals, *Hallel* is not recited (*O.C.* 693:3).

The Torah is read — the passage of וַיָּבֹא עֲמָלֵק (*Exodus* 17:8-16); Half *Kaddish* is recited; the Torah is returned to the Ark; and the *Megillah* is read (*O.C.* 693:4).

The *tefillin* should not be removed before the *Megillah* reading, even if one has completed the *Shacharis* service (*M.B.* 693:6)

27. As at the nighttime reading the reader recites three blessing before reading the *Megillah* (*O.C.* 692:1). The שֶׁהֶחֱיָנוּ blessing of the daytime reading also applies to the other mitzvos of the day — *matanos la'evyonim*, *shalach manos*, and the festive meal (see below). Therefore, both the reader and the listeners should have these *mitzvos* in mind when the blessing is recited (*M.B.* 692:1).

All other laws of the nighttime reading apply to the daytime reading (see #10-11, #13-23, above).

28. After the morning reading, the blessing הָרָב אֶת רִיבֵנוּ is recited; the *piyut* אֲשֶׁר הֵנִיא is omitted, but שׁוֹשַׁנַּת יַעֲקֹב is recited (*O.C.* 692:1).

29. *Shacharis* concludes in the usual weekday manner, except that לַמְנַצֵחַ (psalm 20) is omitted (O.C. 693:3).

❧ Mishloach Manos

30. In recording the mitzvah of mishloach manos (also called shalach manos) the Megillah states וּמִשְלֹחַ מָנוֹת אִישׁ לְרֵעֵהוּ, and for sending food portions each man to his friend (9:22). The plural מָנוֹת, food portions, implies at least two portions, while the singular רֵעֵהוּ, his friend, implies one recipient. Thus the minimum fulfillment of mishloach manos requires the presentation of two foods to one person (O.C. 695:4). Nevertheless, it is praiseworthy not to stint, but to increase both the size of the gift and the number of gifts sent [but see #34 below] (Rambam, Hil. Megillah 2:15).

Moreover, מָנוֹת indicates ready-to-eat food and drink. Therefore it is proper to send cooked meats or fish, baked goods, wine and other beverages, fruit or vegetables (even raw, if that is how they are usually eaten, e.g., apples or cucumbers), deserts, candies, etc. However, food that must be prepared by the recipient [such as raw potatoes, unbaked dough, or coffee power] cannot be used to fulfill the obligation (M.B. 695:20).

31. Both men and women are obligated in mishloach manos. Some women rely upon their husband's shalach manos to fulfill their obligation, and vice versa, but this is not proper. Rather, each spouse should send portions to at least one friend. Moreover, it is improper for a man to exchange

gifts with a woman. Therefore, a man should send to a man, and a woman should send to a woman (O.C. 695:4).

❧ Matanos La'evyonim

32. Purim's special charity obligation is called מַתָּנוֹת לָאֶבְיוֹנִים, gifts to poor people (Esther 9:22). The plural מַתָּנוֹת, gifts, implies at least two gifts (usually money), while the plural אֶבְיוֹנִים, poor people, implies at least two recipients. Therefore, the gifts must be given to two paupers, i.e., a separate gift to each (O.C. 694:1).

33. On Purim one should not investigate whether someone requesting alms is really needy. Rather, 'whoever stretches out his hand to receive, we give him' (O.C. 694:3).

34. Although one can discharge his obligation by giving a single penny to each of two paupers, one should strive to give with an open hand increasing both the quality and quantity of his charity.

When one is presented with the opportunity to increase either his matanos laevyonim or his mishloach manos, but does not have the resources to do both, one should minimize his mishloach manos and maximize his matanos laevyonim. For there is no greater more praiseworthy cause for joy before God than gladdening the hearts of the poor, the orphaned and the widows (Rambam, Hil. Megillah 2:17).

35. One living in an area where there are no poor is not absolved of this mitzvah. He should set aside two sums of money to be given to a poor person when the opportunity presents itself (*O.C.* 694:4). Or he should send a messenger to deliver the money on Purim (*Kitzur Shulchan Aruch* 142:3). Many authorities maintain that when there are no poor people in town the money can be placed into a charity box earmarked for distribution to the poor.

◅§ Seudah

36. Everyone is obligated to eat, drink and be joyous on Purim day. Although the main mitzvah is during the day, it is proper to celebrate to some degree on the preceding night also. However, the nighttime festivities do not replace or fulfill the daytime obligations, for the *Megillah* (9:22) states יְמֵי מִשְׁתֶּה, *fast days* (*O.C.* 695:1).

37. Some customarily eat pulse (seeds, beans, lentils and the like) in remembrance of the foods eaten by Daniel and his comrades in Babylon [see *Daniel* 1:12], and by Esther in Shushan [see *Megillah* 13a] (*O.C.* 695:2).

38. The mitzvos of *mishloach manos, matanos la'evyonim* and *seudas Purim* are all daytime obligations (*M.B.* 692:1). Moreover, since the שֶׁהֶחֱיָנוּ blessing at the *Megillah* reading also applies to these *mitzvos*, it is preferable that they be performed after the reading.

39. *Minchah* should be recited early in the afternoon to allow enough time for the majority of the Purim meal to be eaten while it is yet day. It is also proper that the meal extend a bit into the night (*O.C.* 695:2).

40. When Purim falls on Friday, the *seudah* should be eaten in the morning so that it not interfere with the Sabbath Eve meal (*O.C.* 692:2).

41. Since many aspects of the Purim miracle involved wine — Vashti's downfall at the King's winefest; the banquet at Esther's coronation; Bigsan and Teresh's plot to poison the king's wine; Haman's downfall at Esther's party — the Sages ordained, חַיָב אִינָש לבסומי בְּפוּרְיָא עַד דְּלֹא יָדַע בֵּין אָרוּר הָמָן לְבָרוּךְ מָרְדְכָי, *a man should drink wine on Purim until he cannot distinguish between 'cursed is Haman' and 'blessed is Mordechai'* (*Megillah* 7b). That is, he should drink at least enough more than usual that he should become drowsy, fall asleep, thus being unable to distinguish between Haman and Mordechai (*O.C.* 692:2; *Biur Halachah*).

However, one who is unable to tolerate wine and one who is apprehensive that wine will bring him to neglect the blessings or prayers, or will in any other way weaken his mitzvah observance, should refrain from drinking more than a minimum. Thus, all his actions will be for the sake of Heaven (*Chayei Adam* 155:30).

⮑ Eulogies And Fasting

42. Eulogies and fasting are forbidden on both Purim and Shushan Purim (O.C. 696:3).

⮑ Mourners

43. One who is ר״ל sitting *shivah* is obligated in *mishloach manos* and *matanos laevyonim*, but should not send anything more than simple fare (O.C. 696:6; M.B. 18).

Overt displays of mourning, such as removal of the shoes and sitting on the floor or a low stool, are not performed on Purim. Nevertheless, private acts, such as refraining from cohabitation, are in force (O.C. 696:4; M.B. 12).

Mishloach manos and other presents should not be sent to mourners during their entire mourning period — twelve months after a parent; thirty days after other relatives (O.C. 696:6; M.B. 20).

⮑ Shushan Purim / Walled Cities

44. In a city which is walled since the days of Joshua ben Nun, all the laws of Purim apply to the fifteenth of Adar, rather than the fourteenth (O.C. 688:1). [The only city to which this rule applies with certainty is the Old City of *Yerushalayim*.] Many cities in *Eretz Yisrael* have questionable status. Thus they follow the majority of cities by reading the *Megillah* on the fourteenth of Adar. On the fifteenth, they read it again, but this time without reciting a blessing (O.C. 688:4).

45. The 15th of Adar is called Shushan Purim. When the Jews of Ahasuerus' provinces stood up to defend themselves and destroy their enemies, they fought on the 13th of Adar, then rested and celebrated on the 14th. But the Jews of Shushan were given an extra day to avenge themselves of their foe. They fought on the 13th and 14th, then rested and celebrated on the 15th. Although the special *mitzvos* of Purim do not apply during Shushan Purim (except as detailed in #42-43 above), a vestige of yesterday's festivities does remain: the prayers תַּחֲנוּן אֵל אֶרֶךְ אַפַּיִם, and לַמְנַצֵּחַ (psalm 20) are omitted (M.B. 693:8); some rejoicing and festive eating is customary. However, עַל הַנִּסִּים is not recited. Nevertheless, if עַל הַנִּסִּים was recited by mistake, such recitations not considered an interposition and does not disqualify either *Shemoneh Esrei* or *Bircas HaMazon* (O.C. 693:2; M.B. 6).

⮑ Leap Year

46. In a leap year, Purim is celebrated during the second Adar. Nevertheless, the 14th and 15th of the first Adar are called Purim Kattan. On these days, תַּחֲנוּן אֵל אֶרֶךְ אַפַּיִם and לַמְנַצֵּחַ (psalm 20) are omitted, and eulogies and fasting are prohibited (O.C. 697:1).

⮑ Pesach

47. We ask questions regarding [i.e., we begin studying] the laws of Pesach thirty days before Pesach (O.C. 429:1), on the day of Purim (M.B. 2).

✺§ Observance

Megillas Esther*
Targum Sheni**
Psalm 22***

* This section is reprinted from *The Book of Megillos,* translated and annotated by Rabbi Meir Zlotowitz, Mesorah Publications Ltd.

** This section is reprinted from *Tz'enah Ur'enah,* vol. II, translated by Miriam Stark Zakon, Mesorah Publications Ltd.

*** This section is abridged from *Tehillim,* by Rabbi Avrohom Chaim Feuer, Mesorah Publications Ltd.

A Book for the Ages

One of the great Chassidic masters of the last century remarked that because the festival of Purim was proclaimed during a period of Jewish exile, it has special meaning to Jews in a time of diaspora *(S'fas Emes).* The Book of Esther tells a thrilling, spellbinding story. What a pity that it is so familiar that it no longer thrills us as it should. At the very least, however, let us look at the ancient tale and see how much it speaks to our time, for our Sages saw in it the kind of lessons from which the nation should learn — or which it will be doomed to repeat.

The Twentieth Century has given a new relevance not only to the genocidal intention of Haman, but to his method of pursuing it. No longer can anyone say — as some did a hundred years ago — that modern society could never produce, much less condone, a monster whose announced intention was 'to destroy, to slay, and to exterminate all Jews, young and old, children and women, in a single day ...' *(Esther* 3:13). How naive it now seems that people seriously believed that mass extermination of human beings could never be contemplated by civilized people. Now we know that Haman was the first, but, lamentably, surely not the last. Nor have we recovered from the Holocaust perpetrated by the modern Haman, who came six million souls closer to achieving his goal than did his ancient model.

How striking and ominously familiar were Haman's arguments to gain Ahasuerus' acquiescence. As given briefly in the Book of Esther (3:8-9) and amplified by the Talmudic Sages, Haman's diatribe has been echoed by anti-Semites throughout the ages: Jews are separatists, elitists, racists. They hold themselves apart from all other peoples of the realm. They will not blend into our culture or religion. They are damaging to the unity of the kingdom. Why should the King tolerate their divisive presence — is it worth the price? Would not the world be better served if this nuisance, this friendless nation, were removed from our midst? And, finally, the state will derive an immense economic benefit from the disappearance of this pariah people.

So sophisticated a discourse to justify such a foul end! But it should not surprise anyone. Throughout our history, we have been similarly maligned and our oppressors have indignantly insisted that they were forced to take heroic measures to defend themselves against little Israel. The laws of the Third Reich were carefully phrased in terms that deceived many a naive observer into believing that a tormented nation — call it Persia, Spain, Russia, Germany, or the United Nations — was

אסתר

merely seeking to protect itself from an internal cancer.

What ignited Haman's anger? There are two answers: the obvious one and the true one. The obvious one was Mordechai's obstinacy. Proud Jew that he was, Mordechai refused to bow to Haman, who, as tradition teaches, brazenly paraded with an image of his idol dangling from his neck. Mordechai insisted that there had to be at least one Jew who would not sacrifice dignity on the altar of expediency; would Haman love Israel any more if even Mordechai's knees scraped the ground in obeisance to a pagan deity? The infuriated Haman sought revenge in the annihilation not only of Mordechai but of his entire people. And the pundits of the time surely reveled in the charge that 'stiff-necked' Mordechai was to blame for Israel's catastrophe.

But, as the Sages teach, that was not the *true* reason for the destruction that threatened Israel. Nine years earlier the Jews had ignored the warnings of Mordechai and his fellow sages not to indulge in forbidden foods and acts at the lavish feast of Ahasuerus. Let Jews be loyal to their government — yes; but let them not set aside their Torah to do so. The people would not listen. They argued that Ahasuerus would never understand their abstinence. He would accuse them of disloyalty, of planning secret conspiracies to return to *Eretz Yisrael*. If their loyalties were to Jerusalem rather than Shushan, they would be branded traitors, and the punishment for treason is ...

Dare we antagonize a paranoid, insecure monarch like Ahasuerus? Dare we place our nation's survival at risk by antagonizing a king whose caprices are notorious? And when Ahasuerus ordered the execution of his beloved Queen Vashti simply because she refused to disgrace herself publicly to satisfy his whim — did that not prove that we were wise and right not to provoke his mercurial anger?

On the divine scales, however, Mordechai's judgment was right. Jews do not survive by committing spiritual suicide. For if a Jews lacks pride in his Jewishness, by what virtue does he deserve the right to preserve his separate identity?

The nation had precipitated its own downfall by an act of cowardly faithlessness; only by a parallel act of communal courage could it save itself. Mordechai began the process by defying Haman's decree to bow. *His* knee would not bend. *He* would not grovel. Then came Esther's turn.

Unknown to King Ahasuerus or his viceroy Haman, Queen Esther was a Jewess, and Mordechai demanded that she intercede with the King. She hesitated. Logic dictated that she wait for a more opportune moment to plead with Ahasuerus (see 4:9-11). But Mordechai would

esther

not accept her argument. Could it be that she was somewhat complacent because *she* enjoyed the safety of anonymity and the security of the throne? After all, Ahasuerus had not the slightest suspicion that his beloved was a member of the race he had consigned to the pyre of history. Would she have been so 'rational' if *she* had been in as much jeopardy as her brethren?

Mordechai replied harshly to Esther, 'Do not imagine that you will be able to escape in the King's palace any more than the rest of the Jews. For if you persist in keeping silent at a time like this, relief and deliverance will come to the Jews from some other place, while you and your father's house will perish. And who knows whether it was just for such a time as this that you attained the royal position!' (4:13-14).

A new insight into communal responsibility: To help one's fellow Jews is a privilege, not a chore. The nation will always survive somehow, but the one who spurns its entreaties will himself be doomed. And furthermore, no matter how exalted someone's position or lavish his fortune, let him always regard it as but a means to serve the common good. Now Esther knew why she had been raised to the throne — to save her people, and if she failed to do so she might well be condemning *herself* to oblivion, while another path to salvation would surely open for them.

Esther was more than equal to the challenge, and her bravery, dedication, and cunning precipitated a swiftly moving series of events that brought new glory to her people, and that doomed Haman. But even this is not the primary lesson of Purim.

Amazingly, God's Name does not even appear in the *Megillah* — and precisely that is its lesson: God's ways are not always obvious, His miracles are most often not illuminated by lightning nor punctuated by thunder. In the concisely written 167-verse *Megillah,* no seas split, no heavens roar, no dry bones come to life. But in the truest sense the greatest of all miracles is narrated in the Purim story — the miracle of God's constant supervision and control of events.

With the period of Esther and Mordechai, a new emphasis was added to Jewish history. We had to find God's hand not in the splitting sea or heavenly fire, but in everyday events.

The story of the *Megillah* spanned nine years, and only at the very end did the pieces of God's jigsaw puzzle begin coming together. Suddenly widely separate links began to move together to form a chain and widely separated chains joined to become the anchor upon which Jewish survival was secured. And simple logic turned out to be wrong; Mordechai had been right all along.

One set of links: Ahasuerus' feast led to the execution of Vashti, which led to the coronation of Esther. Because Esther was Queen, she was in a position to approach the King to save her people and she could lull Haman into complacency by inviting him to her private banquet.

Another set of links: Bigsan and Teresh plotted to kill Ahasuerus. Because Esther had secured a royal appointment for Mordechai, he was positioned to overhear them and report the scheme to Esther. She told the King of Mordechai's loyalty. It was inscribed in the royal chronicle, there to lay forgotten until the fateful night when God disturbed the King's sleep.

A third set of links: The King promoted Haman and everyone was required to bow to him, but Mordechai refused. Assured of his power and influence — even with the Queen! — Haman built a gallows and sought royal permission to hang Mordechai, just when Ahasuerus learned that it was Mordechai who had once saved his life.

When the appropriate climactic time arrived, the pieces of God's jigsaw puzzle came together and formed the destruction of Haman and most of Amalek, and salvation for the Jews.

The events of those ancient days determine the mode of Purim's annual observance. The *Megillah* is read morning and evening, and all Jews are required to hear it; its lesson is too important to be restricted only to those who attend the synagogue regularly. Even people who are unable to attend should arrange to have the *Megillah* read for them from a ritually valid scroll. And when we hear the reading, let us remember the eternal lesson beneath the rousing story.

The celebration of Purim is unique among Jewish festivals. Purim is celebrated with an excess of food, drink, and frivolity, because we are marking a time when our *physical* lives were threatened, unlike other festivals that commemorate primarily *spiritual* dangers and salvations.

Furthermore, Purim is a holiday of Jewish fellowship as well, because among the tools that forged the miracle were a sense of communal responsibility, a sense of concern for the plight of every Jew. So the requirements of the day include gifts to friends and to the poor. For indeed, we are one and we must take positive steps to remain one.

As *S'fas Emes* taught, Purim is indeed aimed primarily at Jews without their Temple, for it shows them how to live and survive in a hostile environment where survival is in question, and where God's Presence seems to be absent. Thanks to Purim, we feel more secure about survival and we can 'see' God's hand even where He is invisible.

esther

❊{ BLESSINGS OVER THE MEGILLAH READING / בְּרְכוֹת הַמְּגִלָּה

Before reading *Megillas Esther* on Purim, the reader recites the following three blessings.
The congregation should answer אָמֵן, *Amen,* only [not בָּרוּךְ הוּא וּבָרוּךְ שְׁמוֹ] after each, and should have
in mind that they wish to fulfill the obligation of reciting the blessings themselves.
Absolutely no conversation is permitted from the beginning of the first blessing until the conclusion of
the final blessing following the *Megillah* reading.

בָּרוּךְ אַתָּה יהוה אֱלֹהֵינוּ מֶלֶךְ הָעוֹלָם, אֲשֶׁר קִדְּשָׁנוּ
בְּמִצְוֹתָיו, וְצִוָּנוּ עַל מִקְרָא מְגִלָּה.   (.אָמֵן—Cong.)

בָּרוּךְ אַתָּה יהוה אֱלֹהֵינוּ מֶלֶךְ הָעוֹלָם, שֶׁעָשָׂה נִסִּים
לַאֲבוֹתֵינוּ, בַּיָּמִים הָהֵם, בַּזְּמַן הַזֶּה.   (.אָמֵן—Cong.)

בָּרוּךְ אַתָּה יהוה אֱלֹהֵינוּ מֶלֶךְ הָעוֹלָם, שֶׁהֶחֱיָנוּ, וְקִיְּמָנוּ,
וְהִגִּיעָנוּ לַזְּמַן הַזֶּה.   (.אָמֵן—Cong.)

Blessed are You, HASHEM, our God, King of the universe, Who has sanctified us with His commandments and has commanded us regarding the reading of the Megillah.   (Cong.—Amen.)

Blessed are You, HASHEM, our God, King of the universe, Who has wrought miracles for our forefathers, in those days at this season.   (Cong.—Amen.)

Blessed are You, HASHEM, our God, King of the universe, Who has kept us alive, sustained us, and brought us to this season.   (Cong.—Amen.)

א וַיְהִי בִּימֵי אֲחַשְׁוֵרוֹשׁ הוּא אֲחַשְׁוֵרוֹשׁ הַמֹּלֵךְ מֵהֹדּוּ וְעַד־כּוּשׁ שֶׁבַע וְעֶשְׂרִים וּמֵאָה מְדִינָה:

ב בַּיָּמִים הָהֵם כְּשֶׁבֶת | הַמֶּלֶךְ אֲחַשְׁוֵרוֹשׁ עַל כִּסֵּא מַלְכוּתוֹ אֲשֶׁר בְּשׁוּשַׁן הַבִּירָה:

ג בִּשְׁנַת שָׁלוֹשׁ לְמָלְכוֹ עָשָׂה מִשְׁתֶּה לְכָל־שָׂרָיו וַעֲבָדָיו חֵיל | פָּרַס וּמָדַי הַפַּרְתְּמִים וְשָׂרֵי הַמְּדִינוֹת לְפָנָיו:

ד בְּהַרְאֹתוֹ אֶת־עֹשֶׁר כְּבוֹד מַלְכוּתוֹ וְאֶת־יְקָר תִּפְאֶרֶת גְּדוּלָּתוֹ יָמִים רַבִּים שְׁמוֹנִים וּמְאַת יוֹם:

ה וּבִמְלֹאת | הַיָּמִים הָאֵלֶּה עָשָׂה הַמֶּלֶךְ לְכָל־הָעָם הַנִּמְצְאִים בְּשׁוּשַׁן הַבִּירָה לְמִגָּדוֹל וְעַד־קָטָן מִשְׁתֶּה שִׁבְעַת יָמִים בַּחֲצַר גִּנַּת בִּיתַן הַמֶּלֶךְ:

ו חוּר | כַּרְפַּס וּתְכֵלֶת אָחוּז בְּחַבְלֵי־בוּץ וְאַרְגָּמָן עַל־גְּלִילֵי כֶסֶף וְעַמּוּדֵי שֵׁשׁ מִטּוֹת | זָהָב וָכֶסֶף עַל רִצְפַת בַּהַט־וָשֵׁשׁ וְדַר וְסֹחָרֶת:

ז וְהַשְׁקוֹת בִּכְלֵי זָהָב וְכֵלִים מִכֵּלִים שׁוֹנִים וְיֵין מַלְכוּת רָב כְּיַד הַמֶּלֶךְ:

ח וְהַשְּׁתִיָּה כַדָּת אֵין אֹנֵס כִּי־כֵן | יִסַּד הַמֶּלֶךְ עַל כָּל־רַב בֵּיתוֹ לַעֲשׂוֹת כִּרְצוֹן אִישׁ־וָאִישׁ:

ט גַּם וַשְׁתִּי הַמַּלְכָּה עָשְׂתָה מִשְׁתֵּה נָשִׁים בֵּית הַמַּלְכוּת אֲשֶׁר לַמֶּלֶךְ אֲחַשְׁוֵרוֹשׁ:

י בַּיּוֹם הַשְּׁבִיעִי כְּטוֹב לֵב־הַמֶּלֶךְ בַּיָּיִן אָמַר לִמְהוּמָן בִּזְּתָא חַרְבוֹנָא בִּגְתָא וַאֲבַגְתָא זֵתַר וְכַרְכַּס שִׁבְעַת הַסָּרִיסִים הַמְשָׁרְתִים אֶת־פְּנֵי הַמֶּלֶךְ אֲחַשְׁוֵרוֹשׁ:

יא לְהָבִיא אֶת־וַשְׁתִּי הַמַּלְכָּה לִפְנֵי הַמֶּלֶךְ בְּכֶתֶר מַלְכוּת לְהַרְאוֹת הָעַמִּים וְהַשָּׂרִים אֶת־יָפְיָהּ כִּי־טוֹבַת מַרְאֶה הִיא:

יב וַתְּמָאֵן הַמַּלְכָּה וַשְׁתִּי לָבוֹא בִּדְבַר הַמֶּלֶךְ

1/1. THE FEASTS OF AHASUERUS

— successor to Cyrus toward the end of the 70 years of the Babylonian exile [4th Century B.C.E.].

3. *In the third year:* 3395 from Creation.

According to his (erroneous) calculation, the seventieth year of the Jews' exile had passed, thus belying the prophets who had foretold the exile's end after seventy years, and Ahasuerus rejoiced in this frustration of Jewish hope; he had completed the building of his magnificent throne; he was finally secure in his reign; he took Vashti as his queen. Thus the causes for such a lavish feast *(Midrash).*

6. The letter ת has the numerical value of 8. In the *Megillah* the ת of the word חור, *white garments,* is enlarged to imply that on that climactic day Ahasuerus adorned himself with the eight garments of the High Priest. In punishment for this, he suffered the multiple evils of the resulting episode with Vashti, her death, his embarrassment, and his subsequent depression *(Alkabetz).*

9. VASHTI REFUSES THE KING'S SUMMONS

Vashti was the daughter of Belshazzar, and granddaughter of Nebuchadnezzar.

11. *Wearing the royal crown.* She was to wear *only* the royal crown, i.e., she was to be unclothed *(Midrash).*

Vashti refused, not because of modesty, but because God caused leprosy to break out on her, paving the way for her downfall *(Midrash).*

¹ **A**nd it came to pass in the days of Ahasuerus — the Ahasuerus who reigned from Hodu to Cush over a hundred and twenty-seven provinces — ² that in those days, when King Ahasuerus sat on his royal throne which was in Shushan the Capitol, ³ in the third year of his reign, he made a feast for all his officials and his servants; the army of Persia and Media, the nobles and officials of the provinces being present; ⁴ when he displayed the riches of his glorious kingdom and the splendor of his excellent majesty for many days — a hundred and eighty days. ⁵ And when these days were fulfilled, the King made a week-long feast for all the people who were present in Shushan the Capitol, great and small alike, in the court of the garden of the King's palace. ⁶ There were hangings of white, fine cotton, and blue wool, held with cords of fine linen and purple wool, upon silver rods and marble pillars; the couches of gold and silver were on a pavement of green and white, and shell and onyx marble. ⁷ The drinks were served in golden goblets — no two goblets alike — and royal wine in abundance, according to the bounty of the King. ⁸ And the drinking was according to the law, without coercion, for so the King had ordered all the officers of his house that they should do according to every man's pleasure.

⁹ Vashti the Queen also made a feast for the women in the royal house of King Ahasuerus. ¹⁰ On the seventh day, when the heart of the King was merry with wine, he ordered Mehuman, Bizzetha, Charbona, Bigtha and Abagtha, Zethar, and Carcas, the seven chamberlains who attended King Ahasuerus, ¹¹ to bring Vashti the Queen before the King wearing the royal crown, to show off to the people and the officials her beauty; for she was beautiful to look upon. ¹² But Queen Vashti refused to come at the King's commandment

אֲשֶׁר בְּיַד הַסָּרִיסִים וַיִּקְצֹף הַמֶּלֶךְ מְאֹד וַחֲמָתוֹ
יג בָּעֲרָה בוֹ: וַיֹּאמֶר הַמֶּלֶךְ לַחֲכָמִים
יֹדְעֵי הָעִתִּים כִּי־כֵן דְּבַר הַמֶּלֶךְ לִפְנֵי כָּל־יֹדְעֵי
יד דָת וָדִין: וְהַקָּרֹב אֵלָיו כַּרְשְׁנָא שֵׁתָר אַדְמָתָא
תַרְשִׁישׁ מֶרֶס מַרְסְנָא מְמוּכָן שִׁבְעַת שָׂרֵי | פָּרַס
וּמָדַי רֹאֵי פְּנֵי הַמֶּלֶךְ הַיֹּשְׁבִים רִאשֹׁנָה בַּמַּלְכוּת:
טו כְּדָת מַה־לַּעֲשׂוֹת בַּמַּלְכָּה וַשְׁתִּי עַל | אֲשֶׁר לֹא־
עָשְׂתָה אֶת־מַאֲמַר הַמֶּלֶךְ אֲחַשְׁוֵרוֹשׁ בְּיַד
הַסָּרִיסִים: וַיֹּאמֶר °מוּמְכָן לִפְנֵי °מְמוּכָן ק' טז
הַמֶּלֶךְ וְהַשָּׂרִים לֹא עַל־הַמֶּלֶךְ לְבַדּוֹ עָוְתָה
וַשְׁתִּי הַמַּלְכָּה כִּי עַל־כָּל־הַשָּׂרִים וְעַל־כָּל־
הָעַמִּים אֲשֶׁר בְּכָל־מְדִינוֹת הַמֶּלֶךְ אֲחַשְׁוֵרוֹשׁ:
יז כִּי־יֵצֵא דְבַר־הַמַּלְכָּה עַל־כָּל־הַנָּשִׁים לְהַבְזוֹת
בַּעְלֵיהֶן בְּעֵינֵיהֶן בְּאָמְרָם הַמֶּלֶךְ אֲחַשְׁוֵרוֹשׁ
אָמַר לְהָבִיא אֶת־וַשְׁתִּי הַמַּלְכָּה לְפָנָיו וְלֹא־
בָאָה: וְהַיּוֹם הַזֶּה תֹּאמַרְנָה | שָׂרוֹת פָּרַס־וּמָדַי יח
אֲשֶׁר שָׁמְעוּ אֶת־דְּבַר הַמַּלְכָּה לְכֹל שָׂרֵי הַמֶּלֶךְ
יט וּכְדַי בִּזָּיוֹן וָקָצֶף: אִם־עַל־הַמֶּלֶךְ טוֹב יֵצֵא דְבַר־
מַלְכוּת מִלְּפָנָיו וְיִכָּתֵב בְּדָתֵי פָרַס־וּמָדַי וְלֹא
יַעֲבוֹר אֲשֶׁר לֹא־תָבוֹא וַשְׁתִּי לִפְנֵי הַמֶּלֶךְ
אֲחַשְׁוֵרוֹשׁ וּמַלְכוּתָהּ יִתֵּן הַמֶּלֶךְ לִרְעוּתָהּ
כ הַטּוֹבָה מִמֶּנָּה: וְנִשְׁמַע פִּתְגָם הַמֶּלֶךְ אֲשֶׁר־
יַעֲשֶׂה בְּכָל־מַלְכוּתוֹ כִּי רַבָּה הִיא וְכָל־הַנָּשִׁים
כא יִתְּנוּ יְקָר לְבַעְלֵיהֶן לְמִגָּדוֹל וְעַד־קָטָן: וַיִּיטַב
הַדָּבָר בְּעֵינֵי הַמֶּלֶךְ וְהַשָּׂרִים וַיַּעַשׂ הַמֶּלֶךְ כִּדְבַר
כב מְמוּכָן: וַיִּשְׁלַח סְפָרִים אֶל־כָּל־מְדִינוֹת הַמֶּלֶךְ

conveyed by the chamberlains; the King therefore became very incensed and his anger burned in him.

13. THE KING SEEKS ADVICE

¹³ Then the King conferred with the experts who knew the times (for such was the King's procedure [to turn] to all who knew law and judgment. ¹⁴ Those closest to him were Carshena, Shesar, Admasa, Tarshish, Meres, Marsena and Memuchan, the seven officers of Persia and Media, who had access to the King, and who sat first in the kingdom—) ¹⁵ as to what should be done, legally, to Queen Vashti for not obeying the bidding of the King Ahasuerus conveyed by the chamberlains.

16. MEMUCHAN'S SUGGESTION

'Memuchan is Haman. Why was he called Memuchan? Because he was destined [מוּכָן] for destruction' (Talmud).

¹⁶ Memuchan declared before the King and the officials: 'It is not only the King whom Vashti the Queen has wronged, but also all the officials and all the people in all the provinces of King Ahasuerus. ¹⁷ For this deed of the Queen will come to the attention of all women, making their husbands contemptible in their eyes, by saying: "King Ahasuerus commanded Vashti the Queen to be brought before him but she did not come!" ¹⁸ And this day the princesses of Persia and Media who have heard of the Queen's deed will cite it to all the King's officials, and there will be much contempt and wrath. ¹⁹ If it pleases the King, let there go forth a royal edict from him, and let it be written into the laws of the Persians and the Medes, that it be not revoked, that Vashti never again appear before King Ahasuerus; and let the King confer her royal estate upon another who is better than she. ²⁰ Then, when the King's decree which he shall proclaim shall be resounded throughout all his kingdom — great though it be — all the wives will show respect to their husbands, great and small alike.' ²¹ This

21. VASHTI IS DEPOSED

This proposal pleased the King. 'He gave the order and they brought in her head on a platter' (Midrash).

proposal pleased the King and the officials, and the King did according to the word of Memuchan; ²² and he sent letters into all the King's provinces,

אֶל־מְדִינָה וּמְדִינָה כִּכְתָבָהּ וְאֶל־עַם וָעָם
כִּלְשׁוֹנוֹ לִהְיוֹת כָּל־אִישׁ שֹׂרֵר בְּבֵיתוֹ וּמְדַבֵּר
כִּלְשׁוֹן עַמּוֹ:   אַחַר הַדְּבָרִים הָאֵלֶּה   **ב**   א
כְּשֹׁךְ חֲמַת הַמֶּלֶךְ אֲחַשְׁוֵרוֹשׁ זָכַר אֶת־וַשְׁתִּי
וְאֵת אֲשֶׁר־עָשָׂתָה וְאֵת אֲשֶׁר־נִגְזַר עָלֶיהָ:
וַיֹּאמְרוּ נַעֲרֵי־הַמֶּלֶךְ מְשָׁרְתָיו יְבַקְשׁוּ לַמֶּלֶךְ   ב
נְעָרוֹת בְּתוּלוֹת טוֹבוֹת מַרְאֶה: וְיַפְקֵד הַמֶּלֶךְ   ג
פְקִידִים בְּכָל־מְדִינוֹת מַלְכוּתוֹ וְיִקְבְּצוּ אֶת־כָּל־
נַעֲרָה־בְתוּלָה טוֹבַת מַרְאֶה אֶל־שׁוּשַׁן הַבִּירָה
אֶל־בֵּית הַנָּשִׁים אֶל־יַד הֵגֶא סְרִיס הַמֶּלֶךְ שֹׁמֵר
הַנָּשִׁים וְנָתוֹן תַּמְרֻקֵיהֶן: וְהַנַּעֲרָה אֲשֶׁר תִּיטַב   ד
בְּעֵינֵי הַמֶּלֶךְ תִּמְלֹךְ תַּחַת וַשְׁתִּי וַיִּיטַב הַדָּבָר
בְּעֵינֵי הַמֶּלֶךְ וַיַּעַשׂ כֵּן: אִישׁ יְהוּדִי   ה
הָיָה בְּשׁוּשַׁן הַבִּירָה וּשְׁמוֹ מָרְדֳּכַי בֶּן יָאִיר בֶּן־
שִׁמְעִי בֶּן־קִישׁ אִישׁ יְמִינִי: אֲשֶׁר הָגְלָה   ו
מִירוּשָׁלַיִם עִם־הַגֹּלָה אֲשֶׁר הָגְלְתָה עִם יְכָנְיָה
מֶלֶךְ־יְהוּדָה אֲשֶׁר הֶגְלָה נְבוּכַדְנֶצַּר מֶלֶךְ בָּבֶל:
וַיְהִי אֹמֵן אֶת־הֲדַסָּה הִיא אֶסְתֵּר בַּת־דֹּדוֹ כִּי אֵין   ז
לָהּ אָב וָאֵם וְהַנַּעֲרָה יְפַת־תֹּאַר וְטוֹבַת מַרְאֶה
וּבְמוֹת אָבִיהָ וְאִמָּהּ לְקָחָהּ מָרְדֳּכַי לוֹ לְבַת: וַיְהִי   ח
בְּהִשָּׁמַע דְּבַר־הַמֶּלֶךְ וְדָתוֹ וּבְהִקָּבֵץ נְעָרוֹת
רַבּוֹת אֶל־שׁוּשַׁן הַבִּירָה אֶל־יַד הֵגָי וַתִּלָּקַח
אֶסְתֵּר אֶל־בֵּית הַמֶּלֶךְ אֶל־יַד הֵגַי שֹׁמֵר הַנָּשִׁים:
וַתִּיטַב הַנַּעֲרָה בְעֵינָיו וַתִּשָּׂא חֶסֶד לְפָנָיו וַיְבַהֵל   ט
אֶת־תַּמְרוּקֶיהָ וְאֶת־מָנוֹתֶהָ לָתֵת לָהּ וְאֵת שֶׁבַע
הַנְּעָרוֹת הָרְאֻיוֹת לָתֶת־לָהּ מִבֵּית הַמֶּלֶךְ וַיְשַׁנֶּהָ

to each province in its own script, and to each people in its own language, to the effect that every man should rule in his own home, and speak the language of his own people.

2/1. AHASUERUS SEEKS A NEW QUEEN

He remembered the order he had given her to appear unclothed before him and how she had refused, and how he had been wroth with her and had put her to death *(Midrash)*.

5. MORDECHAI AND ESTHER

This verse is among the four verses recited aloud in the synagogue by the congregation during the public reading of the *Megillah*.

7. The names Hadassah and Esther are both descriptive of her virtues. Hadassah is derived from the Hebrew word הֲדַס — the sweet-smelling 'myrtle'; Esther from אִסְתְּהַר — *'as beautiful as the moon'* (Talmud).

8. ESTHER IS BROUGHT TO THE HAREM

¹**A**fter these things, when the wrath of King Ahasuerus subsided, he remembered Vashti, and what she had done, and what had been decreed against her. ² Then the King's pages said: 'Let there be sought for the King beautiful young maidens; ³ and let the King appoint commissioners in all the provinces of his kingdom, that they may gather together every beautiful young maiden to Shushan the Capitol to the harem, under the charge of Hege the King's chamberlain, custodian of the women; and let their cosmetics be given them. ⁴ Then, let the girl who pleases the King be queen instead of Vashti.' This advice pleased the King, and he followed it.

⁵ There was a Jewish man in Shushan the Capitol whose name was Mordechai, son of Yair, son of Shim'i, son of Kish, a Benjaminite, ⁶ who had been exiled from Jerusalem along with the exiles who had been exiled with Jechoniah, King of Judah, whom Nebuchadnezzar, King of Babylon, had exiled. ⁷ And he had reared Hadassah, that is, Esther, his uncle's daughter; since she had neither father nor mother. The girl was finely featured and beautiful, and when her father and mother had died, Mordechai adopted her as his daughter. ⁸ So it came to pass, when the King's bidding and decree were published, and when many young girls were being brought together to Shushan the Capitol, under the charge of Hegai, that Esther was taken into the palace, under the charge of Hegai, guardian of the women. ⁹ The girl pleased him, and she obtained his kindness; he hurriedly prepared her cosmetics and her allowance of delicacies to present her, along with the seven special maids from the palace; and he transferred her

י וְאֶת־נַעֲרוֹתֶיהָ לְטוֹב בֵּית הַנָּשִׁים לֹא־הִגִּידָה אֶסְתֵּר אֶת־עַמָּהּ וְאֶת־מוֹלַדְתָּהּ כִּי מָרְדֳּכַי צִוָּה

יא עָלֶיהָ אֲשֶׁר לֹא־תַגִּיד: וּבְכָל־יוֹם וָיוֹם מָרְדֳּכַי מִתְהַלֵּךְ לִפְנֵי חֲצַר בֵּית־הַנָּשִׁים לָדַעַת אֶת־

יב שְׁלוֹם אֶסְתֵּר וּמַה־יֵּעָשֶׂה בָּהּ: וּבְהַגִּיעַ תֹּר נַעֲרָה וְנַעֲרָה לָבוֹא ׀ אֶל־הַמֶּלֶךְ אֲחַשְׁוֵרוֹשׁ מִקֵּץ הֱיוֹת לָהּ כְּדָת הַנָּשִׁים שְׁנֵים עָשָׂר חֹדֶשׁ כִּי כֵּן יִמְלְאוּ יְמֵי מְרוּקֵיהֶן שִׁשָּׁה חֳדָשִׁים בְּשֶׁמֶן הַמֹּר וְשִׁשָּׁה

יג חֳדָשִׁים בַּבְּשָׂמִים וּבְתַמְרוּקֵי הַנָּשִׁים: וּבָזֶה הַנַּעֲרָה בָּאָה אֶל־הַמֶּלֶךְ אֵת כָּל־אֲשֶׁר תֹּאמַר יִנָּתֵן לָהּ לָבוֹא עִמָּהּ מִבֵּית הַנָּשִׁים עַד־בֵּית

יד הַמֶּלֶךְ: בָּעֶרֶב ׀ הִיא בָאָה וּבַבֹּקֶר הִיא שָׁבָה אֶל־בֵּית הַנָּשִׁים שֵׁנִי אֶל־יַד שַׁעֲשְׁגַז סְרִיס הַמֶּלֶךְ שֹׁמֵר הַפִּילַגְשִׁים לֹא־תָבוֹא עוֹד אֶל־הַמֶּלֶךְ כִּי

טו אִם־חָפֵץ בָּהּ הַמֶּלֶךְ וְנִקְרְאָה בְשֵׁם: וּבְהַגִּיעַ תֹּר־אֶסְתֵּר בַּת־אֲבִיחַיִל ׀ דֹּד מָרְדֳּכַי אֲשֶׁר לָקַח־לוֹ לְבַת לָבוֹא אֶל־הַמֶּלֶךְ לֹא בִקְשָׁה דָּבָר כִּי אִם אֶת־אֲשֶׁר יֹאמַר הֵגַי סְרִיס־הַמֶּלֶךְ שֹׁמֵר הַנָּשִׁים

טז וַתְּהִי אֶסְתֵּר נֹשֵׂאת חֵן בְּעֵינֵי כָּל־רֹאֶיהָ: וַתִּלָּקַח אֶסְתֵּר אֶל־הַמֶּלֶךְ אֲחַשְׁוֵרוֹשׁ אֶל־בֵּית מַלְכוּתוֹ בַּחֹדֶשׁ הָעֲשִׂירִי הוּא־חֹדֶשׁ טֵבֵת בִּשְׁנַת־שֶׁבַע

יז לְמַלְכוּתוֹ: וַיֶּאֱהַב הַמֶּלֶךְ אֶת־אֶסְתֵּר מִכָּל־הַנָּשִׁים וַתִּשָּׂא־חֵן וָחֶסֶד לְפָנָיו מִכָּל־הַבְּתוּלוֹת וַיָּשֶׂם כֶּתֶר־מַלְכוּת בְּרֹאשָׁהּ וַיַּמְלִיכֶהָ תַּחַת

יח וַשְׁתִּי: וַיַּעַשׂ הַמֶּלֶךְ מִשְׁתֶּה גָדוֹל לְכָל־שָׂרָיו וַעֲבָדָיו אֵת מִשְׁתֵּה אֶסְתֵּר וַהֲנָחָה לַמְּדִינוֹת

and her maidens to the best quarters in the harem. 10 Esther had not told of her people or her kindred, for Mordechai had instructed her not to tell. 11 Every day Mordechai used to walk about in front of the court of the harem to find out about Esther's well-being and what would become of her.

12 Now when each girl's turn arrived to come to King Ahasuerus, after having been treated according to the manner prescribed for women for twelve months (for so was the prescribed length of their anointing accomplished: six months with oil of myrrh, and six months with perfumes and feminine cosmetics) — 13 when then the girl thus came to the King, she was given whatever she desired to accompany her from the harem to the palace. 14 In the evening she would come, and the next morning she would return to the second harem in the custody of Shaashgaz, the King's chamberlain, guardian of the concubines. She would never again go to the King unless the King desired her, and she were summoned by name.

15 Now when the turn came for Esther, daughter of Avichail the uncle of Mordechai (who had adopted her as his own daughter), to come to the King, she requested nothing beyond what Hegai the King's chamberlain, guardian of the women, had advised. Esther would captivate all who saw her. 16 Esther was taken to King Ahasuerus into his palace in the tenth month, which is the month of Teves, in the seventh year of his reign. 17 The King loved Esther more than all the women, and she won more of his grace and favor than all the other girls; so that he set the royal crown upon her head, and made her Queen in place of Vashti. 18 Then the King made a great banquet for all his officers and his servants — it was Esther's Banquet — and he proclaimed an amnesty for the provinces,

14. Having consorted with the King, it would not be proper for any of these girls to marry other men. They were required to return to the harem and remain there for the rest of their lives as concubines, to await the possibility of being crowned Queen if the King found no one better.

17. ESTHER IS CHOSEN QUEEN

יט עָשָׂה וַיִּתֵּן מַשְׂאֵת כְּיַד הַמֶּלֶךְ: וּבְהִקָּבֵץ בְּתוּלוֹת

כ שֵׁנִית וּמָרְדֳּכַי יֹשֵׁב בְּשַׁעַר־הַמֶּלֶךְ: אֵין אֶסְתֵּר
מַגֶּדֶת מוֹלַדְתָּהּ וְאֶת־עַמָּהּ כַּאֲשֶׁר צִוָּה עָלֶיהָ
מָרְדֳּכָי וְאֶת־מַאֲמַר מָרְדֳּכַי אֶסְתֵּר עֹשָׂה כַּאֲשֶׁר

כא הָיְתָה בְּאָמְנָה אִתּוֹ: בַּיָּמִים
הָהֵם וּמָרְדֳּכַי יוֹשֵׁב בְּשַׁעַר־הַמֶּלֶךְ קָצַף בִּגְתָן
וָתֶרֶשׁ שְׁנֵי־סָרִיסֵי הַמֶּלֶךְ מִשֹּׁמְרֵי הַסַּף וַיְבַקְשׁוּ

כב לִשְׁלֹחַ יָד בַּמֶּלֶךְ אֲחַשְׁוֵרֹשׁ: וַיִּוָּדַע הַדָּבָר
לְמָרְדֳּכַי וַיַּגֵּד לְאֶסְתֵּר הַמַּלְכָּה וַתֹּאמֶר אֶסְתֵּר

כג לַמֶּלֶךְ בְּשֵׁם מָרְדֳּכָי: וַיְבֻקַּשׁ הַדָּבָר וַיִּמָּצֵא וַיִּתָּלוּ
שְׁנֵיהֶם עַל־עֵץ וַיִּכָּתֵב בְּסֵפֶר דִּבְרֵי הַיָּמִים לִפְנֵי

ג　א הַמֶּלֶךְ: אַחַר | הַדְּבָרִים
הָאֵלֶּה גִּדַּל הַמֶּלֶךְ אֲחַשְׁוֵרוֹשׁ אֶת־הָמָן בֶּן־
הַמְּדָתָא הָאֲגָגִי וַיְנַשְּׂאֵהוּ וַיָּשֶׂם אֶת־כִּסְאוֹ מֵעַל

ב כָּל־הַשָּׂרִים אֲשֶׁר אִתּוֹ: וְכָל־עַבְדֵי הַמֶּלֶךְ אֲשֶׁר־
בְּשַׁעַר הַמֶּלֶךְ כֹּרְעִים וּמִשְׁתַּחֲוִים לְהָמָן כִּי־
כֵן צִוָּה־לוֹ הַמֶּלֶךְ וּמָרְדֳּכַי לֹא יִכְרַע וְלֹא

ג יִשְׁתַּחֲוֶה: וַיֹּאמְרוּ עַבְדֵי הַמֶּלֶךְ אֲשֶׁר־בְּשַׁעַר
הַמֶּלֶךְ לְמָרְדֳּכָי מַדּוּעַ אַתָּה עוֹבֵר אֵת מִצְוַת

ד הַמֶּלֶךְ: וַיְהִי °בְּאָמְרָם אֵלָיו יוֹם וָיוֹם וְלֹא שָׁמַע °כְּאָמְרָם ק'
אֲלֵיהֶם וַיַּגִּידוּ לְהָמָן לִרְאוֹת הֲיַעַמְדוּ דִּבְרֵי

ה מָרְדֳּכַי כִּי־הִגִּיד לָהֶם אֲשֶׁר־הוּא יְהוּדִי: וַיַּרְא
הָמָן כִּי־אֵין מָרְדֳּכַי כֹּרֵעַ וּמִשְׁתַּחֲוֶה לוֹ וַיִּמָּלֵא

ו הָמָן חֵמָה: וַיִּבֶז בְּעֵינָיו לִשְׁלֹחַ יָד בְּמָרְדֳּכַי לְבַדּוֹ
כִּי־הִגִּידוּ לוֹ אֶת־עַם מָרְדֳּכָי וַיְבַקֵּשׁ הָמָן
לְהַשְׁמִיד אֶת־כָּל־הַיְּהוּדִים אֲשֶׁר בְּכָל־מַלְכוּת

esther 2:19-3:6

19. THE SECOND GATHERING

At Esther's advice, the King appointed Mordechai to sit at the gate and judge the people. Ahasuerus then took counsel of Mordechai as to how he could extract from Esther the secret of her origin. Mordechai suggested that the King once again organize a gathering of beautiful young maidens from thoughout the kingdom. Esther, fearing that she would be replaced as Queen, would certainly divulge her secret. Mordechai made this suggestion because he wanted to ascertain whether Esther's coronation was truly the will of Heaven. If the King could find no one superior to Esther, Mordechai would be assured that her reign was part of God's plan *(Me'am Loez)*.

21. MORDECHAI FOILS A PLOT AGAINST THE KING.

Being a member of the Sanhedrin, Mordechai knew seventy languages. Bigsan and Teresh spoke in their native Tarsian tongue in Mordechai's presence, not expecting him to understand them *(Talmud)*.

3/1. HAMAN IS ADVANCED

Haman was a descendant of Agag, King of Amalek [*I Samuel* 15:9].

2. To make it manifest that the homage due him was of an idolatrous character, Haman had the image of an idol fastened to his clothes, so that whoever bowed down before him worshiped an idol at the same time. Therefore Mordechai would not bow down or prostrate himself *(Midrash)*.

6. HAMAN PLANS THE DESTRUCTION OF ALL THE JEWS

The reaction of Haman to a personal affront is typical of the most rabid anti-Semites throughout the ages.

and gave gifts worthy of the King.

¹⁹ And when the maidens were gathered together the second time, and Mordechai sat at the King's gate, ²⁰ (Esther still told nothing of her kindred or her people as Mordechai had instructed her; for Esther continued to obey Mordechai, just as when she was raised by him.) ²¹ In those days, while Mordechai was sitting at the King's gate, Bigsan and Teresh, two of the King's chamberlains of the guardians of the threshold, became angry and planned to assassinate King Ahasuerus. ²² The plot became known to Mordechai, who told it to Queen Esther, and Esther informed the King in Mordechai's name. ²³ The matter was investigated and corroborated, and they were both hanged on a gallows. It was recorded in the book of chronicles in the King's presence.

¹ After these things King Ahasuerus promoted Haman, the son of Hammedasa the Agagite, and advanced him; he set his seat above all the officers who were with him. ² All the King's servants at the King's gate would bow down and prostrate themselves before Haman, for this is what the King had commanded concerning him. But Mordechai would not bow down nor prostrate himself. ³ So the King's servants at the King's gate said to Mordechai, 'Why do you disobey the King's command?' ⁴ Finally, when they said this to him day after day and he did not heed them, they told Haman, to see whether Mordechai's words would avail; for he had told them that he was a Jew. ⁵ When Haman, himself, saw that Mordechai did not bow down and prostrate himself before him, then Haman was filled with rage. ⁶ However it seemed contemptible to him to lay hands on Mordechai alone, for they had made known to him the people of Mordechai. So Haman sought to destroy all the Jews who were throughout the entire king-

[107] **PURIM** / Its Observance and Significance

ז אֲחַשְׁוֵרוֹשׁ עַם מָרְדֳּכָי: בַּחֹדֶשׁ הָרִאשׁוֹן הוּא־
חֹדֶשׁ נִיסָן בִּשְׁנַת שְׁתֵּים עֶשְׂרֵה לַמֶּלֶךְ
אֲחַשְׁוֵרוֹשׁ הִפִּיל פּוּר הוּא הַגּוֹרָל לִפְנֵי הָמָן
מִיּוֹם | לְיוֹם וּמֵחֹדֶשׁ לְחֹדֶשׁ שְׁנֵים־עָשָׂר הוּא־
ח חֹדֶשׁ אֲדָר: וַיֹּאמֶר הָמָן
לַמֶּלֶךְ אֲחַשְׁוֵרוֹשׁ יֶשְׁנוֹ עַם־אֶחָד מְפֻזָּר וּמְפֹרָד
בֵּין הָעַמִּים בְּכֹל מְדִינוֹת מַלְכוּתֶךָ וְדָתֵיהֶם
שֹׁנוֹת מִכָּל־עָם וְאֶת־דָּתֵי הַמֶּלֶךְ אֵינָם עֹשִׂים
ט וְלַמֶּלֶךְ אֵין־שֹׁוֶה לְהַנִּיחָם: אִם־עַל־הַמֶּלֶךְ טוֹב
יִכָּתֵב לְאַבְּדָם וַעֲשֶׂרֶת אֲלָפִים כִּכַּר־כֶּסֶף
אֶשְׁקוֹל עַל־יְדֵי עֹשֵׂי הַמְּלָאכָה לְהָבִיא אֶל־
י גִּנְזֵי הַמֶּלֶךְ: וַיָּסַר הַמֶּלֶךְ אֶת־טַבַּעְתּוֹ מֵעַל יָדוֹ
וַיִּתְּנָהּ לְהָמָן בֶּן־הַמְּדָתָא הָאֲגָגִי צֹרֵר הַיְּהוּדִים:
יא וַיֹּאמֶר הַמֶּלֶךְ לְהָמָן הַכֶּסֶף נָתוּן לָךְ וְהָעָם
יב לַעֲשׂוֹת בּוֹ כַּטּוֹב בְּעֵינֶיךָ: וַיִּקָּרְאוּ סֹפְרֵי הַמֶּלֶךְ
בַּחֹדֶשׁ הָרִאשׁוֹן בִּשְׁלוֹשָׁה עָשָׂר יוֹם בּוֹ וַיִּכָּתֵב
כְּכָל־אֲשֶׁר־צִוָּה הָמָן אֶל אֲחַשְׁדַּרְפְּנֵי־הַמֶּלֶךְ
וְאֶל־הַפַּחוֹת אֲשֶׁר | עַל־מְדִינָה וּמְדִינָה וְאֶל־
שָׂרֵי עַם וָעָם מְדִינָה וּמְדִינָה כִּכְתָבָהּ וְעַם וָעָם
כִּלְשׁוֹנוֹ בְּשֵׁם הַמֶּלֶךְ אֲחַשְׁוֵרֹשׁ נִכְתָּב וְנֶחְתָּם
יג בְּטַבַּעַת הַמֶּלֶךְ: וְנִשְׁלוֹחַ סְפָרִים בְּיַד הָרָצִים
אֶל־כָּל־מְדִינוֹת הַמֶּלֶךְ לְהַשְׁמִיד לַהֲרֹג וּלְאַבֵּד
אֶת־כָּל־הַיְּהוּדִים מִנַּעַר וְעַד־זָקֵן טַף וְנָשִׁים
בְּיוֹם אֶחָד בִּשְׁלוֹשָׁה עָשָׂר לְחֹדֶשׁ שְׁנֵים־עָשָׂר
יד הוּא־חֹדֶשׁ אֲדָר וּשְׁלָלָם לָבוֹז: פַּתְשֶׁגֶן
הַכְּתָב לְהִנָּתֵן דָּת בְּכָל־מְדִינָה וּמְדִינָה גָּלוּי

dom of Ahasuerus — the people of Mordechai.
⁷ In the first month, which is the month of
Nissan, in the twelfth year of King Ahasuerus,
pur (that is, the lot) was cast in the presence of
Haman from day to day, and from month to
month, to the twelfth month, which is the month of
Adar.

8. HAMAN SLANDERS THE JEWS TO THE KING

Haman said: 'They eat and drink and despise the throne. For if a fly falls into a Jew's cup, he throws out the fly and drinks the wine; but if His Majesty were to merely touch his cup, he would throw it to the ground and not drink from it' (*Talmud*).

9. The price Haman was ready to pay for the right to exterminate the Jews, 10,000 talents, was 24 million ounces, or 750 tons of silver!

10. THE KING CONSENTS TO THE DESTRUCTION OF THE JEWS

⁸ Then Haman said to King Ahasuerus: 'There is a
certain people scattered abroad and dispersed
among the peoples in all the provinces of your
realm. Their laws are different from every other
people's. They do not observe even the King's laws;
therefore it is not befitting the King to tolerate
them. ⁹ If it pleases the King, let it be recorded that
they be destroyed; and I will pay ten thousand silver
talents into the hands of those who perform the
duties for deposit in the King's treasuries.' ¹⁰ So the
King took his signet ring from his hand, and gave it
to Haman, the son of Hammedasa the Agagite, the
enemy of the Jews. ¹¹ Then the King said to Haman:
'The silver is given to you, the people also, to
do with as you see fit.' ¹² The King's secretaries
were summoned on the thirteenth day of the first
month, and everything was written exactly as
Haman had dictated, to the King's satraps, to the
governors of every province, and to the officials
of every people; each province in its own script,
and to each people in its own language; in King
Ahasuerus' name it was written, and it was sealed
with the King's signet ring. ¹³ Letters were sent
by courier to all the King's provinces, to destroy,
to slay, and to exterminate all Jews, young and
old, children and women, in a single day, the
thirteenth day of the twelfth month, which is the
month of Adar, and to plunder their possessions.
¹⁴ The copies of the document were to be promulgated in every province, and be published

14. The strange haste in publishing a decree that would not be executed for eleven months was because Haman was afraid that the fickle King would have a change of heart. Also, he wanted to prolong the agony of the Jews throughout the kingdom by telling them of the impending massacre so far in advance.

טו לְכָל־הָעַמִּים לִהְיוֹת עֲתִדִים לַיּוֹם הַזֶּה: הָרָצִים
יָצְאוּ דְחוּפִים בִּדְבַר הַמֶּלֶךְ וְהַדָּת נִתְּנָה בְּשׁוּשַׁן
הַבִּירָה וְהַמֶּלֶךְ וְהָמָן יָשְׁבוּ לִשְׁתּוֹת וְהָעִיר שׁוּשָׁן

ד א נָבוֹכָה: וּמָרְדֳּכַי יָדַע אֶת־כָּל־אֲשֶׁר
נַעֲשָׂה וַיִּקְרַע מָרְדֳּכַי אֶת־בְּגָדָיו וַיִּלְבַּשׁ שַׂק
וָאֵפֶר וַיֵּצֵא בְּתוֹךְ הָעִיר וַיִּזְעַק זְעָקָה גְדוֹלָה
ב וּמָרָה: וַיָּבוֹא עַד לִפְנֵי שַׁעַר־הַמֶּלֶךְ כִּי אֵין לָבוֹא
ג אֶל־שַׁעַר הַמֶּלֶךְ בִּלְבוּשׁ שָׂק: וּבְכָל־מְדִינָה
וּמְדִינָה מְקוֹם אֲשֶׁר דְּבַר־הַמֶּלֶךְ וְדָתוֹ מַגִּיעַ אֵבֶל
גָּדוֹל לַיְּהוּדִים וְצוֹם וּבְכִי וּמִסְפֵּד שַׂק וָאֵפֶר יֻצַּע
ד לָרַבִּים: °וַתְּבוֹאֶנָה נַעֲרוֹת אֶסְתֵּר וְסָרִיסֶיהָ °וַתָּבוֹאנָה ק׳
וַיַּגִּידוּ לָהּ וַתִּתְחַלְחַל הַמַּלְכָּה מְאֹד וַתִּשְׁלַח
בְּגָדִים לְהַלְבִּישׁ אֶת־מָרְדֳּכַי וּלְהָסִיר שַׂקּוֹ מֵעָלָיו
ה וְלֹא קִבֵּל: וַתִּקְרָא אֶסְתֵּר לַהֲתָךְ מִסָּרִיסֵי הַמֶּלֶךְ
אֲשֶׁר הֶעֱמִיד לְפָנֶיהָ וַתְּצַוֵּהוּ עַל־מָרְדֳּכָי לָדַעַת
ו מַה־זֶּה וְעַל־מַה־זֶּה: וַיֵּצֵא הֲתָךְ אֶל־מָרְדֳּכָי אֶל־
ז רְחוֹב הָעִיר אֲשֶׁר לִפְנֵי שַׁעַר־הַמֶּלֶךְ: וַיַּגֶּד־לוֹ
מָרְדֳּכַי אֵת כָּל־אֲשֶׁר קָרָהוּ וְאֵת | פָּרָשַׁת הַכֶּסֶף
אֲשֶׁר אָמַר הָמָן לִשְׁקוֹל עַל־גִּנְזֵי הַמֶּלֶךְ
ח °בַּיְּהוּדִיִּים לְאַבְּדָם: וְאֶת־פַּתְשֶׁגֶן כְּתָב־הַדָּת °בַּיְּהוּדִים ק׳
אֲשֶׁר־נִתַּן בְּשׁוּשָׁן לְהַשְׁמִידָם נָתַן לוֹ לְהַרְאוֹת
אֶת־אֶסְתֵּר וּלְהַגִּיד לָהּ וּלְצַוּוֹת עָלֶיהָ לָבוֹא אֶל־
הַמֶּלֶךְ לְהִתְחַנֶּן־לוֹ וּלְבַקֵּשׁ מִלְּפָנָיו עַל־עַמָּהּ:
ט וַיָּבוֹא הֲתָךְ וַיַּגֵּד לְאֶסְתֵּר אֵת דִּבְרֵי מָרְדֳּכָי:
י–יא וַתֹּאמֶר אֶסְתֵּר לַהֲתָךְ וַתְּצַוֵּהוּ אֶל־מָרְדֳּכָי: כָּל־
עַבְדֵי הַמֶּלֶךְ וְעַם מְדִינוֹת הַמֶּלֶךְ יֹדְעִים אֲשֶׁר

to all peoples, that they should be ready for that day. [15] The couriers went forth hurriedly by order of the King, and the edict was distributed in Shushan the Capitol. The King and Haman sat down to drink, but the city of Shushan was bewildered.

4/1. MORDECHAI AND THE JEWS MOURN

[1] **M**ordechai learned of all that had been done; and Mordechai tore his clothes and put on sackcloth with ashes. He went out into the midst of the city, and cried loudly and bitterly. [2] He came until the front of the King's gate for it was forbidden to enter the King's gate, clothed with sackcloth. [3] (In every province, wherever the King's command and his decree extended, there was great mourning among the Jews, with fasting, and weeping, and wailing; most of them lying in sackcloth and ashes.)

4. Esther had not yet revealed her origins, but her interest in Mordechai — who had always inquired about her welfare — was well known throughout the palace.

[4] And Esther's maids and chamberlains came and told her about it, and the Queen was greatly distressed; she sent garments to clothe Mordechai so that he might take off his sackcloth, but he would not accept them.

5. Hasach was a great man, Esther's confidant, one who could keep secrets, and whom no one would suspect or dare to question about his mission. In the Talmud he is identified with Daniel.

[5] Then Esther summoned Hasach, one of the King's chamberlains whom he had appointed to attend her, and ordered him to go to Mordechai, to learn what this was about and why. [6] So Hasach went out to Mordechai unto the city square, which was in front of the King's gate, [7] and Mordechai told him of all that had happened to him, and all about the sum of money that Haman had promised to pay to the royal treasuries for the annihilation of the Jews.

8. MORDECHAI ASKS ESTHER TO INTERCEDE

[8] He also gave him a copy of the text of the decree which was distributed in Shushan for their destruction — so that he might show it to Esther and inform her, bidding her to go to the King, to appeal to him, and to plead with him for her people.

10. ESTHER'S RECALCITRANT RESPONSE

[9] Hasach came and told Esther what Mordechai had said. [10] Then Esther told Hasach to return to Mordechai with this message: [11] 'All the King's servants and the people of the King's provinces are well

כָּל־אִישׁ וְאִשָּׁה אֲשֶׁר יָבֽוֹא־אֶל־הַמֶּלֶךְ אֶל־
הֶחָצֵר הַפְּנִימִית אֲשֶׁר לֹֽא־יִקָּרֵא אַחַת דָּתוֹ
לְהָמִית לְבַד מֵאֲשֶׁר יֽוֹשִׁיט־לוֹ הַמֶּלֶךְ אֶת־
שַׁרְבִיט הַזָּהָב וְחָיָה וַאֲנִי לֹא נִקְרֵאתִי לָבוֹא אֶל־
יב הַמֶּלֶךְ זֶה שְׁלוֹשִׁים יֽוֹם: וַיַּגִּידוּ לְמָרְדֳּכָי אֵת
יג דִּבְרֵי אֶסְתֵּר: וַיֹּאמֶר מָרְדֳּכַי לְהָשִׁיב אֶל־אֶסְתֵּר
אַל־תְּדַמִּי בְנַפְשֵׁךְ לְהִמָּלֵט בֵּית־הַמֶּלֶךְ מִכָּל־
יד הַיְּהוּדִים: כִּי אִם־הַחֲרֵשׁ תַּחֲרִישִׁי בָּעֵת הַזֹּאת
רֶוַח וְהַצָּלָה יַעֲמוֹד לַיְּהוּדִים מִמָּקוֹם אַחֵר וְאַתְּ
וּבֵית־אָבִיךְ תֹּאבֵדוּ וּמִי יוֹדֵעַ אִם־לְעֵת כָּזֹאת
טו הִגַּעַתְּ לַמַּלְכוּת: וַתֹּאמֶר אֶסְתֵּר לְהָשִׁיב אֶל־
טז מָרְדֳּכָי: לֵךְ כְּנוֹס אֶת־כָּל־הַיְּהוּדִים הַנִּמְצְאִים
בְּשׁוּשָׁן וְצוּמוּ עָלַי וְאַל־תֹּאכְלוּ וְאַל־תִּשְׁתּוּ
שְׁלֹשֶׁת יָמִים לַיְלָה וָיוֹם גַּם־אֲנִי וְנַעֲרֹתַי אָצוּם
כֵּן וּבְכֵן אָבוֹא אֶל־הַמֶּלֶךְ אֲשֶׁר לֹֽא־כַדָּת וְכַאֲשֶׁר
יז אָבַדְתִּי אָבָדְתִּי: וַיַּעֲבֹר מָרְדֳּכָי וַיַּעַשׂ כְּכֹל אֲשֶׁר־
א צִוְּתָה עָלָיו אֶסְתֵּר: וַיְהִי | בַּיּוֹם הַשְּׁלִישִׁי וַתִּלְבַּשׁ
אֶסְתֵּר מַלְכוּת וַתַּעֲמֹד בַּחֲצַר בֵּית־הַמֶּלֶךְ
הַפְּנִימִית נֹכַח בֵּית הַמֶּלֶךְ וְהַמֶּלֶךְ יוֹשֵׁב עַל־כִּסֵּא
ב מַלְכוּתוֹ בְּבֵית הַמַּלְכוּת נֹכַח פֶּתַח הַבָּיִת: וַיְהִי
כִרְאוֹת הַמֶּלֶךְ אֶת־אֶסְתֵּר הַמַּלְכָּה עֹמֶדֶת בֶּחָצֵר
נָשְׂאָה חֵן בְּעֵינָיו וַיּוֹשֶׁט הַמֶּלֶךְ לְאֶסְתֵּר אֶת־
שַׁרְבִיט הַזָּהָב אֲשֶׁר בְּיָדוֹ וַתִּקְרַב אֶסְתֵּר וַתִּגַּע
ג בְּרֹאשׁ הַשַּׁרְבִיט: וַיֹּאמֶר לָהּ הַמֶּלֶךְ מַה־לָּךְ
אֶסְתֵּר הַמַּלְכָּה וּמַה־בַּקָּשָׁתֵךְ עַד־חֲצִי הַמַּלְכוּת
ד וְיִנָּתֵן לָךְ: וַתֹּאמֶר אֶסְתֵּר אִם־עַל־הַמֶּלֶךְ טוֹב

ה

aware that if anyone, man or woman, approaches the King in the inner court without being summoned, there is but one law for him: that he be put to death; except for the person to whom the King shall extend the gold scepter so that he may live. Now I have not been summoned to come to the King for the past thirty days.'

¹² They related Esther's words to Mordechai. ¹³ Then Mordechai said to reply to Esther: 'Do not imagine that you will be able to escape in the King's palace any more than the rest of the Jews. ¹⁴ For if you persist in keeping silent at a time like this, relief and deliverance will come to the Jews from some other place, while you and your father's house will perish. And who knows whether it was just for such a time as this that you attained the royal position!'

¹⁵ Then Esther sent this return answer to Mordechai: ¹⁶ 'Go, assemble all the Jews to be found in Shushan, and fast for me. Do not eat or drink for three days, night or day; I, with my maids, will fast also. Then I will go in to the King though it's unlawful. And if I perish, I perish.' ¹⁷ Mordechai then left and did exactly as Esther had commanded him.

13. MORDECHAI ENCOURAGES ESTHER

'You may, by some remote twist of fate, manage to save your body. But how will you save your soul?'

15. ESTHER AGREES TO GO UNSUMMONED TO THE KING

16. Esther limited the assembly to the Jews in Shushan because it would have been impossible to assemble Jews living further away on such short notice (Gaon of Vilna).

5/1. ESTHER GOES BEFORE THE KING

The third day — of the fast. It was, according to the Talmud, the first day of Passover.

¹ **N**ow it came to pass on the third day, Esther donned royalty and stood in the inner court of the King's palace facing the King's house while the King was sitting on his throne in the throne room facing the chamber's entrance. ² When the King noticed Queen Esther standing in the court, she won his favor. The King extended to Esther the gold scepter that was in his hand, and Esther approached and touched the tip of the scepter.

4. ESTHER LAYS A TRAP FOR HAMAN

The first Hebrew letters of the words יבא המלך והמן היום form the Holy Name of God. This is one of the several places throughout the Megillah where God's Name is indirectly hinted (Kad HaKemach).

³ The King said to her: 'What is your petition, Queen Esther? Even if it be half the kingdom, it shall be granted you.' ⁴ Esther said: 'If it please the King,

יָבוֹא הַמֶּלֶךְ וְהָמָן הַיּוֹם אֶל־הַמִּשְׁתֶּה אֲשֶׁר־
ה עָשִׂיתִי לֽוֹ: וַיֹּאמֶר הַמֶּלֶךְ מַהֲרוּ אֶת־הָמָן
לַעֲשׂוֹת אֶת־דְּבַר אֶסְתֵּר וַיָּבֹא הַמֶּלֶךְ וְהָמָן אֶל־
ו הַמִּשְׁתֶּה אֲשֶׁר־עָשְׂתָה אֶסְתֵּר: וַיֹּאמֶר הַמֶּלֶךְ
לְאֶסְתֵּר בְּמִשְׁתֵּה הַיַּיִן מַה־שְּׁאֵלָתֵךְ וְיִנָּתֵן לָךְ
ז וּמַה־בַּקָּשָׁתֵךְ עַד־חֲצִי הַמַּלְכוּת וְתֵעָשׂ: וַתַּעַן
ח אֶסְתֵּר וַתֹּאמַר שְׁאֵלָתִי וּבַקָּשָׁתִי: אִם־מָצָאתִי חֵן
בְּעֵינֵי הַמֶּלֶךְ וְאִם־עַל־הַמֶּלֶךְ טוֹב לָתֵת אֶת־
שְׁאֵלָתִי וְלַעֲשׂוֹת אֶת־בַּקָּשָׁתִי יָבוֹא הַמֶּלֶךְ וְהָמָן
אֶל־הַמִּשְׁתֶּה אֲשֶׁר אֶעֱשֶׂה לָהֶם וּמָחָר אֶעֱשֶׂה
ט כִּדְבַר הַמֶּלֶךְ: וַיֵּצֵא הָמָן בַּיּוֹם הַהוּא שָׂמֵחַ וְטוֹב
לֵב וְכִרְאוֹת הָמָן אֶת־מָרְדֳּכַי בְּשַׁעַר הַמֶּלֶךְ וְלֹא־
קָם וְלֹא־זָע מִמֶּנּוּ וַיִּמָּלֵא הָמָן עַל־מָרְדֳּכַי חֵמָה:
י וַיִּתְאַפַּק הָמָן וַיָּבוֹא אֶל־בֵּיתוֹ וַיִּשְׁלַח וַיָּבֵא אֶת־
יא אֹהֲבָיו וְאֶת־זֶרֶשׁ אִשְׁתּוֹ: וַיְסַפֵּר לָהֶם הָמָן אֶת־
כְּבוֹד עָשְׁרוֹ וְרֹב בָּנָיו וְאֵת כָּל־אֲשֶׁר גִּדְּלוֹ הַמֶּלֶךְ
וְאֵת אֲשֶׁר נִשְּׂאוֹ עַל־הַשָּׂרִים וְעַבְדֵי הַמֶּלֶךְ:
יב וַיֹּאמֶר הָמָן אַף לֹא־הֵבִיאָה אֶסְתֵּר הַמַּלְכָּה
עִם־הַמֶּלֶךְ אֶל־הַמִּשְׁתֶּה אֲשֶׁר־עָשָׂתָה כִּי אִם־
אוֹתִי וְגַם־לְמָחָר אֲנִי קָרוּא־לָהּ עִם־הַמֶּלֶךְ:
יג וְכָל־זֶה אֵינֶנּוּ שֹׁוֶה לִי בְּכָל־עֵת אֲשֶׁר אֲנִי
רֹאֶה אֶת־מָרְדֳּכַי הַיְּהוּדִי יוֹשֵׁב בְּשַׁעַר הַמֶּלֶךְ:
יד וַתֹּאמֶר לוֹ זֶרֶשׁ אִשְׁתּוֹ וְכָל־אֹהֲבָיו יַעֲשׂוּ־
עֵץ גָּבֹהַּ חֲמִשִּׁים אַמָּה וּבַבֹּקֶר | אֱמֹר לַמֶּלֶךְ
וְיִתְלוּ אֶת־מָרְדֳּכַי עָלָיו וּבֹא עִם־הַמֶּלֶךְ אֶל־
הַמִּשְׁתֶּה שָׂמֵחַ וַיִּיטַב הַדָּבָר לִפְנֵי הָמָן וַיַּעַשׂ

let the King and Haman come today to the banquet that I have prepared for him.' ⁵ Then the King commanded: 'Tell Haman to hurry and fulfill Esther's wish.' So the King and Haman came to the banquet that Esther had prepared.

6. THE FIRST BANQUET

⁶ The King said to Esther during the wine feast: 'What is your request? It shall be granted you. And what is your petition? Even if it be half the kingdom, it shall be fulfilled.' ⁷ So Esther answered and said: 'My request and my petition: ⁸ If I have won the King's favor, and if it pleases the King to grant my request and to perform my petition — let the King and Haman come to the banquet that I shall prepare for them, and tomorrow I will do the King's bidding.'

⁹ That day Haman went out joyful and exuberant. But when Haman noticed Mordechai in the King's gate and that he neither stood up nor stirred before him, Haman was infuriated with Mordechai. ¹⁰ Nevertheless Haman restrained himself and went home. He sent for his friends and his wife, Zeresh, ¹¹ and Haman recounted to them the glory of his wealth and his large number of sons, and every instance where the King had promoted him and advanced him above the officials and royal servants. ¹² Haman said: 'Moreover, Queen Esther invited no one but myself to accompany the King to the banquet that she had prepared, and tomorrow, too, I am invited by her along with the King. ¹³ Yet all this means nothing to me so long as I see that Jew Mordechai sitting at the King's gate.' ¹⁴ Then his wife, Zeresh, and all his friends said to him: 'Let a gallows be made, fifty cubits high; and tomorrow morning speak to the King and have them hang Mordechai on it. Then, in good spirits, accompany the King to the banquet.' This suggestion pleased Haman, and he had the gallows erected.

8. Esther's ruse worked. When Haman arrived at Esther's first banquet, he was apprehensive of Esther's reason for inviting him. He suspected a connection between the new edict concerning the Jews and his invitation. Only now, having left the first party at which he was overwhelmed with flattery, was he joyous and confident. He was unprepared, therefore, for the consequences of Esther's next banquet (Alkabetz).

9. HAMAN IS INFURIATED BY MORDECHAI

13. Notice that Haman did not mention to his wife and children that he was angry because of Mordechai's refusal to bow down to him; he thought it beneath his dignity to admit that such a minor slight could ruffle him so. Rather he claimed that he was angry because 'the Jew Mordechai was sitting at the King's gate' and he was totally unworthy of such a high honor (Me'am Loez).

ו

א הָעֵץ: בַּלַּיְלָה הַהוּא נָדְדָה שְׁנַת
הַמֶּלֶךְ וַיֹּאמֶר לְהָבִיא אֶת־סֵפֶר הַזִּכְרֹנוֹת דִּבְרֵי
ב הַיָּמִים וַיִּהְיוּ נִקְרָאִים לִפְנֵי הַמֶּלֶךְ: וַיִּמָּצֵא כָתוּב
אֲשֶׁר הִגִּיד מָרְדֳּכַי עַל־בִּגְתָנָא וָתֶרֶשׁ שְׁנֵי סָרִיסֵי
הַמֶּלֶךְ מִשֹּׁמְרֵי הַסַּף אֲשֶׁר בִּקְשׁוּ לִשְׁלֹחַ יָד
ג בַּמֶּלֶךְ אֲחַשְׁוֵרוֹשׁ: וַיֹּאמֶר הַמֶּלֶךְ מַה־נַּעֲשָׂה יְקָר
וּגְדוּלָּה לְמָרְדֳּכַי עַל־זֶה וַיֹּאמְרוּ נַעֲרֵי הַמֶּלֶךְ
ד מְשָׁרְתָיו לֹא־נַעֲשָׂה עִמּוֹ דָּבָר: וַיֹּאמֶר הַמֶּלֶךְ מִי
בֶחָצֵר וְהָמָן בָּא לַחֲצַר בֵּית־הַמֶּלֶךְ הַחִיצוֹנָה
לֵאמֹר לַמֶּלֶךְ לִתְלוֹת אֶת־מָרְדֳּכַי עַל־הָעֵץ
ה אֲשֶׁר־הֵכִין לוֹ: וַיֹּאמְרוּ נַעֲרֵי הַמֶּלֶךְ אֵלָיו הִנֵּה
ו הָמָן עֹמֵד בֶּחָצֵר וַיֹּאמֶר הַמֶּלֶךְ יָבוֹא: וַיָּבוֹא הָמָן
וַיֹּאמֶר לוֹ הַמֶּלֶךְ מַה־לַעֲשׂוֹת בָּאִישׁ אֲשֶׁר הַמֶּלֶךְ
חָפֵץ בִּיקָרוֹ וַיֹּאמֶר הָמָן בְּלִבּוֹ לְמִי יַחְפֹּץ הַמֶּלֶךְ
ז לַעֲשׂוֹת יְקָר יוֹתֵר מִמֶּנִּי: וַיֹּאמֶר הָמָן אֶל־הַמֶּלֶךְ
ח אִישׁ אֲשֶׁר הַמֶּלֶךְ חָפֵץ בִּיקָרוֹ: יָבִיאוּ לְבוּשׁ
מַלְכוּת אֲשֶׁר לָבַשׁ־בּוֹ הַמֶּלֶךְ וְסוּס אֲשֶׁר רָכַב
עָלָיו הַמֶּלֶךְ וַאֲשֶׁר נִתַּן כֶּתֶר מַלְכוּת בְּרֹאשׁוֹ:
ט וְנָתוֹן הַלְּבוּשׁ וְהַסּוּס עַל־יַד־אִישׁ מִשָּׂרֵי הַמֶּלֶךְ
הַפַּרְתְּמִים וְהִלְבִּישׁוּ אֶת־הָאִישׁ אֲשֶׁר הַמֶּלֶךְ
חָפֵץ בִּיקָרוֹ וְהִרְכִּיבֻהוּ עַל־הַסּוּס בִּרְחוֹב הָעִיר
וְקָרְאוּ לְפָנָיו כָּכָה יֵעָשֶׂה לָאִישׁ אֲשֶׁר הַמֶּלֶךְ
י חָפֵץ בִּיקָרוֹ: וַיֹּאמֶר הַמֶּלֶךְ לְהָמָן מַהֵר קַח אֶת־
הַלְּבוּשׁ וְאֶת־הַסּוּס כַּאֲשֶׁר דִּבַּרְתָּ וַעֲשֵׂה־כֵן
לְמָרְדֳּכַי הַיְּהוּדִי הַיּוֹשֵׁב בְּשַׁעַר הַמֶּלֶךְ אַל־תַּפֵּל
יא דָּבָר מִכֹּל אֲשֶׁר דִּבַּרְתָּ: וַיִּקַּח הָמָן אֶת־הַלְּבוּשׁ

6/1. MORDECHAI IS FINALLY REWARDED

¹That night sleep eluded the King so he ordered that the record book, the annals, be brought and be read before the King. ²There it was found recorded that Mordechai had denounced Bigsana and Teresh, two of the King's chamberlains of the guardians of the threshold, who had plotted to lay hands on King Ahasuerus. ³'What honor or dignity has been conferred on Mordechai for this?' asked the King. 'Nothing has been done for him,' replied the King's pages. ⁴The King said: 'Who is in the court?' (Now Haman had just come into the outer court of the palace to speak to the King about hanging Mordechai on the gallows he had prepared for him.) ⁵So the King's servants answered him: 'It is Haman standing in the court.' And the King said: 'Let him enter.' ⁶When Haman came in the King said unto him: 'What should be done for the man whom the King especially wants to honor?' (Now Haman reasoned to himself: 'Whom would the King especially want to honor besides me?') ⁷So Haman said to the King: 'For the man whom the King especially wants to honor, ⁸have them bring a royal robe that the King has worn and a horse that the King has ridden, one with a royal crown on his head. ⁹Then let the robe and horse be entrusted to one of the King's most noble officers, and let them attire the man whom the King especially wants to honor, and parade him on horseback through the city square proclaiming before him: "This is what is done for the man whom the King especially wants to honor." '

10. HAMAN'S HUMILIATION

¹⁰Then the King said to Haman: 'Hurry, then, get the robe and the horse as you have said and do all this for Mordechai the Jew, who sits at the King's gate. Do not omit a single detail that you have suggested!' ¹¹So Haman took the robe

וְאֶת־הַסּוּס וַיַּלְבֵּשׁ אֶת־מׇרְדֳּכַי וַיַּרְכִּיבֵהוּ בִּרְחוֹב
הָעִיר וַיִּקְרָא לְפָנָיו כָּכָה יֵעָשֶׂה לָאִישׁ אֲשֶׁר
יב הַמֶּלֶךְ חָפֵץ בִּיקָרוֹ: וַיָּשׇׁב מׇרְדֳּכַי אֶל־שַׁעַר
הַמֶּלֶךְ וְהָמָן נִדְחַף אֶל־בֵּיתוֹ אָבֵל וַחֲפוּי רֹאשׁ:
יג וַיְסַפֵּר הָמָן לְזֶרֶשׁ אִשְׁתּוֹ וּלְכׇל־אֹהֲבָיו אֵת כׇּל־
אֲשֶׁר קָרָהוּ וַיֹּאמְרוּ לוֹ חֲכָמָיו וְזֶרֶשׁ אִשְׁתּוֹ אִם
מִזֶּרַע הַיְּהוּדִים מׇרְדֳּכַי אֲשֶׁר הַחִלּוֹתָ לִנְפֹּל
יד לְפָנָיו לֹא־תוּכַל לוֹ כִּי־נָפוֹל תִּפּוֹל לְפָנָיו: עוֹדָם
מְדַבְּרִים עִמּוֹ וְסׇרִיסֵי הַמֶּלֶךְ הִגִּיעוּ וַיַּבְהִלוּ
לְהָבִיא אֶת־הָמָן אֶל־הַמִּשְׁתֶּה אֲשֶׁר־עָשְׂתָה
ז א אֶסְתֵּר: וַיָּבֹא הַמֶּלֶךְ וְהָמָן לִשְׁתּוֹת עִם־אֶסְתֵּר
הַמַּלְכָּה: וַיֹּאמֶר הַמֶּלֶךְ לְאֶסְתֵּר גַּם בַּיּוֹם הַשֵּׁנִי
ב בְּמִשְׁתֵּה הַיַּיִן מַה־שְּׁאֵלָתֵךְ אֶסְתֵּר הַמַּלְכָּה
וְתִנָּתֵן לָךְ וּמַה־בַּקָּשָׁתֵךְ עַד־חֲצִי הַמַּלְכוּת
ג וְתֵעָשׂ: וַתַּעַן אֶסְתֵּר הַמַּלְכָּה וַתֹּאמַר אִם־
מָצָאתִי חֵן בְּעֵינֶיךָ הַמֶּלֶךְ וְאִם־עַל־הַמֶּלֶךְ טוֹב
ד תִּנָּתֶן־לִי נַפְשִׁי בִּשְׁאֵלָתִי וְעַמִּי בְּבַקָּשָׁתִי: כִּי
נִמְכַּרְנוּ אֲנִי וְעַמִּי לְהַשְׁמִיד לַהֲרוֹג וּלְאַבֵּד וְאִלּוּ
לַעֲבָדִים וְלִשְׁפָחוֹת נִמְכַּרְנוּ הֶחֱרַשְׁתִּי כִּי אֵין
ה הַצָּר שֹׁוֶה בְּנֵזֶק הַמֶּלֶךְ: וַיֹּאמֶר
הַמֶּלֶךְ אֲחַשְׁוֵרוֹשׁ וַיֹּאמֶר לְאֶסְתֵּר הַמַּלְכָּה מִי
הוּא זֶה וְאֵי־זֶה הוּא אֲשֶׁר־מְלָאוֹ לִבּוֹ לַעֲשׂוֹת
ו כֵּן: וַתֹּאמֶר אֶסְתֵּר אִישׁ צַר וְאוֹיֵב הָמָן הָרָע
הַזֶּה וְהָמָן נִבְעַת מִלִּפְנֵי הַמֶּלֶךְ וְהַמַּלְכָּה:
ז וְהַמֶּלֶךְ קָם בַּחֲמָתוֹ מִמִּשְׁתֵּה הַיַּיִן אֶל־גִּנַּת
הַבִּיתָן וְהָמָן עָמַד לְבַקֵּשׁ עַל־נַפְשׁוֹ מֵאֶסְתֵּר

and the horse and attired Mordechai, and led him through the city square proclaiming before him: 'This is what is done for the man whom the King especially wants to honor.'

¹² Mordechai returned to the King's gate; but Haman hurried home, despondent and with his head covered. ¹³ Haman told his wife, Zeresh, and all his friends everything that had happened to him, and his advisors and his wife, Zeresh, said to him: 'If Mordechai, before whom you have begun to fall, is of Jewish descent, you will not prevail against him, but will undoubtedly fall before him.' ¹⁴ While they were still talking with him, the King's chamberlains arrived, and they hurried to bring Haman to the banquet which Esther had arranged.

13. HAMAN'S DOOM IS FORECAST

7/1. THE SECOND BANQUET: ESTHER PRESENTS HER REQUEST

It was one of God's miracles that, as disturbed as Ahasuerus was, he came to the feast, was cheered by the wine, and regained his good cheer to the extent that he was prepared to fulfill Esther's every wish.

3. The first מֶלֶךְ, *King,* is taken to refer to God, the second to Ahasuerus. 'Esther cast her eyes heavenward and said: "If I have found favor in Your sight, O Supreme King, and if it pleases thee, O King Ahasuerus, let my life be given me, and let my people be rescued out of the hands of the enemy"' *(Targum).*

6. HAMAN IS ACCUSED

7. The King went out to 'cool off' from his anger, part of God's master plan to give Haman the opportunity to incriminate himself even further in the King's absence.

¹ So the King and Haman came to feast with Queen Esther. ²The King asked Esther again on the second day at the wine feast: 'What is your request, Queen Esther? — it shall be granted you. And what is your petition? — Even if it be up to half the kingdom, it shall be fulfilled.' ³ So Queen Esther answered and said: 'If I have won Your Majesty's favor and if it pleases the King, let my life be granted to me as my request and my people as my petition. ⁴ For we have been sold, I and my people, to be destroyed, slain, and annihilated. Had we been sold as slaves and servant-girls, I would have kept quiet, for the adversary is not worthy of the King's damage.'

⁵ Thereupon, King Ahasuerus exclaimed and said to Queen Esther: 'Who is it? Where is the one who dared to do this?' ⁶ And Esther said: 'An adversary and an enemy! This wicked Haman!' Haman trembled in terror before the King and Queen. ⁷ The King rose in a rage from the wine feast and went into the palace garden while Haman remained to beg Queen Esther for his life,

הַמַּלְכָּה כִּי רָאָה כִּי־כָלְתָה אֵלָיו הָרָעָה מֵאֵת
הַמֶּֽלֶךְ: וְהַמֶּ֣לֶךְ שָׁ֗ב מִגִּנַּ֤ת הַבִּיתָן֙ אֶל־בֵּ֣ית | ח
מִשְׁתֵּ֣ה הַיַּ֔יִן וְהָמָ֣ן נֹפֵ֔ל עַל־הַמִּטָּה֙ אֲשֶׁ֣ר אֶסְתֵּ֣ר
עָלֶ֔יהָ וַיֹּ֣אמֶר הַמֶּ֔לֶךְ הֲ֠גַם לִכְבּ֧וֹשׁ אֶת־הַמַּלְכָּ֛ה
עִמִּ֖י בַּבָּ֑יִת הַדָּבָ֗ר יָצָא֙ מִפִּ֣י הַמֶּ֔לֶךְ וּפְנֵ֥י הָמָ֖ן
חָפֽוּ: וַיֹּ֣אמֶר חַ֠רְבוֹנָה אֶחָ֨ד מִן־הַסָּרִיסִ֜ים לִפְנֵ֣י ט
הַמֶּ֗לֶךְ גַּ֣ם הִנֵּֽה־הָעֵ֣ץ אֲשֶׁר־עָשָׂ֪ה הָמָ֣ן לְֽמָרְדֳּכַ֡י
אֲשֶׁ֣ר דִּבֶּר־ט֠וֹב עַל־הַמֶּ֜לֶךְ עֹמֵ֣ד בְּבֵ֣ית הָמָ֗ן
גָּבֹ֥הַּ חֲמִשִּׁ֖ים אַמָּ֑ה וַיֹּ֥אמֶר הַמֶּ֖לֶךְ תְּלֻ֥הוּ עָלָֽיו:
וַיִּתְלוּ֙ אֶת־הָמָ֔ן עַל־הָעֵ֖ץ אֲשֶׁר־הֵכִ֣ין לְמָרְדֳּכָ֑י י
וַחֲמַ֥ת הַמֶּ֖לֶךְ שָׁכָֽכָה: בַּיּ֣וֹם

ח

הַה֗וּא נָתַ֞ן הַמֶּ֤לֶךְ אֲחַשְׁוֵרוֹשׁ֙ לְאֶסְתֵּ֣ר הַמַּלְכָּ֔ה א
אֶת־בֵּ֖ית הָמָ֣ן צֹרֵ֣ר °הַיְּהוּדִ֑ים וּמָרְדֳּכַ֗י בָּ֚א לִפְנֵ֣י °הַיְּהוּדִים ק
הַמֶּ֔לֶךְ כִּֽי־הִגִּ֥ידָה אֶסְתֵּ֖ר מַ֥ה הֽוּא־לָֽהּ: וַיָּ֨סַר ב
הַמֶּ֜לֶךְ אֶת־טַבַּעְתּ֗וֹ אֲשֶׁ֤ר הֶֽעֱבִיר֙ מֵֽהָמָ֔ן וַֽיִּתְּנָ֖הּ
לְמָרְדֳּכָ֑י וַתָּ֧שֶׂם אֶסְתֵּ֛ר אֶֽת־מָרְדֳּכַ֖י עַל־בֵּ֥ית
הָמָֽן: וַתּ֣וֹסֶף אֶסְתֵּ֗ר וַתְּדַבֵּר֙ לִפְנֵ֣י ג
הַמֶּ֔לֶךְ וַתִּפֹּ֖ל לִפְנֵ֣י רַגְלָ֑יו וַתֵּ֣בְךְּ וַתִּתְחַנֶּן־ל֗וֹ
לְהַעֲבִיר֙ אֶת־רָעַת֙ הָמָ֣ן הָֽאֲגָגִ֔י וְאֵת֙ מַֽחֲשַׁבְתּ֔וֹ
אֲשֶׁ֥ר חָשַׁ֖ב עַל־הַיְּהוּדִֽים: וַיּ֤וֹשֶׁט הַמֶּ֙לֶךְ֙ לְאֶסְתֵּ֔ר ד
אֵ֖ת שַׁרְבִ֣ט הַזָּהָ֑ב וַתָּ֣קָם אֶסְתֵּ֔ר וַתַּֽעֲמֹ֖ד
לִפְנֵ֥י הַמֶּֽלֶךְ: וַ֠תֹּאמֶר אִם־עַל־הַמֶּ֨לֶךְ ט֜וֹב וְאִם־ ה
מָצָ֧אתִי חֵ֣ן לְפָנָ֗יו וְכָשֵׁ֤ר הַדָּבָר֙ לִפְנֵ֣י הַמֶּ֔לֶךְ
וְטוֹבָ֥ה אֲנִ֖י בְּעֵינָ֑יו יִכָּתֵ֞ב לְהָשִׁ֣יב אֶת־הַסְּפָרִ֗ים
מַֽחֲשֶׁ֜בֶת הָמָ֤ן בֶּֽן־הַמְּדָ֙תָא֙ הָֽאֲגָגִ֔י אֲשֶׁ֣ר כָּתַ֔ב
לְאַבֵּד֙ אֶת־הַיְּהוּדִ֔ים אֲשֶׁ֖ר בְּכָל־מְדִינ֥וֹת הַמֶּֽלֶךְ:

for he saw that the King's evil determination against him was final. ⁸ When the King returned from the palace garden to the banquet room, Haman was prostrated on the couch upon which Esther was; so the King exclaimed: 'Would he actually assault the Queen while I'm in the house?' As soon as the King uttered this, they covered Haman's face. ⁹ Then Charbonah, one of the chamberlains in attendance of the King, said: 'Furthermore, the fifty-cubit-high gallows which Haman made for Mordechai — who spoke good for the King — is standing in Haman's house.' And the King said: 'Hang him on it.' ¹⁰ So they hanged Haman on the gallows which he had prepared for Mordechai, and the King's anger abated.

9. HAMAN IS EXECUTED

Our Sages ordained that one should always say חַרְבוֹנָה זָכוּר לַטוֹב — 'Charbonah of blessed memory,' because it was Charbonah's swift advice that prevented Haman from possibly talking — or bribing — his way back into the King's good graces.

8/1. MORDECHAI IS APPOINTED PRIME MINISTER

¹ That very day, King Ahasuerus gave the estate of Haman, the enemy of the Jews, to Queen Esther. Mordechai presented himself to the King (for Esther had revealed his relationship to her). ² The King slipped off his signet ring, which he had removed from Haman, and gave it to Mordechai; and Esther put Mordechai in charge of Haman's estate.

3. ESTHER BEGS THE KING TO AVERT HAMAN'S DECREE

³ Esther yet again spoke to the King, collapsed at his feet, and cried and begged him to avert the evil intention of Haman the Agagite, and his scheme which he had plotted against the Jews. ⁴ The King extended the gold scepter to Esther, and Esther arose and stood before the King. ⁵ She said: 'If it pleases the King, and if I have won his favor, and the proposal seems proper in the King's opinion, and I be pleasing to him, let a decree be written to countermand those dispatches devised by Haman, the son of Hammedasa the Agagite, which he wrote ordering the destruction of the Jews who are in all the King's provinces.

ו כִּי אֵיכָכָה אוּכַל וְרָאִיתִי בָּרָעָה אֲשֶׁר־יִמְצָא
אֶת־עַמִּי וְאֵיכָכָה אוּכַל וְרָאִיתִי בְּאָבְדַן
מוֹלַדְתִּי: ז וַיֹּאמֶר הַמֶּלֶךְ אֲחַשְׁוֵרֹשׁ
לְאֶסְתֵּר הַמַּלְכָּה וּלְמָרְדֳּכַי הַיְּהוּדִי הִנֵּה בֵית־
הָמָן נָתַתִּי לְאֶסְתֵּר וְאֹתוֹ תָּלוּ עַל־הָעֵץ עַל
אֲשֶׁר־שָׁלַח יָדוֹ °בַּיְּהוּדִים: ח וְאַתֶּם כִּתְבוּ עַל־ °בַּיְּהוּדִיים ק
הַיְּהוּדִים כַּטּוֹב בְּעֵינֵיכֶם בְּשֵׁם הַמֶּלֶךְ וְחִתְמוּ
בְּטַבַּעַת הַמֶּלֶךְ כִּי־כְתָב אֲשֶׁר־נִכְתָּב בְּשֵׁם־הַמֶּלֶךְ
וְנַחְתּוֹם בְּטַבַּעַת הַמֶּלֶךְ אֵין לְהָשִׁיב: ט וַיִּקָּרְאוּ
סֹפְרֵי־הַמֶּלֶךְ בָּעֵת־הַהִיא בַּחֹדֶשׁ הַשְּׁלִישִׁי
הוּא־חֹדֶשׁ סִיוָן בִּשְׁלוֹשָׁה וְעֶשְׂרִים בּוֹ וַיִּכָּתֵב
כְּכָל־אֲשֶׁר־צִוָּה מָרְדֳּכַי אֶל־הַיְּהוּדִים וְאֶל
הָאֲחַשְׁדַּרְפְּנִים וְהַפַּחוֹת וְשָׂרֵי הַמְּדִינוֹת אֲשֶׁר |
מֵהֹדּוּ וְעַד־כּוּשׁ שֶׁבַע וְעֶשְׂרִים וּמֵאָה מְדִינָה
מְדִינָה וּמְדִינָה כִּכְתָבָהּ וְעַם וָעָם כִּלְשֹׁנוֹ וְאֶל־
הַיְּהוּדִים כִּכְתָבָם וְכִלְשׁוֹנָם: י וַיִּכְתֹּב בְּשֵׁם הַמֶּלֶךְ
אֲחַשְׁוֵרֹשׁ וַיַּחְתֹּם בְּטַבַּעַת הַמֶּלֶךְ וַיִּשְׁלַח סְפָרִים
בְּיַד הָרָצִים בַּסּוּסִים רֹכְבֵי הָרֶכֶשׁ הָאֲחַשְׁתְּרָנִים
בְּנֵי הָרַמָּכִים: יא אֲשֶׁר נָתַן הַמֶּלֶךְ לַיְּהוּדִים | אֲשֶׁר |
בְּכָל־עִיר וָעִיר לְהִקָּהֵל וְלַעֲמֹד עַל־נַפְשָׁם
לְהַשְׁמִיד וְלַהֲרֹג וּלְאַבֵּד אֶת־כָּל־חֵיל עַם
וּמְדִינָה הַצָּרִים אֹתָם טַף וְנָשִׁים וּשְׁלָלָם לָבוֹז:
יב בְּיוֹם אֶחָד בְּכָל־מְדִינוֹת הַמֶּלֶךְ אֲחַשְׁוֵרֹשׁ
בִּשְׁלוֹשָׁה עָשָׂר לְחֹדֶשׁ שְׁנֵים־עָשָׂר הוּא־חֹדֶשׁ
יג אֲדָר: פַּתְשֶׁגֶן הַכְּתָב לְהִנָּתֵן דָּת בְּכָל־מְדִינָה
וּמְדִינָה גָּלוּי לְכָל־הָעַמִּים וְלִהְיוֹת °הַיְּהוּדִיים °הַיְּהוּדִים ק

⁶ For how can I bear to witness the disaster which will befall my people! How can I bear to witness the destruction of my relatives!'

7. PERMISSION IS GRANTED TO OVERRIDE THE DECREE

⁷ Then King Ahasuerus said to Queen Esther and Mordechai the Jew: 'Behold, I have given Haman's estate to Esther, and he has been hanged on the gallows because he plotted against the Jews. ⁸ You may write concerning the Jews whatever you desire, in the King's name, and seal it with the royal signet, for an edict which is written in the King's name and sealed with the royal signet may not be revoked.' ⁹ So the King's secretaries were summoned at that time, on the twenty-third day of the third month, that is, the month of Sivan, and it was written exactly as Mordechai had dictated to the Jews and to the satraps, the governors and officials of the provinces from Hodu to Cush, a hundred and twenty-seven provinces, to each province in its own script, and each people in its own language, and to the Jews in their own script and language. ¹⁰ He wrote in the name of the King Ahasuerus and sealed it with the King's signet. He sent letters by couriers on horseback, riders of swift mules bred of mares, ¹¹ to the effect that the King had permitted the Jews of every single city to organize and defend themselves; to destroy, slay, and exterminate every armed force of any people or province that threaten them, along with their children and women, and to plunder their possessions, ¹² on a single day in all the provinces of King Ahasuerus, namely, upon the thirteenth day of the twelfth month, that is, the month of Adar. ¹³ The contents of the document were to be promulgated in every province, and be published to all peoples so that the Jews should be ready on that day to avenge themselves

8. The Holy One, Blessed is He, now performed an unprecedented miracle. Was there ever in history such a miracle that Israel should wreak vengeance on the other nations and do with their enemies as they pleased? *(Midrash).*

11. Only by organizing and unifying themselves in begging for God's assistance could the Jews be victorious despite being seriously outnumbered.

°עֲתִידִים ק' יד °עֲתוּדִים לַיּוֹם הַזֶּה לְהִנָּקֵם מֵאֹיְבֵיהֶם: הָרָצִים רֹכְבֵי הָרֶכֶשׁ הָאֲחַשְׁתְּרָנִים יָצְאוּ מְבֹהָלִים וּדְחוּפִים בִּדְבַר הַמֶּלֶךְ וְהַדָּת נִתְּנָה בְּשׁוּשַׁן הַבִּירָה: טו וּמָרְדֳּכַי יָצָא מִלִּפְנֵי הַמֶּלֶךְ בִּלְבוּשׁ מַלְכוּת תְּכֵלֶת וָחוּר וַעֲטֶרֶת זָהָב גְּדוֹלָה וְתַכְרִיךְ בּוּץ וְאַרְגָּמָן וְהָעִיר שׁוּשָׁן צָהֲלָה וְשָׂמֵחָה: לַיְּהוּדִים הָיְתָה אוֹרָה טז וְשִׂמְחָה וְשָׂשֹׂן וִיקָר: וּבְכָל־מְדִינָה וּמְדִינָה יז וּבְכָל־עִיר וָעִיר מְקוֹם אֲשֶׁר דְּבַר־הַמֶּלֶךְ וְדָתוֹ מַגִּיעַ שִׂמְחָה וְשָׂשֹׂן לַיְּהוּדִים מִשְׁתֶּה וְיוֹם טוֹב וְרַבִּים מֵעַמֵּי הָאָרֶץ מִתְיַהֲדִים כִּי־נָפַל פַּחַד־הַיְּהוּדִים עֲלֵיהֶם: וּבִשְׁנֵים עָשָׂר חֹדֶשׁ הוּא־חֹדֶשׁ א אֲדָר בִּשְׁלוֹשָׁה עָשָׂר יוֹם בּוֹ אֲשֶׁר הִגִּיעַ דְּבַר־הַמֶּלֶךְ וְדָתוֹ לְהֵעָשׂוֹת בַּיּוֹם אֲשֶׁר שִׂבְּרוּ אֹיְבֵי הַיְּהוּדִים לִשְׁלוֹט בָּהֶם וְנַהֲפוֹךְ הוּא אֲשֶׁר יִשְׁלְטוּ הַיְּהוּדִים הֵמָּה בְּשֹׂנְאֵיהֶם: נִקְהֲלוּ הַיְּהוּדִים ב בְּעָרֵיהֶם בְּכָל־מְדִינוֹת הַמֶּלֶךְ אֲחַשְׁוֵרוֹשׁ לִשְׁלֹחַ יָד בִּמְבַקְשֵׁי רָעָתָם וְאִישׁ לֹא־עָמַד לִפְנֵיהֶם כִּי־ נָפַל פַּחְדָּם עַל־כָּל־הָעַמִּים: וְכָל־שָׂרֵי הַמְּדִינוֹת ג וְהָאֲחַשְׁדַּרְפְּנִים וְהַפַּחוֹת וְעֹשֵׂי הַמְּלָאכָה אֲשֶׁר לַמֶּלֶךְ מְנַשְּׂאִים אֶת־הַיְּהוּדִים כִּי־נָפַל פַּחַד־ מָרְדֳּכַי עֲלֵיהֶם: כִּי־גָדוֹל מָרְדֳּכַי בְּבֵית הַמֶּלֶךְ ד וְשָׁמְעוֹ הוֹלֵךְ בְּכָל־הַמְּדִינוֹת כִּי־הָאִישׁ מָרְדֳּכַי הוֹלֵךְ וְגָדוֹל: וַיַּכּוּ הַיְּהוּדִים בְּכָל־אֹיְבֵיהֶם מַכַּת־ ה חֶרֶב וְהֶרֶג וְאַבְדָן וַיַּעֲשׂוּ בְשֹׂנְאֵיהֶם כִּרְצוֹנָם: וּבְשׁוּשַׁן הַבִּירָה הָרְגוּ הַיְּהוּדִים וְאַבֵּד חֲמֵשׁ ו

on their enemies. ¹⁴ The couriers, riders of swift mules, went forth in urgent haste by order of the King, and the edict was distributed in Shushan the Capitol.

¹⁵ Mordechai left the King's presence clad in royal apparel of blue and white with a large gold crown and a robe of fine linen and purple; then the city of Shushan was cheerful and glad. ¹⁶ The Jews had light and gladness, and joy and honor. ¹⁷ Likewise, in every province, and in every city, wherever the King's command and his decree reached, the Jews had gladness and joy, a feast and a holiday. Moreover, many from among the people of the land professed themselves Jews, for the fear of the Jews had fallen upon them.

15-16. These are among the four verses recited aloud in the synagogue by the congregation during the public reading of the *Megillah*.

16. Rav Yehudah said: אוֹרָה, *light*, refers to Torah; שִׂמְחָה, *gladness*, refers to holiday; שָׂשׂוֹן, *joy*, refers to circumcision; and יְקָר, *honor*, refers to תְּפִילִין, *tefillin* [i.e., they were finally able to resume the study of Torah and the performance of *mitzvos* without hindrance] *(Talmud).*

[Some commentators say that the amusing Purim custom of masquerading in outlandish costumes is derived from this verse. Just as non-Jews 'masqueraded' as proselytes in order to curry favor, so we masquerade merrily to commemorate the miracle.]

9/1. THE TURNABOUT: THE JEWS AVENGE THEMSELVES

¹ **A**nd so, on the thirteenth day of the twelfth month, which is the month of Adar, when the King's command and edict were about to be enforced — on the very day that the enemies of the Jews expected to gain the upper hand over them — and it was turned about: The Jews gained the upper hand over their adversaries; ² the Jews organized themselves in their cities throughout all the provinces of King Ahasuerus, to attack those who sought their hurt; and no one stood in their way, for fear of them had fallen upon all the peoples. ³ Moreover, all the provincial officials, satraps, and governors and those that conduct the King's affairs, deferred to the Jews because the fear of Mordechai had fallen upon them. ⁴ For Mordechai was now preeminent in the royal palace and his fame was spreading throughout all the provinces, for the man Mordechai grew increasingly greater. ⁵ And the Jews struck at all their enemies with the sword, slaughtering and annihilating; they treated their enemies as they pleased. ⁶ In Shushan the Capitol, the Jews slew and annihilated five

ז מֵאוֹת אִישׁ:   וְאֵת |

פַּרְשַׁנְדָּתָא   וְאֵת |

דַּלְפוֹן   וְאֵת |

ח אַסְפָּתָא: וְאֵת |

פּוֹרָתָא   וְאֵת |

אֲדַלְיָא   וְאֵת |

ט אֲרִידָתָא: וְאֵת |

פַּרְמַשְׁתָּא   וְאֵת |

אֲרִיסַי   וְאֵת |

אֲרִידַי   וְאֵת |

י וַיְזָתָא: עֲשֶׂרֶת

בְּנֵי הָמָן בֶּן־הַמְּדָתָא צֹרֵר הַיְּהוּדִים הָרָגוּ וּבַבִּזָּה

יא לֹא שָׁלְחוּ אֶת־יָדָם: בַּיּוֹם הַהוּא בָּא מִסְפַּר

יב הַהֲרוּגִים בְּשׁוּשַׁן הַבִּירָה לִפְנֵי הַמֶּלֶךְ: וַיֹּאמֶר הַמֶּלֶךְ לְאֶסְתֵּר הַמַּלְכָּה בְּשׁוּשַׁן הַבִּירָה הָרְגוּ הַיְּהוּדִים וְאַבֵּד חֲמֵשׁ מֵאוֹת אִישׁ וְאֵת עֲשֶׂרֶת בְּנֵי־הָמָן בִּשְׁאָר מְדִינוֹת הַמֶּלֶךְ מֶה עָשׂוּ וּמַה־שְּׁאֵלָתֵךְ וְיִנָּתֵן לָךְ וּמַה־בַּקָּשָׁתֵךְ עוֹד וְתֵעָשׂ:

יג וַתֹּאמֶר אֶסְתֵּר אִם־עַל־הַמֶּלֶךְ טוֹב יִנָּתֵן גַּם־מָחָר לַיְּהוּדִים אֲשֶׁר בְּשׁוּשָׁן לַעֲשׂוֹת כְּדָת הַיּוֹם וְאֵת עֲשֶׂרֶת בְּנֵי־הָמָן יִתְלוּ עַל־הָעֵץ:

יד וַיֹּאמֶר הַמֶּלֶךְ לְהֵעָשׂוֹת כֵּן וַתִּנָּתֵן דָּת בְּשׁוּשָׁן וְאֵת עֲשֶׂרֶת בְּנֵי־הָמָן תָּלוּ:

טו ﹒הַיְּהוּדִים ק﹒ יִקָּהֲלוּ ﹾהַיְּהוּדִיים אֲשֶׁר־ בְּשׁוּשָׁן גַּם בְּיוֹם אַרְבָּעָה עָשָׂר לְחֹדֶשׁ אֲדָר וַיַּהַרְגוּ בְשׁוּשָׁן שְׁלֹשׁ מֵאוֹת אִישׁ וּבַבִּזָּה לֹא

טז שָׁלְחוּ אֶת־יָדָם: וּשְׁאָר הַיְּהוּדִים אֲשֶׁר בִּמְדִינוֹת

7. The ten sons of Haman and the word עֲשֶׂרֶת, *ten*, which follows, should be said [by the one reading the *Megillah* on Purim] in one breath ... to indicate that they all died together *(Talmud).*

9. The letter Vav [ו] of *Vayzasa* is enlarged in the *Megillah* like a long pole to indicate that they were all strung [one underneath the other] on one long pole *(Talmud).*

10. It was obviously most difficult for poor Jews to restrain themselves from taking spoils. In reward for their restraint, it was established that, throughout all generations, the poor — without exception and investigation as to need — will be the recipients of מַתָּנוֹת לָאֶבְיוֹנִים, *gifts to the poor,* on Purim *(Rebbe of Ger).*

13. THE JEWS IN SHUSHAN ARE GRANTED A SECOND DAY

hundred men. [7] including Parshandasa and Dalphon and Aspasa [8] and Porasa and Adalia and Aridasa [9] and Parmashta and Arisai and Aridai and Vayzasa [10] the ten sons of Haman, son of Hammedasa, the Jews' enemy; but they did not lay their hand on the spoils.

[11] That same day the number of those killed in Shushan the Capitol was reported to the King. [12] The King said onto Queen Esther: 'In Shushan the Capitol the Jews have slain and annihilated five hundred men as well as the ten sons of Haman; what must they have done in the rest of the King's provinces! What is your request now? It shall be granted you. What is your petition further? It shall be fulfilled.' [13] Esther replied: 'If it pleases His Majesty, allow the Jews who are in Shushan to act tomorrow as they did today, and let Haman's ten sons be hanged on the gallows.' [14] The King ordered that this be done. A decree was distributed in Shushan, and they hanged Haman's tens sons. [15] The Jews that were in Shushan assembled again on the fourteenth day of the month of Adar, and slew three hundred men in Shushan; but they did not lay their hand on the spoils.

[16] The rest of the Jews throughout the King's provinces organized and defended themselves

הַמֶּ֫לֶךְ נִקְהֲל֣וּ | וְעָמֹ֣ד עַל־נַפְשָׁ֗ם וְנ֙וֹחַ֙ מֵאֹ֣יְבֵיהֶ֔ם
וְהָרוֹג֙ בְּשֹׂ֣נְאֵיהֶ֔ם חֲמִשָּׁ֥ה וְשִׁבְעִ֖ים אָ֑לֶף וּבַ֙בִּזָּ֔ה

יז לֹ֥א שָֽׁלְח֖וּ אֶת־יָדָֽם: בְּיוֹם־שְׁלוֹשָׁ֤ה עָשָׂר֙ לְחֹ֣דֶשׁ
אֲדָ֔ר וְנ֕וֹחַ בְּאַרְבָּעָ֥ה עָשָׂ֖ר בּ֑וֹ וְעָשֹׂ֣ה אֹת֔וֹ י֖וֹם
מִשְׁתֶּ֥ה וְשִׂמְחָֽה: °וְהַיְּהוּדִ֣ים אֲשֶׁר־בְּשׁוּשָׁ֗ן °וְהַיְּהוּדִים ק׳ יח

יח נִקְהֲלוּ֙ בִּשְׁלוֹשָׁ֤ה עָשָׂר֙ בּ֔וֹ וּבְאַרְבָּעָ֥ה עָשָׂ֖ר בּ֑וֹ
וְנ֕וֹחַ בַּחֲמִשָּׁ֥ה עָשָׂ֖ר בּ֑וֹ וְעָשֹׂ֣ה אֹת֔וֹ י֖וֹם מִשְׁתֶּ֥ה
וְשִׂמְחָֽה: עַל־כֵּ֞ן הַיְּהוּדִ֣ים °הַפְּרָזִ֗ים הַיֹּֽשְׁבִים֙ °הַפְּרָזִים ק׳ יט

יט בְּעָרֵ֣י הַפְּרָז֔וֹת עֹשִׂ֗ים אֵ֠ת י֣וֹם אַרְבָּעָ֤ה עָשָׂר֙
לְחֹ֣דֶשׁ אֲדָ֔ר שִׂמְחָ֥ה וּמִשְׁתֶּ֖ה וְי֣וֹם ט֑וֹב וּמִשְׁלֹ֧חַ
מָנ֛וֹת אִ֖ישׁ לְרֵעֵֽהוּ: וַיִּכְתֹּ֣ב מׇרְדֳּכַ֔י אֶת־הַדְּבָרִ֖ים

כ הָאֵ֑לֶּה וַיִּשְׁלַ֣ח סְפָרִ֗ים אֶל־כׇּל־הַיְּהוּדִים֙ אֲשֶׁר֙
בְּכׇל־מְדִינוֹת֙ הַמֶּ֣לֶךְ אֲחַשְׁוֵר֔וֹשׁ הַקְּרוֹבִ֖ים
וְהָרְחוֹקִֽים: לְקַיֵּם֙ עֲלֵיהֶ֔ם לִהְי֣וֹת עֹשִׂ֗ים אֵ֠ת י֣וֹם

כא אַרְבָּעָ֤ה עָשָׂר֙ לְחֹ֣דֶשׁ אֲדָ֔ר וְאֵ֛ת יוֹם־חֲמִשָּׁ֥ה
עָשָׂ֖ר בּ֑וֹ בְּכׇל־שָׁנָ֖ה וְשָׁנָֽה: כַּיָּמִ֗ים אֲשֶׁר־נָ֨חוּ בָהֶ֤ם

כב הַיְּהוּדִים֙ מֵאֹ֣יְבֵיהֶ֔ם וְהַחֹ֗דֶשׁ אֲשֶׁר֩ נֶהְפַּ֨ךְ לָהֶ֤ם
מִיָּגוֹן֙ לְשִׂמְחָ֔ה וּמֵאֵ֖בֶל לְי֣וֹם ט֑וֹב לַעֲשׂ֣וֹת אוֹתָ֗ם
יְמֵי֙ מִשְׁתֶּ֣ה וְשִׂמְחָ֔ה וּמִשְׁלֹ֤חַ מָנוֹת֙ אִ֣ישׁ לְרֵעֵ֔הוּ
וּמַתָּנ֖וֹת לָֽאֶבְיֹנִֽים: וְקִבֵּל֙ הַיְּהוּדִ֔ים אֵ֥ת אֲשֶׁר־

כג הֵחֵ֖לּוּ לַעֲשׂ֑וֹת וְאֵ֛ת אֲשֶׁר־כָּתַ֥ב מׇרְדֳּכַ֖י אֲלֵיהֶֽם:
כִּי֩ הָמָ֨ן בֶּֽן־הַמְּדָ֜תָא הָֽאֲגָגִ֗י צֹרֵר֙ כׇּל־הַיְּהוּדִ֔ים

כד חָשַׁ֥ב עַל־הַיְּהוּדִ֖ים לְאַבְּדָ֑ם וְהִפִּ֣ל פּוּר֙ ה֣וּא
הַגּוֹרָ֔ל לְהֻמָּ֖ם וּֽלְאַבְּדָֽם: וּבְבֹאָהּ֮ לִפְנֵ֣י הַמֶּ֒לֶךְ֒

כה אָמַ֣ר עִם־הַסֵּ֔פֶר יָשׁ֞וּב מַחֲשַׁבְתּ֧וֹ הָרָעָ֛ה אֲשֶׁר־
חָשַׁ֥ב עַל־הַיְּהוּדִ֖ים עַל־רֹאשׁ֑וֹ וְתָל֥וּ אֹת֖וֹ וְאֶת־

gaining relief from their foes, slaying seventy-five thousand of their enemies — but they did not lay their hand on the spoils. [17] That was the thirteenth day of the month of Adar; and they gained relief on the fourteenth day, making it a day of feasting and gladness. [18] But the Jews that were in Shushan assembled on both the thirteenth and fourteenth, and they gained relief on the fifteenth, making it a day of feasting and gladness. [19] That is why Jewish villagers who live in unwalled towns celebrate the fourteenth day of the month of Adar as an occasion of gladness and feasting, for holiday-making and for sending delicacies to one another.

19. The law of 'Shushan Purim' — celebrating Purim on the fifteenth day of Adar in walled cities in commemoration of the victory in Shushan — is not specifically stated in the Megillah. It is implied in verses 19 and 21 and so established by the Rabbis.

20. MORDECHAI RECORDS THESE EVENTS AND LEGISLATES ANNUAL COMMEMORATION

He wrote this Megillah exactly as it appears in its present text.

22. Sending delicacies to one another — at least two delicacies, i.e., ready-to-eat foods [מָנוֹת being plural] to one person. And gifts to the poor — this means two gifts to two people [one gift to each of the two, the minimum number of the plural word אֶבְיֹנִים, poor, being two] (Talmud).

[20] Mordechai recorded these events and sent letters to all the Jews throughout the provinces of King Ahasuerus, near and far, [21] charging them that they should observe annually the fourteenth and fifteenth days of Adar, [22] as the days on which the Jews gained relief from their enemies, and the month which had been transformed for them from one of sorrow to gladness, and from mourning to festivity. They were to observe them as days of feasting and gladness, and for sending delicacies to one another, and gifts to the poor. [23] The Jews undertook to continue the practice they had begun, just as Mordechai had prescribed to them.

[24] For Haman, the son of Hammedasa the Agagite, enemy of all the Jews, had plotted to destroy the Jews and had cast a *pur* (that is, the lot) to terrify and destroy them; [25] but when she appeared before the King, he commanded by means of letters that the wicked scheme, which [Haman] had devised against the Jews, should recoil on his own head; and they hanged him and

כו בָּנָ֖יו עַל־הָעֵֽץ׃ עַל־כֵּ֡ן קָֽרְאוּ֩ לַיָּמִ֨ים הָאֵ֤לֶּה פוּרִים֙ עַל־שֵׁ֣ם הַפּ֔וּר עַל־כֵּ֕ן עַל־כָּל־דִּבְרֵ֖י הָאִגֶּ֣רֶת הַזֹּ֑את

כז וּמָֽה־רָא֣וּ עַל־כָּ֔כָה וּמָ֥ה הִגִּ֖יעַ אֲלֵיהֶֽם׃ קִיְּמ֣וּ וְקִבְּל֣וּ הַיְּהוּדִים֩ ׀ עֲלֵיהֶ֨ם ׀ וְעַל־זַרְעָ֜ם וְעַ֣ל כָּל־הַנִּלְוִ֤ים עֲלֵיהֶם֙ וְלֹ֣א יַֽעֲב֔וֹר לִֽהְי֣וֹת עֹשִׂ֗ים אֵ֣ת שְׁנֵ֤י הַיָּמִים֙ הָאֵ֔לֶּה כִּכְתָבָ֖ם וְכִזְמַנָּ֑ם בְּכָל־שָׁנָ֖ה

כח וְשָׁנָֽה׃ וְהַיָּמִ֣ים הָ֠אֵלֶּה נִזְכָּרִ֨ים וְנַֽעֲשִׂ֜ים בְּכָל־דּ֣וֹר וָד֗וֹר מִשְׁפָּחָה֙ וּמִשְׁפָּחָ֔ה מְדִינָ֥ה וּמְדִינָ֖ה וְעִ֣יר וָעִ֑יר וִימֵ֞י הַפּוּרִ֣ים הָאֵ֗לֶּה לֹ֤א יַֽעַבְרוּ֙ מִתּ֣וֹךְ

כט הַיְּהוּדִ֔ים וְזִכְרָ֖ם לֹֽא־יָס֥וּף מִזַּרְעָֽם׃ וַתִּכְתֹּ֡ב אֶסְתֵּ֣ר הַמַּלְכָּ֠ה בַת־אֲבִיחַ֧יִל וּמָרְדֳּכַ֛י הַיְּהוּדִ֖י אֶת־כָּל־תֹּ֑קֶף לְקַיֵּ֗ם אֵ֣ת אִגֶּ֧רֶת הַפֻּרִ֛ים הַזֹּ֖את

ל הַשֵּׁנִֽית׃ וַיִּשְׁלַ֨ח סְפָרִ֜ים אֶל־כָּל־הַיְּהוּדִ֗ים אֶל־שֶׁ֨בַע וְעֶשְׂרִ֤ים וּמֵאָה֙ מְדִינָ֔ה מַלְכ֖וּת אֲחַשְׁוֵר֑וֹשׁ

לא דִּבְרֵ֥י שָׁל֖וֹם וֶֽאֱמֶֽת׃ לְקַיֵּ֡ם אֶת־יְמֵי֩ הַפֻּרִ֨ים הָאֵ֜לֶּה בִּזְמַנֵּיהֶ֗ם כַּֽאֲשֶׁר֩ קִיַּ֨ם עֲלֵיהֶ֜ם מָרְדֳּכַ֤י הַיְּהוּדִי֙ וְאֶסְתֵּ֣ר הַמַּלְכָּ֔ה וְכַֽאֲשֶׁ֛ר קִיְּמ֥וּ עַל־נַפְשָׁ֖ם

לב וְעַל־זַרְעָ֑ם דִּבְרֵ֥י הַצּוֹמ֖וֹת וְזַֽעֲקָתָֽם׃ וּמַֽאֲמַ֣ר אֶסְתֵּ֗ר קִיַּ֛ם דִּבְרֵ֥י הַפֻּרִ֖ים הָאֵ֑לֶּה וְנִכְתָּ֖ב בַּסֵּֽפֶר׃

י א וַיָּ֩שֶׂם֩ הַמֶּ֨לֶךְ °אֲחַשְׁרֹ֧שׁ ׀ מַ֣ס עַל־הָאָ֖רֶץ וְאִיֵּ֣י הַיָּ֑ם׃ וְכָל־מַֽעֲשֵׂ֤ה תָקְפּוֹ֙ וּגְב֣וּרָת֔וֹ

ב וּפָ֣רָשַׁ֗ת גְּדֻלַּ֤ת מָרְדֳּכַי֙ אֲשֶׁ֣ר גִּדְּל֣וֹ הַמֶּ֔לֶךְ הֲלוֹא־הֵ֣ם כְּתוּבִ֗ים עַל־סֵ֨פֶר֙ דִּבְרֵ֣י הַיָּמִ֔ים לְמַלְכֵ֖י מָדַ֥י

ג וּפָרָֽס׃ כִּ֣י ׀ מָרְדֳּכַ֣י הַיְּהוּדִ֗י מִשְׁנֶה֙ לַמֶּ֣לֶךְ אֲחַשְׁוֵר֔וֹשׁ וְגָדוֹל֙ לַיְּהוּדִ֔ים וְרָצ֖וּי לְרֹ֣ב אֶחָ֑יו דֹּרֵ֥שׁ טוֹב֙ לְעַמּ֔וֹ וְדֹבֵ֥ר שָׁל֖וֹם לְכָל־זַרְעֽוֹ׃

°אֲחַשְׁוֵרוֹשׁ ק׳

27. *Confirmed and undertook —* i.e., they confirmed what they had undertaken long before at Sinai *(Talmud).*

28. 'Even if all the festivals should be annulled, Purim will never be annulled' *(Midrash).*

29. וַתִּכְתֹּב — *Wrote.* The letter ת in this word is enlarged to indicate that just as the ת is the last letter of the alphabet, so the story of Esther the end of all the miracles to be included in the Bible *(Talmud).*

10/1. EPILOGUE

With the salvation of the Jews, affairs of state returned to normal. Under Mordechai, the empire grew stronger.

3. With the mention of שָׁלוֹם, *welfare* [literally *peace*], and a picture of the stature and security of the Jews under Mordechai, the *Megillah* closes.

The last verse is among the four verses recited aloud by the congregation during the reading of the *Megillah* in the synagogue. Among the reasons offered for this widespread custom are: to popularize the miracle [פִּירְסוּמֵי נִיסָא]; these verses express the essence of the miracle; and to keep the children alert and prevent them from dozing off. The congregation recites the verses loudly as an expression of the joy of the day. The reader then repeats the verses because each verse must be read from a halachically valid *Megillah* scroll.

his sons on the gallows. ²⁶ That is why they called these days "Purim" from the word *"pur."* Therefore, because of all that was written in this letter, and because of what they had experienced, and what has happened to them, ²⁷ the Jews confirmed and undertook upon themselves, and their posterity, and upon all who might join them, to observe these two days, without fail, in the manner prescribed, and at the proper time each year. ²⁸ Consequently, these days should be remembered and celebrated by every single generation, family, province, and city; and these days of Purim should never cease among the Jews, nor shall their remembrance perish from their descendants.

²⁹ Then Queen Esther, daughter of Avichail, and Mordechai the Jew, wrote with full authority to ratify this second letter of Purim. ³⁰ Dispatches were sent to all the Jews, to the hundred and twenty-seven provinces of the kingdom of Ahasuerus — with words of peace and truth — ³¹ to establish these days of Purim on their proper dates just as Mordechai the Jew and Queen Esther had enjoined them, and as they had undertook upon themselves and their posterity the matter of the fasts and their lamentations. ³² Esther's ordinance validated these regulations for Purim; and it was recorded in the book.

¹ **K**ing Ahasuerus levied taxes on both the mainland and the islands. ² All his mighty and powerful acts, and a full account of the greatness of Mordechai, whom the King had promoted, are recorded in the book of chronicles of the Kings of Media and Persia. ³ For Mordechai the Jew was viceroy to King Ahasuerus; he was a great man among the Jews, and popular with the multitude of his brethren; he sought the good of his people and was concerned for the welfare of all his posterity.

If a *minyan* is present for the *Megillah* reading, the following blessing is recited after the reading.

בָּרוּךְ אַתָּה יהוה אֱלֹהֵינוּ מֶלֶךְ הָעוֹלָם, הָרָב אֶת רִיבֵנוּ, וְהַדָּן אֶת דִּינֵנוּ, וְהַנּוֹקֵם אֶת נִקְמָתֵנוּ, וְהַמְשַׁלֵּם גְּמוּל לְכָל אֹיְבֵי נַפְשֵׁנוּ, וְהַנִּפְרָע לָנוּ מִצָּרֵינוּ. בָּרוּךְ אַתָּה יהוה, הַנִּפְרָע לְעַמּוֹ יִשְׂרָאֵל מִכָּל צָרֵיהֶם, הָאֵל הַמּוֹשִׁיעַ. (אָמֵן.—Cong.)

The following poetic narrative of the Purim story is recited only after the evening *Megillah* reading. After the morning reading continue with, שׁוֹשַׁנַּת יַעֲקֹב, below.

אֲשֶׁר הֵנִיא עֲצַת גּוֹיִם, וַיָּפֶר מַחְשְׁבוֹת עֲרוּמִים.

בְּקוּם עָלֵינוּ אָדָם רָשָׁע, נֵצֶר זָדוֹן, מִזֶּרַע עֲמָלֵק.

גָּאָה בְעָשְׁרוֹ, וְכָרָה לוֹ בּוֹר, וּגְדֻלָּתוֹ יָקְשָׁה לּוֹ לָכֶד.

דִּמָּה בְנַפְשׁוֹ לִלְכֹּד, וְנִלְכַּד, בִּקֵּשׁ לְהַשְׁמִיד, וְנִשְׁמַד מְהֵרָה.

הָמָן הוֹדִיעַ אֵיבַת אֲבוֹתָיו, וְעוֹרֵר שִׂנְאַת אַחִים לַבָּנִים.

וְלֹא זָכַר רַחֲמֵי שָׁאוּל, כִּי בְחֶמְלָתוֹ עַל אֲגַג נוֹלַד אוֹיֵב.

זָמַם רָשָׁע לְהַכְרִית צַדִּיק, וְנִלְכַּד טָמֵא, בִּידֵי טָהוֹר.

חֶסֶד גָּבַר עַל שִׁגְגַת אָב, וְרָשָׁע הוֹסִיף חֵטְא עַל חֲטָאָיו.

טָמַן בְּלִבּוֹ מַחְשְׁבוֹת עֲרוּמָיו, וַיִּתְמַכֵּר לַעֲשׂוֹת רָעָה.

יָדוֹ שָׁלַח בִּקְדוֹשֵׁי אֵל, כַּסְפּוֹ נָתַן לְהַכְרִית זִכְרָם.

בִּרְאוֹת מָרְדְּכַי, כִּי יָצָא קֶצֶף, וְדָתֵי הָמָן נִתְּנוּ בְשׁוּשָׁן.

לָבַשׁ שַׂק וְקָשַׁר מִסְפֵּד, וְגָזַר צוֹם, וַיֵּשֶׁב עַל הָאֵפֶר.

מִי זֶה יַעֲמֹד לְכַפֵּר שְׁגָגָה, וְלִמְחֹל חַטַּאת עֲוֹן אֲבוֹתֵינוּ.

נֵץ פָּרַח מִלּוּלָב, הֵן הֲדַסָּה עָמְדָה לְעוֹרֵר יְשֵׁנִים.

סָרִיסֶיהָ הִבְהִילוּ לְהָמָן, לְהַשְׁקוֹתוֹ יֵין חֲמַת תַּנִּינִים.

עָמַד בְּעָשְׁרוֹ, וְנָפַל בְּרִשְׁעוֹ, עָשָׂה לוֹ עֵץ, וְנִתְלָה עָלָיו.

פִּיהֶם פָּתְחוּ, כָּל יוֹשְׁבֵי תֵבֵל, כִּי פוּר הָמָן נֶהְפַּךְ לְפוּרֵנוּ.

צַדִּיק נֶחֱלַץ מִיַּד רָשָׁע, אוֹיֵב נִתַּן תַּחַת נַפְשׁוֹ.

קִיְּמוּ עֲלֵיהֶם, לַעֲשׂוֹת פּוּרִים, וְלִשְׂמֹחַ בְּכָל שָׁנָה וְשָׁנָה.

רָאִיתָ אֶת תְּפִלַּת מָרְדְּכַי וְאֶסְתֵּר, הָמָן וּבָנָיו עַל הָעֵץ תָּלִיתָ.

The following is recited after both *Megillah* readings.

שׁוֹשַׁנַּת יַעֲקֹב צָהֲלָה וְשָׂמֵחָה, בִּרְאוֹתָם יַחַד תְּכֵלֶת מָרְדְּכָי.

תְּשׁוּעָתָם הָיִיתָ לָנֶצַח, וְתִקְוָתָם בְּכָל דּוֹר וָדוֹר.

לְהוֹדִיעַ, שֶׁכָּל קֹוֶיךָ לֹא יֵבֹשׁוּ, וְלֹא יִכָּלְמוּ לָנֶצַח כָּל הַחוֹסִים בָּךְ. אָרוּר הָמָן, אֲשֶׁר בִּקֵּשׁ לְאַבְּדִי, בָּרוּךְ מָרְדְּכַי הַיְּהוּדִי. אֲרוּרָה זֶרֶשׁ, אֵשֶׁת מַפְחִידִי, בְּרוּכָה אֶסְתֵּר בַּעֲדִי, וְגַם חַרְבוֹנָה זָכוּר לַטּוֹב.

esther

If a *Minyan* is present for the *Megillah* reading, the following blessing is recited after the reading.

Blessed are You, HASHEM, our God, King of the universe, Who takes up our grievance, judges our claim, avenges our wrong; exacts vengeance for us from our foes, and Who brings just retribution upon all enemies of our soul. Blessed are you HASHEM, Who exacts vengeance for His people Israel from all their foes, the God Who brings salvation. (Cong.—Amen.)

The following poetic narrative of the Purim story is recited only after the evening *Megillah* reading. After the morning reading continue with, 'The Rose of Jacob,' below.

א Who balked the counsel of the nations and annulled the designs of the cunning,

ב When a wicked man stood up against us,
    a wantonly evil branch of Amalek's offspring.

ג Haughty with his wealth he dug himself a grave,
    and his very greatness snared him in a trap.

ד Fancying to trap, he became entrapped;
    attempting to destroy, he was swiftly destroyed.

ה Haman showed his forebears' enmity,
    and aroused the brotherly hate of Esau on the children.

ו He would not remember Saul's compassion,
    that through his pity on Agag the foe was born.

ז The wicked one conspired to cut away the righteous,
    but the impure one was trapped in the pure one's hands.

ח Kindness overcame the father's error, and the wicked one piled sin on sins.

ט In his heart he hid his cunning thoughts, and devoted himself to evildoing.

י He stretched his hand against God's holy ones,
    he spent his silver to destroy their memory.

כ When Mordecai saw the wrath commence,
    and Haman's decrees be issued in Shushan,

ל He put on sackcloth and bound himself in mourning,
    decreed a fast and sat on ashes:

מ 'Who would arise to atone for error, to gain forgiveness for our ancestors' sins?'

נ A blossom bloomed from a lulav branch — behold!
    Hadassah stood up to arouse the sleeping.

ס Her servants hastened Haman, to serve him wine of serpent's poison.

ע He stood tall through his wealth and toppled through his evil —
    he built the gallows on which he was hung.

פ The earth's inhabitants opened their mouths, for Haman's lot became our Purim,

צ The righteous man was saved from the wicked's hand;
    the foe was substituted for him.

ק They undertook to establish Purim, to rejoice in every single year.

ר You noted the prayer of Mordecai and Esther;
    Haman and his sons You hung on the gallows.

The following is recited after both *Megillah* readings.

ש The Rose of Jacob was cheerful and glad,
    when they jointly saw Mordecai robed in royal blue.

ת You have been their eternal salvation, and their hope throughout generations.
To make known that all who hope in You will not be shamed; nor ever be humiliated, those taking refuge in You. Accursed be Haman who sought to destroy me, blessed be Mordecai the Jew. Accursed be Zeresh the wife of my terrorizer, blessed be Esther [who sacrificed] for me — and Charbonah, too, be remembered for good.

תרגום שני

Targum Sheni on Megillas Esther

Megillas Esther

(Based on *Targum Sheni*)

◄§ Ten Mighty Rulers

It was in the days of Achashverosh (Esther 1:1), ruler from India to Ethiopia, one hundred and twenty-seven lands. הוּא אֲחַשְׁוֵרוֹשׁ — *This is Achashverosh* (Ahasuerus), one of the ten kings who reigned, or who shall reign, over the entire world.

The first of these kings was the King of Kings (May His reign soon extend over us all!). Nimrod was second, Pharaoh, third. Shlomo (Solomon), king of Israel, was fourth, and the fifth was Nebuchadnezzar, king of Bavel (Babylon). The sixth was Achashverosh; the seventh, Alexander of Greece; the eighth, the emperor of Rome. The ninth will be the 'King *Mashiach*, and the tenth will once again be the King of Kings.

◄§ The Prince of the Pursuit of Power

With the death of Nebuchadnezzar, king of Bavel, there was great internal strife, and the kingship seemed destined for oblivion. The people of Bavel simply did not know whom to crown as their king.

Nebuchadnezzar's son, Evil Merodach, hoped to assume the kingship, but the people did not want him and rebelled. They told him: "We admit that by right the kingship should be yours, but remember that God once punished your father by crazing him, sending him naked to run mindlessly through the forest for seven years, eating grass like a beast, his hair and nails grown long and wild. All thought him dead, but after seven years his sense returned.

"When he returned to his city, riding on a mighty lion, he found his son ruling in his stead. He killed his son immediately together with many of his servants.

"If you become king, perhaps your father will return once again, and seeing you ruling, will kill both you and us! Perhaps he will return, perhaps you have told us that he is dead merely to further your own ambitions for kingship!"

When Evil Merodach heard their words, he replied, "You have spoken correctly, but I can assure you that there is no need to fear.

He is most certainly dead, and that body which we buried was indeed that of my father."

"You are a good man," they replied, "and we believe you. Still, we are in terror of him. We have not seen the corpse, so how can we be certain that it was him? You are aware of the terror which the entire world felt at the mere sound of his voice. We do not know what to do!"

When Evil Merodach saw their determination, he ran to the cemetery and brought the body back to the city, dragging it in chains through the streets. Now everyone could see that it was indeed Nebuchadnezzar, and what had become of his mortal remains. Relieved that his son had complied with their request, they crowned him king.

◄§ Achashverosh

הוּא אֲחַשְׁוֵרוֹשׁ — *He is Achashverosh* (1:1). He is Achashverosh, who sold the impoverished Jews (רָשׁ — "poor"); he is that same Achashverosh who darkened (שָׁחוֹר — "black") the Jews' faces with sorrow like a burnt pot; he is Achashverosh who gave orders to bring cedar wood from Lebanon and gold from Ophir, and never did [for Achashverosh is identified by some of the Sages with Coresh; and see *Ezra* chs. 3 and 4 on the building of the Second *Beis HaMikdash*]; he is Achashverosh, in whose times were fulfilled the words of the rebuke: *You shall have no assurance of your life (Devarim* 28:66).

The expression *he is* (הוּא) appears in reference to five wicked men, and five righteous men. The righteous men were: Avraham, Moshe, Aharon, Chizkiyahu and Ezra. The wicked men were: Nimrod, Esav, Dasan and Aviram, King Achaz, and Achashverosh.

He is Achashverosh, who never fulfilled what he had promised to do. As a result his kingdom was made smaller. First he ruled מֵהֹדּוּ וְעַד כּוּשׁ, *from India to Ethiopia* (1:1), which includes virtually the entire world. Later, he ruled only שֶׁבַע וְעֶשְׂרִים וּמֵאָה מְדִינָה — *one hundred and twenty-seven provinces* (1:1).

He is Achashverosh, who murdered his wife Vashti because of his admirer Haman, and who murdered Haman because of his wife Esther.

◄§ The Extent of his Empire

He is Achashverosh, who ruled from India to Ethiopia. This is difficult to understand, though, for Hodu and Cush are lands which are close to each other — what was the great accomplishment, then? The verse lets us know that just as he ruled powerfully over those two, so did he rule over 127 nations.

This same metaphor is expressed in King Shlomo's case. He ruled the whole world, and the verse tells us that he ruled "from Tifsach to Azah," although they were close to one another. Just as he ruled over those two places, so did he rule over the entire world.

There were four kings who ruled from one end of the earth to the other; two were Jews and two were not. Shlomo and Achav were the Jews, Nebuchadnezzar and Achashverosh were the other two. But ultimately Achashverosh's kingdom was lessened, until he ruled over 127 nations only.

He merited ruling over those 127 nations because of Esther, his future wife, granddaughter of Sarah, who lived for 127 years.

❧ The Greatness of Shlomo

בַּיָמִים הָהֵם כְּשֶׁבֶת הַמֶּלֶךְ אֲחַשְׁוֵרוֹשׁ עַל כִּסֵּא מַלְכוּתוֹ אֲשֶׁר בְּשׁוּשַׁן הַבִּירָה —
In those days, when King Achashverosh sat on his throne of majesty in Shushan the capital (1:2). Our Sages say that the throne did not belong to Achashverosh or to his ancestors. It was actually the throne of Shlomo, built for him by Chiram (Hiram), king of Tyre.

This was Shlomo, beloved of God, chosen by Him even before his birth. God revealed many secrets to him, and granted him great wisdom, the wisdom to discern truth in judgment. Like his father before him, beauty and charm radiated from his face; the crown of majesty sat proudly upon his head.

He was crowned at the age of thirteen, and he was called Yedidyah, meaning "friend of God"; and Shlomo, because there was peace (*shalom*) during his reign. Ben was his name, for he built (*banah*) the Temple, and Itiel ("God is with me"), for God Himself attested to his superior wisdom. Yakeh, too, was his name, because he was the ruler of the world and all the nations feared him [Derivation of this interpretation: untraced].

The demons themselves fell into his hands, and fish and birds and beasts brought him tribute. When he made a banquet the beasts would come to the kitchen and offer themselves for slaughter.

He was very wealthy, possessor of much gold and silver. He revealed deep secrets, and his enemies became his friends; kings obeyed him and wanted to meet him. God raised him to greatness because of his father David. His name was renowned by all the kings, and his wisdom repeated by all the sages.

ᴥᔥ The Marvelous Throne

This was Shlomo, who [owned] the marvelous throne. When Shlomo would sit in judgment upon his throne, crown on his head, he could delve into the hearts of the complainants and see by their faces who was guilty, who was innocent, and whose testimony was false. For this reason the verse says that Shlomo sat on *God's chair* — for God guarded the chair as if it were His own.

The throne itself was miraculously built. It had twelve golden lions upon it, and twelve golden eagles, the paw of a lion opposite the wing of an eagle. There were six stairs to climb upon, each with six golden lions and six golden eagles. They were made of elephant bones (i.e., ivory). The golden lions numbered 72 *(sic)*, with 72 eagles as well.

On the first step was a golden ox opposite a golden lion. On the second step lay a wolf of gold opposite a golden sheep. The third step had a panther facing a golden camel; the fourth a golden eagle facing a golden peacock. On the fifth step was a golden cat opposite a golden chicken, and on the sixth was a hawk facing a golden dove. All of this showed that in matters of justice the weak does not have to fear the strong.

All the animals were crafted with great skill and cunning. It worked this way. When Shlomo placed his right foot on the first stair, the ox extended him his foot, and he grasped it. When he placed his other foot on the first step, the lion extended his paw. Then the ox would display a scroll with the following verse inscribed upon it: *It is forbidden to take bribes;* and the lion would show a scroll with another verse: *Do not recognize anyone in judgment* — that is, do not recognize a person, even if he once did you a favor or if he is rich or important or pious or poor, by judging in his favor.

All the other animals did likewise, lifting Shlomo up with one foot and displaying their judicial maxims with the other.

ᴥᔥ The King Enthroned

Shlomo would sit at the summit of the throne. There was a golden dove there, holding a hawk, for Israel is compared to a dove. On the very top of the throne was a *Menorah* (candelabrum), crafted with lights and branches and cups and flowers. Facing it were seven gold branches, bearing upon them the likenesses of the seven forefathers — Adam, Noach, Shem, Avraham, Yitzchak and Yaakov, with Iyov

(Job) in their midst. On the other side were seven gold branches bearing the likenesses of seven righteous men — Levi, Kehas, Amram, Moshe, Aharon, Eldad and Medad, and Chur; some say that Chaggai was among them.

On the tip of the *Menorah* was a golden pitcher full of the oil which was burned in the Temple. Underneath stood a large golden bowl, with a likeness of Eli the priest carved upon it. Two branches extended from it, bearing likenesses of his sons Chofni and Pinchas, and from these two other branches came out, bearing likenesses of Aharon's two sons, Nadav and Avihu.

There were two chairs there, one for the High Priest and one for his deputy. There were seventy chairs surrounding them, for the seventy members of the Sanhedrin, and there they sat in judgment before the king.

Near the approach to the throne there were two doves. Over the throne 24 golden branches were built, to shade the king. Wherever he turned, he was always protected by the shade.

When Shlomo reached the sixth step a golden eagle would seat him on the throne. The actual place where Shlomo sat was covered with silver leaf.

When other nobles and kings heard of Shlomo's throne they came and bowed down to him and said: "There is no king in the entire world who owns such a throne, no craftsman who could build such a marvel."

When Shlomo sat down a golden eagle, crafted with great skill and wisdom, held the crown over his head, without touching him, so that he should not be uncomfortable. The golden eagles and lions were made with great cunning, gathering around the king and providing shade for him. A golden dove would descend from the pillars and open the holy Ark, remove a tiny Torah scroll and place it into King Shlomo's hands, so that he could fulfill the admonition (cf. *Devarim* 17:18-20): the Torah shall be with him for all of his days, so that his reign, and the reign of his children, shall be long.

The High Priest and the Elders would come to greet the king. The judges and the Sanhedrin sat on his right and left sides to judge the people. When a person would testify falsely, the king would cause wheels to spin, oxen to low, lions to roar, and bears to pounce as if ready to tear something apart. Each of the animals of the throne would make his noise, as if he were truly alive. All this was done to terrify the perjurer, so that he would think to himself: "Why should I testify falsely, and lose such a world with my sin?"

When the animals opened their mouths to shout, a wonderful

fragrance, the fragrance of Eden, would pour out. It was a fragrance of spices, of all the wonderful smells which God created.

◄§ The Fate of the Throne

When Israel sinned Nebuchadnezzar came and laid waste to all of *Eretz Yisrael*, looting the holy city of Yerushalayim and burning the Temple (May God yet have mercy upon us!). Nebuchadnezzar then led the people into exile, taking the throne with him.

Nebuchadnezzar wanted to seat himself upon the throne, but he did not know how to ascend it. When he put his foot on the first step, the golden lion rose in order to help him climb up. But Nebuchadnezzar did not know what to do, and so the lion kicked him with his left foot, striking him on the right thigh and leaving him crippled for the rest of his life.

When Alexander the Great of Macedonia conquered Babylonia he took the throne with him and brought it to Egypt. He was pious and revered the throne as very holy, and refused to sit upon it. After his death Sheshak, king of Egypt, tried to sit on the throne, and the same fate befell him as had befallen Nebuchadnezzar before him. He was crippled for the rest of his life, and was called Pharaoh Necheh, Pharaoh the Lame.

Then Aniphonus, son of Antiochus, came and removed the throne from Egypt. He put it into a ship and brought it to his land. During the voyage one foot of the throne broke off, and he could not, in all of his lifetime, find a craftsman skilled enough to repair it. There was no king at this time who could have had such a throne built.

The throne found its way into the possession of Coresh of Persia, and because he allowed the Temple to be rebuilt he merited being able to sit upon the throne without harm.

בִּשְׁנַת שָׁלוֹשׁ לְמָלְכוֹ — *In the third year of his reign* (1:3). Achashverosh made a feast for all of his nobles and servants of Persia and Media, and all the governors of his provinces came to him.

In the third year of Nebuchadnezzar's reign the people of Israel wept and sighed, saying: "Woe to us since Nebuchadnezzar has prevailed over us, humiliating our land and destroying our nation, leading us into exile. Whatever injustice he could mete out, he did, chaining our elders in iron fetters, banishing our nobles, striking down our youth, and taking the smallest children into captivity. He has removed the crown of pride from our heads."

⋅≶ The King and the Birds

Before the destruction of the *Beis HaMikdash,* David rose to rule Israel, and his son Shlomo reigned after him. God placed Shlomo as ruler over the entire world: over the beasts of the field, the birds under heaven, and the reptiles of the sands; over the demons and shades. He understood all their languages. When he was merry he had the beasts and birds, the shades and demons, brought before him, to dance for him and for visiting kings, in order to prove his dominion over them. All came without need of persuasion, and none were coerced.

Once he asked the birds if all of them were there. The birds looked around to see if anyone was missing, and they discovered that the moor cock was not there. They told Shlomo, who in great wrath ordered that he be brought before him. He was brought to the king, and fell before him in terror.

He said to Shlomo: "I beg for mercy, my beloved lord, O king! It is a long while now that I eat my food in tears, and drink in trembling. I flew out into the world, seeking a place where you do not have dominion. Finally I came to a country whose capital city is called Kitor, whose land is covered with gold. Its trees are like the trees of Eden. A woman rules over this nation, and they worship the sun. If you wish I can assemble all the birds of prey, fly there, and destroy them."

King Shlomo demurred, but immediately called for his scribe, and dictated this letter: "From King Shlomo to the queen of the land of Kitor — peace to you and to your nobles. Be it known to you and to them that God, blessed is He, has made me ruler over all the peoples, the birds and beasts and demons and shades. I therefore wish you to bear my name as well. Send a tribute to me, as all the kings do. If you do so, you shall live in peace, but if you refuse, I shall send a great host to destroy you and your kingdom. Not soldiers alone, but wild birds and badgers and demons shall attack your kingdom and destroy it. Send me your answer with this bird, and peace to you."

⋅≶ The Queen of Sheba

They clipped the letter to the moor cock's wing and, together with an escort of many birds of prey, it flew to Kitor, to the Queen of Shva (Sheba). They arrived very early, right after sunrise. The queen arose to bow down as she normally did, but there were so many birds that the sun was obscured. Terrified, she rent her garments. The moor cock then flew down with his letter, and when she had read its uncompromising message she once again tore her clothing.

She immediately summoned her nobles and told them the contents of the letter, but they did not want to listen, and said that they did not recognize King Shlomo or his rule.

The queen did not rely on their opinion, and sent a ship laden with silver and gold, precious gems and fine wood. She chose 6,000 boys and girls of particular beauty, who had all been born on the same day, and dressed them all in identical clothing of silk and purple wool.

She sent a letter with the sailors, which said: "From the Queen of Kitor to my lord, King Shlomo, and all his nobles. Peace to you. Please accept my gift. I beg of you to appoint a time for me to come to you, for you know that it is a matter of seven years' journey. I hope to come and bow down to your rule in three years (sic)."

The Sages say that she knew, through stargazing, that the young children whom she had sent would die within a year. Shlomo too foresaw this, and sent them back to her with shrouds, with this message: "If you have sent these to me because of a lack of shrouds, here they are; now take them back. You may come to speak with me."

◆§ Her Visit

At the end of three years she came. When Shlomo heard that she was approaching, he sent his courtier, Benayahu ben Yehoyada, a very handsome man. When she saw him she dismounted her horse and bowed low, for she thought that he was Shlomo. "I am not Shlomo," he assured her, "just one of his servants."

She returned to her nobles and said: "You have not yet seen the lion. If one of his servants looks like this, imagine what Shlomo himself looks like!" And Benayahu brought her to Shlomo.

When the king heard of her arrival he sat in a room made of glass. She bowed down before him, and he treated her courteously. Later, she said to him: "My beloved lord, I want to ask you three riddles. If you know the answers, I will know that you are truly wise; if not, you are just like other men." She asked him her questions, and he gave her the very answers which she had been thinking of.

The king gave her all that she desired. Then she bade him goodbye and returned with her retinue to her land.

◆§ Nebuchadnezzar Defiles the Temple

When any of the kings of the world would hear the name of

Shlomo they would tremble, and all sent the best produce of their land to him.

Had Israel listened to the prophet Yirmeyahu, and repented, they would not have been exiled. Yirmeyahu prayed to God the entire time that he was in Yerushalayim, and he was able to hold Nebuchadnezzar at bay and keep him from destroying the city. But then he went to the land of Binyamin, and Nebuchadnezzar sent his general Nevuzaradan, who immediately breached the walls, and afterwards, together with Nebuchadnezzar, came to the *Beis HaMikdash*.

They could not enter it, because the gates had locked themselves. When Nebuchadnezzar saw that no one could open them, he wanted to break them down. He broke many axes upon them to no avail, for they would not open. Then a man by the name of Parnutos came and slaughtered an impure animal, sprinkling its blood on the *Beis HaMikdash* and defiling it. The doors then opened of their own accord. Nebuchadnezzar entered, and saw God's wonders before him.

One of the things he saw was blood on a rock, seething without rest. He asked the elders what it was, and they answered that it was the blood of sacrifices, but he soon realized that they were lying. Then he said: "If you reveal the secret, well and good; if not, I will tear your flesh with burning pincers."

Then they told him the truth — that among them had been the prophet Zechariah, who continually rebuked them. They did not listen to him, and finally stoned him on a *Shabbos* — which was the Day of Atonement was well — in the *Beis HaMikdash* itself. From that time on his blood would not rest.

"Why did you not wash the blood away?" asked Nebuchadnezzar.

"We have washed it away many times," they answered, "but it does not help. It comes right back. We have broken away the stones and replaced them with others, but nothing helps; the blood keeps returning."

⋖§ Massacre

Then Nebuchadnezzar called his general Nevuzaradan and ordered him to still the blood. He took many thousands of priests and slaughtered them on top of the blood, but to no avail. He slaughtered the Sanhedrin and the elite of Israel, but still the blood would not rest. Then he slaughtered the young schoolchildren, but still the blood seethed. Finally he had pity, and said to the blood: "Zechariah, Zechariah, I have massacred the best of the Jews upon your blood. Be still now, or I will slaughter all of Israel on your account." And then, finally, the blood quieted down and sank into the earth.

Then Nevuzaradan thought to himself: "The Jews killed only one man, and God punished them so harshly. I have killed so many beautiful Jews — what will happen to me?" He fled, and ultimately became a righteous convert.

When the High Priest and the other *Kohanim* saw that the *Beis HaMikdash* and all within it was in flames, they threw themselves together with their harps into the fire.

When Nebuchadnezzar tried to enter the Holy of Holies, the doors locked themselves shut, until a heavenly voice rang out and said: "Open up your doors, Temple, and let the fire burn." Then they opened of their own volition. When that evil man entered and saw the glory of God, and the holy vessels of the Temple, which righteous kings used to use, they vanished before his eyes. The wicked man stormed out in a rage and killed, through our sins, many Jews. Many others were bound in chains and led, naked, bearing heavy burdens of sand, into painful servitude.

⋽ The Prophet Intercedes

The prophet Yirmeyahu accompanied them until he reached the graves of the Patriarchs. He fell upon their tombs and wept: "O merciful fathers, Avraham, Yitzchak, and Yaakov, rise up and see how they lead your children into exile, naked and barefoot, bent under heavy loads!"

Then he ran to the tombs of Sarah, Rivkah, Rachel and Leah. He wailed and said: "Arise, you mothers, and see how your children are being led naked into exile, and how bitter is their lot." Then he sped to the graves of Moshe, Aharon and Miriam, and said: "See how they are leading your flock into exile. You watched over them carefully; now see how the cruel wolves prey upon them and tear them apart, leading them naked and barefoot over the mountains and through the cities, laden with heavy burdens, while the wicked ones harass them without mercy."

Finally, he hastened once again to the forefathers, who asked him: "Why did you not pray that such a fate not befall them? Now you come to us to tell us the terrible news?"

And so the captives continued on their way until they reached a place called Beis Kuri. There Nebuchadnezzar commanded that their burdens be removed and they be given clothing. It was there that the prophet Yirmeyahu told Nebuchadnezzar: "You will go and boast in your idolatrous temple, and say that your might did this. But the truth is, and remember this well — what happened to those before you will happen to you, too."

Yirmeyahu went with the Jews, wailing and lamenting, until they reached a place called Yichud Medinta, where Nebuchadnezzar commanded that the chains be removed from the neck of King Tzidkiyahu, and new clothing be brought to him.

◄§ An Oriental Banquet

בְּהַרְאֹתוֹ אֶת עשֶׁר כְּבוֹד מַלְכוּתוֹ — *When he (Achashverosh) displayed the riches of his glorious kingdom* (1:4). Achashverosh displayed the utensils and vessels of the *Beis HaMikdash*. When the Jews saw these vessels they wanted to leave the feast. Achashverosh was told that the Jews were crying and lamenting when they saw the vessels; he responded that they were right, and ordered that they be seated in a separate place.

וּבִמְלוֹאת הַיָּמִים הָאֵלֶּה — *And when these days were fulfilled* (1:5), one hundred and eighty days, the king made a feast for all the people in the capital city of Shushan, from great to small. It was a seven-day feast in the court of the palace garden. This feast was followed by still another seven-day feast for the residents of Shushan alone.

חוּר כַּרְפַּס — *White hangings and fine cotton* (1:6). Linen, white as pearls, hung from one tree to the next, woven with threads of green, blue, and silk. A hanging of purple encircled it, bound all around with golden chains.

וְהַשְׁקוֹת — *And they gave them to drink* (1:7) in golden cups, with no two cups identical. Once one had drunk from a cup, it was used no more; each drink was served in a new cup. But when they displayed the vessels of the *Beis HaMikdash*, the other vessels seemed like copper in comparison. Each person drank as much as he wanted, and each was given wine the same age as he — wine in abundance, according to the king's bounty.

וְהַשְּׁתִיָּה — *And the drinking* (1:8) was voluntary, so that no one would be harmed. It was customary at that time, when making a feast, that a person would be brought an enormous goblet of wine called the *piska*. Whoever was given this goblet by the butler was forced to drink the entire contents, though only Achashverosh was capable of such a feat. Whoever could not drink it was forced to give a huge sum of gold to the butler. In this way the butlers became very wealthy. But during this feast Achashverosh forewent this custom, and everyone drank whatever they wished, and no more.

◆§ The Queen is Summoned

גַּם וַשְׁתִּי הַמַּלְכָּה — *Queen Vashti, too* (1:9), made a feast for the women, in the palace. She served them black and red wines, and seated them in the king's palace, because she wanted to flaunt the king's wealth. "Where does the king sleep? Where does he eat?" they asked, and she showed them all that was to be seen, for women are very curious.

בַּיּוֹם הַשְּׁבִיעִי — *On the seventh day* (1:10) of the feast, when the king's heart was merry with wine, he spoke with Mehuman, Bizsa, Charvona, Bigsa, Avagsa, Zesar and Carcas, the seven chamberlains who were constantly with him. As they sat eating and drinking, the talk turned to women. The kings of the west said that the women of their lands were the most beautiful. The kings of the east said that their women were more attractive. Then the wine in Achashverosh began to speak, and he boasted that the women of Bavel were the most beautiful of all. "If you don't believe me," he said, "I will call for the queen."

"Yes, for we want to know the truth," the men replied, "but bring her in naked, so that we can truly see her beauty."

The king ordered that the queen be brought to him with the crown of majesty, to show the people her beauty. The king told his nobles, "Go to Queen Vashti and tell her to stand up from her throne, and undress herself totally. Let her put the golden crown upon her head, a golden bowl in her right arm, and a golden goblet in her left hand, and let her come before me and the 127 kings who are sitting with me, so that they will see that she is the most beautiful of all women."

וַתְּמָאֵן הַמַּלְכָּה וַשְׁתִּי — *Queen Vashti refused* (1:12) and haughtily told her servants: "I am Vashti, daughter of the kings of Bavel, descendant of Belshazzar. My father could outdrink a thousand men, and the wine would never cause him to say such foolish things."

King Achashverosh was told that the queen had defied him, and his fury burned within him.

◄§ Vashti's Downfall

וַיֹּאמֶר הַמֶּלֶךְ — *The king said* (1:13) to the wise men, who knew the temper of the times: "What shall be done to Queen Vashti, because of her disobedience?"

וַיֹּאמֶר מְמוּכָן — *Memuchan said* (1:16). This is Daniel. He was exiled to Bavel with the tribe of Yehudah, and through him great miracles and valorous deeds were performed. He was "prepared" *(muchan)* from heaven to be the instrument of Vashti's downfall, and so was called Memuchan.

As was customary, the king used to first consult with the least important of his advisers, and therefore he began with Memuchan. This adviser had a Persian wife of great importance, who wanted him to speak her language, and he sought a pretext to force her to speak his. Therefore he said: "Not only has Vashti behaved badly to the king, but to all of the nobles of all of the provinces of Achashverosh. When the words of the queen shall be known to all the other women, they will humiliate their husbands, for they will say, 'Are you, then, more important that Achashverosh, who commanded that the queen come before him and who was not obeyed?'

וְהַיּוֹם הַזֶּה — "*And on this day* (1:18) the princesses of Persia and Media will tell their husbands, when they hear what the queen did, and there will be much humiliation to be furious over."

אִם עַל הַמֶּלֶךְ טוֹב — *If it please the king* (1:19). When Memuchan suggested the decree he was afraid that the king would not follow his advice, and then Vashti would take revenge upon him. Therefore he saw to it that the following edict was immediately written in the laws of Persia and Media: "Since the queen refused to appear her position will be given to someone better than she. And this decree and action shall be heard in the entire kingdom, and all the women will respect their husbands, great and small."

This solution pleased the king, and he did as Memuchan had suggested.

וַיִּשְׁלַח סְפָרִים — *He sent letters* (1:22) to all the provinces of the kingdom, to each nation in its script, each people in its language, to let all know and understand the contents: that each man should be a ruler in his house, and women should speak the language of their husbands.

◄§ The King Relents

אַחַר הַדְּבָרִים הָאֵלֶּה — *After these things* (2:1), when the king's wrath had abated, he sent for his advisers and said: "Not only was I furious with Vashti, but now I am furious with you, too. When I was drunk you ought to have silenced my anger until I had come back to my senses, but you made me even more angry, and gave me the idea of killing her." When he had put them to death he remembered Vashti, and realized that she was innocent of any wrongdoing. This was all God's doing, for He wanted to destroy the descendants of Nebuchadnezzar.

The king's young servants said: "Let us search for a beautiful young maiden to be the king's wife. Let the king appoint men in all of his provinces to choose young and beautiful maidens, and let them be brought to the women's house in Shushan, under the care of the king's adviser Hegai, the custodian of the women. He will give them their cosmetics, and the girl who shall most please the king, shall be set up by the king in Vashti's place." And thus did the king do.

◄§ Mordechai and Esther

אִישׁ יְהוּדִי — *A Jewish man* (2:5) was in Shushan, the capital city. His name was Mordechai, and he was called *Yehudi* (the Jew) because he truly feared God. Targum translates the name Mordechai as meaning "pure spices." He was the son of Yair, son of Shim'i, son of Kish, from the tribe of Binyamin, who had been banished in the previous exile.

וַיְהִי אֹמֵן — *And he had raised* (2:7) Hadassah, that is, Esther. She was called Hadassah because the strong and fragrant smell of the *hadas*, myrtle, is not lost, even when it grows among thorns. So, too, did she retain her Jewishness when among the pagans. She was called Esther because her deeds were lovely and good. [The Talmud says that the pagans called her Estahar on account of her beauty, סַהַר ("the moon") being a common metaphor for the epitome of beauty.]

When the king's words were heard, and his decree was made known, many lovely young girls were assembled in the king's house, under the protection of Hegai, custodian of the women. When Mordechai heard of this he hid Esther away from the royal messengers, but the daughters of the Amalekites fussed and beautified themselves so that they should be taken.

The servants collected together all the young women, and saw that Esther was not among them. Long before they had remarked upon her goodness and beauty. They then told the king: "We have fatigued ourselves for no purpose, for the most beautiful girls have been hidden from us."

When the king heard this he decreed that anyone who had hidden his daughter and would not give her out would be hanged upon his own doorway. Then Mordechai saw what would come out of this, and that this was God's hand, and he took her out and led her to the palace. She was led to the other maidens.

וַתִּיטַב הַנַּעֲרָה בְעֵינָיו — *The young girl pleased* (2:9) Hegai, and he treated her kindly. He gave her cosmetics and all that she needed, as well as seven young girls of the palace; and he showed his preference for her and her maidens. Esther never revealed her nationality nor her descent, according to Mordechai's instructions.

וּבְכָל יוֹם וָיוֹם — *And every day* (2:11) Mordechai would go in front of the women's house to find out Esther's welfare, and what was happening to her, and what miracles would occur through her.

When the time came for Esther, daughter of Avichayil, uncle of Mordechai who had taken her in as a daughter, to come to the king, she asked for nothing to accompany her, taking only that which Hegai, the women's custodian, pressed upon her. Esther charmed all who saw her, and she was taken to the palace of King Achashverosh in the tenth month, that is Teves, in the seventh year of his reign.

◆§ The King's Curiosity

וַיֶּאֱהַב הַמֶּלֶךְ אֶת אֶסְתֵּר — *The king loved Esther* (2:17) more than the other women, for she found grace and favor in his eyes. He placed the crown of majesty upon her head and made her queen in Vashti's stead. The king made a great feast for her.

He was exceedingly curious about Esther's origin, who her family was and what sort of people she stemmed from, and he tried to flatter the information out of her.

"Who are your people?" he asked her. "I would like to appoint them nobles."

"My dear king," she answered, "I do not know my people and my family. My father and mother died when I was very young, and I have not been able to find out who they were. Only Mordechai had mercy on me. If it were God's will that I know my family, I would certainly tell you."

Since Achashverosh could not find out who her relatives were, and thus could not lavish upon them the gifts which he wished to give, instead he freed the entire land of tribute for her sake, for he felt that her family must be somewhere in his land.

◆§ A Dark Conspiracy

בַּיָּמִים הָהֵם — *In those days* (2:21), when Mordechai was sitting in the doorway of the palace, Bigsan and Teresh, two chamberlains of the king who were the guardians of his threshold, grew angry at their master, saying: "From the time that he has become king, we have no peace." They conspired to put snake venom into the goblet from which the king drank after waking from his sleep.

וַיִּוָּדַע הַדָּבָר — *And the matter became known* (2:22) to Mordechai through divine inspiration, and he told the queen, who told the king, in the name of Mordechai.

וַיְבֻקַּשׁ הַדָּבָר — *The matter was investigated* (2:23) and found to be true, so both were hanged on a gallows, and the incident was recorded in the king's book of chronicles.

◆§ The Villain Rises to Power

אַחַר הַדְּבָרִים הָאֵלֶּה — *After these things* (3:1), King Achashverosh promoted Haman, son of Hamdasa the Agagite, over all the other nobles.

The words *after these things* shows us that our God, blessed be He, prepares the cure before the plague — Esther was appointed queen on account of her beauty, and Mordechai saved the king from death; and only then was Haman, who hated the Jews because he was descended from Amalek, raised to greatness.

וְכָל עַבְדֵי הַמֶּלֶךְ — *And all the king's servants* (3:2) who lived in the king's palace would bow and scrape to Haman, for the king had so ordered. But Mordechai refused to bow or kneel.

The king's servants said to Mordechai: "Why are you greater than we, that you refuse to bow to Haman, while we bow down?" Mordechai answered: "I will bow before our beloved Master, the Lord, Blessed is He, for He created the entire world with His might."

וַיַּרְא הָמָן — *When Haman saw* (3:5) that Mordechai would not bow nor kneel to him, he was filled with rage. It was contemptible to him to simply cast his hand at Mordechai alone. He had been told who Mordechai's people were, and he determined to destroy all of the Jews, Mordechai's people, throughout the whole empire of Achashverosh.

◄§ Haman Casts Lots

In the first month, that is Nissan, in the twelfth year of the king's reign, Haman cast lots to see when to destroy the Jews. Then a heavenly voice rang out and said: "Congregation of Israel, you have no reason to fear, if only you return in repentance! Then Haman will fall into your hands!"

Haman ordered Shamshai, the king's scribe, to cast lots for the day of the week. But this could not succeed, for on Sunday heaven and earth were created, on Monday the waters separated, on Tuesday the Garden of Eden came into being. On Wednesday, the sun, moon, seven stars, and twelve constellations were created; on Thursday the Leviathan and moor cock were created, prepared for the great feast of the future, when *Mashiach* comes. Adam and Chavah were created on Friday, and *Shabbos* is a testament between God and Israel. As a result, Haman despaired of the lottery of days, and began a lottery of months.

So reasoned Haman: "In Nissan I cannot prevail because of the merit of the Pesach sacrifice. Iyar, too, is not good for they have the merit of the *man* (manna), which began to fall in that month. In Sivan the Torah was given, and Tammuz, too, is eliminated, for in that month the walls of Yerushalayim were breached, and, having had one sorrow in that month, God will not put them through another. Av, too, is not good, for in that month the deaths in the desert ended, and the Divine Presence once again spoke to Moshe. In Elul Moshe ascended Mt. Sinai for the second set of Tablets. Tishrei is not good, for God forgives their sins then, and Cheshvan is out of the question because the great flood began in that month, and Noach and his children were saved, together with everything in the ark. Kislev is out, for they repaired the Temple then, and many miracles occurred in that month. Teves, too, is not good, for in that month the Jews already underwent much sorrow, for Nebuchadnezzar went up to Yerushalayim and besieged it. Shevat contains the New Year for Trees, and they bring the offering of the first fruits."

When he came to the twelfth month, the month of Adar, Haman said: "Now they will fall into my power as easily as a small fish does when eaten by a large fish" [for the zodiacal sign of Adar is the fish]. What Haman did not know was that the Jews were the children of Yosef, whose blessing had been that his children would increase like fish of the sea.

৺§ Persuading the King

Then Haman told the king: "There is among us a people — the Jews, spread among the nations in all of the provinces of your kingdom. They are haughty, and they go after all of the pleasures. In the winter month of Teves they bathe in warm water, in hot Tammuz they drink cold drinks. All their ways are different than the others.

אִם עַל הַמֶּלֶךְ טוֹב — *"If it please the king* (3:9), let him record that they are to be destroyed. I will give one hundred gulden for each Jew. When they left Egypt they numbered 600,000, which would total to 10,000 silver talents, and I will give that amount to the king's treasure houses. Let the king simply give me his signature so that I can write whatever I want concerning their fate."

God then said: "When Israel left Egypt they each gave half a shekel, which also totalled 10,000 talents of silver. You have no right to buy them, nor you, Achashverosh, to sell them."

וַיָּסַר הַמֶּלֶךְ — *The king removed* (3:10) his signet ring and gave it to Haman son of Hamdasa, enemy of the Jews. And the king said to Haman: "I give you the silver, and do what you will with the people." But God said: "You most certainly have not sold them!"

৺§ The Edict of Annihilation

וַיִּקָּרְאוּ סֹפְרֵי הַמֶּלֶךְ — *The scribes of the king were summoned* (3:12) on the thirteenth day of the month of Nissan, and all that Haman asked for was written down and sent to the king's nobles and to the governors of every province. It was sent to each nation in its writing, to each people in its language, signed with the king's name and inscribed with his seal.

Couriers swiftly ran everywhere with the news, and the letter was openly displayed in the city of Shushan. The king and Haman sat down to drink, while the city of Shushan wept and wailed.

וּמָרְדְּכַי יָדַע — *And Mordechai knew* (4:1) through divine inspiration *(ruach hakodesh)* what was going to happen. God had sent three of His righteous servants — the prophets Chagai, Zechariah, and Malachi — to prophesy in the Chamber of Hewn Stone in the *Beis HaMikdash*, the seat of the Sanhedrin, that 72 towers would yet be built in Yerushalayim. This alluded to the 70 members of the Sanhedrin, together with its head, and the *nasi*. This prophecy in fact foretold the rebuilding of the *Beis HaMikdash* in the time of Ezra.

The evil Achashverosh sent for 127 scribes, from each of his 127 provinces each with book in hand, and they wrote down harsh decrees against the Jews. The first message was written in the name of the king, stamped with his seal, and was sent by couriers throughout the kingdom.

This is what it said: "Announce in my name, King Achashverosh, in all the land, each to his own language — peace to you. I want to announce to you that a man has come to us. He is not from our city, nor from our land, and he wishes to strengthen us so that we prevail over our enemies. He is Haman, son of Amalek, son of Reuel, son of Eliphaz. He bears a great heritage, is a great nobleman, rich in wealth. This man has asked a small thing of me in regard to the Jews. He has shown that they are not fair-dealing, and has offered me 100 gulden for each person. I have therefore sold these people to be killed and taken the money. In truth the idea pleases me greatly, and may you, too, eat and drink and be as merry as I."

◆§ The Tzaddik Rallies his People

וַיִּקְרַע מָרְדְּכָי — *Mordechai tore* (4:1). After reading this letter Mordechai tore his garments, clothed himself in sackcloth and put ashes on his forehead. He ran through the city and cried bitterly, and said: "My beloved Lord, have mercy upon Your people, Israel. They have not made the decree on one half of us, nor on one quarter. They want to tear out the entire garden!"

When the Jews heard and saw this they grew terrified and did not know what was befalling them. They ran to Mordechai to find out what had happened. Many Jews gathered together, and Mordechai stood up and said: "Beloved brothers, people of Israel: have you not heard what Achashverosh and Haman have commanded and sealed? To destroy us from under the heavens, throughout the entire world! We have no king to rely on for succor, nor have we a prophet to beg for us and show us what to do. We have no land, no city to run to. We have only God: may He have pity upon us and help us. We are like sheep with no shepherd, a ship without a captain, orphans without a father, nursing infants with no mother."

Everyone started to cry. They took the holy Ark and carried it through the Jewish streets. They covered the Torah scroll with sackcloth and placed ashes upon it and they read the passage in *Parashas Vaeschanan* which begins: בַּצַּר לְךָ — *When you are in trouble ... (Devarim* 4:30). Then Mordechai stood up once again and exhorted the people to repent. As he spoke he cried, and tears ran down his cheeks. He cried: "Woe to you, O Israel, for this terrible decree," and once again ran, with bitter weeping, through the streets.

וַיָּבֹא — *He came* (4:2) up to the king's gate, for the king had decreed that one could not enter that gate clothed in sackcloth. At this time a certain Jew came to an Amalekite and begged him to buy him, his wife, and his children, so that they would remain alive. The Amalekite answered: "We cannot buy the Jews, for we must kill them." That moment saw the fulfillment of the verse in the Torah which warned that *you shall sell yourselves to your enemies as servants and maids, and they will not buy (Devarim 28:68).*

Every day the Jews could see exactly how much time was left for them to live, thus fulfilling the dire words of the Torah: *And your life shall hang in doubt (Devarim 28:66).*

וּבְכָל מְדִינָה וּמְדִינָה — *And in each province* (4:3), in each place where the king's words reached, there was a great wailing among the Jews, with fasting and lamentation, and many lying in sackcloth and ashes.

∝§ Esther Rises to the Occasion

וַתָּבוֹאנָה נַעֲרוֹת אֶסְתֵּר — *Esther's maids came* (4:4) and told her, and she trembled. She sent clothing for Mordechai to put on in place of the sackcloth, but he refused them.

Then Esther called to Hasach, one of the king's chamberlains, and ordered him to go to Mordechai, to find out what was going on.

Hasach went out to Mordechai, into the street which stood before the king's gates, and Mordechai told him all that had happened, and of the money which Haman had promised the king in exchange for the Jews' lives.

וַיָּבוֹא הֲתָךְ — *And Hasach came* (4:9) to Esther and told her Mordechai's words, and Esther sent her reply: לֵךְ כְּנוֹס — *"Go and assemble* (4:16) the Jews of Shushan. No one shall eat or drink for three days and nights. I and my maidservants shall do likewise. Then I shall go, unsummoned but willingly, to the king. Even if I (God forbid) lose this world for your sakes, I shall still have the World to Come."

∝§ Her Plea

וַיְהִי בַּיּוֹם הַשְּׁלִישִׁי — *It was on the third day* (5:1) of their fasting that Esther stood up from her ashes and mourning, at first still stooping. She then dressed herself beautifully, in the fashion of a queen, in clothing of silk and fine gold from Ophir, with pearls and diamonds brought from Africa. She placed the crown upon her head and then prayed: "O great God of Avraham, Yitzchak, and Yaakov, God of Binyamin my father! Although I have no merit before You, I go for the sake of Your people Yisrael, lest they be doomed. For if they are destroyed, who shall say before You, three times a day, three times 'Holy'? Just as you helped Chananiah, Mishael and Azariah in the fiery furnace, and Daniel in the lions' den, help us also. Let me find favor in his eyes."

She said these words with tears in her eyes, and then continued: "I beg you, my God, hear my prayers. If it has been decreed upon us that the warning in the Torah is to be visited upon us — that we will be sold as slaves and no one will even want to buy us, and if it has been decreed that we die because of our sins, and thus we have fallen into the hands of Haman, wicked son of Amalek, then remember, Master of the World, how Avraham, our father, took hold of the neck of his son Yitzchak with his left hand, and with his right hand took the knife to slaughter him, just for his love for You. He fulfilled Your commands: heed our pleas!

"Open your windows, heaven, and let the merciful angels, too, pray for us. You, angels, cry with a mighty wail: 'Woe to the world if it be destroyed.' I have cried out to You — answer me, as You answer all those who are in anguish. You see our agony, and You are called 'Merciful and Forebearing' — have mercy upon us. You are called the One who 'bestows lovingkindness upon the thousands' — to the thousandth generation. You have been merciful to our forefathers. Is this, then, the vow which You swore to them? Just as You heard the agony of Yonah (Jonah) when he was in the fish, so hear us today.

"We are like a woman in the severest throes of childbirth. Help us out of our plight and remove it from us. I have fasted three fasts. What else can I do, Master of the World? More fasts I would fast, but I fast only three, so that You will recall the merit of Avraham, who walked for three days with Yitzchak in order to offer him for a sacrifice. You promised him that when his children were in trouble You would remember the merit of the *akedah*, the binding of his son. The three days also represent the *Kohanim*, Levites, and Israelites who accepted Your Torah, and said 'We will do and we will hear.' For their sake, save us from this sorrow.

"God, the Lord of Hosts," she continued, "remember the merit of Avraham, Yitzchak, and Yaakov; do not turn away from my pleas and do not refuse my request."

⋅§ In the Throneroom

וַיְהִי כִרְאוֹת — *When the king saw Esther* (5:2) standing in the forecourt she charmed him, and he extended the golden scepter in his hand towards her. Esther approached and touched the tip of the scepter.

The king said to her: "What is it, Queen Esther, and what is your desire? It shall be given to you, even up to half my kingdom."

When Esther heard the king's offer of up to half his kingdom, out of great joy she mustered courage and answered, "If it pleases the king, let the king and Haman come to a feast which I have prepared."

The king commanded that Haman be called to the feast. At the wine feast, the king said to Esther, "What is your desire, and it will be given to you; what is your request, and it shall be done, up to half my kingdom?"

"My beloved master," she answered, "my request is this: if I have found favor in your eyes, then come to another feast of mine."

⋅§ Haman is Vexed

וַיֵּצֵא הָמָן — *And Haman went out* (5:9) on that day, merry and joyous, but when he saw Mordechai sitting by the king's gate, refusing to stand up for him or bow down, he was filled with rage. He came quickly to his home, and called for his friends and his wife Zeresh. He told them of his great wealth and of the glory with which the king had honored him, and how the king had raised him up over all the other nobles and courtiers. Then he said, "Queen Esther, too, did not invite anyone to her feast, just the king and me. Tomorrow, again, the king and I are invited. But all of this means nothing to me when I see the Jew Mordechai sitting by the king's gate. I can have no joy in my heart."

וַתֹּאמֶר לוֹ זֶרֶשׁ — *Zeresh told him* (5:14), and all of his admirers: "You cannot incinerate him in fire, for his father Avraham, and also Chananiah, Mishael and Azariah, were saved from the fiery furnace, while those who threw them in were burned. You cannot kill him by sword, for his father Yitzchak was saved from the knife. Your cannot drown him, because Moshe Rabbeinu and all of Israel at the Red Sea were saved from drowning. You cannot throw him to the lions, because the prophet Daniel was saved from them. You cannot stone him, for King David killed the Philistine Goliath with a stone. There is no way to kill Mordechai, except by building a gallows fifty cubits high, for his ancestors have never been tried with this. Go to the king tomorrow morning and ask him to command you to hang Mordechai."

The suggestion pleased Haman, and he built the gallows — but it was built for himself!

◈ The Slumberless Night

בַּלַּיְלָה הַהוּא — *That night* (6:1) the wails of the Children of Israel reached up to the blessed God, like the cries of little goats. The heavenly angels were disturbed, and stood in terror, and one said to the other: "For certain, the time for the world's destruction is at hand." They gathered together and went to God, and He asked them: "What is this cry of young goats that I hear?"

The Attribute of Mercy answered Him: "This is not the cry of sheep, it is the wail of the Children of Israel, who have been sold to their deaths through the wicked Haman."

God was at once filled with pity, and spoke compassionately of His people Israel, and ordered that the seal of their doom be broken. Then He commanded the angels in charge of confusion and disturbance to go and disturb the slumber of Achashverosh.

The king awoke very agitated, and told his scribe Shamshai to bring his book of chronicles, and see what had been the fate of the kings of Persia and Media, and what events had overcome his people throughout history.

When Shamshai came to the page which described how Mordechai had saved the king from the plot of Bigsan and Teresh, he tried to skip the pages, and did not want to read them. But by the will of God the pages would not be skipped over, and read themselves to the king.

וַיִּמָּצֵא כָתוּב — *It was found recorded* (6:2) how Mordechai had informed the king that his two chamberlains, Bigsan and Teresh, had plotted his assassination.

◈ The Tables are Turned

The king said: "Who is out in the courtyard?" The young courtiers answered that it was Haman, who had come just then into the outer yard in order to ask the king's permission to hang Mordechai upon the gallows. The king ordered that Haman be admitted, וַיָּבוֹא הָמָן — *and Haman came in* (6:6).

"What honor should be done to a person whom the king wishes to honor?" asked the king.

"Whom would the king wish to honor, more than me?" thought Haman to himself.

Then Haman told the king: "The man whom the king wishes to honor should be brought royal garb, which the king has worn, and the horse which the king has ridden. The crown should be placed upon his head. The horse should be given to one of the king's nobles, who should dress the person and lead him on horseback through the streets of the city, crying before him: 'This shall be done to the person whom the king wishes to honor!' "

This suggestion pleased the king, and he decided to show Mordechai this honor. The king said to Haman: "Run to my treasure house and take all that you mentioned. Then go and dress the Jew Mordechai, and show him the honor which you described."

"My dear king," protested Haman, "there are many Jews called Mordechai. Which one shall I go to?"

"To that Mordechai who sits by my gate."

When Haman heard that the king meant Mordechai, his arch-enemy, he trembled, and his face grew dark. His mouth twisted, and his very organs quivered. His knees knocked together, and he said: "But mighty king, there are many gates. I do not know which gate you mean."

"I clearly told you that I meant the gate of my palace, near the entrance to the women's quarters."

"That Mordechai is my mortal enemy, and his forefathers were my ancestors' enemies. Therefore, my beloved lord, my king, I will give you ten thousand silver talents, but do not show him this honor."

"You shall give him the ten thousand talents," the king retorted, "and you must show him this honor."

"My dear king," Haman continued, "let my ten sons run before him, but do not show him this honor."

"You, your wife, and all of your children shall be made subservient to him," responded the king, "but this honor you must show him."

"But my beloved king," Haman protested, "you have sent letters to all of the lands, announcing that you wish to destroy his people. Now, if you do him such honor, it will seem that you want to rescind your decree. What will the people say? Since you cannot rescind the decree, you cannot show him this honor."

"If it comes to that, we shall rescind the decree," the king replied, "but the honor shall be done to him."

Then the king turned and shouted at Haman: "Go now, and do not delay. Do all which you spoke of to my faithful Mordechai, and do not omit anything!"

When Haman saw that his words were having no effect on the king, he went sadly to the king's treasure house and took out all which the king had commanded. Then he went into the stalls and took the best horse and all of its finery. He carried the garb of majesty on his shoulders, and led the horse by its golden bridle, to Mordechai.

◂§ Mordechai and his Students

All of this was destined by God, and this was what the king had ordained. But when Mordechai saw the wicked man from afar, he told his students: "Whoever of you can flee should do so, for here comes the wicked Haman to kill me. Do not be killed for my sake."

"We shall all die together," answered his pupils.

"Then let us learn," said Mordechai, "and we will die in our studies and our prayers."

This was the 16th day of Nissan, and they studied how the grain offering of the *Omer* had been brought on that day, when the Temple still stood. Haman stood from afar and then asked the children what they were learning.

"When we were in our land," they answered, "we used to bring the *Omer* on this very day."

"What is the *Omer?*" Haman asked. "Was it made of silver or of gold?"

"Neither," answered the students. "It was nothing more than a small amount of barleymeal."

"Your meal has been of more help to you," said Haman, "than the ten thousand talents of silver which I offered to give to the king, and which he refused. You are beloved of your God, who helps you against your enemies."

◂§ Haman Encounters Mordechai

Then Haman told Mordechai: "Stand up, beloved Mordechai, righteous child of Avraham, Yitzchak and Yaakov. Stand up and remove your sackcloth and ashes. Your prayers have helped more than the ten thousand silver talents which I offered the king, in order to spare me this humiliation. Praised be your God, who has planned this. Put on this royal garb which has been sent to you. You must ride this noble horse. See what great honor God has heaped upon you."

Mordechai thought that the wicked man was mocking him, for he never thought that he could act so gently, and he told Haman: "You, Haman, descendant of Amalek, let me eat my bitter bread and drink my bitter water in peace, and then do with me what you will."

"Come, beloved Mordechai," Haman repeated, "dress yourself at once, and ride this horse, and do not defy the king's words."

"How can I do this? I have been fasting now for three days and three nights," Mordechai answered. "I have been rolling in ashes, and am covered with dust. I must clean myself."

Then Haman ran swiftly to the king's warehouses and brought back sweet-smelling balsam, and anointed him. He served him food from Esther's feast, and then Mordechai rode the king's horse.

◈§ Esther Witnesses the Miracle

Esther sent 27,000 chosen young men out of the palace, with golden goblets in their right hands and golden pitchers in their left, and they praised Mordechai and said: "So is done to the man whom the king wishes to honor." When the Jews saw what was happening to Mordechai, they said: "So shall be done to the man whom God wishes to honor."

When Esther saw Mordechai riding on the king's mount, dressed in the royal garb, crown upon his head, she praised God for His great help. She had previously seen him in torn garments, with ash upon his clothing, and now she saw him in his greatness.

She said: "Today the verse in *Psalms*, מֵאַשְׁפֹּת יָרִים אֶבְיוֹן — *from the dirt He lifts up the needy (Tehillim 113:7), has been fulfilled.*"

Mordechai, too, praised God, and said: הָפַכְתָּ מִסְפְּדִי לְמָחוֹל לִי" — *You have turned my mourning into dancing (ibid. 30:12). I praise You God, my redeemer, for You have not allowed my enemies to rejoice.*"

◈§ Haman Returns to his Kinsmen

וַיָּשָׁב מָרְדְּכַי — *Mordechai returned* (6:12) to the king's gate, while Haman, deeply distressed, returned to his home in a great depression, his head covered.

He had been humiliated by four menial tasks: he had been Mordechai's barber, having cut his hair; Mordechai's valet, having bathed him; Mordechai's driver, having led the horse; and a town crier, having cried out that this is what was done to the man whom the king wished to honor.

Haman came back to his house, and recounted all that had happened, and his wife and friends said: "If Mordechai is of Jewish descent, you should know that God performs miracles for them all the time. He performed miracles for Daniel when he was thrown into the lions' den, and enabled him to leave it unharmed. When

Chananiah, Mishael and Azariah were thrown into a furnace He helped them, and the people standing outside the furnace were incinerated. Therefore, we fear that you will not be able to harm him, and may even continue to fall before him."

◆§ The Fateful Banquet

While they were still speaking the king's servants came to bring Haman to the banquet which Esther had prepared. The king and Haman came to drink with Esther, and the king said to her at this wine feast on the second day: "What is your request, Queen Esther, and it shall be granted; and what is your desire? Up to half the kingdom will be given to you."

And Esther answered: "If I have found favor in your eyes, and if it pleases the king, let him give me my life as my request, and my people's lives as my desire; כִּי נִמְכַּרְנוּ — *for we have been sold* (7:4), I and my people, to be killed and destroyed. Had we simply been sold into slavery I would have held my peace, for the humiliation would not have warranted bothering the king."

Then the king told the interpreter to ask Esther who and where was the man who had set his heart to do this, and Esther answered: "The evil man, Haman, your enemy, who wanted to strike out against God's children, the Jews!" (The *Midrash* says that the name הָמָן can be seen as comprising the two Aramaic words הָא מָן, meaning, "[This is] he who [sought to kill God's children].")

Haman grew terrified before them, and the king, in a rage, left the feast and walked into the garden. Strong trees were felled in order to quell his anger, but to no avail. In the meantime, Haman stood before the queen to beg for his life, for he saw that he was about to feel the full measure of the king's wrath.

The king returned to the feast from the garden, while Haman had fallen upon the couch where the queen reclined.

"Will you seduce my queen in my own house?" roared the king, and Haman's face grew shamed.

◆§ Haman is Hanged

Charvonah, one of the king's retainers — this Charvonah is generally remembered unfavorably, but in one matter is remembered with kindness — was one of those involved in the plot to hang Mordechai, but when he saw that Haman's plot was not working out, he went to the king and said: "My master, the king, Haman wishes to destroy you and take away your kingdom. If you do not believe me, send someone to see the gallows which he has prepared for Mordechai, who has done such good for the king. It stands in the court of his house, fifty cubits high."

Then the king commanded that Haman be hanged upon it. Through Mordechai was fulfilled the verse which says that he whom God loves will see his enemies turn into friends.

Then the king told Mordechai: "Stand up, and take this wicked Haman, oppressor of the Jews, and hang him upon the gallows which he himself built. Do with him what you will."

Then Mordechai took Haman from the king's gate and told him: "You, wicked Haman, oppressor of the Jews, I will hang you upon the gallows which you built for yourself." They hanged Haman on his gallows, and God's wrath was stilled. With Mordechai was fulfilled the divine promise that the righteous will be rescued from anguish while the evil man comes in his place.

◆§ A Further Request

בַּיּוֹם הַהוּא — *On that day* (8:1) king Achashverosh gave Haman's house into Queen Esther's hands. Mordechai came before the king, for Esther had told him that he was her relative. The king took the signet ring which he had taken back from Haman, and gave it to Mordechai, and Queen Esther appointed Mordechai over Haman's household.

Then Esther spoke to the king again, and fell before him, crying. She begged him to undo the evil which Haman the descendant of Agag had planned, and to foil his schemes against the Jews — *for how can I see the evil which will overtake my people? How can I watch as my people are doomed?*

The king told Queen Esther and Mordechai: "You yourself are guilty, for when I asked you at the feast about your ancestry, when I wanted to make your family nobility, you answered that your parents had died when you were young and unaware of it. Still, I give Haman's house to you. Haman has already been hanged, for he dared to strike against the Jews. And now write whatever you wish concerning the Jews, using the king's name, and seal it with the king's seal, for a letter written with the king's name and sealed with his seal cannot be revoked."

◆§ The Second Prolcamation

וַיִּקָּרְאוּ סֹפְרֵי הַמֶּלֶךְ — *The king's scribes were called* (8:9) on the 23rd day of the third month, that is Sivan, and all that Mordechai the Jew requested was recorded. It was sent to all of the nobles and governors of 127 nations, each nation in its writing, each people in its language, and to the Jews in their language. It was written and sealed with the king's name, and it was sent out with couriers who rode horses and swift camels and young mules, that the king had given permission to the Jews of each city to assemble and destroy all of their oppressors, their wives and their children, and permission to keep their booty — on one day, on the 13th day of the twelfth month, that is, Adar.

פַּתְשֶׁגֶן הַכְּתָב — *The text of the letter* (8:13) was such, and was displayed to all of the people: "To all of the population of my kingdom, those dwelling on land and those in the sea, peace and prosperity. I today announce and write to you as follows. You know that God gave me dominion over many nations and people, on land and in the sea. He has made me king over all of them. You know well that I have not done harm to any of you. I have ruled over you with goodness and sincerity, and have let all those under my rule live in peace and friendship.

"Now I let you know that evil men approached me and insinuated themselves with me, until I entrusted them with the rule of the entire kingdom. I let them do as they saw fit, for I thought that they would deal truthfully and with goodness, but they were false and evil and tricked me, doing whatever they fancied.

"They had me write a letter which was wicked in the eyes of God and man. The desire of the evil men was that I should destroy many righteous men, men who never did any act of evil, and who were toally innocent of wrongdoing. These are Esther and Mordechai and their people. Esther is praised with all that is good, and Mordechai is outstanding in all manner of wisdom and nobility, and no one can find fault with either.

"When Haman told me to kill all the wicked Jews, I thought that he meant some other nation who were also called Jews, for he could not mean those Jews, who are called the children of Him Who created the heaven and the earth and all that is in the world, and Who performs miracles for them all the time, He Who is more awesome and greater and more mighty than all of the kings of the earth. How could I ever have thought of selling such a people?

"But the evil Haman urged me on, in order that the people should not respect me, for he schemed to take my kingdom away from me. Once I became aware of what was going on, I gave him his just deserts, and hanged him on his own gallows. Know, then, that He Who created heaven and earth has repaid him well, him and his evil comrades."

The king's message was delivered in great haste by couriers to all the corners of his kingdom, and was made known as well in Shushan the capital.

◆§ Shushan Exults

וּמָרְדְּכַי יָצָא — *Mordechai went out* (8:15) from the presence of the king wearing a white kingly garment of linen and a robe of purple wool, and a golden crown, and all the city of Shushan was merry and joyful.

The Jews had light and gladness, laughter and glory; and in each city where the king's words and his orders reached, there was rejoicing and laughter for the Jews, and many feasts and happy days. Many of the people around them converted, for the fear of the Jews had fallen upon them.

◆§ The Jews Defend Themselves

וּבִשְׁנֵים עָשָׂר חֹדֶשׁ — In the twelfth month (9:1), that is Adar, on the thirteenth day, as the king had commanded, the Jews assembled against their enemies, who had hoped to destroy them. Their plans were turned about, and it was the Jews who prevailed. The Jews assembled in their cities in all the provinces of King Achashverosh, to strengthen themselves against those who had planned to do evil to them. No one stood before them, for a fear of the Jews had fallen upon the land. All of the nobles of the provinces and those who followed the orders of the king upheld the Jews, for the fear of Mordechai was upon them. Mordechai was greatly honored in the king's house, and his name was known throughout the provinces.

The Jews struck at all of their enemies with their swords, and they did whatever they wished to their foes. In the capital city of Shushan the Jews killed five hundred men. Parshandasa, Dalfon, Aspasa, Porasa, Adaliah, Aridasa, Parmashta, Arisai, Aridai, and Vayzasa — the ten sons of Haman son of Hamdasa, the oppressor of the Jews — were killed. But the Jews did not put out a hand to plunder the spoils.

On that day the number of dead in Shushan came to the attention of the king. He called to Esther and told her: "See what the Jews have done in Shushan. I know well that in Shushan they have killed five hundred men. See what they have done in the other cities. If this is not sufficient for you, Esther, tell me your desire and it will be fulfilled."

"If it pleases the king," Esther said, "let tomorrow, too, be given to the Jews in Shushan, so that they can do what they did today. And let Haman's ten sons be hanged on the gallows."

The king commanded that this be done, and Haman and his ten sons were hanged on the gallows. Mordechai saw them hanging, and said: "You planned to do evil things to Israel, but God, Blessed is He, knows what man schemes. He repaid you well. You wanted to take us out from under God's wing, therefore you now have your children under your wing, on the gallows."

The Jews assembled on the fourteenth day of the month of Adar and killed three hundred men in Shushan, but no one put out a hand to take booty. The other Jews, of the provinces, fought for their lives and destroyed their enemies, and killed 75,000 men, but there too no one touched the spoils. That was on the thirteenth day of Adar, and they rested on the fourteenth day, making it a day of feasting and joy. The Jews repeat this every year, on the fourteenth day of Adar, just as on the day that they rested from their foes.

⋅§ A Miracle to Remember

It was a month of turnabouts — their tears turned to joy, their mourning to happiness. Therefore we must make it merry and joyous, and every person should send gifts to his friend and give charity to those in need.

The Jews took it upon themselves to do what Mordechai had written, for Haman, son of Hamdasa, descendant of Agag, had schemed to destroy the Jews. But when Esther had approached the king she said: "Our Torah commands us to stamp out the descendants of Amalek. Haman knew this, and that is why he hatched his plot." But God turned his schemes upon his own head, and he and his sons were hanged. For this reason, these days are called "Purim" from the word *pur* — the lots which Haman cast.

Esther, daughter of Avichayil, and Mordechai the Jew, wrote to confirm the second letter of Purim. And they sent word to the Jews of the 127 provinces of King Achashverosh, with friendship and love, to celebrate the days of Purim in their rightful time, as Mordechai the Jew and Queen Esther had celebrated them. And Esther's words were fulfilled, and the episode of Purim, with its fasts and prayers, was written down.

King Achashverosh imposed a tribute on his lands and on the islands of the sea. All of his might and strength, and the honor and greatness of Mordechai, whom the king had honored, is written down in the chronicles of the kings of Persia and Media.

Mordechai was the second-in-command to King Achashverosh, a

chamberlain of the Sanhedrin and a noble over all the peoples of the kingdom. His words were respected from one end of the world to the other. This is the Mordechai who is likened to an aromatic spice, and to the star called Nogah (Jupiter), for it is brighter than all other stars. He is likened to a rose which blooms early. He was a teacher to the Jews and a friend to the Sanhedrin, bringing good to the people and speaking of peace to all of his children.

❁ ❁ ❁

(The Torah reading on Purim morning is from Sh'mos 17:8-16. See pages 373-374.)

תהלים כ״ב

Psalm 22

אֵלֶת הַשַּׁחַר, מִזְמוֹר לְדָוִד. בּ אֵלִי אֵלִי א לַמְנַצֵּחַ עַל
לָמָה עֲזַבְתָּנִי, רָחוֹק מִישׁוּעָתִי דִּבְרֵי שַׁאֲגָתִי. ג אֱלֹהַי,
אֶקְרָא יוֹמָם וְלֹא תַעֲנֶה, וְלַיְלָה וְלֹא דוּמִיָּה לִי. ד וְאַתָּה
קָדוֹשׁ, יוֹשֵׁב תְּהִלּוֹת יִשְׂרָאֵל. ה בְּךָ בָּטְחוּ אֲבֹתֵינוּ,

◄§ Psalm 22

This Psalm, although entitled
מִזְמוֹר לְדָוִד, *A song of David*, deals
primarily with events which were
destined to occur hundreds of years
after David's time. David, with his
holy spirit foresaw the bleak Babylonian and Persian exiles in general,
and in particular, the terrible threat of
Haman and Ahasuerus against the
entire Jewish nation as personified by
Queen Esther. Although there are
countless events in Jewish history
which David does not discuss in the
Book of Psalms, *Alshich* explains that
David dedicated a psalm to Esther
because he personally had a hand in
the salvation of Israel in her days.
When David fled from Absalom,
Shimi ben Gera of the tribe of Benjamin viciously cursed David. Yet,
David would not allow his men to kill
Shimi although he deserved death for
blaspheming the king (*II Samuel*
16:5-13). The Talmud (*Megillah* 13a)
says that David foresaw that
Mordechai [and Esther] was destined
to descend from Shimi [*Mordechai,
son of Yair, son of Shimi* (*Esther* 2:5)]
and being that the salvation of Israel
was at stake, David forfeited his own
dignity for the sake of saving his
people.

Therefore, David was inspired to
compose a psalm in honor of the
Purim miracle, for without him it
could not have come to pass.

It was the custom of the Vilna
Gaon to recite this psalm as the שִׁיר

שֶׁל יוֹם, *the Song of the Day*, on Purim
(*Maaseh Rav* 250).

1. אַיֶּלֶת הַשַּׁחַר — *Ayeles Hashachar*.

The commentaries offer numerous
explanations for these words.

Many say that this was a type of
musical instrument (*Rashi; Radak;
Ibn Ezra; Metzudos*). Or, this refers
to the dawn (*Rashi*) or the morning
star (*Radak*).

Meiri combines these interpretations explaining that these very melo-
dious instruments start with a subtle,
low sound and slowly gather
strength and volume, just as the light
of early dawn rises slowly until it
reaches a climax with the appearence
of the dazzling sun.

Rashi comments that it is also a
term of endearment towards Israel
which is called אַיֶּלֶת אֲהָבִים, *a lovely
hind* (*Proverbs* 5:19). At the same
time the word אַיֶּלֶת denotes strength
and salvation as in (below, v. 20)
אֱיָלוּתִי לְעֶזְרָתִי חוּשָׁה, *O my Strength,
hasten to my assistance* (*Rashi;
Radak*).

Ultimately, all of these themes find
expression in the personality of Esther, who represents the slow dawn-
ing of the light of redemption for the
Jews who were engulfed in the dark-
ness of exile. *Midrash Shocher Tov*
explains that immediately before the
rise of the morning star the night is at
its darkest, for the moon and bright
stars have already begun to fade and
recede. Similarly, Esther arrived at
Israel's darkest hour. Through her

¹ For the Conductor, on the Aiyeles Hashachar, a psalm by David. ² My God, my God, why have You forsaken me; why so far from saving me, from the words of my roar? ³ O my God! I call out by day — and You answer not; and by night — but there is no respite for me. ⁴ Yet You are the Holy One, enthroned upon the praises of Israel! ⁵ In You our fathers trusted, they trusted and You delivered them. ⁶ To You they

great love for God (אַיֶּלֶת אֲהָבִים) she gathered the tremendous strength (אֱיָלוּתִי) to fast for three days and to enter Ahasuerus' court unsummoned although this meant certain death.

Furthermore, the Talmud (*Yoma* 29a) adds: Just as the female deer (אַיָּלָה) is always enticing to her mate, so did the lovely Esther arouse Ahasuerus' passions at each meeting as if it was the first time he was with her. Also, just as the horns of a deer continue to grow as it ages, the prayers of the righteous are more readily heard the more they recite them. Finally, just as אַיֶּלֶת הַשַּׁחַר, *the morning star*, marks the end of the night, so does the miracle of Esther mark the last of the miracles recorded in the Scriptures.'

Yalkut Shimoni (*Megillas Esther* 1053) explains that the name Esther is derived from *Istahar*, a very bright star.

2. Esther's Prayer

Now it came to pass on the third day, Esther donned royalty (*Esther* 5:1). The Talmud (*Megillah* 15a) explains that this refers not only to royal apparel but also to spiritual royalty, i.e., the holy [prophetic] spirit clothed her. But on her way to the king's throne room Esther passed through a chapel filled with the king's idols — and suddenly the holy spirit departed from her. In her anguish she uttered these words: אֵלִי אֵלִי.

לָמָה עֲזַבְתָּנִי, *My God, my God, why have You forsaken me?*

רָחוֹק מִישׁוּעָתִי דִּבְרֵי שַׁאֲגָתִי — *Why so far from saving me, from the words of my roar?*

Esther emphasized that her concern was not for herself, but for all of Israel. She declared: 'My anguished roar is motivated by thoughts far removed from concern over my personal salvation' (*Turei Zahav*).

Esther lamented: 'Ordinarily, God does not reject the fasting and prayers of an entire congregation. Rather, *Before they call, I already answer* (*Isaiah* 65:24). But here, even after I roar there is no answer, and salvation is far off' (*Baalei Bris Avrohom*).

3. אֱלֹהַי אֶקְרָא יוֹמָם וְלֹא תַעֲנֶה וְלַיְלָה וְלֹא דוּמִיָּה לִי — *O my God! I call out by day and You answer not; and by night — there is no respite* [lit. 'silence'] *for me.*

Rabbi Joshua ben Levi derived the following law from this verse: A person is obligated to recite the Megillah in the evening and then repeat it again on the following day (*Megillah* 4a); this recalls the circumstances of the miracle when they cried out continually in their distress, day and night (*Rashi*).

4. וְאַתָּה קָדוֹשׁ יוֹשֵׁב תְּהִלּוֹת יִשְׂרָאֵל — *Yet You are the Holy One, enthroned upon the praises of Israel.*

According to *Rashi* יוֹשֵׁב literally

בָּטְחוּ וַתְּפַלְּטֵימוֹ. ‏ אֵלֶיךָ זָעֲקוּ וְנִמְלָטוּ, בְּךָ בָטְחוּ וְלֹא
בוֹשׁוּ. ‏ וְאָנֹכִי תוֹלַעַת וְלֹא אִישׁ, חֶרְפַּת אָדָם וּבְזוּי עָם.
ח כָּל רֹאַי יַלְעִגוּ לִי; יַפְטִירוּ בְשָׂפָה, יָנִיעוּ רֹאשׁ. ט גֹּל
אֶל יהוה יְפַלְּטֵהוּ, יַצִּילֵהוּ כִּי חָפֵץ בּוֹ. ‏ כִּי אַתָּה גֹחִי
מִבָּטֶן, מַבְטִיחִי עַל שְׁדֵי אִמִּי. יא עָלֶיךָ הָשְׁלַכְתִּי
מֵרָחֶם, מִבֶּטֶן אִמִּי אֵלִי אָתָּה. יב אַל תִּרְחַק מִמֶּנִּי כִּי
צָרָה קְרוֹבָה, כִּי אֵין עוֹזֵר. יג סְבָבוּנִי פָּרִים רַבִּים,

means *sitting*, i.e., God sits to hear praises. *Radak* and *Metzudas David* maintain that the word יוֹשֵׁב is used figuratively to denote the permanence of God's strength which remains *sitting*, i.e., unchanged, for all eternity.

After reading the *Megillah* in the evening, the congregation recites the prayer וּבָא לְצִיּוֹן גּוֹאֵל, *A redeemer shall come to Zion*, omitting the opening verses and beginning with וְאַתָּה קָדוֹשׁ יוֹשֵׁב תְּהִלּוֹת יִשְׂרָאֵל, *You are the Holy One...* (*Orach Chaim* 693:1).

This custom is derived from our psalm. The preceding verse which speaks of the obligation to read the *Megillah* is followed immediately by this verse which begins וְאַתָּה קָדוֹשׁ (*Hagohos Maimoni*).

8. כָּל רֹאַי יַלְעִגוּ לִי — *All who see me deride me.*

The preceding verses describe the Jews in Esther's times. They put their faith in God and shouted and fasted to nullify Haman's decree. Esther displayed her unswerving faith by fearlessly coming to the king, unsummoned. The present verse depicts the vicious sons of Haman who derided the Jews by shaking their hands and taunting, 'Tomorrow you shall die!' (*Midrash Shocher Tov*).

10. כִּי אַתָּה גֹחִי מִבָּטֶן — *For You are the One Who drew me forth from the womb.*

Esther alludes to the tragic circumstances of her birth. When Esther's mother conceived her, her father died. At childbirth her mother died (*Megillah* 13a). Thus, as she was leaving her mother's womb, her life was in mortal danger, and only because God drew her out of the birth passage did she survive (*Alshich*; *Midrash Shocher Tov*).

In truth, her orphan status was an asset many years later. For, the *Megillah* tells us that *Esther would not reveal her birthplace and her nation* (*Esther* 2:19). The enigma of her silence intrigued Ahasuerus and made her even more attractive to him. Thus, the *Talmud* (*Megillah* 13a) says: 'Every nation of the empire claimed her to be its own.' Hence, her true identity was shrouded, and therein rested the key to salvation (*R' Avrohom Chaim Feuer*).

11. עָלֶיךָ הָשְׁלַכְתִּי מֵרָחֶם — *I was cast upon You from birth.*

As explained in the preceding verse, Esther was an orphan from birth and God is *the father of orphans* (*Psalms* 68:6).

מִבֶּטֶן אִמִּי אֵלִי אָתָּה — *From my*

cried out and they were rescued, in You they trusted and they were not shamed. ⁷ *But I am a worm and not a man, scorn of humanity, despised of nations.* ⁸ *All who see me, deride me; they open wide with their lips, they wag their heads.* ⁹ *One who casts [his burden] upon* HASHEM — *He will deliver him! He will save him, for He desires him!* ¹⁰ *For You are the One who drew me forth from the womb, and made be secure on my mother's breasts.* ¹¹ *I was cast upon You from birth, from my mother's womb You have been my God.* ¹² *Be not aloof from me for distress is near, for there is none to help.* ¹³ *Many bulls surround me,*

---

mother's womb, You have been my God.

Esther has already cried out אֵלִי twice (v. 2). Now she addresses God with this Name for the third time. *Midrash Shocher Tov* says that she wished to allude to the fact that she had always scrupulously observed the three commandments which God designated specifically for women נִדָּה, חַלָּה, הַדְלָקַת הַנֵּר, *niddah, separating challah, and lighting the Sabbath candles* (see Mishnah *Shabbos* 2:6).

12. אַל תִּרְחַק מִמֶּנִּי — *Be not aloof from me.*

You have been close to me since my conception and birth, and You have continued to guide me throughout my development. Please do not suddenly desert me in my distress (*Radak*).

כִּי צָרָה קְרוֹבָה — *For distress is near.*

Midrash Shocher Tov describes the circumstances under which Esther said this:

When she dared to approach the king's throne room unsummoned, she had to pass through seven antechambers. She passed through three of them unharmed, but when she

entered the fourth (the middle one) Ahasuerus her noticed and began to gnash his teeth in wrath. He cried, 'Alas, I sorely miss the former queen who is gone but not forgotten. When I called for Vashti [to display herself] she maintained her dignity and refused to come. But this one, Esther, comes on her own, like a low woman soliciting for herself!'

At that moment Esther froze in fear. Sentries appeared from all sides and wished to pounce on her, but the middle ante-chamber was not under their jurisdiction and they were forced to pause. Esther called to God, 'Be not aloof from me, for distress is near.'

13. סְבָבוּנִי פָּרִים רַבִּים — *Many bulls surround me.*

This refers to Ahasuerus' soldiers and bodyguards (*Midrash Shocher Tov*).

According to *Alshich*, this alludes to the many agents who were sent out by Ahasuerus to circle (סבב) the city, to bring in the most beautiful maidens for the competition to decide who would be the queen. One of these searches uncovered Esther who was taken forcibly, against her will, to the palace.

[173] **PURIM** / Its Observance and Significance

אֲבִירֵי בָשָׁן כִּתְּרוּנִי. יד פָּצוּ עָלַי פִּיהֶם, אַרְיֵה טֹרֵף וְשֹׁאֵג. טו כַּמַּיִם נִשְׁפַּכְתִּי, וְהִתְפָּרְדוּ כָּל עַצְמוֹתָי; הָיָה לִבִּי כַּדּוֹנָג, נָמֵס בְּתוֹךְ מֵעָי. טז יָבֵשׁ כַּחֶרֶשׂ כֹּחִי, וּלְשׁוֹנִי מֻדְבָּק מַלְקוֹחָי; וְלַעֲפַר מָוֶת תִּשְׁפְּתֵנִי. יז כִּי סְבָבוּנִי כְּלָבִים; עֲדַת מְרֵעִים הִקִּיפוּנִי, כָּאֲרִי יָדַי וְרַגְלָי. יח אֲסַפֵּר כָּל עַצְמוֹתָי, הֵמָּה יַבִּיטוּ יִרְאוּ בִי. יט יְחַלְּקוּ בְגָדַי לָהֶם, וְעַל לְבוּשִׁי יַפִּילוּ גוֹרָל. כ וְאַתָּה יהוה אַל תִּרְחָק, אֱיָלוּתִי לְעֶזְרָתִי חוּשָׁה. כא הַצִּילָה מֵחֶרֶב נַפְשִׁי, מִיַּד כֶּלֶב יְחִידָתִי. כב הוֹשִׁיעֵנִי מִפִּי אַרְיֵה, וּמִקַּרְנֵי רֵמִים עֲנִיתָנִי. כג אֲסַפְּרָה שִׁמְךָ לְאֶחָי, בְּתוֹךְ

כִּתְּרוּנִי — Encircle me [lit. they crown me].

This refers to the agents who discovered Esther and sought to have her crowned (Alshich).

14. אַרְיֵה — Like a lion.

The agents who forcibly brought Esther to the palace saw that she was miserable. They tried to cheer her up, saying, 'You have won the most coveted prize, the royal crown! Why don't you roar for joy like the lion who has seized his prey?' (Alshich).

15. כַּמַּיִם נִשְׁפַּכְתִּי — I am poured out like water.

Esther's reaction to the news of Haman's decree against the Jews is described as, וַתִּתְחַלְחַל הַמַּלְכָּה מְאֹד, and the queen was greatly distressed (Esther 4:4) [lit., she became full of hollow spaces].

The Talmud explains this in two ways. Rav said: She became a niddah. Rav Yirmiyah said: Her stomach was loosened (and melted like water) (Megillah 15a).

According to the Midrash she was pregnant and miscarried (Esther Rabbah 8:3).

17. כִּי סְבָבוּנִי כְּלָבִים — For dogs have surrounded me.

This refers to the sons of Haman (Midrash Shocher Tov). The Rabbis often equated the seed of Amalek with that of a dog. He is called עֲמָלֵק because it is a contraction of the words עַם שֶׁבָּא לָלוּק, the nation that came to lick, the blood of the Jews, like a blood-thirsty dog (Tanchuma Ki Seitzei),

Yalkut Shimoni illustrates the obligation to remember Amalek's wickedness with this parable: A king placed a mad dog at the entrance of his orchard to guard against thieves. Once the king's favorite secretly went to steal some fruit and the mad dog pounced on him and ripped his clothing. Whenever the king wished to remind his favorite of this incident (without embarrassing him too much), he would say, 'Remember how crazy that dog was, the one that

Bashan's mighty ones encircle me. ¹⁴ They open their mouths
against me like a tearing, roaring lion. ¹⁵ I am poured out like
water, and all my bones became disjointed; my heart is like
wax, melted within my innards. ¹⁶ My strength is dried up
like baked clay, and my tongue cleaves to my palate; in the
dust of death You set me down. ¹⁷ For dogs have surrounded
me; a pack of evildoers has enclosed me, like a lion's prey
are my hands and my feet. ¹⁸ I can count all my bones —
they look on and gloat over me. ¹⁹ They divide my clothes
among themselves, and cast lots for my clothing. ²⁰ But You,
HASHEM, be not far from me. O my Strength, hasten to my
assistance! ²¹ Rescue my soul from the sword, my only one
from the grip of the dog. ²² Save me from the lion's mouth as
You have answered me from the horns of the reimim. ²³ I will
proclaim Your Name to my brethren; in the midst of the

ripped your clothing!' Similarly, the
Jews once cried out, 'Is HASHEM in
our midst or is He not? (Exodus 17:7).
They thought Hashem was not
watching over them just as the favorite thought that the king's orchard
was not watched. Immediately they
were attacked by Amalek! (ibid. v. 8).
Moshe did not want to embarrass
them by reminding them of their lack
of faith, so he said, 'Remember what
Amalek did to you' (Deuteronomy
25:17), like that mad dog by the gate!

יַחְלְקוּ בְגָדַי לָהֶם .19 — They divide my
clothes among them.

When Esther began to walk to the
king unsummoned, she apparently
sealed her doom. All of the palace
courtiers eyed her valuables cov-
etously. One said, 'I will take her
garments.' Another said, 'I want her
jewels!' A third said, 'Her necklaces
are mine!' (Midrash Shocher Tov).

וְעַל לְבוּשִׁי יַפִּילוּ גוֹרָל — And [they]

cast lots for my clothing.

According to Midrash Shocher
Tov this specifically refers to the most
significant article of clothing, the
royal mantle, which may be worn
only by the royal family.

הַצִּילָה מֵחֶרֶב נַפְשִׁי .21 — Rescue my
soul from the sword.

Abudraham notes that the initials
of these three words form the name
הָמָן, Haman. The initials of the next
three words form מַכִּי, who smites me.

מִיַּד כֶּלֶב — From the grip of the dog.

This too refers to Haman for the
Talmud equates the slanderer to a
dog, 'Whoever speaks evil gossip,
deserves to be thrown to the dogs'
(Pesachim 118a). The Talmud
(Megillah 13b) also says that there
was never anyone who could spread
slander as well as Haman (Tehillah
L'David).

אֲסַפְּרָה שִׁמְךָ לְאֶחָי בְּתוֹךְ קָהָל אֲהַלְלֶךָּ .23
— I will proclaim Your Name to my

קְהָל אֲהַלְלֶךָ. כד יִרְאֵי יהוה הַלְלוּהוּ, כָּל זֶרַע יַעֲקֹב כַּבְּדוּהוּ, וְגוּרוּ מִמֶּנּוּ כָּל זֶרַע יִשְׂרָאֵל. כה כִּי לֹא בָזָה וְלֹא שִׁקַּץ עֱנוּת עָנִי, וְלֹא הִסְתִּיר פָּנָיו מִמֶּנּוּ; וּבְשַׁוְּעוֹ אֵלָיו שָׁמֵעַ. כו מֵאִתְּךָ תְּהִלָּתִי בְּקָהָל רָב, נְדָרַי אֲשַׁלֵּם נֶגֶד יְרֵאָיו. כז יֹאכְלוּ עֲנָוִים וְיִשְׂבָּעוּ, יְהַלְלוּ יהוה דֹּרְשָׁיו; יְחִי לְבַבְכֶם לָעַד. כח יִזְכְּרוּ וְיָשֻׁבוּ אֶל יהוה כָּל אַפְסֵי אָרֶץ, וְיִשְׁתַּחֲווּ לְפָנֶיךָ כָּל מִשְׁפְּחוֹת גּוֹיִם. כט כִּי לַיהוה הַמְּלוּכָה, וּמֹשֵׁל בַּגּוֹיִם. ל אָכְלוּ וַיִּשְׁתַּחֲווּ כָּל דִּשְׁנֵי אֶרֶץ, לְפָנָיו יִכְרְעוּ כָּל יוֹרְדֵי עָפָר, וְנַפְשׁוֹ לֹא חִיָּה. לא זֶרַע יַעַבְדֶנּוּ, יְסֻפַּר לַאדֹנָי לַדּוֹר. לב יָבֹאוּ וְיַגִּידוּ צִדְקָתוֹ, לְעַם נוֹלָד כִּי עָשָׂה.

brethren, in the midst of the congregation will I praise You.

The Talmud (Megillah 14a) explains that one reason we do not recite the Hallel on Purim, even though the salvation from death would warrant such a recital, is because the reading of the Megillah itself takes the place of Hallel. Therefore, Esther said: 'I will proclaim Your Name to my brethren [i.e., equivalent to reciting Hallel], in the midst of the congregation will I praise You (Alshich).

24. כָּל זֶרַע יַעֲקֹב כַּבְּדוּהוּ וְגוּרוּ מִמֶּנּוּ כָּל זֶרַע יִשְׂרָאֵל — All of you, the seed of Jacob, glorify Him! Be in awe of Him, all you seed of Israel.

Seed of Jacob refers to his first eleven sons. Seed of Israel refers to the tribe of Benjamin. Benjamin was the only one of the tribes born after Jacob wrestled with the angel who bestowed upon him the additional name, Israel, which denotes sover-

eignty (Ha'amek Davar, Bereishis 33:7).

Maharal adds that Benjamin was the only one of Jacob's sons who was born in the Land Of Israel. Therefore, the holy spirit dwelled in Benjamin's territory and it was there that the Temple was built.

Benjamin was also the only son who was not humiliated by bowing down before Esau in fear, because Benjamin had not been born. The Midrash (Esther Rabbah 7:9) explains that precisely for this reason Mordechai, the Benjaminite, refused to bow down before Haman, the descendant of Esau.

27. יֹאכְלוּ עֲנָוִים וְיִשְׂבָּעוּ — The humble will eat and be satisfied.

Radak explains that the humble are the Jews who were downtrodden in exile by the haughty Babylonians. When the Babylonian Empire was overthrown by Darius and Cyrus, Cyrus took the treasures of the Beis *congregation I will praise You. ²⁴ You who fear HASHEM, praise Him! All of you, the seed of Jacob, glorify Him! Be in awe of Him, all you seed of Israel. ²⁵ For He has neither despised nor loathed the supplication of the poor, nor has He concealed His face from him; but when he cried to Him, He heard. ²⁶ From You is my praise in the great congregation; I will fulfill my vows before those who fear Him. ²⁷ The humble will eat and be satisfied, those who seek HASHEM will praise Him — your hearts will live forever. ²⁸ All the ends of the earth will remember and turn back to HASHEM; all the families of the nations will bow before You. ²⁹ For the kingship belongs to HASHEM, and He rules the nations. ³⁰ All the fat of the land will eat and bow down, all who descend to the dust will kneel before Him, but He will not revive his soul. ³¹ About the seed of those who have always served Him, it will be told of the Lord to the latter generation. ³² They will come and relate His righteousness, to the newborn nation that which he has done.*

HaMikdash which had been the proud possession of the Babylonians and returned them to the Jews along with permission to rebuild the Temple. Thus Israel will *eat and be content* with the return of its most precious possession.

It was Ahasuerus, the successor of Cyrus, who commanded that the construction of the Temple come to a halt. Esther prayed that she should have the power to influence Ahasuerus to rescind his decree. Ahasuerus never did this. Nevertheless, Esther ultimately did realize her wish when Darius II, the son she bore to Ahasuerus, ascended the throne and gave orders to renew construction of the Temple in the year 3408.

יְהַלְלוּ ה׳ דֹּרְשָׁיו — *Those who seek HASHEM will praise Him.*

Only a handful of people responded to Cyrus' invitation to return to Israel (which was then desolate) to rebuild the Temple. These hardy pioneers may be called *those who seek HASHEM*. The rest sought the security and comfort of their established homes. Mordechai was amongst those who returned with Zerubavel in the year 3390 to rebuild the Temple. However, the construction was quickly halted as a result of the vicious slander (accusing the Jews of treason) spread by Haman and his sons (R' *Avrohom Chaim Feuer*).

יְחִי לְבַבְכֶם לָעַד — *May your hearts be alive forever.*

Midrash Shocher Tov states that Haman's downfall, his treasures were divided into three parts. One third went to Mordechai and Esther. One third went to those who toiled in Torah study. And one third went towards construction of the Temple. All three are implied in this verse, *The humble will eat and be satisfied*, refers to Mordechai and Esther. *Those who seek HASHEM will praise Him*, refers to those who toil in Torah study. *May your hearts be alive forever*, refers to the Temple of which it says elsewhere, *My eyes and heart shall be there forever* (*II Chronicles* 7:16).

This verse may also refer to the mitzvos of Purim: *The humble will eat* is an allusion to *matanos laevyonim* (alms for the poor) [עֲנָיִים, *humble ones*, is cognate with עֲנִיִים, *paupers*]; *mishloach manos* (food portions exchanged); and the Purim *seudah* or banquet. *Those who seek HASHEM will praise Him*, alludes to the reading of the *Megillah*, which is compared to reciting *Hallel*.

And *May your hearts be alive forever*, refers to the festival of Purim, which will *never cease* among the Jews (*Matzreif Dahava*).